BENNETT'S GUIDE TO JURY SELECTION AND TRIAL DYNAMICS IN CIVIL AND CRIMINAL LITIGATION

By

CATHY E. BENNETT
Cathy E. Bennett & Associates, Inc.
Jury and Trial Consultants
Galveston, Texas

and

ROBERT B. HIRSCHHORN
Cathy E. Bennett & Associates, Inc.
Jury and Trial Consultants
Galveston, Texas

Edited by Eda Gordon

ST. PAUL, MINN.
WEST PUBLISHING CO.
1993

ISBN 0-314-01168-4

Bennett-Jury Selection Text Vol.

This work is dedicated to Cathy "Cat" Bennett. She taught us to be better lawyers, but more importantly, she taught us to be better human beings. Cat is gone now, but her spirit shall live forever. We must carry on her message of love and justice for all.

ROBERT B. HIRSCHHORN

*

INTRODUCTION

The late Marvin Teague, a Justice on the Texas Court of Criminal Appeals, succinctly stated the biggest problem with jury selection:

> "If one thing is clear from our published opinions in this area of the law it is that potential jurors frequently misunderstand the questions put to them by attorneys during *voir dire*. The problem is often exacerbated by the questions themselves."

Hernandez v. State, 757 S.W.2d 744, 747 (Tex.Cr.App.1988). This difficulty permeates all of our relationships—those with clients, judges, witnesses, friends, family and juries.

This guide is intended for experienced and novice litigators, social scientists, jury consultants and legal staff. Criminal defense lawyers, prosecutors, plaintiff's counsel, civil defense attorneys and judges should equally benefit from this collaborative effort. This book is based on over thirty (30) years we've collectively spent in courtrooms throughout America. Having assisted with jury selection and trial strategy in over 850 civil and criminal trials, every single idea discussed in this guide has been tried and tested in the courtroom.

Drawing on our courtroom experiences, we have attempted to include as many ideas as possible. Each and every time we assist with jury selection or trial strategy we learn something new. Effective jury selection and trial presentation are ongoing learning processes. Learning from previous mistakes and keeping an open mind to new methods will enhance the lawyer's ability to effectively communicate with the jurors and other trial participants.

Many trial lawyers feel that jury selection is the most difficult part of the trial. It is easy to understand this concern: trial lawyers have been taught it is good lawyering to carefully think out every aspect of the case, from Opening Statement to Closing Argument. Lawyers are reasonably certain what the witnesses will say and can prepare accordingly. Jury selection is quite the opposite. The lawyer knows what questions to ask but has no idea what answer the prospective juror will give. The fear of the unknown, or worse yet, the bad answer, has caused many attorneys to shy away from the intended purpose of *voir dire* and turn it into a perfunctory process where little or no information is learned about the potential jurors.

While some lawyers may be good speakers, they often are not good listeners. For this reason, we've included coverage of the client interview, depositions, grand juries, numerous aspects of *voir dire*, and other related matters in this book. It is the combination of speaking and listening skills that give the lawyer a trial foundation. We advise adding a jury and trial consultant to the legal team to aid with this—someone who can be the lawyer's eyes and ears, someone who is aware of what people are feeling and thinking, and someone sensitive to the emotions and preconceptions behind what they are saying. The consultant, as you will see, wears many hats and can be whatever the lawyer wants or needs, short of a stand-in. This book, however, speaks predominantly to "you", the lawyer, who with or without the help of a consultant will conduct a better *voir dire* and create the conditions for a better result, if you incorporate these techniques in your trial practice.

There are lawyers who would argue that the first twelve people on a jury panel would be as likely to render a favorable verdict as the twelve who are selected after careful investigation and *voir dire*. We would strongly disagree. Many years of trial experience have convinced us first, that jury selection is the most critical aspect of a jury trial, and second, of the importance of adopting a "jury" perspective from the beginning of the case starting with the client interview. This means not only winning the case participants' hearts and minds but getting inside their thoughts and feelings. It also includes awareness and sensitivity to your client's emotions and ideas.

This guide sets out the various options available to the lawyer in no budget, low budget or unlimited budget litigation. Whether you are litigating a rear end collision, complex commercial issue or a death penalty case, this guide contains ideas and techniques that will improve your trial and people skills. The authors personally have used the tools outlined in this book in cases with no money, as well as, those with large budgets.

There are a variety of problems associated with jury selection: 1) jurors are reluctant to talk; 2) jurors do not disclose their honest thoughts and feelings when they do talk; 3) some jurisdictions do not allow attorney participation during *voir dire*; and, 4) time limitations being placed on *voir dire*. This guide seeks to address these issues and a host of other matters and problems associated with being a lawyer. Our goal is to improve the quality and quantity of information obtained during all aspects of trial practice.

Our suggestions are what we know at this time, the outgrowth of experience. We find that like the law, our theories evolve and change with our exposure to new situations. The ideas we share with you are based on our present knowledge and as with all evolutions may change with new information and input. The process is dynamic, like all relationships. Our desire is to take the mystery out of what we do as consultants and pass our philosophy on to you. We do not feel any of our ideas are the only way to be your best at lawyering—just a spark to ignite your creativity.

Because of the every-changing nature of the law, we cannot guarantee that the case law cited in the text and in sample motions and memoranda is up-to-date. Legal analysis, where included, is current as of publication, to the best of our knowledge. The sample pleadings provided in the Appendices span many years of creative lawyering in prominent, and not so prominent cases. They are the "state of the art" in content but not definitive in case law. All cites should be Shepardized to assure their applicability in your case.

Our desire in writing this work was to define our philosophy of communication that which we believe has proven effective. Most of us think we are good communicators and yet, listen far less than is necessary. We've striven to give you the guts of how we prepare for and assist during a case. We ask that your read our thoughts with an open mind and an open heart.

CATHY E. BENNETT
ROBERT B. HIRSCHHORN

Galveston, Texas
April, 1992

*

ACKNOWLEDGEMENTS

We would like to thank family members, friends, and organizations who have been instrumental in the formation of this work. We do not claim any part of this book as having been any original thought of ours but a collection of philosophies and feelings we have learned through the years from our family, loving friends, teachers, spiritual and psychological leaders, jurors, law office staff members, lawyers and judges.

Eda Gordon, our editor, to you we are deeply indebted because without your guiding hand, organizational skills and loving ways this work would have never come to fruition. Your touch, brilliance, kindness and endearing spirit is the pulse of the entire book. We are on our knees in your honor for this hope we have in this chronicle.

Three people volunteered their valuable knowledge to read through our book and lend their precious observations. Joan Cheever, Richard Kammen, and Rebecca Christy, on short notice, jumped in and helped us. Thank you from the bottom of our hearts.

We would like to thank Cat's Mom, Jimmie Ellis, whose non-judgmental way has shown her the way to treat other people; her Dad, Glenn Ellis, for teaching her how to feel comfortable speaking in front of people and the importance of communicating well on your feet, and for his special love; her brother and sister-in-law, Bill and Gail Ellis, for being supportive; and her sister, Rebecca Christy, who has been a very loving and caring friend.

We are grateful to Robert's Dad and Step-Mom, Leo and Evelyn Hirschhorn, for their constant prayers and love for us. Thelma Hirschhorn, Robert's Mom, for her kindness. Richard and Gail Epstein, Neil and Alice Hirschhorn, and Joel and Evie Hirschhorn for their love and support.

We would like to thank our special little son, Matthew, for being the sweetest boy in the entire universe. And to Spirit, our loyal Weimaraner friend, for truly exemplifying unconditional love.

Clients are the backbone of this book and the impetus for its being written. Some special clients are the American Indian Movement, who were our first clients and who taught us about the earth and spiritual communication. Our death penalty clients who taught us about the value of all people and that each person has meaning. Our middle class clients who taught us we are all the same and there is no station in life. And, of course, the poor who suffer for us all.

We especially remember Dr. Will Smith who came into our lives at a time when we needed a good friend and healer, and who has remained inspirational to us personally. We would also like to thank Will Smith's entire family for opening up their home amd hearts to us and making our family feel a part of theirs when we needed a circle of love.

The following organizations and people associated with them have been our touchstone. First and foremost, the National Association of Criminal Defense Lawyers and its numerous presidents, board of directors, and executive directors have been extremely helpful. Especially Keith Stroup, the Executive Director, who has been a strong believer in jury and trial consultation and its sweet loving Deputy Executive Director, Cynthia (Cindy) Magill, who has been a long time friend and motivational colleague. The National Criminal Defense College which has been the most spectacular training institute in America for lawyers and has done more to educate trial attorneys than any other group. Deans John Ackerman and Deryl Danzler have been two of the most instrumental people nationally in encouraging lawyers to look at the sensitive side of their natures.

Other organizations that have been helpful in spreading the positive message have been Byron McCoy's University of Houston Trial Advocacy Institute for Civil Lawyers, Wyoming Trial Institute which has been headed by Justice Robert Rose and presently Justice Joe Cardine, California Attorneys for Criminal Justice, Texas Criminal Defense Lawyers Association, and Georgia Legal Services. The Legal Services Training Program in Washington, D.C. and Georgia Legal Services were the first two groups to recognize the importance of listening skills in the law and to them and their ground-breaking awareness, the authors will forever be indebted.

The courage to fight the good fight has always been exemplified by Morris Dees and the Southern Poverty Law Center's litigators through the years, such as Judge John Carroll, Dennis Balske and Richard Cohen. Their valiant work with the death penalty and civil rights litigations involving the struggle against racism and prejudice in this country has taught us all lessons. Thank you, Morris, for being such a special friend and inspiration to us all.

Friends who have been loving and supportive personally, professionally, and in other ways, are too numerous to list, but a few have shown like sparkling stars through the years:

The philosophy that is communicated in this book has come from such psychological giants as Dr. Robert North, who was Cathy Bennett's psychology and counseling teacher, and Carl Rogers, Ph.D., one of the founders of the field of humanistic psychology. Santa Fe Community College in Gainesville, Florida, West Georgia College in Carrollton, and University of Florida gave Cathy her most important psychology instructions.

Louise Yearwood, thank you very much for being the first one to believe in Cat professionally and to have dedicated your keen people and managerial skills back in the beginning when there was only love and no money to pay you for all your hard work. You stood beside Cat and encouraged Cat to keep going because you felt this mission was valuable.

Dr. Rusty London for your spiritual encouragement and support in teaching us the valuable lesson that no one is in charge as much as we would like to think that someone is.

Dr. John McConahay, thank you for being our survey consultant. You have worked with us longer than anyone and always with enthusiasm. Your instincts and awareness of our society has helped many clients.

Thank you, Juanita Brooks for being there always and being the softness of a real friend. Brenda Hampton and Dr. Bob for assisting in our daily spiritual growth. Wendy Eaton for being an example of what "friendship" really means. Cee Cee Glenn for always knowing how to cheer us up. Becky Lynn for being a great friend and colleague. Richard and Laurie Tegtmeier, Mike Norris, Robert Fogelnest, Bart Sheela, Alan Silber, Alan and Debbie Caplan, Shari Marger, Aunt Pat and Uncle Jerry, Aunt Kat, Aunt Johnnie, Stanley Schneider, Jim Jenkins, Andrea Lyons, Martha Garrett, Dawn Eden, Wayne Pressel, Skip Glenn, Michael Christy, Roy Black, Nancy Hollander, Jeff Weiner, Tony Cueto, Mike Dowd, David Lewis, Mark Donatelli, Marian and Karen Rosen, Reber Boult, Jim and Gilda Shellow, Lillian Sumerall, and John Boston, thank you for your help through the years.

We'd like to thank the countless medical people who have been extremely supportive of us, but especially Dr. Aman Buzdar, Dr. Eva Singletary, and Dr. Carl Simonton for their caring and healing energies.

Lew Gerwitz, Bruce Ellison, William Kunstler, Dan Jackson, John Lowe, Jack Swartz, Bob Robideau, Paulette D'Auteil, Leonard Peltier, Dino Butler and many other Native American leaders and believers who have paved the path and been the path.

The following group of law students performed our legal research under the direction of a finc lawyer, David Norris. We would like to thank them for their help: Thomas Peters, Alan Ryan, David McLenachen, Thomas Cashman, Carol Repasky, Dem Hopkins, William "Biff" Johnson, Dennis De Caro, Jay W. Stein, and Art Gasey.

Our appendices are a collection of motions, memorandums of law, affidavits and other work produced by some of the best people in the business. We would like to thank them for being so generous with all of us and for knowing that their labor will help many of you out there in the field. The following is what we hope is a complete list of those folks. If we have inadvertently left anyone out, we hope you will forgive us.

Harry Nass
Danny Davis
Janet Clow
Robert Fogelnest
Michael Mears
Roger Finzel

Theodore Wells
Paul Grand
Alan Silber
Joseph Hayden
Fred Hafetz
John Arseneault

ACKNOWLEDGEMENTS

Gerald Lefcourt
Stephen Berlin
Marisa Mendez
Mark Schnapp
William F. Bryan
Robert Buckout, Ph.D.
Morris Dees
Bruce Lyons
Robert Shapiro
Geena Eichenberg
Pat Mika
John Cotsirilos
Robert Willman
Mark Donatelli
David Stafford
Steve Bright
Althea Buafo
Robert Schwartz
Frank Cox
Roy Black
Mark Seiden
Holly Skolnick
John McConahay, Ph.D.
Richard Cohen
Juanita Brooks
Alan Caplan
David Lowe
Richard Tegtmeier
Jay Grossman
Elizabeth Missakian
Cynthia LeBourgeois
Joseph Beeler
Don Re
Gerald Christensen
Reber Boult
Steven Feldman
Kathryn Lund Ross
Richard Zimmer
Terry McCarthy
Mike Millman
Tim Ford
Skip Gant
Robert B. Hirschhorn
Howard Weitzman
Larry Biggam
John Gallagher
Barry Tarlow
Timothy Rutherford
Michael Thorman
Kevin McNalley
Karina Wicks
Richard Davis

Thank you Susan Johnson Watt, Jackie Puentes, Mary Ann Bustamante, Wanda Reed, and Bonnie Louvierre for your countless hours typing and organizing the book.

We regret all of you whom we failed to mention. You know how we love you and the warm breeze you are to us.

Most timely, we would like to thank all that is—The Great Spirit for giving us the time and space to complete this message.

A message we listen to each day, each moment, is that we are all the same—we all want the love in our lives, that gentle is easier than tough, that ego is an inhibitor to flow, that quiet is better than loud, and letting "being", be all that is. . .

CATHY E. BENNETT
ROBERT B. HIRSCHHORN

Galveston, Texas
(409) 763–0700
April, 1992

SUMMARY OF CONTENTS

*

TABLE OF CONTENTS

CHAPTER 3. GRAND JURIES

CHAPTER 6. SURVEYS

CHAPTER 7. IMPROVING *VOIR DIRE* CONDITIONS

CHAPTER 8. QUESTIONNAIRES

TABLE OF CONTENTS

CHAPTER 12. *VOIR DIRE* STRATEGY

TABLE OF CONTENTS

CHAPTER 13. RELATING TO JURORS

CHAPTER 14. VOICE INFLECTION/BODY LANGUAGE/ NON-VERBAL COMMUNICATION

TABLE OF CONTENTS

TABLE OF CONTENTS

*

APPENDICES VOLUME CONTENTS

APPENDICES TO CHAPTER 1. JURY AND TRIAL CONSULTANTS

APPENDICES TO CHAPTER 3. GRAND JURIES

APPENDICES TO CHAPTER 5. FOCUS GROUPS AND MOCK TRIALS

APPENDICES VOLUME CONTENTS

APPENDICES TO CHAPTER 7. IMPROVING *VOIR DIRE* CONDITIONS

APPENDICES VOLUME CONTENTS

APPENDICES TO CHAPTER 8. QUESTIONNAIRES

APPENDICES VOLUME CONTENTS

APPENDICES VOLUME CONTENTS

APPENDICES VOLUME CONTENTS

BENNETT'S GUIDE
TO
JURY SELECTION AND TRIAL DYNAMICS
IN
CIVIL AND CRIMINAL LITIGATION

Chapter 1
JURY AND TRIAL CONSULTANTS

Table of Sections

§ 1.1 Overview

The booming field of jury and trial consultation was started by a handful of people from around the country who believed that people with a social science background could be helpful to attorneys in jury selection and other trial-related matters. They began working with lawyers on surveys, mock trials, jury selection, questionnaires, witness preparation, trial observation, design of opening and closing arguments and other matters related to the "people" aspects of trying a lawsuit. The field has now grown to sizeable proportions, drawing people from a variety of backgrounds, including psychology, counseling and sociology, acting and communication.

§ 1.2 The Necessity of a Consultant

In the age of massive TV consumption, "law and order" hysteria, the war on crime and tort reform, the need for someone to assist lawyers in jury selection and other emotional parts of a case has become paramount. Television floods American living rooms each night with images of missing people, lawyer and detective dramas and rampant "shoot-em-up" sagas. These have a profound influence on the average American, which can resonate in the jury box and magnify already strong feelings about lawyers, their clients and the issues in litigation. Lawyers have, therefore, come to realize that trial consultants are no longer a frivolous luxury, to be used in the highly publicized, sensational case. A consultant can give invaluable feedback and guidance from the standpoint of someone who thinks more like a juror than like a lawyer.

Some law firms and state law offices have actually hired an in-house jury and trial consultant. This, the authors believe, is the wave of the future. Most large offices have in-house accountants and in-house experts; it only makes sense to have an in-house jury and trial consultant. For the smaller law firm, having a sounding board to confer with on jury and trial issues is very important. An hour or two of a consultant's time can help the lawyer phrase *voir dire* questions and take a fresh look at case issues.

§ 1.3 In Court Versus Out of Court

Some lawyers and consultants are more comfortable with the jury and trial consultant only being involved outside of the courtroom. This would mean that they would assist lawyers in case analysis, *voir dire* questions and presentation, surveys, witness preparation, mock trials and other aspects of trial strategy. They would not appear at any time in the courtroom. In some cases, this can be advantageous to the attorney because the other side may not otherwise consider hiring its own jury and trial consultant. There is a disadvantage, however, since much of the assistance that a trial consultant can offer comes into play when the consultant has a chance to actually eye-ball the jurors with the lawyer and evaluate in-court perceptions against the pre-trial research that has been compiled. How the lawyer uses the consultant is ultimately a matter of personal preference and resources.

The fear that jurors will resent lawyers who have jury and trial consultants should not be a factor in having the consultant in the courtroom. Jurors interviewed post-trial have consistently said that the jury and trial consultant's presence during the trial made them feel the necessity to be even more fair in looking at and verbalizing their biases and prejudices. They felt that the jury and trial consultant had special training in non-verbal language and could detect someone who is not telling the truth. This impact is a favorable one. Jurors have also said that though they may have felt some resentment during the course of jury selection, once they were sworn in they felt special because they had been approved by one of those "new-fangled things" called a jury and trial consultant. In hundreds of cases it has been the rare juror who has ever continued to hold resentment toward the lawyer for hiring a consultant. Most of them realize the difficulty lawyers have in not only getting jurors to discuss their thoughts and feelings openly, but also in presenting a case to a group of strangers.

§ 1.4 The Consultant and *Voir Dire*

Jury and trial consultants can assist lawyers during in-court jury selection and in developing a strategy for getting *voir dire* expanded. Their other main role is to assist in the design of *voir dire* questions that will ferret out people's true thoughts and feelings to help develop cause challenges and effectively use peremptory challenges. Prior to trial, they meet with the lawyer either via telephone or in person regarding the facts of the case and advise the lawyer on the main subjects on which the jury needs to be questioned. This means boiling down the complicated issues of the case to four or five subjects that are the most relevant. At trial, they normally sit next to the lawyer during jury selection. They keep track of verbal and non-verbal responses and contrast them with any investigative information; suggest questions to unmask a particularly inscrutable juror; they compare last-minute notes on cause and peremptory challenges; and generally help the lawyer use his or her time in the most productive way.

§ 1.5 The Consultant and the Client Interview

Should you find a consultant, or even better, have worked with a consultant whose impressions you value, it is worthwhile to have the consultant sit in on a client interview. Not only will you want your client to meet the person who will be evaluating the jury panel and to understand the importance of jury selection in the outcome of his or her trial, but the consultant's skills can immediately come into play.

The consultant can explore and put into perspective background information and other details about the client that will affect the case strategy. The consultant, from experience, can identify the characteristics of the client that jurors will find acceptable and unacceptable, and guide the lawyer on how to best present the client. On a personal level, consultants are generally more natural at "hand-holding" and can therefore further the lawyer's rapport with the client and the client's family and friends.

(*See* Appendix 1A for a sample motion requesting the court to appoint and authorize funds for a jury and trial consultant in a death penalty case. The format may be adapted for a non-capital case, as well as civil cases.)

§ 1.6 Evaluating a Consultant—Generally

As with the legal profession, different consultants have different philosophies about ways to work. Attorneys should carefully interview the consultants under consideration, not only to determine the scope of their experience, but to gauge if their philosophy is compatible. Find out how they think and feel, and how they believe they can be of assistance to you. Some consultants, for example, believe in giving the lawyer only a juror profile, while others feel that it is preferable to work with a whole perspective on the case. Instead of offering a quick fix, they will help the lawyer explore more effective ways to tackle each step. Your choice should be the consultant you can get along with, who will also challenge your case theories.

§ 1.7 Evaluating a Consultant—Experience

Experts learn their trade at different rates. In retaining a trial consultant, it is important to find out the number of cases the consultant has worked on and the specific role he or she played in those cases. Given the attorney-client and expert work-product privileges, consultants may not be able to tell you about some of their cases. You should listen carefully to what they say about what they did on hypothetical cases to determine their true experience. This is essential because you will soon come to realize that many jury and trial consultants are extremely good communicators. They can "talk up" their experience, way beyond their abilities. Others will admit to limited experience but have incredibly keen instincts. You should listen for that as well. The key is to observe the consultant's awareness of your jury issues and to listen for the ability to give constructive and insightful assistance. Consultants can be of help to you by the fact that their ears and eyes are trained to "think" on a different level.

§ 1.8 Evaluating a Consultant—References

It is important to ask jury consultants for references and to follow up. Do not call just the references the consultant lists on a résumé.

You should ask for specific cases the consultant has worked on and the names and telephone numbers of the lawyers involved. This will aid you in finding out what those lawyers' experiences were with the consultant and in determining the consultant's scope of expertise and credibility.

§ 1.9 Evaluating a Consultant—Fee Schedules

Carefully discussing fees with the consultant is imperative. The flat rate, hourly fee or daily rate, as well as out-of-pocket expenses, should be discussed in advance and agreed upon. This will prevent problems midstream. As with any unpaid professional, consultants who feel they have not been paid according to their understanding of the agreement can become frustrated, which can drain the energy and focus you are counting on to assist you in trial. Therefore, taking care of financial business beforehand is very important to everybody concerned.

§ 1.10 Letter of Employment

A letter of employment is beneficial when a jury and trial consultant is brought in on a case. First, it establishes the breadth of services that the lawyer and consultant have agreed the consultant will provide, and second, it confirms that the consultant has been hired by the lawyer and is protected under the work-product privilege. The lawyer should send a letter of employment to the consultant with the retainer and a copy should be placed in the case file. This will protect the client should the trial consultant ever be subpoenaed along with his or her work product. The letter of employment also should stipulate what obligation the attorney will assume to compensate the consultant if there is any litigation regarding the consultant's work. (*See* Appendix 1B for a sample letter of agreement.)

§ 1.11 Contracts

Most jury and trial consultants have decided that any major work with an attorney should be covered by a contract. This assures that everyone is clear about the terms of payment, time of payment, amount of payment and how expenses will be determined. Additionally, the contract should delineate how the consultant's fee will be calculated should the case settle and what will be done should the consultant be subpoenaed by opposing counsel. The consultant should prepare the contract with the advice of his or her own attorney, after thorough discussion of these matters with the hiring counsel, and not begin work until the contract is signed.

§ 1.12 Attorney–Client Privilege

It is vital that the consultant be included in the attorney-client privilege because he or she must have information about the client and the facts of the case in order to adequately advise the attorney how to handle jury selection. The attorney-client privilege would apply in direct discussions about potentially damaging aspects of the client's background, specific case issues to be covered in *voir dire,* and survey and mock trial results as well as any other discussions or documents the consultant is made privy to in learning about the case.

The lawyer should make sure that the consultant, whether a veteran or neophyte, understands the scope and meaning of the attorney-client privilege. It should be made crystal clear if and when the consultant can discuss a case with outsiders and what role he or she played.

§ 1.13 Work Product

Written materials prepared or compiled by the consultant in anticipation of trial should likewise be protected from discovery under the work-product exception. Once again, it is the lawyer's obligation to let the jury and trial consultant know what materials are considered work product and which are not. A rule of thumb for the consultant is to mark every piece of paper transmitted to the lawyer, "Attorney–Client and Work–Product Privileges." If any documents arrive at the lawyer's office unmarked, they should immediately be stamped "Work Product," to ensure the privilege is in place.

§ 1.14 Where to Find a Consultant—Generally

The best place to find a consultant is through lawyers that have used the services of a particular consultant and been pleased with their work. Another good way to locate a consultant is by attending a seminar where a consultant is on the program. Check advertisements of national, state and local bar associations for mention of a consultant lecturing on jury issues. Go to the seminar and listen to the ideas and talk with the consultant, when possible, after the lecture.

You can also find consultants through the American Society of Trial Consultants [1], which publishes a directory. This is a national association of trial consultants whose membership includes many, but not all, of the country's leading consultants. Other good sources for consultants are the national offices of the National Association of Criminal Defense Lawyers and the American Trial Lawyers Association, the state branches of these organizations and state and local bar associations.

§ 1.14

1. American Society of Trial Consultants, Towson State University, Towson, Maryland 21204. Phone: (301)830–2448.

§ 1.15 Where to Find a Consultant—Undergraduate and Graduate School

Local colleges and universities are also a source of consultants to assist you on either a temporary or long-term basis. You should check both the undergraduate and graduate programs in departments that have the kind of training and skills that you are seeking.

§ 1.16 Where to Find a Consultant—Undergraduate and Graduate School—Psychology

The psychology department is the obvious place to begin your search for a jury and trial consultant. Contact the head of the department, or a professor you know, and ask if they have any bright, sensitive, intuitive and hard-working students that are interested in learning about a new and exciting field. You will almost always have someone bite that hook and you will find that most professors are eager to find placements for their students. This helps both you and the professor.

Psychology students should be interviewed by you personally to find out what type training they have had in non-verbal communication, small groups, one-on-one behavior, interviewing skills, language and voice intonation. If they have been trained in experimental psychology, they probably have very little understanding of the skills that you will need in your case preparation. If they are social psychology students, then they have probably had training in some statistical matters that can be of help if you desire to do a limited survey. Ask whether the students have any background in statistics and if not, what their specialization has been. Humanistic and clinical psychology students are a good bet for having the training in good observation, group and interviewing skills. Ask whether they have had any courses in listening and communication skills. Once again, your needs should determine the kind of student you seek.

§ 1.17 Where to Find a Consultant—Undergraduate and Graduate School—Sociology

Depending upon the school and the training curriculum, sociology students generally have had some kind of training or background in group behavior. This can be helpful since a jury is nothing more than a small group. You should further explore their knowledge of interviewing, non-verbal language and other observation skills. Observe them and watch for signs of effective relating and good intuition.

§ 1.18 Where to Find a Consultant—Undergraduate and Graduate School—Anthropology

If you are planning to do a background search on jurors, anthropology students can be helpful because of their interest in the study of the human animal and its environment. Once again, you should conduct a probing interview to determine how they will be helpful to you.

§ 1.19 Where to Find a Consultant—Undergraduate and Graduate School—Drama

Drama students have learned a lot about non-verbal language, tone of voice and body positioning. They can be helpful to the lawyer not only in determining which jurors to put on the case, but also in terms of gauging juror reactions to the lawyer's non-verbal communication. In preparation for trial, drama students can help evaluate the effectiveness of demonstrative evidence and suggest tactics to keep the jurors' interest.

§ 1.20 Where to Find a Consultant—Undergraduate and Graduate School—Art

Art students can assist with demonstrative aids. Marketing and/or graphic design experience can be invaluable in deciding how best to get your evidence across.

§ 1.21 Where to Find a Consultant—Undergraduate and Graduate School—Professors, Practicums, Internships, Class Projects

In discussing who will help you on a case, you will find many professors themselves who are interested. Explore the professors' credentials, time and availability, and interest in the project, as well as their rates for research, consultation and in-court testimony, if necessary. You will also want to know if they have given expert testimony and in what areas they have qualified as an expert, such as authenticating survey results in an evidentiary hearing or a pre-trial publicity motion, and the outcome of those cases.

While a professor may not be able to become personally involved, he or she may be willing to supervise a student on a practicum or internship basis. This arrangement would give the student incentive to work without your having to pay any money out of your pocket. You may feel it is appropriate to pay an hourly wage or some other kind of limited fee in order to help students through difficult times. Most of them, however, will be willing to work for the experience alone.

Having students do your jury selection research or participate in your jury selection for a class project can be very productive as well. Many professors will give interested students class credit to assist in a jury selection, write *voir dire* questions or sit as observers in a witness preparation session and thus learn about the field.

§ 1.22 Where to Find a Consultant—Legal Resources

Within the legal community there exists a fountain of expertise as well as a constituency eager for trial experience. Working, however, with colleagues trained in the law, or in training, can undermine your primary interest in getting the "people's view" of your case. Always consider their feedback in light of their experienced, yet jaded, eye.

§ 1.23 Where to Find a Consultant—Legal Resources—Law Schools

Law schools can lend a tremendous amount of assistance, not only in jury selection, but also in trial preparation. This valuable resource often goes untapped. Law professors will eagerly provide students to help with juror observation and juror investigation. Law students can also be used as mock jurors for feedback on opening statements and closing arguments, as well as your client's testimony. The caveat with using law students is that their perceptions have been altered through the reprogramming of law school. Some students escape the dehumanization process; many do not. You should use your instincts to determine whether or not you are working with a law student whose "juror" reactions have been affected by learning how to become a lawyer.

§ 1.24 Where to Find a Consultant—Legal Resources—Law School Clinics

Law students participating in mock trial competitions or legal clinics at law school are often more interested in litigation-related matters such as jury selection, opening statement, closing argument, witness and trial preparation. Given their natural interest, you can often approach clinical programs to recruit volunteers or students who will work for minimum wage. You will also find that many clinical professors are more than happy to allow you to use their mock courtroom, video equipment and video staff, an added help in preparing witnesses or conducting a mock trial. In exchange for using the facilities, clinical students who sign a confidentiality form can watch the mock trial from a viewing room as part of their education. Many law professors are not only interested but excited about this quid pro quo.

§ 1.25 Where to Find a Consultant—Legal Resources—National Association Student Divisions

The National Association of Criminal Defense Lawyers (NACDL) and the American Trial Lawyers Association (ATLA) have arms specifically for law students. Students who have joined these two associations tend to be more eager to be involved in litigation-related matters. Just the opportunity to work side by side with a practicing lawyer can draw some exciting talent.

§ 1.26 Where to Find a Consultant—Legal Resources—State and Local Bar Associations

You should not overlook litigation-related associations when seeking volunteers to assist you in trial preparation projects, such as mock trials and witness preparation sessions. The criminal law and young lawyers sections of the state bar, the local bar and specialty law associations can be excellent sources of help. Criminal defense lawyers and prosecutors, for instance, will have no problem finding interested participants for their projects within the criminal law association. Those who join the association are often eager to work hands on with practitioners for litigation experience.

§ 1.27 Where to Find a Consultant—Lay Assistance

The resources available are myriad. You should obviously seek assistance from traditional sources such as other lawyers, law students and lawyer associations but do not overlook valuable lay assistance from community people. Community people not only mirror the pool from which jurors are chosen, but also have knowledge of specific jurors and issues in the community that may affect those jurors in the jury box. This community-based input is discussed at length in Chapter 5, "Focus Groups and Mock Trials."

Chapter 2

CLIENT INTERVIEW

Table of Sections

§ 2.1 Overview

The initial client interview is the backbone of good legal representation. It is important to think of your client as your most important resource person—the person who knows the most about his or her life experiences, and facts that can assist in proving the case. Unfortunately, very few lawyers know how to conduct an effective client interview. Many lawyers leave this vital part of trial preparation to a paralegal, associate, or someone else in the law firm. This can be a grave mistake because the rapport between lawyer and client must be established from the beginning.

It is a well-known fact that clients consider the most difficult part of legal representation to be the relationship with their lawyer. Lawyers, likewise, consider the most difficult part of representing someone to be their relationship with the client. Both feel they have a hard time communicating with the other. This can be remedied by the lawyer giving emphasis and thought to the client interview. An effective interview is a state of mind—one that requires the lawyer to become the counselor at law, the adviser who listens *effectively* to what the client has to say. Effective listening is the type of communication that requires the interviewer to actively and sensitively *hear* what the client is saying. This means that the interviewer encourages the interviewee to do most of the talking and the interviewer listens and feeds back to the client what is being said.

The problem is that law school does not train lawyers to listen except as an adversary, ready to pounce for an objection or on cross-examination. In fact, law school drums out of most litigators the capacity for empathy and heart-felt warmth toward clients that is necessary in order to hear what may be the key to helping them. Establishing a strong relationship and good rapport with a client means removing the callus over your heart and allowing your feelings to surface. Responding from your heart as well as your head will make your client feel acknowledged and understood, and save you, your secretary, your associates and investigator much time in the long run preparing the case.

§ 2.2 Setting the Stage—Generally

How to conduct the client interview depends on the individual client and the circumstances—whether the client is emotionally upset, in physical pain, evasive, verbose, free or in jail. Whether the case is a civil or criminal matter may also have some bearing. The bottom line is not to attempt to maintain control of the interview too early. Trying to control prematurely can stifle building rapport and put you in a tug-of-war with the client. The best way to get the information you need and instill confidence in your ability to handle the case is to approach the client warmly and acknowledge the client's fears. Then begin to structure how to tackle the client's problem.

§ 2.3 Setting the Stage—Office Interview

Make your client feel comfortable. Nine times out of ten your client will feel like a stranger in a strange land on arrival at your office. Your front office staff should be instructed to "cut the ice" with a warm greeting, a handshake and an offer of something to drink. The client and any accompanying family members should be escorted to a seat and told, if possible, how long they must wait. None of us like to wait, and our anxiety level tends to increase if we have been given no indication of the amount of time we will be expected to wait. It is the same frustrating experience of waiting endlessly in a doctor's office. The client feels no different coming to see a lawyer for help. As you know, pain of a legal nature can be as bad as any physical pain a person can experience.

When you are ready, the client and family members should be shown to your office. You should introduce yourself and shake hands. Your office should be arranged so that you can sit next to the client as opposed to having the desk between you. It is a simple detail that will create a stronger rapport and a more open discussion with the client and family members. To establish rapport in the beginning of the interview, it is best not to take notes, so you have no need for the desk. If later in the interview you decide to take notes, you can move back behind the desk.

§ 2.4 Setting the Stage—Jail Interview

It is important that you make every effort to have a lawyer room during your first meeting with a client in jail. The client's anxiety level and fear are tremendous and having to speak to you through a glass or mesh wire, often in proximity of other inmates and guards, obviously erects a physical and psychological barrier. If necessary, file a motion in court for an attorney room.

Once your privacy is arranged, start by introducing yourself, shaking the client's hand and offering your business card. If you are an appointed lawyer or a public defender, you obviously have something to overcome because the client did not choose you. Do not hesitate to assure clients that their rights, liberties and welfare are what matter to you. They are your responsibility and sole interest at the moment, and you answer to them, as their representative. Tell the clients how you value having the privilege of representing them and how much you enjoy being a trial lawyer. Explain how you have been trained to try cases and that you like winning.

§ 2.5 Setting the Stage—Hospital Interview

A hospital visit is both trying and necessary. It should go without saying that a lawyer should *never* initiate contact with a client in the hospital without a specific request from the client or family. Those who solicit business in hospitals give all hard-working lawyers a bad name.

The initial consultation with a hospitalized client should be done personally by the attorney—not a secretary, paralegal, legal assistant or investigator—unless the client has an established working relationship with the attorney. The quickest way for the attorney to build rapport is by showing enough concern to see the client personally. At the hospital the attorney should find out how the client is being treated and what can be done to make sure the hospital is attending to the client's needs. We also recommend that the attorney consult the family and hospital staff about the medications the client is taking. If the client is on pain medication, the attorney should not even raise the issue of signing a retainer agreement.

The initial hospital interview should be limited in time and scope, depending on the circumstances. The primary goals should be comforting the client and family and accumulating the minimal amount of information necessary to start preparation for litigation. Again, as with all initial interviews, you should use open-ended questions to obtain the information. Be mindful of the fact that the client may very well have a different agenda. "What is going to happen to me?" may be the more important question to the client than the attorney's inquiry, "What happened to you?" If you find that the client is not able to assist in the fact-finding process, you may want to seek answers from the family, hospital staff, paramedics, or other witnesses. In the end, however, your primary source of information should be the client. A subsequent interview should be set up as soon as possible.

Though the hospital interview may not be totally fruitful, and more than likely a hardship on everyone, do not underestimate its value. Taking the time to comfort a client at this critical stage pays huge dividends in building the attorney-client relationship.

§ 2.6 Setting the Stage—Corporate Clients

Corporations can be the largest fee-generating clients and the most demanding, but they do not fit a pattern. In our experience, they run a wide gamut. Some of our most informal, congenial clients have been Fortune 500 companies, while the more formal, demanding ones have been small, though hugely successful, businesses. To create a favorable first impression, and a lasting relationship, find out whom you are dealing with and make every effort to accommodate their needs. For instance, some lawyers always insist on meeting at the lawyers' office during normal working hours. We would encourage flexibility. By offering the client the opportunity to set the agenda—where and when to meet—you will show consideration for your client. Seeing you take them into account, they often not only allow you to make this initial scheduling decision but begin trusting your input in substantive matters.

§ 2.7 Laying the Groundwork

It is important that clients understand what the focus and direction of the interview is going to be. Tell them how you intend to conduct the interview. Explain that initially you would like to get to know them and something about their background and family, and that later in the interview you will be asking more specific questions about the case. It is important that you tell them how long you expect the interview to last so that when it comes time to close they have some forewarning. You might also tell them that you will be taking notes later in the interview and the purpose of those notes.

Tell them that you will be discussing with them the legal process their particular case will follow. If it is in civil court, you should discuss depositions, interrogatories and other terms the client needs to know to understand the stages of litigation. If it is a criminal case, it is important that you discuss the preliminary hearing, grand jury, motions, etc. It is imperative that you presume the client knows nothing about the legal system. If a client says, "Oh, I know what that is, let's move on," you should ask what he or she understands the term to mean. It has often been found that clients misinterpret what is happening in the course of the legal process and become confused because no one has taken the time to explain the process properly.

§ 2.8 Discovering the Problem

It is important that you get the client to tell you the problem as opposed to you defining the problem initially. This means that you must listen to what the client says and refrain from voicing your opinions during this initial interview. Your non-verbal language is as important in this process as your words. Something as simple as nodding your head in affirmation as the client talks will encourage the client to continue revealing information to you. Another useful non-verbal technique is to move your hand in a circular motion as if you were pulling information out of the client. Make sure that your feet are on the ground and that your hands are in an open posture. Avoid crossing your arms over your chest, crossing your legs, or clenching your hands. All of these gestures communicate being closed rather than open to what your client is saying, and can make the difference between a shallow and fruitful interview.

§ 2.9 Acknowledging Feelings

Opening an interview requires *open-ended questions* that encourage the client to speak and bring his or her feelings to the surface. You might say:

1) *Tell me what brings you here today?* or
What's on your mind? or
What is bothering you?

2) (In a criminal case) *Why did the police arrest you? What is incorrect about what they say happened? What would you like me to know about your case?* or *What would you like me to know about the situation in which you find yourself?*

3) (In a civil case) *Tell me what happened. When did you first start feeling pain?*

These are examples of open-ended questions that will open up communication and get to the information you need from your client.

Carl Rogers, father of humanistic psychology, discovered in 1937 that there were basic ingredients necessary to get someone to open up in any kind of relationship. These response types can be categorized. The number one response type to get people to talk with you is the *open-ended question,* discussed above, which is a *what, why, when, where* and *how* kind of question. *See* Section 2.16, *infra,* for a list of open-ended questions that can be used in initial client interviews.

Reflection, the second response type, involves giving feedback, based on what you have heard the client say. This is an extremely important interview technique because, like peeling an onion, as you acknowledge feelings you can proceed to a deeper level with that client. However, unless you acknowledge the first layer of feelings, you will not get to the next layer. You must take the time to mirror your clients' feelings so they can see their own experience through your eyes. It helps clients to hear how their representations of their life, the facts of the case, and other circumstances that may assist or hamper their case sound to someone else, and will eventually sound to a jury.

This exchange will also help clients feel safe with you, and the more secure they feel, the more apt they are to reveal important issues and feelings. In the process, you get to know them as human beings so that you can be a more effective advocate and they can feel that you truly care about what is happening to them. Once the client begins unfolding his or her story, you can begin acknowledging the feelings, expressed or unexpressed. This means that when you see the client is nervous, you say to the client, "You appear to be nervous, tell me about that." If the client appears angry, you can say, "You are angry, tell me about that". If the client is expressing depression or sadness, again you can respond, "You appear down or sad, tell me about that."

Another of Carl Rogers' important ingredients for opening up an interview is *clarification.* Here you express to clients that you have heard them say one thing at one point in the interview and something else at another point in the interview. You would explain, for example:

You say that you are not angry with that person and yet I notice that when you talk about them, you grit your teeth and your fist is in a ball. This indicates to me that you do have some anger. Will you tell me about that?

Clarification, in other words, requires the interviewee to give more information to the interviewer. In this instance, you, the lawyer, are the interviewer; you must put before the client what you are hearing so that he or she can clarify the issues. Many lawyers get into trouble here when they begin to jump to conclusions as to what the client means. It is your job not to jump to *any* conclusions during this initial interview, but instead listen to what the client has to say.

The next response type that Carl Rogers discusses is called *self-disclosure.* This ingredient is probably the most difficult for attorneys because it requires them, once again, to be human, to discuss with the client how *they* feel about what is happening. For example, if a client says that a brother was severely injured in an automobile accident and that truly makes you feel sad, it is important that you tell the client. Likewise, if you are uncomfortable with something the client says, it is important that you say to the client, "This makes me feel uncomfortable." It is essential that you are truthful with the client, who will read your non-verbal language and know that you're feeling something different from what you're expressing. Clients also misjudge your true feelings unless you give them some guidance. This can lead to mistrust and misunderstanding, and destroy the good rapport you have worked to build.

Carl Rogers also identified four response types which tend to shut down an interview and inhibit further communication. These ingredients do have their place in some interviews, but generally are used sparingly in an initial client interview because they preclude opening and encourage closing. (*See* Sections 2.34 through 2.38, *infra,* for "parting words" that elicit closed-ended responses.)

§ 2.10 Taking Notes—Generally

Note taking is advisable at some point during the initial interview. If you have limited time, however, the notes should always be taken after you leave the interview as opposed to taking up your precious time by jotting down notes. Let the client know if you will need to take notes in a more lengthy interview. There are some specific rules on note taking as covered in the following sections.

§ 2.11 Taking Notes—Tell the Client the Purpose of the Notes

Clients have no reason, in the initial interview, to trust you. They may even fear that your notes will be shown to someone who could harm them. You must reassure them that you are worthy of their trust. Stress that the notes are confidential and used only by you and your staff to recall important points. This reassurance will make your clients more comfortable and gain you respect.

§ 2.12 Taking Notes—Do Not Begin Any Interview by Taking Notes

The client is always going to be more interested in what you are writing on the piece of paper than the question you are asking. At the least, your note taking will be a distraction, inhibiting the client's responses. You are best served by asking open-ended questions for at least the first 15 to 30 minutes of an interview or until you see the client beginning to trust you. Then tell the client you need to take some notes because what they have to say is very important to you and you want to remember all of their points.

§ 2.13 Taking Notes—Note Only Important Facts; Otherwise Pay Attention

Many times when lawyers are first getting to know their clients, or if they are nervous, they tend to take more notes than are necessary. They then get more involved in what they are writing than what the client is saying. Often they wind up missing important cues as to what is happening in this client's life. The client's eye contact, voice, body language and other non-verbal and verbal exchanges are pieces of the puzzle that require a close watch. Paying attention is a greater priority than writing notes.

§ 2.14 Taking Notes—Offer to Give Your Client a Copy of Your Notes

Clients will rarely want your notes, but offering them a copy will make them feel more secure. Remember the goal is to save yourself time in the long run. A few extra courtesies help build a strong foundation between you and the client and facilitate further communication.

§ 2.15 Asking Open-Ended Questions—Generally

Below is a list of open-ended questions to open up avenues of discussion in an attorney-client interview and invite the client to elaborate rather than give a simple yes or no answer. Obviously, not all of these questions will be asked during the first interview, but they are the kind of questions that you should use in a lengthy interview. Given that each client is different, the lawyer must judge how far to delve at this early stage.

§ 2.16 Asking Open-Ended Questions—Background Questions

1) Tell me about your background.

2) Where did you grow up and what was your family like?

3) What is your relationship with your family now?

4) What is your relationship with your spouse, girlfriend or boyfriend?

5) How do your children see you?

6) What kind of jobs have you held in the past?

7) Describe your relationship with your present employer.

8) What kind of things will your present employer say about you?

9) Have you ever sued anyone in the past?

10) Has anyone ever sued you in the past? If so, tell me about that.

11) What can I read that will help me understand more about you or the company you work for?

§ 2.17 Asking Open-Ended Questions—Self-Description

1) Describe yourself to me.

2) What is your military background?

3) What would you be doing for work if you could do something other than what you're presently doing?

4) What are your strengths?

5) What are your weaknesses?

6) What kind of skeletons do you have in your closet that I should know about?

7) What are your hobbies?

8) What are your talents?

9) What kinds of books and literature interest you?

10) What were the happy parts of your childhood?

11) What were the painful parts of your childhood?

12) All of us have been a victim at some time in our lives. Please tell me about something that has happened to you that made you feel like you were a victim.

§ 2.18 Asking Open-Ended Questions—Jail Conditions

1) What has it been like for you here in jail?

2) What can I do to make it easier for you?

3) How have the guards been treating you?

4) How have your cellmates been treating you?

5) *Have you been able to receive a phone call? With whom have you spoken and what have they said about their willingness to help you?*

§ 2.19 Asking Open-Ended Questions—Trial Preparation

1) *Who are some people I can call who can help me locate your witnesses?*

2) *What confuses you about the court system?*

3) *What else would you like to know about the case now?*

§ 2.20 Asking Open-Ended Questions—Follow-up Questions

1) *What was that like for you?*

2) *Tell me more about that.*

3) *How did that affect you?*

4) *What else should I know about you?*

§ 2.21 Setting Parameters for What You Do and Do Not Want to Discuss

Sometimes a client has no trouble revealing what the lawyer needs to know to prepare the case. Other times a client is not willing to talk about the case, or is not ready to be honest about the facts. A good way to avoid starting on the wrong foot is to tell the client you are not interested in hearing the specifics during your first visit. Say at this point and time you are more interested in getting to know him or her. As the interview progresses, you can decide if it is opportune to go into more detail.

Cross-examining a client during the first interview is *absolutely* inappropriate. There will be plenty of time to make the client feel uncomfortable and intimidated. This is the time to open communication and build trust. If some inconsistencies arise during the course of the interview, and you, as counsel, feel you need to get to the bottom of this rapidly, tell the client, but do not attack. You should state what you feel and think. For example:

1) *I feel that it is important that we start off with an honest relationship.*

2) *I feel that there are some things that you are hiding from me.*

3) *This makes me feel uncomfortable, because unless I have all the information, I cannot represent you in the way I would like.*

4) *Please be honest with me so that I can do the best job that I can.*

This is different from cross-examining a client; this is being honest and direct, and provides a role model for the client, reflecting your hope and expectation of the client-attorney relationship.

§ 2.22 The Five Basics—Generally

Carl Rogers defined five basic ingredients that will result in open communication. They are as follows:

§ 2.23 The Five Basics—Empathy

To empathize is not the same as to sympathize. When you feel sympathy, you in essence feel sorry for someone. When you empathize, you put yourself into someone else's experiences and feelings in order to better understand that person. Empathy implies equality in a relationship as opposed to a superior/subordinate dynamic. For example, you probably will never know how it feels to be a truck driver, but you do know what it feels like to own your own business. You may never be in the position of a battered wife, but you know what it is like to be afraid. So there is a point of understanding that you need to reach. Time spent working with your client, sharing your understandings and how they affect you will help your client begin to open up to you. Empathy is very important in any interview situation.

§ 2.24 The Five Basics—Warmth

Lawyers must realize that being warm does not make you weak or susceptible to a client's whims. You can be a person and a lawyer at the same time. This is a fundamental concept that will be brought up throughout this book.

§ 2.25 The Five Basics—Respect

No one will voluntarily disclose information to someone that he or she does not respect or feels is disrespectful. If you think of someone in your own life that you felt comfortable talking to, undoubtedly it will be someone who gave you respect and, in turn, whom you respected. So you must treat clients respectfully, no matter what their station in life, and convey that you are a person you hope they will eventually respect.

§ 2.26 The Five Basics—Concreteness

Concreteness is similar to a topic sentence. If you have a question of a sensitive nature, explain to the client the necessity of the question so that the client understands in what direction you are going. Concreteness is nothing more than an explanation or statement that keeps an interview on track. It will save much confusion between you and the client and negate the client's feeling that you are prying into unnecessary territory. A little explanation will save a lot of resistance.

§ 2.27 The Five Basics—Congruence

Congruence is expressing on the outside what you are feeling on the inside. This is the honesty variable on the lawyer's part. This means if you are anxious, you tell the client that you are feeling anxious; if you are happy, you tell the client you are feeling happy. Once again, how can you expect the client to be open with you if you are not open?

§ 2.28 Summarizing the Content of the Interview

Once you have completed the bulk of the interview, it is important that you summarize with the client what you have learned. You should make sure that you have noted necessary information correctly and that the client feels that you have heard the important things that were said. Normally, as you summarize, the client will volunteer additional information that he or she did not feel comfortable giving you earlier in the interview. This is therefore a very important step.

§ 2.29 Assigning the Client Tasks to Help You

All of us are more apt to feel we are an important part of a team if we are given some responsibility. At the end of each interview the lawyer should have some things that the client can do to help prepare the case. We call this a "to do list." It accomplishes several things: It helps clients become part of their own representation; it makes them feel included and valued; and it helps them realize that hiring a lawyer does not mean turning over their life to the lawyer. You should also give interested family members some things they can do to help their loved one. The more input and helpers, the better off for everyone. If you are a privately retained lawyer, this may also dissuade clients from thinking that you just want to run up the bill. If they realize that they are cutting expenses by assisting you and that they can actually be helpful, this builds their trust in you and strengthens your relationship. Make a copy of the "to do list" for your client and family members and keep a copy for yourself so that when you next meet, you can make sure there has been follow-up.

Keeping your client's confidence strong is a very important part of any lawyer-client relationship. You should make it clear, however, that whatever is done regarding the case should be done with your advice and consent to assure that your client's interests are protected.

§ 2.30 Laying Out the Next Steps

At the end of the meeting, it is important to summarize what will happen next. Always remember that you understand the process but the clients and their family members may not. So, let them know what to expect in the future as far as court settings, investigation, interviews, etc. This will once again save your office staff and yourself unnecessary calls that could have been avoided by taking a little extra time to explain what the next steps will be.

§ 2.31 Keeping Promises and Appointments

Follow-through is as important as the interview itself. As in any relationship, if the lawyer promises something and does not come through, the client will feel neglected. It is especially frustrating if the client is in jail and feels he or she has no control over the events in his life. If you say you are going to bring cigarettes to the jail, do so. If you arrange to meet your client at his place of business to see how the corporation works, keep that appointment and be on time. If something occurs where you cannot keep a commitment, make sure that the client is informed. Make every effort to fulfill every promise you make to the client, or as many as possible, so that the client knows that you truly are a person of your word.

§ 2.32 Identifying Witnesses and Family

Names will invariably be mentioned as your client unravels his or her story. Make sure, before the close of the interview, that you have noted the important names—witnesses and family members, and any other persons with pertinent knowledge. Do not leave the interview without obtaining addresses and telephone numbers in your client's possession. While this information may be erroneous or out of date, it will give you a head start on the investigation of the case and provide leads that may not have been so readily accessible. You may also want to involve your client in paving the way for these interviews, if you think a prior introduction would help open communication.

§ 2.33 Ask What Else You Need to Know

Closure in an interview is as important as the opening. Close your interview by asking the client and family members what else you need to know about them or the situation that may help in preparing the case. Eliciting this information may take some additional time. When the client is through speaking, determine a mutually convenient time to meet again. Note the date in your calendar, and make every effort to keep that appointment. Write the time, date and place of the next appointment on the back of your business card and hand it to your client.

§ 2.34 Parting Words—Generally

As mentioned in Section 2.9, Carl Rogers identified four response types that tend to close communication. They are: advice, reassurance, closed-ended questions and interpretation.

§ 2.35 Parting Words—Advice

Advice has very little place in most relationships because it basically suggests to another person that you know more than he or she does. There are times when you will have to be direct with the client, but be careful of your approach. It is easy to put someone on the defensive. You should generally wait until the end of an interview to offer advice. Helpful advice is:

1) *Call me with questions.*

2) *Do not talk with others about your case unless you clear it with me.*

3) *Write down other things about yourself and the case that come to mind and write "Attorney-Client Privilege" at the bottom of each page.*

4) *Let me worry about your case.*

§ 2.36 Parting Words—Reassurance

Most clients do not feel reassured early in the relationship with their lawyer because they are too afraid. When lawyers say "everything is going to be okay"—generally to make *themselves* feel better—most clients feel this is false reassurance, and that everything is not going to be okay. So, ending an interview with "everything is going to be okay" will probably fall on deaf ears. Instead, assure the client that you are concerned about the situation, that you care, and that you are going to do everything in your power to make everything okay. Most importantly, do not lie to clients or give them false hopes. You will both be disappointed.

§ 2.37 Parting Words—Closed-Ended Questions

"Do you have any feelings about something?" Or, "Did this ever happen to you?" Those are closed-ended questions and do nothing but imply the answer to the client. Whenever possible, avoid closed-ended questions because they have the answer you expect within them and leave the client with very little room to elaborate. Instead close the interview with:

1) *What other questions do you have?*

2) *What are you thinking and feeling?*

3) *What else should I know about you and the case?*

§ 2.38 Parting Words—Interpretation

Another possible response is interpretation or analysis. When used inappropriately, this response tends to label a person by giving reasons for his or her feelings. It also assumes things about the person without enough data, leaving the person feeling misunderstood and judged. For example, in an effort to quell the fears of a client who says, "I'm afraid the police are following me," a lawyer might respond, "You sound like the typical paranoid client." Certainly, this is a way to shut down the lines of communication between client and counsel.

§ 2.39 Including a Consultant in the Client Interview

The client interview is the lawyer's opportunity to establish rapport with the client. Once some level of trust has been reached, it may be helpful to introduce the jury and trial consultant, who not only can explain the rigors of a jury trial but assist the lawyer in identifying case themes for *voir dire*. Observing how the lawyer listens to the client, the consultant may also be able to give the lawyer some pointers for relating to jurors. If the lawyer cannot listen to the client, it is likely the lawyer will have similar difficulty listening to jurors during jury selection. *See* Section 1.5, "The Consultant and the Client Interview," for further discussion on the consultant's potential input from participating in the client interview.

Chapter 3

GRAND JURIES

Table of Sections

---

§ 3.1 Overview

Grand juries hear testimony from victims, suspects, law enforcement officers and material witnesses. Lawyers representing anyone appearing before the grand jury must focus on protecting their client's rights. How many times has a client testified before a grand jury believing he was a witness and ended up being indicted? What could the lawyer have done to prepare the client that could have prevented the indictment or limited self-incrimination? What steps could the lawyer have taken to assure that the grand jury proceeding was fair?

Lawyers must be more creative with their approach to grand juries and not merely follow custom. Grand jury challenges, *voir dire,* investigation and documentary evidence are among the opportunities for creativity that could help divert indictment or reduce the indictable offense.

§ 3.2 Grand Jury *Voir Dire*—Generally

People forget that grand juries are nothing more than a body of citizens with their own biases, prejudices and reactions. This means that criminal lawyers need to pay particular attention to what kind of influences have preyed upon the open-mindedness of the grand jurors who will decide whether or not to render a true bill. Be creative in the use of this forum. Like any other jury proceeding, creative thinking can make a difference.

§ 3.3 Grand Jury *Voir Dire*—Uncovering the Effects of Publicity

Like petit jurors, grand jurors have read about events in their community. They understand the local pressures and forces at work. You should therefore file a motion to *voir dire* the grand jurors about the effects of the publicity upon their ability to hear the case with an open mind. The motion should request a hearing before a judge to present evidence supporting the need for *voir dire* in order to obtain an impartial grand jury, given the potential impact of the publicity. Ideally, extensive *voir dire* should be conducted by the attorney on an individual basis, in a sequestered setting. Should the court allow questioning, you will want to *voir dire* jurors in an open-ended manner using the following kinds of questions:

1) *What have you heard about this case through T.V., radio, newspapers, or word of mouth?*

2) *What was your reaction when you heard about this incident?*

3) *What was the reaction and feeling of the person who told you about this incident?*

4) *What do you think the members of our community feel about this case?*

5) *How do you think people would feel if the grand jury chose not to indict?*

6) *How would you feel about telling your neighbors, friends and family that you chose not to indict this particular person?*

7) *How many people have not been indicted since you've been on this grand jury?*

8) *Let's be honest with each other. There's pressure in the community to do what people want to see done. How do you think this pressure will affect your ability to be open to returning a no bill?*

§ 3.4 Grand Jury *Voir Dire*—Uncovering the Effects of Potential Contact With Parties

You should pay particular attention to the fact that the grand jurors know many people in the community. This means that they may have had some kind of personal or official relationship with people involved in prosecution of the case, such as the district attorney. File motions requesting the opportunity to examine grand jurors on this. If granted, you should *carefully voir dire* the grand jury on this subject. The kind of questions that should be asked of the grand jurors are:

1) *Who do you know that's involved in this case?*

2) *How do you know them?*

3) *What effect do you think this knowledge will have on you or them?*

4) (Read witness list) *Do you know any of the witnesses in this case?* (If yes) *Please tell us about this person.*

5) *What have you heard about the witnesses, their employers or family members?*

6) *What else should we know of your knowledge about any of the parties in this case?*

In addition, at the time of trial, you may want to file a motion to disclose the relationships between the grand jurors and state agencies in any way connected to the indictment. (*See* Appendix 3A for sample motion.)

§ 3.5 Grand Jury *Voir Dire*—Uncovering the Effects of a Co-defendant's Indictment

If one grand jury has already indicted a co-defendant, it is not unusual for another or the same grand jury to indict a second suspect. Grand jurors may have been exposed to publicity about the first indictment, coupled with their inclination to "go along with" the previous grand jury or their previous decision. It is your job to request the right to *voir dire* this grand jury on the effect of another grand jury's indictment or their prior indictment of a co-defendant. You should *voir dire* the grand jurors in the same manner you would a petit jury regarding influences on their view of the case. The kind of questions that should be asked on this subject are:

1) I'm sure that you've heard that my client's co-defendant was indicted by another grand jury. What did you think when you heard this? What was your reaction?

2) I am afraid that because you've already indicted another defendant, you may feel it is your obligation to indict my client as well. What do you think about my fear?

3) Why should I believe this grand jury is going to be fair to my client when another grand jury on similar evidence indicted a co-defendant?

4) Why do you think I should not fear that you will ignore things that would point to my client's innocence?

§ 3.6 Gathering Documents

Investigation should begin as soon as your client has hired you. Part of this investigation is gathering all the documents that you believe are going to be presented to the grand jury. If you discover documents favorable to your client's case that you believe the prosecutor will not present to the grand jury, you should file a motion requesting that these documents be submitted to the grand jury. Begin gathering documents as quickly as possible so that they can be preserved and presented to the grand jury if you feel they will assist your client.

§ 3.7 Preparing Fact Witnesses

Finding out what evidence will be presented to the grand jury is another priority. Learn who the fact witnesses are and what will be their testimony. Fact witnesses are sometimes represented by counsel, whom you should contact immediately to arrange interviews in their presence. At the interviews, you will want not only to ascertain the scope of the witnesses' testimony, but probe the witnesses' memory for other information important to the case that they may have otherwise omitted. Often witnesses are terrified of appearing before the grand jury and, out of fear or ignorance, do not realize they should tell all they know, not just the information the district attorney asks of them. It is also in your client's interest to assure them that it is okay to include helpful, as well as unhelpful, testimony about the accused. You should ask the witness (and his/her counsel) for permission to record this interview.

§ 3.8 Deciding Whether or Not Clients Should Testify—Generally

There have been numerous cases where a client testifying before the grand jury has resulted in a no bill. There are just as many cases where clients have testified and not only been indicted, but their testimony was used against them. This is obviously a judgment call only the lawyer can make in light of all the circumstances. The decision should be based, among other things, on: the client's prior record; his ability to speak in public; his ability to listen and respond to questions that will be asked by the prosecuting attorney or grand jurors; the relative weight of the incriminating and exculpatory evidence and whether or not he has a clear defense supported by the evidence and witnesses; the credibility of the witnesses; and generally, whether his testimony will leave a positive or negative impression.

In the rare instance where you decide your client's testimony may be helpful to set the record straight, you should be sure that your client understands the risk, and then take the time to adequately prepare him for the stand.

§ 3.9 Deciding Whether or Not Clients Should Testify—Prior Record

If your client has a prior criminal record, you should realize the impact this will have upon a grand jury. Like other jurors, they will be influenced by a client's lack of credibility in the past. If you are able to *voir dire* the jury you will have the opportunity to delve into this problem; if not, this should weigh in your decision whether or not your client should testify.

Obviously, other things about your client's nature, presence and overall verbal ability should also be taken into account to avoid character assassination. For instance, if your client has a chip on his shoulder or an attitude that says, "It is ridiculous that I am being charged," the grand jury may interpret this belligerence as guilt, or at least a lack of respect for the process, and deny him the benefit of the doubt. Again, preparation is the key.

§ 3.10 Preparing the Client for Testimony—Generally

You should prepare clients to testify before the grand jury with as much gusto as you would prepare for a petit jury. This means that you should take them through a Q & A session so they know what to expect from the prosecutor. It has proven helpful to have several lawyers conduct the examination so the client is prepared for different approaches and styles of questioning. Such preparation should be done diligently over several sessions to guarantee the best results when your client testifies.

§ 3.11 Preparing the Client for Testimony—Scope of Questions

The client should also understand when it is advisable to request assistance from counsel in the grand jury and when it is best to fly on his own—what areas are suitable for questioning and what areas are not. You should specifically discuss with the client the importance of knowing when the questions asked have exceeded the rules of evidence.

This will necessitate a mini-course in law, but will help your client recognize when to ask for leave to confer with you about whether or not to answer a particular question.

§ 3.12 Preparing the Client for Testimony—Requesting Assistance of Counsel

If in doubt, the client should always request assistance. In preparation, the client should go through the procedure of making the request and coming out to speak with counsel. He or she should have no hesitation or discomfort about exercising the right to confer with counsel. However, the client should be respectful when making the request. For example, "I mean no disrespect to the grand jury, but I respectfully request the opportunity to discuss this question with my attorney."

§ 3.13 Preparing the Client for Testimony—Scope of Investigation May Expand

It may be appropriate for the client, while testifying, to suggest to the grand jury that the investigation be expanded. Counsel should carefully consider how this suggestion should be made. It is your responsibility to ensure that clients are not put in a position of indicating that they have knowledge of facts which they actually do not have.

§ 3.14 Preparing the Client for Testimony—The Fifth Amendment

Your client may find it necessary to plead the Fifth Amendment, rather than testify, as a protection against self-incrimination. This should be done in a way that is least offensive to the grand jurors. Remind the client that common courtesy applies even in a grand jury proceeding. The client can exercise his right merely by saying, "With all due respect to this grand jury, upon advice of counsel, I must rely on my Fifth Amendment right and decline to answer this question."

§ 3.15 Preparing the Client for Testimony—The Intimidation Factor

Intimidation is built into the grand jury process, by the sheer fact that the district attorney runs the show and his mission is to get an indictment. Unless you, as counsel for the accused, are granted the opportunity to present evidence, only one side of the story may be told. The investigating officer and hostile witnesses may be the only others present in the proceeding beside the grand jurors themselves. For your client, this "them versus me" setup will undoubtedly be unnerving. If your client plans to testify, the intimidation factor can multiply, with disastrous consequences. Out of nervousness, the client may become overwhelmed and say too little, or worse yet, too much. Or, the client may react, rather than respond, to a hostile question and lose control.

In preparation, point out to your client the intimidating aspects of the grand jury process and how to relax in the face of them, or at least lessen their impact. Also, do not overlook your client's subjective reality—the fear of public speaking, the fear of letting family members down, the firm belief that the grand jury will automatically indict.

A rule of thumb for a client taking the stand is: *Never jump to answer a question. Pause. Make sure you understand the question. If you don't understand, ask to have the question repeated. Then answer directly and succinctly, and respond to only what is asked.*

§ 3.16 Counsel Should Be Present—Generally

Counsel for the accused should always be present outside the grand jury room at all grand jury proceedings. This will help clients feel protected and reassured that they may seek assistance if needed.

Protecting the anonymity of the grand jurors has been the reason for excluding counsel from the grand jury room. You could propose an audio feed into another room where counsel for the testifying witness could hear the testimony. If the witness left the stand to request assistance of counsel, the lawyer would immediately understand the context of the question at issue and save the grand jury time. This request should be filed along with other grand jury motions.

§ 3.17 Counsel Should Be Present—Observing Improprieties

In addition to bolstering your client, your presence is important so that you can observe any improprieties that occur during the grand jury process. It would be improper, for instance, if unauthorized persons were allowed into the grand jury room, if there were fewer than the statutorily required number of grand jurors present, or if the prosecutor were present when the grand jury is voting or failed to take a grand jury oath. In a case which affected a large segment of the community, like the 1980 New Mexico prison riot, the grand jury pool may include more than the usual number of citizens with a potential conflict of interest or an actual connection with state agencies involved in the prosecution.

You would be surprised at how many improprieties do occur. Had the lawyer not been there to observe, there would probably be no record and no recourse. When improprieties are found, a record should be made by filing a protective order with the court to stay the grand jury proceedings until the grand jury is in compliance with the statutory authority. At the time of trial you may also file a motion to dismiss the indictment on the basis of grand jury improprieties (*see* Appendix 3B for a sample motion), or to discover information regarding the grand jury proceedings that may lead to disclosure of constitutional defaults (*see* Appendices 3C and 3D). You may also want to file a motion for inspection of records used during selection of both the grand jury that returned the indictment and the panel of prospective jurors to be selected in your case. (*see* Appendix 3E for a sample motion and memorandum of law in support of the motion.) Though this information may be useful in establishing grounds for improprieties, you should be sure that it does not reach the jury at trial. A motion in limine, as contained in Appendix 3F, could preclude prejudicial information, including the action of the grand jury and the indictment itself, as well as the identity of the grand jurors.

§ 3.18 Confirming the Date and Time

You should write a letter to the foreperson and the district attorney confirming the specific date and time of the grand jury proceedings. You will want to know the duration of the entire proceeding, not just when your client will testify. This will assure that you and your client are prompt and will show respect for the process and courtesy toward the participants. Also, being present outside the room throughout the proceeding will confirm your interest. This can do nothing but put you in good light before the grand jury.

§ 3.19 Putting on Evidence—Generally

You should request to introduce, at the grand jury proceeding, evidence which the district attorney has withheld or does not have in his possession. The fact that this is not usually done does not mean that it cannot be done. What is needed is a change in the present grand jury structure, which would allow for more than one side of the story to be heard. This is another opportunity for creative lawyering. Take the initiative to present affidavits from former grand jurors as to the impact of hearing one side of the story. Encourage local graduate schools to research the effects on decision making when people hear only one side of a claim. This documentation can put a new perspective on the parameters of the grand jury and work to revise the strictures that prevent the accused from presenting evidence.

§ 3.20 Putting on Evidence—Evidence Should Be Limited

When you decide to submit evidence to the grand jury, you should be cognizant that every document, exhibit and affidavit will be thoroughly scrutinized by the district attorney's office. If you submit every document in your file and the grand jury returns a no bill, your openness will have been to your client's benefit. On the other hand, if the grand jury returns an indictment, the district attorney's file will now contain invaluable discovery that they ordinarily would not be privy to until the trial. They will know your theory of the case, your witnesses and the substance of their testimony. They will have sufficient time to digest the materials, pull out any inconsistencies or gaps and prepare a thorough cross-examination. Such a posture may place the defense at a severe disadvantage.

Defense counsel should also keep in mind the grand jury's perspective. It should come as no surprise that the average grand jury is a rubber stamp for the prosecution. The average grand juror feels that if the police arrest someone, that person must have done something wrong. Furthermore, the accused or their witnesses rarely appear before the grand jury and the grand jury hears only one side of the case. It is therefore not unusual that indictments are returned in marginal cases.

Still, this should not discourage you from presenting evidence that may discourage an indictment. It is generally counter-productive to produce volumes of material. Except in the extraordinary or highly publicized case, it is doubtful the grand jury will devote the hours or days necessary to review documents, exhibits, affidavits or prior recorded testimony and put it in context. Your submissions should be limited in scope and quantity. All superfluous or tangential documents should be eliminated and only the most compelling and unimpeachable exhibits should be presented. Limited and powerful presentations will always be more effective than expansive dissertations. Your clients will fare much better if the grand jury concentrates on the heart of the matter, rather than engaging in a time-consuming quest for what is relevant.

As a final note on the issue of submitting materials to the grand jury, we strongly recommend that any attached exhibits or documents be *very* legible. You should consider enlarging the documents and highlighting the portions to which you want the grand jury to pay attention, but except in the most extraordinary circumstances, do not blow up documents or exhibits to poster size. Poster board presentations are best saved for the petit jury, in the event the grand jury relies on the minimal standard of probable cause and indicts your client.

§ 3.21 Putting on Evidence—Summary of Events

To aid the grand jury in deciding what really happened, counsel should prepare a summary of events. This summary should include all the events, parties, places, dates and times, with attached documents or exhibits that pointedly substantiate the defense position.

The summary should be short, simple and self-explanatory, since you will not be able to discuss it with the grand jury. Even if you present a witness who can explain the summary, most jurisdictions allow the grand jurors and prosecutor to question the witness. Unless the witness is adequately prepared and intimately familiar with all the events, you could wind up doing more harm than good.

The summary will put into perspective all the events surrounding the incident. Human nature dictates that we see and recall events in a light most favorable to our position. A classic example is the police beating of an African American motorist in Los Angeles. If you relied solely on the police reports, it appeared that the motorist, Mr. King, was recalcitrant, resisting arrest, and the police used reasonable force under the circumstances. Regardless of the motivating factors, this is how the police chose to see this event. A neighbor's videotape, on the other hand, captured the essence of what happened without the frailty of human subjective interpretation.

Your summary should work like a video camera. Let it capture the essence of what happened without subjective interpretation. The facts should be black or white, not grey. Grey facts are for a petit jury or judge to decide. The less interpretation or explanation in the summary, the more attention the grand jury will pay to the facts and begin to question what really happened.

§ 3.22 Putting on Evidence—Client Affidavit or Statement

You may find that it is more helpful for your client to prepare an affidavit or a statement rather than testify. You should carefully review this affidavit or statement with your client to ensure that the language truly reflects your client's intent. Many clients, unfortunately, do not have the verbal skills we would wish. It is therefore imperative that the attorney work with the client on his or her language. It may be helpful to solicit the assistance of someone with lay writing skills or effective people skills, who is more apt to communicate in a grand juror's language. This person could be a jury consultant, a secretary, a teacher, or anyone who effectively understands lay language. After the affidavit or statement is written, review it with the client to make sure it contains all the information that should be included and is expressed in the most effective and sensitive way. Remember, people relate at a feeling level, not at an intellectual one. Your client's feelings—fear, sadness, anger, horror, etc.—should be as much a part of the story as the facts he or she wishes to present.

A client's words have a way of coming back to haunt the case, if not in the grand jury room, later at trial. As counsel, you should take particular care to scrutinize the statement or affidavit for any language that might be construed as an admission of guilt for the crime under investigation or any lesser included offenses, or in any way shows intent to commit an act which has criminal consequences.

In most cases, counsel will not be provided with discovery from the prosecution's file until after the Grand Jury has indicted the client. Potentially winnable cases have been lost by virtue of false, incredulous or incriminating statements made by clients when they appeared before the Grand Jury. An inconsistent, impeachable or untruthful statement by the client (or the defense witnesses) can be the death blow to your case. It is supremely important that counsel spend the time necessary to be thoroughly familiar with every aspect of the facts. Witness preparation for Grand Jury testimony is absolutely essential since you can not effectively protect your client as you would during a trial. Your client or witnesses may be subjected to improper, irrelevent or objectional questioning. You must anticipate this and the client accordingly. If such questioning begins, your client should politely request to be given the opportunity to write down the question and confer with counsel. At that point, you can take the question up with prosecutor or the presiding Judge if necessary. A good rule of thumb is that the client should *not* testify or submit an affidavit unless you have a complete grasp of the facts and the client and witnesses have been thoroughly prepared for what they are about to face.

§ 3.23 Putting on Evidence—A Packet for Each Grand Juror

All written materials that you are going to request be presented to the grand jury, including the client's statement or affidavit and a summary of the events relevant to the case, should be compiled in a packet for each grand juror. This will make the jurors feel you are communicating with them individually and, in turn, expect their individual attention. Also, if each grand juror has a packet, no one person has power or control over your presentation. This is always a good policy.

As mentioned above, you should highlight the portions of the documents on which you would like the grand jurors to focus. Care should be taken that each of the packets is highlighted the same. Double checking always helps when it comes to matters of this importance.

§ 3.24 Preparing a Client for a True Bill

The counselor at law portion of your title comes into play when you must prepare a client for a true bill. Building clients' confidence and giving them false expectations often cause lawyers problems down the road. Be honest with clients. Express your concerns about the potential for indictment. Explain that most grand juries indict, even innocent people, and why. Describe how the prosecutor runs the show, there is no right to cross-examination to undercut the prosecutor's side of the story, and the grand jury uses a lower standard of proof.

As in the initial client interview, you should listen to what your clients have to say and let them express their emotions. This will save you a lot of time in the long run, while continuing to reinforce a positive attorney-client relationship.

§ 3.25 Obtaining the Grand Jury Transcript

Obtain a transcript from the grand jury proceeding as soon as possible. You will have to file extensive motions to obtain it, but transcripts have been released in many jurisdictions. Once in hand, make sure someone analyzes the transcript for areas of investigation, inconsistencies, witness statements to be taken, and the prosecutor's theory of the case. Begin immediately to organize your own case file.

§ 3.26 Grand Jury Challenges—Generally

One of the best ways to rattle the system is to file for a grand jury challenge. This is an important step when you have the resources. Several kinds of challenges, as discussed below, can be filed.

§ 3.27 Grand Jury Challenges—Grand Jury Panel

The composition of the grand jury can be challenged on demographic grounds. How representative are the grand jurors of the community at large? How do they compare in gender, ethnicity and age with the census data for the jurisdiction? Also, was this grand jury chosen in accordance with the jurisdiction's requirements for grand jury selection? Interview the court clerk or court administrator to find out the procedure and get a copy of written materials that describe the procedure.

Census data are generally available from the state university or state library, as well as other sources. For a scientifically acceptable analysis, you should compile statistics from a number of grand juries over a period of years. What constitutes a sound sample would be an important question to ask the analyst or pollster who assists you in compiling the demographic analysis for the challenge. The clerk of court will provide you, sometimes reluctantly, with the questionnaires from previous grand jury panels from which you can ascertain sex and age, as well as education and homeowner versus tenant status—two other fruitful areas to challenge. Other areas for challenge are: Hispanic surnames, which can be checked against an official list of Spanish surnames adopted by the U.S. Bureau of Census and compared with census data on Spanish origin; and Native American representation on federal grand juries in areas with a large urban Native American population or areas close to Native American reservations.

§ 3.28 Grand Jury Challenges—Grand Jury Foreperson

To challenge the composition of the grand jury foreperson, once again you must look at the demographics. How closely does the gender, ethnicity and age of the foreperson match the census data? Also, how was the foreperson chosen? Was he or she elected or appointed by the judge and on what basis?

§ 3.29 Grand Jury Challenges—Random Computer

Like petit jurors, grand jurors are supposed to be chosen by random selection. You should see how random the selection has been. Do not take the word of a clerk that a computer makes the selection so that it is random. Seek out the data and determine whether or not in your opinion you have reason to doubt the process.

In one Dallas jurisdiction, for example, it was discovered that the last names were randomly chosen, but the first names were abbreviated, excluding whole sections of the Hispanic population by the abbreviations used.

Again, you may want to consult a computer analyst or statistician to understand how the selection can be skewed, what clues to look for in reviewing the data, and what would comprise a "random selection."

§ 3.30 Reconsideration of Grand Jury Action

Under certain circumstances, you may want the grand jury to reconsider its action. If the case has been presented to the grand jury without notifying you, after you have specifically requested notice, a request for reconsideration may be appropriate. For example, in a situation where your client has been arrested but you do not know when the grand jury will review the case, you might send the foreperson a registered letter to forestall the grand jury's consideration of the case without your input. The letter would state whom you represent and that you would like seven days' notice of the proceeding because you have critical documents or witnesses to present. A copy of the letter must be sent to the prosecutor assigned to the grand jury and the court which assembled the grand jury. A mere telephone call to the prosecutor will not suffice.

If the letter is sent timely, yet the case is presented to the grand jury without notifying you, a second letter to the grand jury requesting reconsideration is in order. The reconsideration letter should be courteous, short, sweet and to the point. (*See* Appendix 3G for a sample reconsideration letter and supporting documents.)

§ 3.31 Preliminary Hearing

In some jurisdictions the determination of probable cause is made by a judge at a preliminary hearing, instead of by the grand jury. In anticipation of the preliminary hearing, you should do or have done a thorough investigation of the facts of the case, and prepare the witnesses as you would for trial. This is your only shot to avoid the indictment and in the case of first offenders, save your client from a criminal record. You should view the preliminary hearing not as a fact-finding opportunity, but like a deposition—an opportunity to hammer down the testimony of the other side.

Chapter 4

DEPOSITIONS

Table of Sections

---

§ 4.1 Defining the Purpose of the Deposition—Generally

A deposition has several functions: for discovery purposes; to suppress or control unfriendly witnesses; and to advance the theory of your case. It is to your advantage to decide at the outset the purpose of the deposition, which in turn will dictate your demeanor with the witness. Your goals should be carefully thought out so you make maximum use of the time in deposition. Remember, it is important to vary the style, depending on the witness. With some witnesses you can be soft. With others, you can be more forceful, particularly if they are being evasive.

§ 4.2 Defining the Purpose of the Deposition—Taking a Deposition for Discovery

Invariably, you will use the deposition as a discovery tool, to explore what witnesses for the other side have to tell you about the case and to assess the strength of their case. For discovery purposes, you will want to ask open-ended questions—the *how, when, why, who, tell me about it, describe for me, give me an example of,* kind of questions that require the interviewee to give you information. Establish a rapport, as you would in any good interview. Let go of the power in the deposition; give it over to the witness. The witness should perceive you as the good guy, not an adversary. Set a comfortable pace. Put the witness at ease so that there is no question that you are truly interested in what the witness has to say. If the deposition is to be videotaped, the crew should be instructed to film the witness, not you.

Your non-verbal language as well as your verbal language should communicate openness. Be sure that you do not sit with your arms or legs crossed, and wear relaxed clothing. Everything about you should say, "Tell me all you've got to tell me." The information should flow.

§ 4.3 Defining the Purpose of the Deposition—Closed-Ended, Leading Questions

When you use a deposition to set the tone that you are in charge, ask the witness more closed-ended, leading questions. These are the kind of questions that have the answer built in. You do the leading, and the witness basically answers yes or no. Be cautious about using this type of questioning. Use it only in situations where you know what the witness's answers are to all the questions.

§ 4.4 Defining the Purpose of the Deposition—Controlling the Witness

You should be in control of the witness at all times. The deposition is used to nail down facts. Adopt a tone of voice and an assertive stance that leaves the witness no doubt who is in charge. If this is a videotaped deposition that could be shown at trial, be cautious of the angle of the camera and the impression you make. You do not want to appear aggressive or suggest to the jury by your non-verbal language or tone of voice that you were being unfair or overly demanding with the witness.

§ 4.5 Defining the Purpose of the Deposition—Don't Play All Your Cards With a Trial Witness

If the witness will testify at trial, do not play all your cards at the deposition. Save some of your punch lines for the case. Do not assume, however, that you know how the witness will communicate on all subject matters. Be circumspect.

§ 4.6 Defining the Purpose of the Deposition—Advancing the Theory of Your Case

If you desire to expose the theory of your case, you may decide on an open-ended style, or you may want to control the witness. You can also advance your theory of the case by making statements and getting the witness to agree with them. This can be very helpful in developing your litigation strategy. It is an opportunity to test the waters to see if your theory will float.

§ 4.7 Defining the Purpose of the Deposition—Combining Approaches

You may decide that an effective tactic is to start with a more open-ended style to find out where the witness is coming from, then hammer down to see how he or she copes with cross-examination. This approach will give you a glimpse of how the witness behaves when relaxed and when tense. It is useful for purposes of drawing out the various personalities that the witness can portray.

§ 4.8 Criminal Cases, In Particular

If you are fortunate to live in such states as Florida and Oregon, you have the opportunity to take depositions in criminal cases. Texas allows depositions under certain circumstances. This is extremely helpful in gathering information pre-trial and is your strongest arm of investigation. There is, unfortunately, a movement to eliminate this process, which would be a great loss to the states that have it. Criminal lawyers in states that do not allow depositions should be fighting for this opportunity, which is helpful not only to the defense, but to the prosecution as well. Depositions tend to expedite settlement pre-trial, and help both sides to present their most effective front.

§ 4.9 Civil Cases, In Particular

Depositions are definitely a fact-finding tool for civil litigants. Lawyers should be careful, however, of using abusive tactics on witnesses in front of the camera. If the deposition is introduced in the courtroom, jurors will resent this treatment and hold you accountable. Remember, you should be the nice guy, not the person that they find offensive.

§ 4.10 Think Like the Judge or Jury

You should envision that the judge and jury are always there with you and keep your deposition questions short, simple, and well thought out. It is your responsibility to make sure that a judge or jury will understand the path you are taking. The theory of your case should be woven throughout the questions. It is helpful to have a list of questions or areas for questioning as a checklist to make sure that you have covered all your bases. It is not necessarily suggested that you follow this list question by question, but that you have it for reference so no areas are inadvertently left unexplored.

It would be a good idea to space your questions on the page to allow room to jot down the witness's answers or make note of particular information to follow up. The checklist, with answers, is helpful later in reviewing a tape or videotape of the deposition.

§ 4.11 Minimize Lawyer Words

The deposition is a chance for you to pay attention to the lawyer words you should avoid at trial. Jurors do not understand many of the terms that lawyers use, and you do not want your language to interfere with the points you are trying to make or the sensitive impression you are trying to give. Remember to talk like a person, not like a lawyer. The deposition should come across in a friendly and understandable manner in anticipation that it will be entered into evidence.

§ 4.12 Run Facts by a Former Judge and/or Lay People

In preparing for the deposition you should have lay people and/or a former judge analyze your approach and suggest questions. You would be surprised at the kinds of things they would be interested in learning from this witness. Given that a deposition is frequently used in situations where a witness will not be testifying, make sure that the questions on the jurors' minds are answered. Getting a second opinion, as it were, can be of great assistance.

§ 4.13 Preparing the Witness—Generally

You should prepare your witness to testify in a deposition in the same manner you would prepare someone for court testimony. This process is too often neglected and brushed over by trial lawyers. It is your job to work with those witnesses so they understand what the content of the deposition is likely to be. You should take the time to explain the rules of depositions and how deposition testimony differs from testifying in court. Unless adequately prepared, witnesses who have given court testimony before could become confused at the deposition and believe that they should not offer information and should not ask whether or not they should answer a question.

§ 4.14 Preparing the Witness—Demeanor

Whether or not it is taped, the witness should see the deposition as a dress rehearsal for court. Witnesses should remember to sit up in their chair, not pick at their face or clothing and show respect as the process unfolds. This is a time to experience the adversary system at work and practice at being put on the spot. Witnesses should be reminded to pay particular attention to non-verbal language at a videotaped deposition so that, if the videotape is introduced at trial, the jury is left with a favorable impression.

§ 4.15 Preparing the Witness—Dress

It can be harmful to present one image in a deposition and try to repair that image during trial. Witnesses should dress appropriately for deposition, in court clothes. As counsel, you should be very specific in explaining what court clothes are. This will cancel assumptions that "dress up" means his black leather jacket or her biggest gold earrings. It can also prevent a diamond pinky ring flashing in the eye of the camera that would convey an image you would like to avoid.

§ 4.16 Recording the Deposition

It is, of course, imperative that a court reporter be present during all depositions. Counsel should also bring a tape recorder to record the deposition, when allowed, so you can review the tape at a future date for your own benefit.

§ 4.17 Videotaping—Generally

You may find it even more helpful to videotape the deposition, if opposing counsel agrees. Videotaping allows you not only to review the content, but to judge the demeanor and style of the witness. The tape will also be useful to a trial consultant in determining a witness's strengths and weaknesses. A consultant may notice areas where the witness feels on weak ground and other areas where the witness appears to be firmly convinced of the truth of the matter. This will be helpful in strategizing the handling of the witness on the stand, whether to be hard or soft, when to attack and when to soothe. With this preparation, your style and presentation will be compatible and effective with witnesses.

§ 4.18 Videotaping—Lighting

You should make sure when videotaping a deposition that the lighting is technically adjusted to provide not only a comfortable atmosphere for the parties, but proper contrast so that you do not have green people in a blue room. Also, lighting plays an important role in whether jurors perceive a witness as favorable or unfavorable. Be sure the lighting for your witnesses is warm and friendly. If, however, some of their witnesses have particularly offensive facial expressions or gestures, good lighting can capture them in their full glory. Use your judgment on these dynamics. Of course, if you prefer that the witness not make the best appearance in court, lighting should not be a concern.

§ 4.19 Videotaping—Angles

The camera angle can be very important. Work with an experienced video crew to determine the best way to present your witnesses, or detract from theirs. In preparation, pay attention to the different angles used by politicians in presenting themselves to the American public, and consult with the video crew as to how this imaging may be adapted for the benefit of your witnesses.

§ 4.20 Videotaping—Volume

Each speaker in the videotape should be hooked to an auxiliary microphone. Relying on a video camera microphone can be disappointing if you should need to use the videotape in court. The video crew should conduct a sound check before each deposition begins to be sure the speakers can be heard loud and clear.

§ 4.21 Transcripts Coupled With Videotapes Hammer Points Home

If deposition testimony is to be presented at trial, you should make sure that a copy of the transcript is provided to each of the jurors. In this way, jurors have the choice whether to watch the videotape, if there is one, or read the transcript. It is often suggested that jurors not receive the written transcript until after they have watched the videotape, to assure their attention. This is a decision for the individual lawyer. Having the videotape and the transcripts available at the same time would allow auditory jurors to watch the tape and visual jurors to follow the tape with the aid of the transcript.

§ 4.22 Reading of Depositions at Trial—Generally

Deposition reading should be considered an art form. It can be very helpful when you are going to introduce depositions in court to have either an actor or an animated reader do the reading. Nothing is more frustrating than a person droning along page after page. Find someone who fits the profile of the person who has been deposed, and who can best communicate the subject matter to the jury. When the subject matter is rough and gruff, you may want a sensitive-looking reader to portray your witness and soften the impact. If the witness is for opposing counsel, you may want a tough-looking reader to play it for all it is worth.

§ 4.23 Reading of Depositions at Trial—Rehearsal

Make sure that you rehearse the reading so that you have a rhythm with the person playing the witness. This is important so that there is a flow and a reality to the deposition.

§ 4.24 Reading of Depositions at Trial—Intonation

You should change your voice during the reading so that the jury does not go to sleep or tune out. Intonation and expression are extremely important.

§ 4.25 Reading of Depositions at Trial—Do Not Be Overly Dramatic

On the other hand you do not want to appear to be hamming it up. The jury will think that you are being a clown, and discount the importance of the evidence and the seriousness of your case.

§ 4.26 Reading of Depositions at Trial—Demonstrative Aids

Demonstrative aids have been used in court in conjunction with deposition testimony. Demonstrative aids help explain or emphasize information in the deposition as it is being read. This gives the jury an easy reference. You should also have smaller copies of these demonstrative aids in a packet or a jury book that is distributed to each juror for closer inspection in the jury box and later review during deliberations.

§ 4.27 Reading of Depositions at Trial—Taking a Break

It is your job to keep an eye on the jury. If you see the jurors fidgeting in the jury box, you should request a break. If you notice a juror is sleeping, request a break without embarrassing the juror. Ideally your deposition reading will be dynamic enough to keep the interest of the jurors.

Chapter 5
FOCUS GROUPS AND MOCK TRIALS

Table of Sections

---

§ 5.1 Overview

Focus groups are not new to the marketing industry. They have been used to test everything from corn flakes to hotel decor. Their purpose is to get feedback from real people—consumers—about a particular product. This tool can also be used in a legal context. Like it or not, you are selling a product, and it is important to know what real people, in this instance the jury, think of your goods and your sales pitch. The focus group involves gathering a cross-section of the community with demographics similar to actual jurors and testing parts of your case. The format can be expanded into a mock trial which summarizes the entire case.

Jury and trial consultants consistently hear from lawyers that the most educational day of their legal career was viewing a mock trial in a case in which they were involved. Many veteran trial lawyers are amazed at things they have given no thought to after all their years of litigating. New York would never consider putting a play on Broadway without a dress rehearsal. The fact that lawyers go to trial with people's lives and financial welfare in their hands without a dress rehearsal is shocking. One lawyer, who initially resisted the idea, later concluded it verged on ineffective assistance of counsel *not* to run a mock trial. Seeing a mock trial in progress, he was overwhelmed by its educational and strategic value.

§ 5.2 Formats—Generally

The format you choose will be determined by your resources, priorities and time available. Some projects will require you to carefully think through your case from *voir dire* to instructions, others will focus only on the case themes.

§ 5.3 Formats—Focus Groups

The difference between a focus group and a mock trial is one of length and scope. The focus group is very helpful in examining a specific aspect of a case, whereas the mock trial presents the whole case in summary form. The focus group centers on the opening and closing statements, a particular witness, a point of defense, a demonstrative aid or the theory of the case. If you are wondering how the jury will react to a witness or if a line of argument will hurt or help your client, where your case may be most favorably filed or which defendants are most likely to be held liable, the focus group is appropriate and practical for this analysis.

§ 5.4 Formats—Focus Groups—Issue Analysis

The focus group is an opportunity to brainstorm about the impact of a specific issue in your case. For instance, you would ask them, "So what would you think if you learned this piece of evidence and then this piece of evidence and then that piece of evidence?" You could also present opening statements, witness summaries or closing arguments and then brainstorm with the focus group their ideas about the case.

§ 5.5 Formats—Focus Groups—Arguments Only

By presenting just the opening or closing arguments for both sides, you can get a good feel for people's thoughts about the case issues, as well as your own presentation. Many people feel that your case is 80% won or lost by the end of jury selection and the opening statement. Being such an important part of your case, there is no room for error in the opening statement. It is advisable to run several opening statements on video and have a skilled facilitator debrief the focus group on which presentation was the most effective. Obviously, the arguments are not what totally turns the case, and the group's reaction should be weighed in light of the strength of the evidence. Still, you will get some powerful feedback, which may even reveal the holes in your case before it is too late.

§ 5.6 Formats—Focus Groups—Demonstrative Aid Testing

Many lawyers spend fortunes on visual effects artists, only to find out after trial that there was something about their demonstrative aid either that the jurors did not understand or that contradicted their case. In some instances, they will find that omitting a piece of evidence on a chart or diagram to emphasize their case only served to undermine their credibility. The jury was left with the impression that the attorney was trying to hide something. The focus group or mock jury is an opportunity to find out if your demonstrative aid is as self-explanatory, and helpful, as you think. You can see from the jurors' viewpoint what does and does not make sense, and how to put this powerful tool to its best use.

§ 5.7 Formats—Focus Groups—Case Theory Analysis

Determining if your case makes sense to real people will guide you toward an intelligent strategy and presentation at trial. If you are the plaintiff's lawyer, the focus group provides an opportunity to test several theories of your client's claim to determine which is most palatable and understandable to a group of lay people. You can also analyze the strengths and weaknesses of a variety of defenses through the focus group, whether this is your side or your opponent's.

With a lay analysis of the theory of the case, lawyers are better armed to make the hard decision of whether to consider a plea bargain for their criminal client or settle their civil client's case pre-trial. For a more accurate calculation of the odds, it is often advisable to run at least two focus groups, in order to get the input of a larger cross-section. The objective, however, is to gather as much information as possible to facilitate these critical decisions.

For criminal lawyers particularly, focus groups can also be helpful in determining if you should put on a defense at all. Research shows that generally you do want to present a defense in a criminal case so that the jurors who favor your client have concrete issues to argue with the jurors who lean towards a guilty verdict. As much as we would all like to believe in the inviolability of the presumption of innocence and the burden of proof, in reality we know that jurors frequently believe the government would not bring a case unless there was something to it. In their minds, where there's smoke, there's fire. It therefore becomes necessary in many cases to present evidence to help the jurors understand your client's perspective. This thinking equally applies in civil cases.

§ 5.8 Formats—Mini-Mock Trial

To assess the impact of a specific witness, a mini-mock trial is useful. You can present opening statements, the videotaped testimony of a major witness with both direct and cross-examination, then read some other witness statements before the closing arguments. This format can produce honest feedback on the one specific witness, plus other aspects of the case, and assist in witness preparation. You can learn first impressions of the witness and reactions to the witness's dress, non-verbal language and tone of voice, as well as what did and did not make sense about the witness's testimony.

Some lawyers have the witness present at the mock trial; others choose not to, based on the stability of the witness and whether it will be a help or a hindrance. Beating a witness over the head with juror reactions can be devastating to an insecure witness and a reality-check for an arrogant one. You should make the judgment call as to whether your witness can handle this feedback or whether it would be best to incorporate the jurors' input as you prepare the witness on your own.

§ 5.9 Formats—Full-Blown Mock Trial

A full-blown mock trial involves *voir dire* of the panel, opening statements for both sides, three witnesses for each side, closing arguments, judge's instructions and jury deliberations. This is the preferred method of conducting a mock trial because the mock jurors are more apt to get the full flavor of the case.

Some lawyers are skeptical of this approach. They say, "This case is going to last a month or six weeks, and there's no way to boil it down to one day." You would be surprised at how, even in complicated litigation, there is generally no more than eight hours of information that really has an impact on a jury. The task at hand is to think through carefully who are the key witnesses for each side, to make maximum use of the mock trial.

§ 5.10 Formats—Super Mock Trial

To get feedback from a larger cross-section of the community, you can stage the mock trial in an auditorium before a group of 50 or more people, who at the end of the day will divide up for deliberations. Again, you would present the opening statements, three witnesses for each side and closing arguments. The obvious problem with this format is that it requires someone to review all the deliberations and analyze the material. With a single or dual mock trial, the lawyers on the case can personally be present and glean the important points of the deliberations as they are in progress.

§ 5.11 Formats—Dual Mock Trials

The cadillac of mock trials is to present two trials simultaneously with different case presentations, or to run one mock trial on one weekend, make changes based on the jurors' reactions and deliberations, and run another mock trial the following weekend incorporating the changes. In this way, you can gauge the impact of what you learned from the first mock trial and whether or not the changes that seemed to be indicated were really as important as they appeared to be. It is advisable, if there is adequate funding, to run two mock trials with the same theory on one weekend and another two mock trials on a second weekend, incorporating changes indicated from the prior mock trials. Observing reactions to different strategies is the key.

§ 5.12 Presentations—Generally

There are three basic types of mock trial presentations: live, videotaped and combination. Each approach has its pros and cons.

§ 5.13 Presentations—Live

In a *live* mock trial, the jury sees the litigants and witnesses in person. This allows for feedback on the substance of the testimony and arguments as well as the non-verbal language of the participants. The inherent problem with the live mock trial is that the jurors are usually reluctant to give honest criticism when they know the participants are present or close at hand. While there is opportunity for more flexibility in the presentation itself, this flexibility has a flip side. The case often gets side-tracked on irrelevant matters; objections and bench conferences occur; arguments by the attorneys go over the allotted time or are poorly delivered or read monotonously; witnesses give rambling or unintelligible answers which confound the cross-examination. Though the live presentation is widely used by lawyers and jury and trial consultants, the problems are sufficiently grave to detract from the overall benefits.

§ 5.14 Presentations—Videotaped

In the authors' opinion, the most productive mock trial is one that has every segment videotaped. With this approach, arguments and examinations are thoroughly prepared and effectively presented, objectionable or irrelevant materials are redacted and time limitations can be followed. Three additional benefits are: 1) Jurors will fairly and honestly evaluate the lawyers, witnesses and arguments; 2) counsel can concentrate on observing rather than performing; and 3) the consultant can give the attorneys immediate feedback and ideas.

Even the videotaped mock trials have their detractors, however. The most common criticism of this approach is that, unlike the actual trial, attorneys have no chance to bond with the jury. Also, the lack of spontaneity may affect juror reaction to a witness. Two other concerns are noteworthy: The videotapes are potentially discoverable under the theory that recorded statements of the witness are subject to discovery, and it takes more time to prepare and execute an effective videotaped mock trial.

Despite these criticisms, the authors firmly believe that when properly prepared, the videotaped mock trial is the best way for the attorney to try out his arguments and the direct and cross-examinations of witnesses. A classic example was the mock trial run by the defense in a murder case. The lawyer had felt that intoxication was the only defense. The mock jurors on the other hand saw elements of self-defense. The lawyer re-evaluated the issues and tried a self-defense case. The real jury acquitted on the murder charge and found the client guilty of unlawful use of a firearm.

§ 5.15 Presentations—Combination

The *combination* mock trial is primarily used when counsel is concerned about the discoverability of a witness's recorded statements. This problem is resolved when counsel puts arguments on tape and has witness examinations transmitted by live feeds. The direct and cross-examinations are conducted in an adjoining room and fed to the jury on the monitor in the jury room. To the jury it looks like a tape, when in reality it is a live presentation.

The advantages and disadvantages of a combination mock trial are the same as for live and videotaped mock trials. There is an additional benefit when you are conducting mock trials back to back and want to make changes but do not have the time or money to make new videotapes. The combination mock trial, then, is the best approach if there are discovery concerns or if counsel wants the option of making immediate modifications to the presentation.

§ 5.16 Finding Mock Jurors—Generally

There are a number of sources for mock jurors. Each has its value. Your budget, and the community pool from which you are choosing, will determine the best sources.

§ 5.17 Finding Mock Jurors—The Unemployed

If you contact the local unemployment agency and say you are running some research on the jury system, the agency will be more than happy to put together 30 to 40 people, who must then be screened to obtain the most representative cross-section of the community. One method is to hire a screener who will screen applicant calls and select the ten people needed for each group. Another way is to have the unemployment agency set up interviews every 30 minutes at their offices, where you can use an employer room to screen for a day or two until you get the number of mock jurors you need. Either way is effective as long as a good screening instrument has been designed and the screener has been trained in what to look and listen for.

§ 5.18 Finding Mock Jurors—Newspaper Advertising

You can place a classified ad in a local newspaper advertising a one- or two-day research project, or you can publish a public service announcement free of charge. Newspaper advertising usually produces some very interesting participants. The obvious problem is that someone from the other side of the case may read the newspaper that day and be alerted to the fact that a mock trial is being run. The other disadvantage is that people who read the newspaper are a definitive group. Respondents should be carefully screened to make sure that you are not putting only one kind of person on the mock jury.

§ 5.19 Finding Mock Jurors—College Students

Students can be very helpful and eager participants in a mock trial. A professor may be more than willing to devote the necessary time to use the mock trial as a class project. The obvious problem with student mock jurors is that generally they are all in a similar age bracket and have similar socio-economic characteristics. You must factor in these similarities in determining the validity of the results. Nevertheless, when you have a tight budget, this can be a very helpful route to get feedback on your case.

§ 5.20 Finding Mock Jurors—Law Students

Law students would obviously be interested in participating in a mock trial. They are willing to put in the time that it takes to watch your case unfold and are very eager to give feedback, not only on the case issues, but on the lawyer's skills. When using law students, however, you must also be careful of the desensitization and built-in bias that can be a by-product of a legal education. Nonetheless, law students should not be overlooked as a resource when you are on a restricted budget.

§ 5.21 Finding Mock Jurors—Senior Citizens

Since more and more senior citizens are called to jury duty, you should involve senior citizens in your mock trials. Residents of retirement homes and members of senior citizen groups are generally happy to volunteer, or work for a small fee, and turn out to be very active participants. The experience of elders in the community may also give you valuable input into your case strategy.

§ 5.22 Finding Mock Jurors—Houses of Worship

If you call churches or synagogues in the community and ask to be put in contact with members who would want to participate in a research project, either on a volunteer or on a paid basis, you can generally get an interesting cross-section of people. Involving people of different religious denominations can create provocative influences on the mock jury and put new light on the case.

§ 5.23 Finding Mock Jurors—Social Clubs

Social clubs, fraternal organizations and ethnic community centers are another good source of mock jurors because their members come from different walks of life. The diversity of your mock jury can be as broad as the diversity of the clubs you contact.

§ 5.24 Finding Mock Jurors—Family Members and Friends

In some instances, where time and money are limited, you can call upon family members and friends. Though obvious biases arise when mock trials are run before friends or family members, if cautioned, they can be objective and put themselves in the role of being real jurors in a real case. Many times they become very involved and forget this is role play. If there are funds available, you can always offer payment, but most friends and family members will be more than willing to assist just for the thrill of being able to work with you and to get a better understanding of what you do for a living.

§ 5.25 Finding Mock Jurors—Neighbors

Once again, in instances where you have limited time and resources, you can use neighbors you do not know very well to participate. The mock trial can be conducted informally at your home or law office and can be done on a very low budget, as a fun event. Like family members and friends, neighbors tend to have an inherent bias. They should be cautioned to be objective and to make their determination regardless of you, so that you get their honest feedback. You should let them know that they will not hurt your feelings if they are critical of either you or your case.

§ 5.26 Finding Mock Jurors—Office Staff/Other Firms

Your staff may be willing to sit on a mock trial, but you should be aware that first and foremost you are the boss, and it is very difficult for employees to be critical of their boss. You are in a position of power and you control the purse strings. If, however, you openly solicit their help and assure them that you want their honest feedback, they are often willing to suspend their fears and be forthright. Sometimes they even enjoy this added participation in your case, and it can make for good on-the-job training. As a rule, though, you should turn to your staff only when you do not have time to carefully screen for participants who have no vested interest in the outcome.

You may get a somewhat more realistic view using the staff of other law firms. Once again, because of their involvement in law and because they know more than the average juror, their input may not be as realistic as that of real people. Nevertheless, it is an opportunity for analysis, and when your time and money is limited, you should use whatever resources you have available.

§ 5.27 Finding Mock Jurors—Old Jury Lists

A prime source for obtaining potential mock jurors is from old jury lists that are normally retained by the district or county clerk's office.

It is critically important that the jurors have completed their jury service. You should not, under any circumstances, attempt to recruit as a mock juror someone who is currently on jury duty or a person who has received a summons for jury duty. The appearance of impropriety, or worse yet jury tampering, must be avoided at all cost.

The jury lists retained by the clerk's office generally have the juror's name, address and telephone number. When using this method for obtaining potential mock jurors, you should be aware of certain pitfalls. Some jurors will resent being contacted and occasionally some jurors have been known to make an official complaint. There is nothing morally, ethically or legally wrong with drafting jurors who have completed their jury service but you run the risk that the other side will learn about your research. Despite this potential disadvantage, our experience has been very good when using this method of finding mock jurors.

§ 5.28 Screening Mock Jurors—Generally

Mock jurors need to be properly screened. This is a job for a professional interviewer. The best route is to hire a professional jury and trial consultant who has run mock trials and focus groups. They know how to properly screen participants and can save you the headache of this laborious part of the project. Should you choose not to hire a consultant, you will want to hire someone who is organized and dependable and has a warm telephone personality. It is always advantageous to have someone who has a background in telephone interviewing, psychology, counseling or law. Paralegals, law students and psychology majors are among the best candidates. They should receive careful instruction about their job responsibilities and the importance of follow-up.

Some lawyers prefer to use a marketing firm to supply their mock jurors because they have a ready data bank of research participants. If time is of the essence, it may be worth the considerable fee these firms charge. You must weigh the speed with which they can assemble a group against the value of conducting your own screening process and getting fresh participants. Generally, a marketing firm uses the same participants over and over in different kinds of research. Just as you would be leery of a juror who had sat on many cases, you should also avoid research participants who have been through many mock trials or other research projects. Consider carefully the costs and benefits of taking the easier route.

§ 5.29 Screening Mock Jurors—The Screening Sheet

If your screening process is conducted in-house, rather than conducted professionally by a jury consultant or marketing firm, you should be sure to provide *pre-screens.* Pre-screens indicate whether or not someone should be accepted on your panel of mock jurors. Customary pre-screens are:

1) *Are you a registered voter?* In many jurisdictions voter registration is a requirement for jury duty.

2) *Are you currently on jury duty, or do you have a family member who is or has been subpoenaed for jury duty?* If the answer is yes in either case, you should thank the person for his or her time and discontinue the interview. You do not want to be accused of interfering with the jury system.

3) *Do you or a family member work in the media?* If so, the person should also be excluded from the pool, because no doubt he or she would have too much information and could also expose the fact that you are conducting this research.

The importance of screening cannot be overemphasized. Nor should you underestimate the need for a screener with savvy who knows what you are seeking. In Appendix 5A you will find a sample screening sheet for use in mock trial preparation.

§ 5.30 Screening Mock Jurors—Mirroring the Composition of a Jury

In order to properly instruct your screeners, you need to know what a cross-section of the community would be and the composition of juries in the jurisdiction. For example, if you know that generally in any group of ten jurors you will find five women and five men, the screener should attempt to organize that kind of grouping. (*See* the following section, "Screening for a Cross-section," for other important demographics to consider in screening for mock jurors.) In district court, the court administrator or clerk of court can inform you of the general composition of a jury in the jurisdiction, if you do not know. You should also contact lawyers who try a number of cases in that district to find out what their experience has been with juries.

In federal court, there is a jury plan available from the jury commissioner for the federal courts or the clerk of courts. If you are from outside the jurisdiction, this plan can be helpful in determining where the jurors are drawn from in that federal district.

§ 5.31 Screening Mock Jurors—Screening for a Cross-section

The demographics important to consider in screening for mock jurors are generally: age, sex, occupation, race, socio-economics, and neighborhood. The census data are a good resource for information on the population in the community, to determine a representative cross-section. Census data are generally available from the state university or local library. There may also be other categories specific to a certain community or relevant in a specific case. For example, in cases involving patents, hobbies could be important to determine if a person is a tinker. The screening sheet should reflect these categories, and the screener should be alert to organizing the mock juries to accurately reflect a cross-section of the community.

§ 5.32 Screening Mock Jurors—Age

The screener should know that there should not be more people from a certain age bracket than what you would normally see impaneled in a real jury.

§ 5.33 Screening Mock Jurors—Sex

There should be a good balance of the sexes so gender will not become an issue in the case deliberations.

§ 5.34 Screening Mock Jurors—Occupation

A variety of occupations should be represented in order to get a feel for how people from different walks of life see your case.

§ 5.35 Screening Mock Jurors—Race and Ethnicity

You should have the balance of race and ethnicity that you would normally see on a real jury.

§ 5.36 Screening Mock Jurors—Socio-Economics

To give you some idea how people of different socio-economic backgrounds view your case, you should have mock jurors in a variety of economic brackets. Socio-economic status may influence a juror's view not only of financial claims in a civil suit, but of guilt versus innocence in a property crime.

§ 5.37 Screening Mock Jurors—Neighborhoods

Having an assortment of neighborhoods represented allows you to see what incidents in a neighborhood can affect your case. As obvious an influence as a high incidence of crime, or a singular occurrence of police brutality, can taint a juror's judgment of the facts.

§ 5.38 Screening Mock Jurors—A Pool of 40

Ten participants is a good-sized group to work with. Six participants is too few and 12 can take too long to debrief effectively in a one-day mock trial. A screener must generally talk to about 40 people in order to find ten participants that are appropriate for a mock trial. He or she should be instructed to screen down to 15 or 20 participants and then discuss with you the final selection before it is made. This is an important step in the mock trial procedure to assure that you are satisfied with the cross-section.

§ 5.39 The Ideal Mock Juror—A Verbal Leader

In screening for a mock trial, you are not looking for the two leaders and eight followers you would typically find on a jury. Rather, the goal of the screening is to find people who would be power brokers on a jury, perhaps the foreperson. These would be people who are comfortable taking charge, people who have held positions of power in the past, people who seize the opportunity to speak out about things that bother them, people whom others generally like. (*See* Chapter 16, "Power Brokers and Followers," for an in-depth discussion of power broker attributes.) You want to get input from ten leaders so that you can determine what kind of leader to choose for the real case when you go to trial.

The mock trial is to uncover ideas, attitudes and feelings about a particular aspect of your case or about the entire case strategy. You need people who will speak up about what they think and feel and not be shy in a group. The screener should look for people who are assertive and articulate, or at least willing to state their opinions.

§ 5.40 The Ideal Mock Juror—Trustworthiness

The screener should also listen during an interview for clues that the person may be apt to divulge information about the case and violate a confidentiality oath. A screener with experience and/or intuition usually can ferret out those who cannot be trusted.

§ 5.41 Confidentiality

It is important, before they hear any of the evidence in the case, that the mock jurors be instructed about the necessity of keeping confidential all information that they learn in this mock trial, and sign a confidentiality form. (*See* Appendix 5B for a sample.) They should be told that in exchange for their keeping confidential what they have learned during the case, you will not reveal their name or any information that you have learned about them in any written research or data. They should also be reminded that it may or may not be a real case, but they should view it as one.

§ 5.42 Compensating Mock Jurors

While there may be instances in which you will find volunteers, generally you should pay mock jurors anywhere from $50 to $125 per day. It is important for the screener to tell the jurors that they will be paid at the end of the day, and that they must complete the day in order to be paid. This will prevent losing people halfway through the process.

§ 5.43 The Venue

There are several advantages to running a mock trial in the jurisdiction where the case will be heard: 1) You get insight into how pre-trial publicity has affected potential jurors. 2) You get a sense of the positive and negative influences your client or your client's employer or business has on the community. 3) You find out more about opposing counsel and their reputation in the community. 4) Likewise, you learn about the credibility of witnesses in the community. 5) You can begin developing a juror profile for that jurisdiction. If you and your client live in that jurisdiction, the logistics are easier. On the other hand, if you are away from home, you and your staff can remove yourself from your normal distractions. It has been shown that when mock trials are run out of town, lawyers put more into the mock trial and, logically, get more out of it.

There are also disadvantages of running a mock trial in the same jurisdiction. The obvious disadvantage is that if it involves a case or a company with a high profile, you run the risk of people exposing your research. If it is held in a community that does not have a tie to the case, there is less likelihood of exposure to people you would prefer not to know about the case. Also, if you or your consultant lives in another jurisdiction, it is more difficult to put together the mock trial when you are not familiar with available hotels, video crews and sources of mock jurors. It saves the client time and money when the mock trial is run in a convenient place for the jury and trial consultant who is conducting the research.

Whether it is run in or out of a particular jurisdiction is really not as important as the effectiveness of how it is run. You are seeking as many ideas, attitudes and feelings about your case as possible from real people from different walks of life. Focus groups and mock trials have been extremely valuable in getting feedback to assess the validity of case issues and the credibility of trial witnesses.

The venue does become important in a case that has received a great deal of publicity or involves an influential employer or large company. As discussed, there are benefits and risks of running a mock trial in a venue where a considerable percentage of the panel will have heard about the case or the parties. It can be helpful, however, to determine whether or not your thoughts and feelings about local awareness are accurate. Lawyers often forget that they travel in circles of people whose values and thoughts may or may not be the same as people in the community. Focus groups and mock trials have often led lawyers to rethink their preconceptions about people's impressions of their case.

For example, a series of focus groups were run in the Mormon Will trial in Las Vegas, Nevada. Some of the lawyers representing the plaintiffs assumed it would be ludicrous to think that people in Las Vegas could have believed that Howard Hughes was wandering around in the desert giving away money to gas station attendants like Melvin Dummar. After a series of focus groups, it became quite evident that the local people not only did believe that Howard Hughes was wandering around in the desert, but most of them contended that either they or someone they knew had seen Hughes out and about at the time in question. This was a critical issue in the case and one the lawyers discovered had to be addressed in the case presentation.

§ 5.44 Site Location

The best places to run a focus group or mock trial are neutral places—a hotel conference room or a law school or college facility. The worst place, for obvious reasons, is a lawyer's office. The participants may realize which side is conducting the research and may hedge their responses as a result. You should give the location careful consideration to avoid any contamination of the participants.

It is best to have two adjacent rooms, one for the mock trial and one for observers. If the mock trial is to be videotaped, the room where the mock trial is run should be large enough, approximately 25 by 30 feet, so that the camera can get a wide-angle shot of all the jurors. The rooms should be hard walled so that there is no interference between the observers and the mock jurors. Most hotels are happy to set up two meeting rooms rent-free or at least at a substantially reduced rate in exchange for catering.

§ 5.45 How to Set up the Room

The main room should be set up in a U-shape or V-shape with a table at the mouth of the U or V for the facilitator. There should be a table in the back for the video crew and another table for demonstrative aids that will be used in the mock trial. Food should be served for the breaks either in another room or at scheduled times to prevent the caterers from entering during the mock trial. This is very important so as not to violate the confidentiality of the mock trial and not to disrupt the process.

§ 5.46 Videotaping

It is recommended that you videotape the focus group or mock trial for subsequent analysis. Find a video crew that understands the process and the need for confidentiality. It is advisable for the video crew to sign a confidentiality form, like the mock jurors. Also, they should be reasonable in their price structure. They should include in the cost all equipment, videotape and services. To encourage their cooperation, you should explain that mock trials are run on a regular basis, and if they do a good job, they will get more business, not only for future mock trials, but for videotaped depositions and witness preparation.

§ 5.47 Catering

The schedule for an all-day focus group or mock trial should include two meals and at least two breaks. There should be a continental breakfast in the morning, a morning break, a lunch meal and an afternoon break. Some lawyers also offer a late afternoon snack such as brownies, fruit or cheese. You should provide decaffeinated drinks for those people who are sensitive to caffeine, and make sure that there is water in the room. Whether to allow smoking should be discussed with the mock jurors. Some mock jurors do not care if there is smoking in the room, others do. This is important for everyone's comfort and concentration, as well as a practical consideration of whether or not to provide ashtrays.

You should also ask catering to provide name tags and pens or pencils and pads for the mock jurors to take notes. Note taking is critical because you want the mock jurors, in their debriefing, to have the facts and figures straight.

§ 5.48 Breaks

You will want to give the mock jurors numerous breaks. This is important to maintain their attention span and to keep them from getting tired. It is also important because if they are distracted by wanting to use the restroom or to smoke a cigarette, they will not pay attention to your presentation or to the facilitator's questions. As in an actual trial, mock jurors should be cautioned not to discuss the case with the other jurors during the break.

§ 5.49 Research Standards

Some lawyers feel that in order to meet a true research standard they need to run two, three or four mock trials so they can get input from a good cross-section of people. Others realize that it is important to get feedback even if it is from just one mock trial. You should determine what is appropriate in your instance. In any case, you should have a well-thought-out design for your mock trial in order to get a clear sense of how your case should be handled. Appendix 5C provides a sample letter to lawyers outlining what they should do in preparing for a mock trial.

It is definitely the lawyer's responsibility to make sure there is a balanced presentation of the ideas and theories of each side of the case. If the presentation is not balanced, the feedback is lopsided. Your goal is to get accurate feedback; this can best be done when both sides have been presented in a strong and forceful manner. We strongly encourage lawyers to make the strongest possible presentation for the other side, including evidence that may or may not be admissible.

§ 5.50 Lawyer Preparation—Generally

The lawyer should prepare the opening statement, witnesses, instructions and arguments in advance. We recommend that the most efficient way to organize the presentation is to do jury instructions and the witnesses first, then do the arguments. If the case presentation is to be done on videotape, the lawyer and his or her assistants should make sure that there is an outline of the contents of each videotape so that the mock trial will run smoothly. Each of the tapes should be rewound to the beginning after use.

§ 5.51 Lawyer Preparation—Demonstrative Aids

The lawyer should also prepare in advance any demonstrative aids on which he or she desires feedback. Some lawyers find it helpful to do a makeshift version of the demonstrative aid in-house so that they have the input of the mock jurors before they submit it to a graphic artist for final design. This is up to the lawyer and his pocketbook.

§ 5.52 The Facilitator's Role—Generally

The facilitator is the most important person in the mock trial process. This is the person who holds the event together and to whom the mock jurors, lawyers and hotel staff look for guidance. Hiring an experienced jury and trial consultant is the best way to assure that the mock trial will run smoothly and effectively. Consultants have run many groups and understand how to juggle and coordinate many complex and unusual situations at once. They wear the hats of conference director, group leader, counselor, lawyer's assistant, and can assume numerous other roles on demand.

Ideally, there should be two facilitators to run a mock trial: one, to focus on the mock jurors; and the other, on the lawyers. While the one facilitator debriefs each mock juror, it is important for the other facilitator in the lawyer observation room to be pointing out how this information can be used, the non-verbal reactions of mock jurors and other related issues, such as the impact of witness positioning, changes called for in the opening statement, holes in the case strategy, changes or modifications to the case theme and demonstrative aides to be designed.

It is also helpful to have someone assist the facilitator in coordinating the breaks and attend to miscellaneous tasks during the mock trial. This person should be present at 7:00 a.m. to greet the jurors when they arrive and hand out the mock juror questionnaire, a one- to two-page sheet that asks about personal background, spouse's background and other demographics, as well as some case-specific questions that will save time during the *voir dire* process. This questionnaire will give you a brief overview of the mock jurors to compare with their responses in the mock trial. (*See* Appendices 5D through 5H for sample questionnaires used in assorted criminal and civil mock trials.)

You can, of course, run a mock trial in-house, without the assistance of a consultant. This is normally much less formal and sometimes less informative, but is still worth the effort. With limited time and resources, as discussed above, you should make use of whatever opportunities exist to get feedback on your case before it goes to court.

§ 5.53 The Facilitator's Role—Conducting *Voir Dire*

The facilitator asks questions of the mock jurors in order to make them more comfortable with one another and to uncover issues that may affect their deliberations. This process is important in later analyzing what caused these people to be for or against you. Some responses may even prompt you to exclude a juror before the start of the mock trial. It should be explained to mock jurors that it is common for one side or the other to excuse some jurors peremptorily. Of course, you should pay the excused jurors for their time. The screener should have prepared the mock trial participants for the possibility of being excused after jury selection, just as in a real trial.

Of course, the skill of the jury and trial consultant in asking effective *voir dire* questions comes into play. The sample questionnaires in Appendices 5D through 5H suggest types of *voir dire* questions to ask in a criminal or civil mock trial. Note that you should always include four or five open-ended case-specific questions to ascertain how the mock jurors think about the issues of the case.

Spending an hour and a half or so getting the mock jurors to talk about themselves and the issues creates a bond that will pay off in deliberations. Injecting some humor will also help to dispel any tension.

§ 5.54 The Facilitator's Role—Debriefing

The facilitator should debrief the jurors after opening statements, each witness, and again after deliberations. This is a very important step because you want to learn as much as possible about what affected the mock jurors as the mock trial progressed. If you wait until the end of the mock trial, you have left many stones unturned. The facilitator should carefully go around the circle to make sure each juror gives input.

Mock jurors may be debriefed in three different ways: 1) after each stage except closing arguments; 2) after critical stages only; or 3) post-verdict. The most fruitful process is to debrief the jurors after opening statements and each witness. Given short-term human retention of vast quantities of new information, you want reaction as close to the event as possible. You will then get the most accurate and honest feedback. Critics argue that oral debriefings will "taint" the other jurors. This is not, however, a good enough reason to lose this valuable information. To lessen the potential for taint, the consultant should remind the jurors after each debriefing session not to form an opinion until all the evidence and arguments have been heard. If counsel still is concerned about tainting the jurors, a written evaluation can be given to the jurors. (*See* Appendix 5I for a sample evaluation form used in a patent case and Appendix 5J for a sample witness evaluation.)

Debriefing after critical stages is a second option that offers the benefit of feedback, but not simultaneously with the event. With this approach, debriefing is done after both opening statements, after the plaintiff's or state's case and after the defendant's case. Our research shows that there will be more thorough feedback on the last argument or last witness, consistent with the primacy/recency principle. This problem can be prevented by encouraging the jurors to take notes.

The final option is to eliminate debriefing altogether and rely solely on deliberations and post-verdict debriefing. Our experience has shown this approach to be the least fruitful. Since the jurors are screened to maximize the number of power brokers, the potential for tainting or polluting the mock jury is minimized. Again, if counsel insists on pursuing this approach, the jurors should be encouraged to take copious notes and evaluation forms should be used and collected prior to deliberations.

The debriefings yield some of the most valuable insight the mock trial has to offer. We learn how jurors feel at each stage, what witness or argument has influenced them and what are the best or worst parts of the presentation. This feedback should be sought at every possible opportunity. Regardless of the approach, jurors must be thoroughly debriefed after deliberations.

§ 5.55 Questions During Deliberations

A copy of the verdict form you intend to request in the actual trial should be given to each of the mock jurors for use in deliberations. (*See* Appendices 5K, 5L and 5M for sample civil and criminal verdict forms.) Once the mock jurors begin deliberating, the camera people should be appointed hypothetical "bailiffs" in the case. The mock jurors should be told that if they have any questions as they deliberate, the foreperson should write down the question and hand it to the camera crew who are now "bailiffs." The "bailiffs" will then take the question to the facilitator, who has assumed the role of judge. If the question can be answered, without commenting on the evidence, it should be answered.

§ 5.56 Lawyer Observation Room

In the lawyer observation room, you are observing everything as it progresses. When a mock juror has a question, you should begin answering that question as if you were the judge. You should be very careful not to do more than what you would expect a real judge to do. The tendency to get the mock jurors back on track or to influence their deliberations should be avoided at all costs.

§ 5.57 Final Debriefing Session—Generally

The final debriefing is used to ask mock jurors how they decided the issues. The questions that occurred to you while the mock trial was in process should be asked in this debriefing. This is also the time to discuss how other pieces of evidence might have changed the mock jurors' vote. Generally, all the questioning should be done by the facilitator.

§ 5.58 Final Debriefing Session—Juror Feedback on Lawyers

After the mock jurors have reached a verdict, it is important in the final debriefing to ask the mock jurors what they thought of the lawyers. This can be very helpful in determining your effect on real people. Mock jurors have been known to say he is "too slick" or she was "too quick in her delivery." They can be extremely candid and are encouraged to be so by the facilitators. You should be grateful for the opportunity to find out how you come across before trial, rather than in a post-trial interview.

§ 5.59 Final Debriefing Session—Juror Feedback on the Case

During the post-deliberation debriefing, mock jurors are also asked for feedback about the strengths and weaknesses of each side. To get concrete information, they each need to be asked to talk about what affected them the most in determining their verdict. This can be very helpful in summarizing the impact of the entire process.

§ 5.60 Final Debriefing Session—Debriefing Questions

The following are sample questions that you may want the facilitator to ask at the close of the mock trial:

1) What was your first reaction to lawyer A?

2) What was your first reaction to lawyer B?

3) How did your reactions to lawyers A and B change as the case progressed?

4) What was the main strength of each side's case?

5) What was the main weakness of each side's case?

6) What more did you want to hear from side A?

7) What more did you want to hear from side B?

8) What did you feel were the most important issues?

9) *What kind of evidence do you think may have changed your verdict?*

10) *What was a mystery to you about the case?*

11) *What puzzled you most about what you heard?*

§ 5.61 Lawyer's Turn to Ask Questions

Some lawyers choose to remain in the lawyer observation room and not to be recognized by the mock jurors. Others feel that they would like to come in and ask questions themselves. The general rule of thumb is that it is best for the lawyers not to intervene. Any questions that the lawyers have should be written down and asked by the facilitators during the debriefing. If it is important to the lawyers to do their own questioning, they should realize the risk that the mock jurors will probably now know it is a real case and begin asking who paid for the research.

§ 5.62 Arranging for Follow-up

The mock jurors should be told that there may be further questions, and asked for permission to be contacted in the future. In that way, they will not be taken by surprise should they be called at a later date.

§ 5.63 Subsequent Analysis

Some lawyers feel that the analysis that has been gleaned from actually watching the mock trial in process is sufficient. Generally you will have learned enough from that one day's experience. Other lawyers feel that they want the facilitators to invest additional time to analyze the tapes and write a report. Once again, it is the lawyer's decision how much subsequent analysis he or she desires.

§ 5.64 Additional Mock Trials

You may want to make changes in the opening statement, witness presentation, closing arguments, instructions or other parts of the case and run a second mock trial on the following day. Many attorneys find this process to be helpful and commit a two-day span of time.

Others find it more helpful to make the changes in the mock trials and run them on a weekend in the future, such as the following weekend or a month later. This gives them time to make thorough adjustments and absorb the input from both mock trials.

Still others prefer to run two or three mock trials simultaneously. This is a good way to proceed and produces lots of information. The obvious down side of this approach is that it is difficult to have three mock trials running at once. With a team of lawyers working on the case, however, one can be at each of the monitors so there is constant firsthand review of the proceedings. Being an eyewitness to your own trial is, after all, the prime benefit of the focus group and mock trial.

§ 5.65 Protecting Work Product

Federal Rule of Civil Procedure 26 (hereinafter cited as Fed.Rules Civ.Proc.Rule) governs the scope of discovery. In general it permits inquiry into "any matter, not privileged, which is relevant to the subject matter involved in the pending action." Anything concerning the case is discoverable unless prohibited by specific limitations on its scope. Rules 27 through 36 prescribe the devices, such as oral depositions, written interrogatories, the production of documents and things, and physical and mental examinations of parties or persons.[1] Rule 37 provides for sanctions.

The work-product doctrine is a qualified protection against the discovery of material prepared for litigation by or for the opposing party. The purpose of this protection is to prevent a party from unduly benefitting from the legwork of the other side. The doctrine was essentially established in *Hickman v. Taylor*,[2] which recognized the need for an exception to the expanding scope of discovery. Under *Hickman,* the protected work product covers a lawyer's notes and memoranda and whatever else reflects his or her "mental impressions, conclusions, opinions, or legal theories," including oral or written statements that the opposing lawyer takes from witnesses.[3]

In order for a civil party to claim work-product protection from discovery, three elements are necessary.[4] The same three requirements are equally applicable in criminal discovery proceedings.[5] First, there must be specific tangible items that are sought to be protected. That is, it is impermissible to claim the work-product doctrine as a blanket protection for all discovery conducted. Second, the tangible items must be prepared in anticipation of litigation. That is, the items or documents to be protected cannot have been prepared during the normal course of business; they should be directed toward a specific question or issue to be resolved in upcoming litigation. Third, the items should be prepared by another party for that party's representative. Courts are more apt to find that an item is not protected by the work-product doctrine when its preparation is not closely supervised by an attorney or submitted in response to a question by an attorney regarding upcoming litigation.[6]

§ 5.65

1. Fed.Rules Civ.Proc.Rules 30, 33, 34, 35.

2. 329 U.S. 495, 67 S.Ct. 385, 91 L.Ed. 451 (1947).

3. *Id.* at 508–510, 67 S.Ct. at 392–393.

4. *See* Fed.Rules Civ.Proc.Rule 26(b)(3).

5. Fed.Rules Crim.Proc.Rule 16(b)(2).

6. *Westhemeco Ltd. v. New Hampshire Ins. Co.,* 82 F.R.D. 702 (S.D.N.Y.1979); *see also Sterling Drug Inc. v. Harris,* 488 F.Supp. 1019 (S.D.N.Y.1980).

Once the elements of the work-product doctrine are established, protected items are discoverable by the opposing party only upon a showing of substantial need and the inability to obtain its equivalent without undue hardship. However, work product that reveals the attorney's mental processes ("opinion work product") requires a far greater showing of necessity and unavailability by other means.[7] Some courts also give an even more important role to the work-product doctrine in criminal proceedings.[8] There is, however, no additional constitutional right protecting criminal defendants from the disclosures of expert reports.[9]

Rule 26(b) protects the mental impressions, conclusions and theories not only of the attorney but of a representative who does investigation in anticipation of possible litigation. Rule 26(b) protects communications with an expert who is "informally consulted" in anticipation of possible litigation for he may be interpreting the facts of the case to the hiring attorney. If a report or other document contains the "mental impressions" of the attorney or other representative, these impressions are deleted when the report is disclosed.[10] If a witness statement taken by an attorney or investigator records the impression of the attorney or representative and it is too difficult to separate the witness's statement from these impressions, even the statement may be immune from discovery.

Southern Pacific Transp. Co. v. Banales[11] is a case in point. John Percival, the real party in interest, originally brought suit for hearing loss he sustained while employed by Southern Pacific Transportation Company. The Company hired Dr. Thomas Sumnar to assist in conducting a hearing conservation program. As part of his preparation to testify by videotaped deposition, the Company taped a practice session, which Percival's attorneys learned about during the course of Dr. Sumnar's actual deposition. When they requested that the videotape be produced, the Company objected that it contained the mental impressions of the attorneys and was privileged under the work-product doctrine and as a witness statement.[12] The trial court refused to review the videotape *in camera,* as requested by the Company, and ordered the Company to produce the tape. In finding that Judge Banales abused his discretion by failing to review the videotape *in camera,* the Texas Court of Appeals clarified the application of the work-product doctrine to trial preparation materials:

7. *Upjohn Co. v. United States,* 449 U.S. 383, 101 S.Ct. 677, 66 L.Ed.2d 584 (1981).

8. *United States v. Nobles,* 422 U.S. 225, 238, 95 S.Ct. 2160, 2170, 45 L.Ed.2d 141 (1975), on remand 522 F.2d 1274 (9th Cir. 1975).

9. *See,* for example, *United States ex rel. Edney v. Smith,* 425 F.Supp. 1038 (E.D.N.Y.1976), affirmed 556 F.2d 556 (2d Cir.1977), cert. denied 431 U.S. 958, 97 S.Ct. 2683, 53 L.Ed.2d 276 (1977).

10. Fed.Rules Civ.Proc.Rule 26(b)(3).

11. 773 S.W.2d 693 (Tex.App.—Corpus Christi 1989).

12. Vernon's Ann.R.Civ.P., Rule 166b(3)(a) and (c).

> *Liberal discovery has been encouraged to allow all parties to obtain full exposure of the issues and facts of a case. However, we believe the work product of an attorney is equally deserving of protection. We also believe that a videotape of this nature could easily contain information which could be classified as work product. It was incumbent upon the trial court to examine the contents of the video to discern whether it contained strategy, evaluation of the strengths and weaknesses of the case or mental impressions which would be protected. Likewise, the trial court should view the videotape to determine whether it contained information tending to mold the witness' testimony, which would not be worthy of protection.*[13]

Often a trial consultant may assist in trial preparation but not testify. If such an expert has been "retained or specially employed ... in anticipation of litigation or preparation of trial, a discovering party can approach him only if he shows special necessity."[14] In other words, the rule differentiates between experts "specially employed" to testify and those who are "informally retained" and consulted.

If an expert is "employed" or subpoenaed to testify as a witness at trial, his or her opinion could be discovered upon a showing of good cause, of a need which other means cannot fill. The court may also impose conditions on and restrict discovery, and may in its discretion require the compensation of the party who originally retained the expert, a measure intended to discourage abusive practices.[15] If the "other representative" is a non-attorney, his opinion may possibly be more discoverable, although some jurisdictions treat "other representatives" on a par with attorneys.[16] Federal Rule 19 precludes discovery of an expert who was "informally consulted" in preparation for trial, but not retained or specially employed. He is differentiated from an expert who is simply a general employee of the party not specially employed on the case.

Through interrogatories under Rule 33, a discovering party can compel an adverse party attorney to disclose: 1) the identity of each expert witness it expects to call at trial, 2) the subject of the testimony, 3) the substance of the fact and opinion, and 4) a summary of the grounds for the opinion.[17] If special need exists, the discovering party can also examine the expert by deposition.

13. 773 S.W.2d at 6.

14. Fleming James, Jr. and Geoffrey C. Hazard, *Civil Procedure,* § 5.1 at 228 (3d ed. 1985) at 255.

15. Fed.Rules Civ.Proc.Rule 26(b)(4)(A). Proposed amendments to the Federal Rules of Civil Procedure Relating to Discovery, 48 F.R.D. 504 (1970). 8 Wright and Miller, *Federal Practice and Procedure,* § 2033; 4A *Moore's Federal Practice,* § 26.-66[3] at 26–416 (2d ed.).

16. James and Hazard, *Civil Procedure,* § 5.11 at 254.

17. Fed.Rules Civ.Proc.Rule 26(b)(4)(A)(1).

Experts fall into four categories: [18]

1) Informally consulted experts whose identity need not be disclosed and who cannot be examined by any discovery device.

2) Those specially employed but not expected to be called as witnesses (non-testifying).

3) Those employed to give expert testimony at trial (testifying).

4) Persons who happen to be experts and who personally observed or participated in the events giving rise to the litigation (percipient or perceiving witness) who are subject to discovery in the same manner as any other witness.

The court in *Virginia Elec. & Power Co. v. Sun Shipbuilding & Dry Dock Co.*,[19] held that an "in-house expert" should be treated as an ordinary witness, that an employee who is, has been, and will be an employee of defendant without regard to pendency of the claim, is not protected by Rule 29(b)(4), since an expert cannot be partisan and must owe his allegiance to his calling. It added that "specifically employed" does not include the assigning of a person already an employee to work on the matter at issue.

A discovering party may obtain the independent expert opinion from experts in any of the first three categories without running the risk of adverse discovery: [20]

1) After identifying a potentially favorable expert, the party retains him/her informally, and obtains a preliminary opinion. If the opinion is unfavorable, the party retains the expert as an informal consultant. His identity and opinion are then non-discoverable.

2) If the opinion is favorable, but the expert will not be a very effective witness, the party may retain him in anticipation of litigation. Since the party does not anticipate that the witness will be testifying, a showing of "exceptional circumstances" would be necessary for discoverability.[21]

3) If the opinion is favorable and the party expects to use the expert at trial, he becomes a "trial expert" witness. The adverse side then has a right to a summary of the substance of the expert's testimony, and to further discovery upon a showing of good cause.[22]

18. James and Hazard, *Civil Procedure*, § 5.11 at 255.

19. 68 F.R.D. 397, 408 (E.D.Va.1975).

20. James and Hazard, *Civil Procedure*, § 5.11 at 256.

21. *Id.* at 256.

22. *Id.* at 256.

Often jury and trial consultants may assist at trial but not testify. Experts who have been retained or specially employed in anticipation of litigation or preparation for trial, but are not expected to be called as a witness, fall in a separate category under the Rules of Civil Procedure.[23] Under its provisions, opposing counsel may discover facts known or opinions held by such an expert only upon a showing of exceptional circumstances, where it is impracticable to obtain facts or opinions on the same subject by other means.[24] This precludes not only the information but the identity of experts informally consulted but not those retained or specially employed.[25] It also rejects case law bringing expert information within the work-product doctrine,[26] and instead adopts the "unfairness" doctrine.[27] Generally, where the expert has been specifically retained in anticipation of litigation and will not be called for trial, the burden is distinctly on the other side to establish entitlement to discover facts known or opinions held by that expert.[28]

As discussed in Chapter 1, attorneys may call a range of experts—psychologists, sociologists, communication specialists, pollsters, and others—for assistance in jury selection. The sociological and psychological techniques at their command are community attitudinal analysis, mock juries, investigation of prospective jurors, in-courtroom assessment and witness review. Eventually the techniques, in combination with the expert's perception and previous experience, are used to form a "report," oral or written, short or long, informal or formal, which the expert communicates to the attorney. The questions, then, are: How much of what the expert finds or reports is protected and how much is discoverable? Must the attorney disclose the identity of the jury consultant? Is an in-house memorandum by the expert discoverable? According to the 1970 Amendments to the Discovery Rules, the discovery of "materials" prepared by an attorney is not afforded special treatment, but the court shall protect against disclosure of the "mental impressions, conclusions, opinions or legal theories of an attorney or other representative of a party concerning the litigation." [29]

Absent exceptional circumstances, the Rules of Civil Procedure do not permit discovery of the names or opinions of experts that a party does not intend to call at trial. At the same time, however, the Rules do not say whether an adverse litigant may use that expert opinion as

23. Fed.Rules Civ.Proc.Rule 26(b)(4)(B).

24. *See Ager v. Jane C. Stormont Hospital and Training School for Nurses,* 622 F.2d 496 (10th Cir.1980).

25. *See Perry v. W.S. Darley & Co.,* 54 F.R.D. 278, 280 (E.D.Wis.1971).

26. *See United States v. McKay,* 372 F.2d 174, 175–177 (5th Cir.1967).

27. *See United States v. 23.76 Acres of Land, More or Less, in Anne Arundel County, State of Md.,* 32 F.R.D. 593, 597 (D.Md. 1963).

28. *See Barkwell v. Sturm Ruger Co., Inc.,* 79 F.R.D. 444, 446 (D.Alaska 1978).

29. 8 Wright and Miller, *Federal Practice and Procedure,* § 2026.

evidence at trial where obtained through means other than discovery. This was the gap which concerned the court in *Graham v. Gielchinsky.*[30]

The plaintiff alleged that the defendant physician had negligently departed from accepted medical standards in failing to remove pacemaker wires implanted in the patient's chest during cardiothoracic surgery and in failing to take the proper cultures which would have shown that a foreign body was causing the infection. Graham's first attorney had sent Graham to a physician expert for an examination. His conclusion was that the defendant had not been negligent. Graham's second attorney sent him to a second physician expert who concluded that the defendant had been negligent. In some undisclosed manner, the defense attorney obtained the first expert's opinion report and asked him to testify on the defendant's behalf. Before the opening statement Graham moved to bar the testimony. In the absence of controlling precedent and because of the unexpected manner in which the issue arose, the court allowed the defendant to use the expert opinion favorable to him and the jury returned a favorable verdict.

On appeal, the plaintiff argued that the court had erred in allowing the first referral physician to testify as a defense expert, that he had violated the trial court's ruling which prohibits him from disclosing the identity of the party who had first retained him, and that in his summation, defense counsel had made improper remarks about the first expert's impartiality. The appellate majority held that the trial court had not erred in permitting the first expert to testify, and that his testimony did not prejudice the case.

The United States Supreme Court reversed the lower decisions and granted plaintiff a new trial at which the first expert's testimony would be excluded. The United States Supreme Court held that the lower court majority had embraced an undesirable proposition of law and a violation of well-established work-product and contract principles. The majority had detracted from and distorted the fact-finding process. It held that the testimony of the first expert was improperly presented as objective although he was appearing voluntarily, not under compulsion of subpoenas. To present his expert opinion and to argue in the summation that the doctor was an impartial unbiased witness was a gross distortion of the truth, so prejudicial that it had the clear capacity to produce an unjust result. Noting its holding in a preceding case, *Genovese v. New Jersey Transit Rail Operations, Inc.,*[31] which barred plaintiff from using a conditioned deposition of defendant's expert, the court achieved an additional step by offering: "With rare exception, the

30. 126 N.J. 361, 599 A.2d 149 (1991). The United States Supreme Court reversed the earlier New Jersey superior court case of the same name, *Graham v. Gielchinsky,* 241 N.J.Super. 108, 574 A.2d 496 (1990), judgment affirmed 126 N.J. 361, 599 A.2d 149 (1991).

31. 234 N.J.Super. 375, 560 A.2d 1272 (1989), certification denied 118 N.J. 195, 570 A.2d 960 (1989).

testimony of an expert originally retained by one side should be excluded for use by the other side. Allowance of such testimony is fraught with a high potential for mischief. It is a diversion from the jury's fact-finding mission." [32] While this case does not directly apply to jury and trial consultants, its holding is instructive.

In a historical paragraph, the *Graham* court said that the premise for relaxing the discovery process is the theory that no party should build its case by foraging through opinions from the experts of the other party. It cited the work product rule in *Hickman* as insulating the efforts of an attorney to develop a client's case from discovery. In addition, the *Graham* court added, the attorney-client privilege prevents both the discovery and the use of such evidence on the basis that the expert was the client's messenger conveying privileged information to the attorney.

In *Sporck v. Peil,*[33] the court further held that an attorney's selection and compilation of documents in preparing for pre-trial discovery is highly protected opinion work product, even if the individual documents making up the grouping are not attorney work product. This is because "identification of the documents as a group will reveal defense counsel's selection process and thus his mental impressions." *Id.* at 315. The *Sporck* court thus rejected the argument that all documents used in preparing a witness are discoverable. Likewise, the Court in *Shelton v. American Motors Corp.,*[34] found that an attorney's acknowledgment of the existence of documents she had identified, examined and selected from her client's files in preparation for trial reflected her judgment as an attorney and was protected from discovery under the work-product doctrine despite the general rule that the mere existence of documents is generally discoverable.

The rules themselves seem to offer clear answers to what is discoverable and what is not. According to the "work-product" rule, every attorney should feel free to investigate all aspects of a case, without fear that the opposing party could easily obtain unfavorable matters and put them to one-sided use. This general principle alone should preclude discoverability of the work of the expert jury consultant. Moreover, jury consultants do not create facts; they analyze information and give impressions to the lawyer.

Consultants assist lawyers in designing theories of trial presentation. The focus of the trial consultant is working with the employer-lawyer on better ways to communicate the case to the jury. This is different in every way from an expert fact witness who knows specific,

32. *Graham v. Gielchinsky,* 574 A.2d at 501.

33. 759 F.2d 312 (3d Cir.1985), cert. denied 474 U.S. 903, 106 S.Ct. 232, 88 L.Ed.2d 230.

34. 805 F.2d 1323, 1328 (8th Cir.1986).

unique facts that may not be determinable by the other side in the litigation. Each party can hire a jury and trial consultant to aid in forming impressions and developing strategies, should the party so desire.

Courts differ, however, on whether the work-product doctrine extends to the preparation work only of lawyers. The *Hickman* case left this issue open since the statements in that case were taken by a lawyer. Courts also differ on whether Rule 26 permits discovery of the identity of non-testifying retained experts without the required showing of exceptional circumstances, although the only court to have considered the issue has held that the rule prohibits such discovery.[35]

A court may conclude that trial preparation materials are not work product because they are not the result of the lawyer's work, and yet hold that they are not discoverable because "good cause" has not been shown. The "good cause" requirement for discovery is "a showing that the party seeking discovery has substantial need of the material in the preparation of his case and that he is unable, without undue hardship, to obtain the substantial equivalent of the materials by other means." [36] When the decisions on "good cause" are taken into account, most authority affords protection of the preparatory work of both lawyers and non-lawyers (though not necessarily to the same extent) by requiring more than a showing of relevance to secure production. Courts have specifically found that the good cause exception is not applicable to any material revealing an attorney's impressions, conclusions or legal theories.[37]

Because of the lack of specificity of Rule 26(b)(3), courts have generally taken three approaches in defining the protection afforded opinion work product: 1) absolute protection; 2) a balancing test to determine discoverability; and 3) a "strict protection" standard. In *Duplan Corp. v. Moulinage et Retorderie de Chavanoz,*[38] the court denied all discovery of opinion work product:

> *In our view, no showing of relevance, substantial need or undue hardship should justify compelled disclosure of an attorney's mental impressions, conclusions, opinions or legal theories. This is made clear by the Rule's use of the term "shall" as opposed to "may."*

Id. at 734.

In *Xerox Corp. v. International Business Machines Corp.,*[39] the court balanced the right of privacy of an attorney's notes against the critical

35. *Cox v. Piper, Jaffray & Hopwood, Inc.,* 848 F.2d 842, 845 (8th Cir.1988).

36. Fed.Rules Civ.Proc.Rule 26(b)(3).

37. *See Kenford Co. v. Erie County,* 55 A.D.2d 466, 390 N.Y.S.2d 715 (1977).

38. 509 F.2d 730 (4th Cir.1974), cert. denied 420 U.S. 997, 95 S.Ct. 1438, 43 L.Ed.2d 680 (1975).

39. 64 F.R.D. 367, 381 (S.D.N.Y.1974).

need for information by the attorneys and the court. The court concluded that while the work-product doctrine announced in *Hickman* protected documents containing an attorney's opinion work product, it nonetheless required the disclosure of non-privileged facts. This balancing approach weighs the extent to which the lawyer's mental processes are reflected in the materials sought against the needs of the discovering party.

The "strict protection" standard, applied by the majority of the courts, was described in *In re Murphy.*[40] The *Murphy* court stated that "opinion work product enjoys a nearly absolute immunity and can be discovered only in very rare and extraordinary circumstances."[41] The Court permitted the discovery of documents containing the opinion work product of attorneys representing drug producers because of rare situations that might arise in the future where the attorney's opinion work product may need to be discoverable.

Rules 33 and 36 have been revised in order to permit discovery calling for opinions, contentions, and admissions relating not only to fact but also to the application of law to fact. Under those rules, a party and his attorney or other representative may be required to disclose, to some extent, mental impressions, opinions, or conclusions. But the rules protect documents or parts of documents containing these matters. Even though a party may ultimately have to disclose in response to interrogatories or requests to admit, he is entitled to keep confidential documents containing such matters prepared for internal use.

40. 560 F.2d 326 (8th Cir.1977).

41. *Id.* at 336.

Chapter 6
SURVEYS

Table of Sections

§ 6.1 Overview

Surveys are extremely helpful to gauge the community's attitudes and prejudices about your case. They can be used to analyze the effect of publicity and current events, and with a properly designed instrument can unearth ingrained biases. They can help evaluate whether to seek a change of venue and to what jurisdiction, and perhaps most importantly, educate the judge on the necessity of expanding the *voir dire* conditions. They can also assist in isolating the values and demographics that will determine the profile of the best and worst jurors for your case.

You may want to confer with a consultant to determine if a survey can help clarify your case strategy. Keep in mind, however, that the term "survey" means different things to different consultants. You should carefully define your goals before choosing a consultant to make sure you tap the right skills for the job you want done.

Surveys are generally done over the telephone, but some consultants prefer to conduct their surveys face to face. In either case, if you intend to present the survey results in court, it is important that the sampling and interviewing process be done with a high degree of accuracy. A scientifically accurate sample will normally require 450 or more completed interviews.

§ 6.2 Community Analysis

Community analysis is a systematic approach to interviewing people representative of a jury panel to explore the range of responses jurors may have, based on their background and life experience. The interviews offer a valuable opportunity to test case theories and explore the interaction between commonly held attitudes in the community and issues specific to the case.

Generally, 200 to 300 names are randomly pulled from the telephone book. The sample may also be drawn from old jury lists, voter registration lists or city directories. The main concern is that the people interviewed be eligible for, but not summoned to, jury duty and not currently serving on a jury. In most jurisdictions, they would qualify if they are registered voters, though some jurisdictions also include people with only a driver's license.

Once the sample is drawn, the interviewing can begin. The interviews may be done face to face or by telephone. After asking a set of qualifying questions, the interviewer reads a case summary, which the respondents then analyze through a series of open-ended questions. The interview ends with a demographic inquiry. The responses are recorded on printed answer sheets.

There is a difference between a community analysis and a survey. In a community analysis, a facilitator or jury and trial consultant reviews the answer sheets and decides from the responses what impact the media coverage, case-specific issues and other defined factors have had on the community. In contrast, survey data are compiled by computer to correlate statistically accurate information.

The community analysis effectively asks people to be "jurors" during the interview so that attorneys can develop an understanding of their case through those "jurors'" eyes. Many important ideas have come from community analysis. For instance, attorneys defending members of the Irish Republican Army learned from a community analysis done pre-trial that prospective Jewish jurors in the Eastern District of New York must be carefully examined because of a tendency to compare the IRA with the Palestine Liberation Organization. This was new information to the attorneys, which made the community analysis well worthwhile.

§ 6.3 Case Analysis

In preparing for trial, attorneys frequently confer with their colleagues about contradictions and inconsistencies in their case. As mentioned earlier, because of their training, lawyers are the people least likely to sit, or think, as jurors. A lot more can be learned from the systematic use of case analysis interviews.

In contrast to community analysis, case analysis is a small-scale endeavor involving 25 to 35 interviews of people representative of a jury panel. Generally, this analysis is done via the telephone. The interviewer briefly describes the competing case theories and lays out the facts of the case and the information anticipated from the testimony of key witnesses. In more complex cases, the interviewer will begin with a summary of the undisputed facts. Following the case summary, the respondents are asked a series of open-ended questions. The questions first call for general reactions, then delve into more specific issues. The interview ends with a set of questions on the respondent's background demographics.

The interview data exposes the impact of community attitudes on case issues and highlights the strengths and weaknesses of a case from a lay perspective. For example, you might learn that the victim's reputation is well known in the community.

A prerequisite for writing the case analysis interview is a thorough understanding of the case facts, legal issues and competing theories, as well as agreement on the focus of the analysis, since interviewers can relay only a finite amount of information. The case analysis instrument demands time, effort and skill in development. Without a clear, concise picture of each side's case, the interviews will not produce reliable data for analysis.

§ 6.4 Hybrid Analysis

Community and case analyses can be neatly combined when time and resources are short or when a complete community analysis is unnecessary or impossible.

On home turf, or in an area where a community analysis has already been done, incorporating aspects of the community analysis format into a case analysis interview provides an opportunity to test your assumptions about the community and examine correlations between attitudes and demographic characteristics pertinent to both jury selection and case presentation. In a foreign jurisdiction, starting with a few community analysis interviews will expand your contacts and overview of the community to help select an appropriate sample for case analysis. Community analysis may also indicate where the case analysis interview should be modified to reflect, for example, the content of the local media coverage. When developing a hybrid, be aware of the scope of your questions, so the interviews do not become unwieldy.

§ 6.5 Publicity Analysis

Before you run a survey, it can be very helpful to have a specialist analyze the publicity to distill the inflammatory words or phrases and determine how many times your client's name or company was mentioned in the local media. The findings of the analysis can be reduced to an affidavit, which may encourage judges to open up the *voir dire,* change the venue or take other necessary measures to assure a fairer jury selection process. Local universities are a source of communication analysts who have studied the media and know its impact on community attitudes. If the publicity analysis does not succeed in persuading the court of the taint on the community, a survey may provide further ammunition for your argument.

§ 6.6 Surveys—Generally

It is important to understand that you cannot try the entire case through a survey. This is not the purpose of a survey; it is more to examine the major issues and determine how the publicity has affected a local community. A survey also identifies what broad groups of people will tend to be more for you than against you, based on their attitudes toward case-specific issues and the parties involved, particularly a local company or its executives.

Another strength of surveys is that they can be run in such a way that the interviewees are not in any way influenced by the interviewer. This will give you a realistic look at how people view issues in your case.

Surveys have their weaknesses, as well. While you can get feedback on your case strategy, you cannot try your case in a survey, as you can in a mock trial. The majority of survey questions must be closed-ended, limiting the respondent to yes-no or a multiple-choice answer, which, in turn, limits the information you ultimately receive. The information you do glean, however, can be helpful in obtaining a change of venue or in selecting a favorable jury.

§ 6.7 Surveys—Change of Venue

One of the best known uses of the survey is in connection with a change of venue. There are two different forms of a change of venue survey. One simply measures the predisposition in the community in which the lawsuit is being tried. The second compares community attitudes in the scheduled venue with those in potential venues, should a change of venue be granted. In either case, the survey should be run prior to filing a motion for change of venue. The reason is obvious: If you run a change of venue survey in the jurisdiction and find an overwhelming number of potential jurors have formed opinions about the case, you have a powerful exhibit in support of your motion. On the other hand, if the results do not show a predisposition against your case or your client, you could then use the survey results for a jury profile.

Multi-district surveys help to indicate whether or not you are making the right decision in requesting a change of venue. You may be more likely to obtain a fair jury in the jurisdiction you are in than in another venue. This point was classically illustrated in *State of Florida v. William Kennedy Smith.* Despite the massive and generally negative publicity surrounding the rape allegations, there was a lower percentage of citizens in Palm Beach County that thought he was guilty than the potential jurors in three other Florida jurisdictions (Tampa, Orlando and Jacksonville). In John DeLorean's cocaine case, a change of venue survey run in both San Francisco and Los Angeles determined that what little difference existed between the two cities made San Francisco less advantageous to DeLorean. Hence, it did not make sense to change the venue to San Francisco. Similarly, a survey in Santa Fe, New Mexico, after a bloody prison riot, showed that respondents had enough questions about the cause of the riot and conditions at the prison that it would be possible to obtain a fair and impartial jury to review the facts of the subsequent prosecutions.

With any survey effort, it is necessary to do a statistically accurate survey in order to convince the judge that the evidence is relevant. There must be a sufficient sample and enough questions asked to fend off any challenge that it is representative, based on current census data. This is another judgment call, particularly if the intention is to translate the survey results into a jury profile without doing any further polling.

§ 6.8 Surveys—Jury Selection Survey

A jury selection survey can determine such issues as: 1) What are the most important jury selection questions? 2) What do people from different socio-economic groups, races, ages, occupations, etc. think about your issues? 3) What about your case does not make sense or is not believable to people?

The jury selection survey can be especially helpful in jurisdictions with limited *voir dire,* where you do not have the opportunity to question prospective jurors about attitudes relevant to your case. A survey will define the attitudes of people with similar demographics, which can be compared with background information from the juror questionnaire. Your criteria can be further refined if the survey is run in tandem with a mock trial. (*See* Section 6.19.) The survey data provide a guide for designing the mock juror questionnaire and a foundation for requesting the court to authorize an expanded questionnaire at trial.

In close calls, survey data may help resolve whether or not to keep or reject a particular juror. You should keep in mind, however, that jury selection surveys give you only broad demographics. The data should always be supplemented by in-court observation to determine whether or not a person fits the profile you have developed through the survey. It has often been noted that someone who looked great on paper turned out to be biased in court, and vice versa.

§ 6.9 Surveys—Expanding *Voir Dire* Conditions

Many jurisdictions limit *voir dire.* A survey can help you educate the judge about the importance of expanding the *voir dire* in order to ferret out biases that the survey indicates the jury panel may have. (*See* Chapter 7 for a discussion of customary limits on *voir dire* and ways to improve *voir dire* conditions.) Without a survey, you often cannot substantiate the necessity to expand the *voir dire* conditions. An expert will be left open to challenge on cross-examination, that he or she does not really know the community and is basing his or her judgment on jurors in general and not on the specific jurisdiction. To make sure that the request for expanded *voir dire* conditions is preserved, it is important to run the survey. You will be surprised at how many judges will listen to the evidence and give you something that you have requested. Your measure of success should always be that if you can get just one additional question you did not think you would get, it was worth the effort. For example, in the McMartin day care case in Los Angeles, the change of venue motion was not granted, but the lawyer was given wide latitude in his *voir dire* questions.

§ 6.10 Surveys—Dual Purposes

Generally you cannot use the same survey to evaluate change of venue and jury selection. The reason is that it is counter-productive to include demographics in a change of venue survey because on cross-examination the expert who testifies about the survey will be asked whether or not the numbers of people interviewed match the most recent census data. This is partially because it is so hard to explain "sampling error" to non-statisticians and because census figures are irrelevant when a jury is drawn from registered voters.

You need to understand the limitations of each kind of survey and make a choice. Many lawyers find it useful to run two separate surveys.

§ 6.11 Surveys—Predicting the Size of the Panel

Surveys can also be used to determine the size of a jury panel. They will help answer the question: Given this kind of publicity and the impact on the community, as documented by the survey, how many people must we interview in order to get a fair jury?

§ 6.12 Questionnaire Design—Generally

Designing a survey instrument requires a great deal of knowledge and skill. It is advisable to hire an expert pollster with experience in survey design for lawyers, and particularly for jury selection analysis. Many jury and trial consulting companies work directly with a pollster in much the same way as the authors have worked with the highly skilled Dr. John McConahay of Duke University. This solid working relationship is important to assure complete coordination on the design of the survey.

Lawyers should dialogue with the pollster to assure that all the important issues are covered in the questionnaire. Take into account, however, that respondents will stay on the telephone line only a certain amount of time. You cannot try your entire case through a survey. The purpose is to look at change of venue, expanded *voir dire* or trial themes.

§ 6.13 Questionnaire Design—Short Versus Lengthy Survey

If you are seeking a change of venue or expanded *voir dire* conditions, you may find it appropriate to run a short survey. This will cut the cost of the survey and will be succinct in terms of analysis. If you are trying to discover complicated issues for jury selection purposes, then the survey must obviously be longer and more involved. For instance, you may cross-tabulate several sections to determine how one issue affected different groups of people. Again, it is important to define the goals of the survey and frame questions to have particular bearing on your case.

§ 6.14 Sampling

There are agencies that will provide a computer-generated list of telephone numbers so you have a random sample in the jurisdiction where you are running a survey. You may also be able to persuade the agency which tabulates the list of registered voters in the jurisdiction to run a random list of names. This approach eliminates the need for prescreening for voter registration, but involves the added, time-consuming task of looking up telephone numbers, and not all registered voters have listed numbers. In either case, it is important that the sample be random to produce scientifically accurate results that can hold up in court.

§ 6.15 Pre-screens and Exclusions

There should also be a pre-screening process to make sure that there is ample information to determine whether or not a respondent falls within a particular cross-section so that you wind up with a good sample. The most obvious pre-screen is for registered voters or for English-speaking respondents in jurisdictions where these are requirements for jury duty.

Ask at the beginning of your survey: "Are you or any family member currently serving on a jury, or have you or they been subpoenaed for jury duty?" If the answer is yes, the person should be excluded from your survey sample to avoid any appearance of impropriety. There may be other exclusionary questions you will want to add if you have concerns about particular issues. For example, in a discrimination case, you would want to pre-screen for people who work or have worked for a company involved in a similar suit. (*See* Appendix 5A for a sample screening sheet used in mock trial preparation that can be adapted for survey use.)

§ 6.16 Pre-test

Where time allows, it can be important to run an initial 50 interviews as a pre-test for length and comprehension, and then analyze what questions, if any, are not working. In this way, you can make changes before the bulk of the interviews have been done and get a far more accurate final result.

§ 6.17 Timing

When to run a survey depends on the purpose of the survey. For example, if a case has generated a tremendous amount of publicity, it is appropriate to run a survey in the aftermath of the publicity and then perhaps consider a follow-up closer to trial. If you intend to introduce the data in court, you will want to allow enough time from the beginning of the survey to the hearing so that the expert has time to prepare properly for affidavits and testimony and to write a thorough report, if desired.

A common mistake among lawyers is not realizing the time involved in preparing a good survey and waiting a couple of weeks before trial to begin. Though surveys can be run on short notice, it is always advisable to give your pollster plenty of time to prepare the instrument and assure that everyone is agreed that the issues are covered adequately. The jury and trial consultant should always secure the lawyers' approval *in writing* so there is never any question that this is the instrument the lawyers want used in their case.

§ 6.18 Follow-up Surveys

You may find that it is necessary to run a second survey in the same jurisdiction because the publicity has changed in tenor. The survey will indicate whether or not it is the publicity that has affected your community or the essence of the case itself.

You may also want to run a second survey because you are running two different kinds of surveys—one for jury selection purposes and one for change of venue.

§ 6.19 Mock Trials Run in Tandem With Surveys

Once a survey has been run it can be very helpful to run a mock trial to analyze the data produced by the survey. The mock trial and survey—the brother and sister of research—are vehicles that in tandem can give you tremendous insight into jury selection and case strategy.

§ 6.20 Court Prevention or Interruption of a Survey

It is rare for a court to prohibit or interrupt a survey. If the court does attempt to block your survey, you should request a full evidentiary hearing to argue the validity and value of the survey in determining the strategy of the case at bar and whether or not changes in the venue and *voir dire* conditions are necessary to obtain a fair trial for your client.

A survey conducted on behalf of counsel is, in our opinion, protected under the work-product privilege and should not be disclosed to the opposition unless counsel chooses. Furthermore, should the opposition seek to prohibit or enjoin counsel from conducting surveys, counsel should argue, as was successfully done in *U.S. v. Ledher–Rivas,* that such proposed action would amount to an unconstitutional prior restraint on the defendant's First Amendment right to free speech. *United States v. Ledher–Rivas,* 667 F.Sup. 827 (M.D.Fla.1987).

§ 6.21 Finding an Expert

You should carefully comb the country to find the expert that has the best reputation for the kind of survey that you are running. There are any number of excellent pollsters. Your jury and trial consultant will be a good source for recommendations.

You need to find one who is also experienced in writing affidavits and testifying in court. If you are on a low budget, you can generally find a statistician or pollster at a good university who has run some kind of survey on some other matter. In that case, you should carefully discuss what you are trying to accomplish with the survey and review the kind of instrument that he or she suggests should be run. You should find out who will be conducting the interviews and how they will be supervised.

Inquire as to the exact methodology your pollster will be using. Different pollsters have different ways of analyzing statistics. You should know whether or not they are using the standard methodology that will be accepted as scientifically accurate. Knowing how the survey will be conducted and analyzed is particularly important if you intend to introduce the instrument and survey results in court or call the pollster as an expert witness in connection with a motion for change of venue or expanded *voir dire.*

§ 6.22 Basics of Survey Analysis

Analyzing a survey requires that you learn some basics about percentages, means and other statistical information. Feel comfortable asking your pollster to describe the analytical terms to you.

§ 6.23 Identifying Your Kind of Juror

Surveys have led to interesting insights into human nature that will benefit you in jury selection. For example, you would think that people would not truly know whether they are flexible or rigid. Research has shown, however, that people interviewed on surveys who indicate that they are flexible in fact tend to be more flexible. This is an important discovery because it gives you a sense of who is more likely to be your kind of juror. In some cases you are going to want the flexible juror; in others, the rigid. It depends on your case and your case strategy.

§ 6.24 Preparing for Hearing

Once armed with your survey data, it is important that you prepare thoroughly for your hearing before the court. Your expert witnesses should be taken carefully through direct testimony and cross-examination, and alerted to bring all exhibits they will present in support of their analysis. It is important that you establish a rhythm with each expert.

Ask your experts to identify the weaknesses in their testimony and deficiencies in their curriculum vitae. Also ask, if they were employed by the other side, would the same conclusion have been reached, what areas pose potential problems, and what kinds of questions would likely upset the apple cart. There may be something about your expert that you do not know. In other words, be prepared for the ambush before it happens. Many things occur in a hearing that could have been prevented if the lawyer had just taken the extra hour or two to prepare properly. Use the same rigor with your experts that you would in preparing your client to take the stand. To avoid impeachment by a prior inconsistency, you should request all articles or books that the expert has written on this topic covered in the testimony. If the list is too voluminous, you should carefully discuss each book or article with the expert to avoid having his or her credibility being attacked.

Chapter 7

IMPROVING *VOIR DIRE* CONDITIONS

Table of Sections

---

§ 7.1 Overview

Voir dire conditions should be carefully analyzed in your search for the fairest jury possible. The standard jury selection process and questions used in many jurisdictions do not adequately provide an atmosphere and foundation for uncovering latent biases. The following are examples of conditions that are worthy of your consideration and recommendation to the court in the form of oral or written motions. You may want to request a hearing to argue the importance of expanding *voir dire* in one or more of the following ways.

§ 7.2 Types of Conditions—Individual Sequestered

Jurors speak more honestly when interviewed individually out of the presence of the rest of the panel. They are less apt to hide their opinions and admit to having been exposed to issues or publicity that may affect their view of the case. For this reason, you should request the opportunity to question jurors individually in a sequestered setting. This is imperative in highly publicized cases or cases involving sensitive issues, when you fear the panel will be influenced by other jurors' responses. (*See* Appendix 7A for a sample motion for individual sequestered *voir dire* by counsel in federal court and Appendix 7B for a sample motion and memorandum of points and authorities in support of a motion for individual sequestered *voir dire* and related jury matters in state court.) The American Bar Association offers some ammunition for your argument. ABA Standard for Criminal Justice 8.35 (2d Ed.1980) requires interrogation of each juror individually regarding pre-trial publicity if there is a substantial possibility that exposure to prejudicial material will render a juror ineligible to serve on a jury.

In military court you should request individual sequestered *voir dire* as you would in civilian court. The military encourages its forces to hold back their emotions and not make a public display. This ups the ante for having individual sequestered *voir dire* on sensitive issues, to provide an opening for jurors who would be less likely to express their true feelings at the risk of being judged by those who subscribe to the same rigid code. (*See* Chapters 12, 15 and 18 for further discussion of the value of individual sequestered *voir dire.*)

§ 7.3 Types of Conditions—Attorney Conducted

Clearly jurors are more open to answering questions from lawyers than judges in most instances. This is because there is less social distance between a juror and a lawyer than between a juror and a judge. Additionally, lawyers know the issues of their case and can choose the appropriate questions more effectively than the court. (*See* Chapter 11 for further discussion on judge-conducted *voir dire,* and Chapter 12 for a step-by-step approach to attorney-conducted *voir dire. See also* Appendix 7C for a sample motion and memorandum of law for attorney participation in *voir dire.*)

§ 7.4 Types of Conditions—Questionnaire

A questionnaire designed for your particular case can provide critical juror information that would not have been evident from the standard court questionnaire, and will save *voir dire* time for follow-up questions and case-specific matters. (*See* Chapter 8 for an in-depth discussion on the design and use of supplemental juror questionnaires and Appendix 8JJ for a sample motion to submit a questionnaire.)

§ 7.5 Types of Conditions—Sensitive Issues

The court needs to be educated about jurors' difficulty discussing sensitive matters in front of the rest of the panel. Matters such as finances, problems with drugs or alcohol or sex abuse are embarrassing for jurors to discuss in public and extra measures must be taken to overcome this problem. (*See* Chapters 11, 12 and 15 for further discussion on the questioning of jurors about sensitive issues.)

§ 7.6 Types of Conditions—Small Group

Should the court turn down your request for individual sequestered *voir dire,* you should consider requesting the opportunity to interview jurors in small groups of three to six. This can be a good fallback position that allows the chance to observe jurors in a more intimate environment and protects them from feeling exposed to the public. It can also be helpful to see how jurors relate to a few of their other panel members and how they react in a group.

Courts in many instances are more open to this approach than individual sequestered *voir dire* because they accept the argument that it expedites the jury selection process. (*See* Appendix 7D for a sample motion for small group and individual *voir dire* and employment of the struck system of jury selection and memorandum of law in support.)

§ 7.7 Types of Conditions—Media Exclusion From Sequestered Sessions

It is a well-known fact that the presence of the media inhibits jurors from being open during *voir dire.* In a case in Wisconsin where jurors were questioned about the presence of the press in sequestered sessions, many said it would affect their candidness and be intimidating. You should prepare a comprehensive argument to exclude the press during individual sequestered *voir dire* for the protection of the jurors' privacy. (*See* Appendix 7E for a sample motion and memorandum of law in support of the motion to prohibit televising or photographing of the jury venire and prospective jurors, and to prohibit the publication of the names of jurors, their addresses and place of business.)

§ 7.8 Types of Conditions—Additional Peremptory Challenges

If you have sought a change of venue, expanded *voir dire* or other improvements in the jury selection environment, and the court has denied each request, you may want to ask for additional peremptory strikes. Discuss with the court that given the extreme bias or prejudice that exists because of media coverage, the nature of the case or events that would color the jurors' view of the evidence, additional peremptories could be helpful in assuring your client a fair trial.

If you are working on a criminal case with multi-defendants or a civil case with multiple parties, you should request that additional and separate peremptories be given so that each party will have the opportunity to exclude from the jury those jurors they find objectionable. (*See* Appendix 7F for a sample motion and Chapter 17 for an in-depth discussion on the effective use of peremptory challenges.)

§ 7.9 Types of Conditions—Arizona Struck System

The Arizona Struck System is a method of clearing jurors for cause before exercising peremptory challenges. Counsel counts twelve jurors (the typical number on a jury, or six in states such as Florida) plus the total number of peremptories for each side before the striking begins. A strike sheet is passed back and forth between the litigants until each side has either passed or used all peremptories. You can strike anywhere in the list that you deem appropriate. This method is far superior to other methods like the blind strike system that prevent your full view of the panel. Those other methods require, for example, that each side strike privately, not knowing who the other side has struck, or that each side strike as each juror is cleared for cause.

Many courts have not adopted the Arizona Struck System as a striking option because they have never seen it used or had a lawyer ask for it, or because they do not understand it. Courts tend to be more open to this process if it is explained that it aids in intelligently exercising peremptory challenges and can save time. (*See* Appendix 7D for a sample motion requesting employment of the struck system.)

§ 7.10 Types of Conditions—Seating of Alternates

It is important when seating alternates that you know the order in which the jurors will move into the jury box. It will strongly affect your strategy for striking the alternates. You may, for example, want to strike the first and the second alternate so that alternate # 3 would become alternate # 1 and thus be the first alternate juror to be seated. Many courts use the process of not numbering the alternates so no one will know who will actually move into the box. This can be dealt with by not informing the jurors as to who is alternate # 1, 2, 3 and 4, but telling them that they all could end up serving on the jury. This method will help the lawyers give thought to the choice of the alternates, while keeping the alternates involved in the trial.

§ 7.11 Types of Conditions—Shuffle Panel

If all the minorities are seated in the back of the panel or there is an apparent unequal distribution of the panel, some states, such as

Texas, allow the clerk to shuffle the panel, if one of the parties requests it. Whether or not this is a custom in your state, you should make the request, stating that you feel there is an unequal distribution of a cognizable group. (See Appendix 7G for a sample motion.)

§ 7.12 Types of Conditions—Change of Venue

A change of venue is normally an important request in the face of extensive pre-trial publicity. There are several reasons to seek a change of venue:

1) Survey findings document that the current venue is worse than an alternative venue the court could designate;

2) A change of venue will normally delay the trial, giving time to lessen the impact of the pre-trial publicity; and

3) If the change of venue is denied, you may have greater success at improving *voir dire* conditions—getting a juror questionnaire, for instance, or individual sequestered attorney-conducted *voir dire* on sensitive issues.

You are best served by conducting a change of venue survey to document the effects of the media coverage on the community. (*See* Chapter 6, *supra,* for a full discussion on possible types of surveys and how to use a survey for the best results in court.) The change of venue survey can be used either to supplement a media analysis or in lieu of a media analysis to show the impact of publicity on community attitudes and views of your case and client.

In circumstances where time or resources prohibit a survey, a media analysis can be run alone. You can analyze the publicity yourself by tracking the headlines, the number of articles, the publications in which they have appeared, the use of your client's name and any negative references. Or you can retain an expert who specializes in assessing the impact of inflammatory words and the volume and duration of negative press. The expert can file an affidavit regarding the findings of the media analysis and later be called to testify at the hearing on the motion for change of venue. (Appendix 7H contains an excellent model for a change of venue motion based on media analysis.)

Notwithstanding the finances of your client and the willingness of experts to lend their expertise, you should garner as much documentation as possible through either of these two vehicles. Should you have an extremely limited budget and be unable to locate experts who would work at a reduced fee or pro bono, you have the option of getting affidavits from community leaders and residents who can attest to the impact of publicity and word-of-mouth knowledge on perceptions of your case.

§ 7.13 Types of Conditions—Time Limitations

It is obviously imperative that you fight for reducing the time limitations that the court imposes. It flies in the face of reality to believe that you can, for example, interview 45 people in 20 minutes. You can improve your *voir dire* conditions by requesting that the court either give you additional time, a questionnaire, or by thoroughly making your record when the court shuts you down. You should write down a succinct list of questions that you would have asked the jury had you been granted enough time to adequately conduct your *voir dire.* This should be made a part of the record before the jury is sworn. (*See* Section 11.14, *infra,* for further discussion of *voir dire* time limitations and Appendix 7I for a sample motion and memorandum of law in support of a motion for additional time to conduct *voir dire.*)

§ 7.14 Types of Conditions—Client Participation

In some instances you may find that having the client participate in *voir dire* either in a major or in a minor role can be quite helpful. You may want to request that your client be allowed to ask only one question regarding his race, his occupation or the ability of the jurors to assure him a fair trial. Invariably, this humanizes your client and allows you to read the jurors' verbal and non-verbal reactions to your client. (*See* Section 13.7, "Humanizing Yourself and Your Client," for additional suggestions on how to include your client in the jury selection process and improve his or her relationship with the jurors.)

§ 7.15 Types of Conditions—Co-counsel Participation in *Voir Dire*

Your co-counsel should participate in *voir dire.* The lawyers in the case should all have an opportunity to relate to the jurors before opening statement. This can be achieved by either dividing the issues or the panel so that the questioning is not redundant. Should one lawyer be more effective at *voir dire* than the other, then perhaps the stronger communicator should take the lead and the other play a minor role. In any case, each lawyer should have some exposure to the panel. (*See* Sections 12.17 through 12.26, "Sharing *Voir Dire* with Co–counsel," for an in-depth discussion of the ways to divide up the *voir dire.*)

§ 7.16 Types of Conditions—The Anonymous Jury

The anonymous jury has become a problem for trial lawyers throughout the United States in the way it thwarts effective jury selection. Its purpose, of course, is to keep criminal defense lawyers and their clients from knowing the identity of the jurors, where they live and what they do for a living. The jurors, especially those who have served on other cases, soon realize that something is unusual about this procedure. They are likely to assume that the prosecution and the trial judge believe that the defendant is dangerous and that the jury is in jeopardy if their identity is revealed. There is no larger barrier against the presumption of innocence than the court calling for an anonymous jury. It should be fought tooth and nail. Affidavits, as well as experts and polls, can underscore the negative effect of the anonymous jury—the implication of guilt or of the threat of violence—and dissuade the court from this severe cloud over the fairness of the process.

§ 7.17 Affidavits—Generally

Affidavits can impress upon the court the need to expand *voir dire* conditions. Your imagination should be your guide as to the kinds of affidavits that are possible to get your *voir dire* expanded. A variety of sources have been tapped and arguments put together. This chapter gives you some suggestions on where to begin your search for people and ideas.

§ 7.18 Affidavits—Community Affidavits

Ironically, the community itself is a well of support for your arguments to expand *voir dire.* The collected opinions of registered voters, community leaders, media representatives and the local bar, among others, will be difficult for the court to discount in assessing the climate in which the case will be heard. The more prominent the affiants, and the larger the numbers, the greater the influence should be on the judge's decision.

§ 7.19 Affidavits—Registered Voters

Affidavits from 50 to 100 registered voters would be persuasive. The affidavits should state that the publicity or the nature of the case has influenced their feelings about whether or not your client can get a fair trial in the community. This can be done by door-to-door canvassing or by setting up a stand at a mall or some other public place, where one-page form affidavits can be made available for signature or the affiant can make an individualized statement. Make sure a notary public is present to notarize the affidavits so that they are admissible in court.

§ 7.20 Affidavits—Civic Leaders

It is important to get the opinion of people who have lived in the community for a period of time and have a pulse on community sentiment. You should seek affidavits from city, county, state and other government officials and people with position and name recognition in the private sector.

§ 7.21 Affidavits—People With Extensive Community Contact

Members of clubs, organizations and churches are an integral part of the social fabric of the community, and usually in touch with a broad base of people. They could give feedback on what about your case would affect people's ability to be fair and impartial jurors.

§ 7.22 Affidavits—Other Lawyers

You should never overlook the resource that attorneys in your community offer. They will know about local juries and have an educated opinion about whether or not your client can get a fair trial, given the climate and circumstances of the case. Most lawyers, if they believe the evidence is there, will be happy to sign an affidavit in support of your motion for expanded *voir dire*. (*See* Appendix 7J for sample affidavit of attorney William F. Bryan in support of a motion of individual sequestered *voir dire* in a criminal case.)

§ 7.23 Affidavits—People Respected by the Judge

If at all possible, you should try to include among the affiants people with legal, political or professional experience whose opinion the judge will value. Seek out people who have held positions in the judicial system such as former judges, prosecutors and court clerks. Once people have resigned or retired from a prominent post, they are usually more open to voicing their views about adversarial issues. Seek them out and ask them for their valued opinion. Explain that all you want is a fair trial for your client.

§ 7.24 Affidavits—The Media

Media personnel have an idea about the community because they are "in the field" and interview so many of us. You should contact the media and get affidavits from reporters and broadcasters who have an opinion as to whether or not your client can get a fair trial in this community. Retired media people may be more open to expressing their opinions than those still in the business.

§ 7.25 Affidavits—Prior Jurors

You should find people in the community who have served on juries in the past. Run through the facts of your case and ask whether or not they think your client can get a fair trial, based on what they learned of juror attitudes from prior jury service. It is important that they compare their previous jury experiences with what they know of your particular case. Their opinion will shed light on the potentiality for a fair trial in that community, and give weight to your claim that *voir dire* should be expanded to expose any hidden biases.

§ 7.26 Expert Affidavits—Generally

A second valuable source of affidavits are the experts—the people who focus on community behavior and are trained to get an accurate picture.

§ 7.27 Expert Affidavits—Jury and Trial Consultants

Jury consultants in most instances have seen more jury trials than any ten lawyers. Their affidavits can be written with the flavor of extensive jury selection experience. They can compare your case with others in terms of the facts and issues of the case, the publicity and the influences on the community. They can discuss the social significance of the case and other factors that will affect jurors' ability to be fair. They can also deduce, based on prior observations, what *voir dire* conditions would help to secure a fair trial. (*See* Appendix 7K for a sample affidavit of Cathy E. Bennett in support of a motion for attorney-conducted individual sequestered *voir dire* filed by the defendant.)

§ 7.28 Expert Affidavits—Social Scientists

If there is not a jury consultant with whom you have a rapport or one who has been referred to you, then contact sociologists or psychologists in your community who will look at the circumstances of your case and evaluate how the *voir dire* should be expanded in order to get a fairer trial. Many social scientists, either on a volunteer basis or for a small fee, will gladly render an opinion in an affidavit. (*See* Appendices 7L and 7M for sample affidavits of John B. McConahay, a professor of public policy studies, and Robert Buckhout, a professor of psychology, analyzing survey results in a child molestation case and a drug-related case, respectively.)

§ 7.29 Expert Affidavits—Investigators

It is the work of investigators to talk to people in the community about their ideas and feelings about a particular case. No doubt they will require a fee to delve into community sentiment and prepare an affidavit of their findings. Their affidavit should describe how the investigation was done and what they found to be the effects of the publicity and the case issues on the community. There should also be a clear statement that the affidavit is based upon their investigative experience and upon what they have learned investigating the community on this case.

§ 7.30 Expert Affidavits—Media Analysts

You should hire a media expert to analyze the effect of the media upon the community. This person should be trained in evaluating the impact of inflammatory words and repetitious coverage that could color the perception of your client and the case. The affidavit prepared from the media analysis should be clear, concise and free of professional jargon.

§ 7.31 Expert Affidavits—Pollsters

Pollsters can be hired to conduct a survey on the issues of your particular case, as discussed in Chapter 6. Pollsters who have run a survey in your community relative to the issues in your case can also extrapolate the information gleaned from their polls and prepare an affidavit for the court. Care should be taken that the affidavit covers only those issues surveyed that would further your argument for expanded *voir dire,* for example, where the survey indicated obvious bias toward similar facts or issues. You do not want to document so broad a range of inquiry that the court could discount its relevance.

To oppose use of an anonymous jury, a survey would randomly poll citizens and ask what they would think if they were on a jury where their names, addresses and occupations were not allowed to be discussed. What would they think if they were a number, not a name? You may also want to get permission to poll jurors who have been through jury duty and ask how they would respond if they learned that they were to serve on a jury that was to be anonymous. This would be the most accurate sample for a survey. Again, these results should be put into affidavit form and presented to the court along with expert testimony.

It may be further persuasive to introduce interviews with jurors who have sat on anonymous juries asking what conclusions they drew from being anonymous. Obviously, you will want to check the local rules and law in that jurisdiction to make sure that you are not in violation by conducting post-trial interviews.

§ 7.32 Waiver of *Voir Dire* Errors—Generally

The failure to propose questions aimed at discovering a juror's bias or prejudice or to take necessary steps to preserve *voir dire* errors for appeal usually results in waiving *voir dire* errors as a basis for a new trial. In *Turner v. Murray,* [1] the Supreme Court found that a defendant cannot complain that the trial court failed to question prospective jurors on racial prejudice or bias unless he specifically requested such questioning.

§ 7.32

1. 476 U.S. 28, 37, 106 S.Ct. 1683, 1689, 90 L.Ed.2d 27 (1986).

As articulated in *United States v. Gibbons,*[2] the trial court has "broad discretion" to determine the scope and form of *voir dire.* Appellate courts are reluctant to disturb judicial discretion except in extreme cases. For example, *United States v. Hill*[3] found an abuse of discretion when the *voir dire* fails "to properly test the qualifications and competency of the prospective jurors to sit on the trial of case." In *Emmons v. State,*[4] the appellate court ruled that the trial judge had abused his discretion when he denied defendant's repeated requests that *voir dire* be recorded. Even when the trial judge conducts *voir dire* questioning, determines the specific areas to be pursued, and actually formulates the questions asked, the attorney has the burden of making specific objections on the record in order to raise *voir dire* issues on appeal. In *Horsey v. Mack Truck, Inc.,*[5] the court stated at footnote 19 at page 848:

> *It is incumbent upon counsel to make his record for appeal even if he believes that objecting to the actions of judge or counsel will give offense to the court or the jury.*

If particular *voir dire* questions are essential, counsel must inform the court and state reasons on the record before *voir dire* is complete or the issue is waived.

The following circumstances may constitute waiver:

1) Failure to object to the standard *voir dire* questions used by various district courts.

In *Horsey v. Mack,*[6] the court could not determine whether Horsey had called the trial judge's attention to the requirement of *Kiernan v. Van Schaik,*[7] that a judge in a personal injury case ask jurors about any connection with the insurance company. The court also found no evidence on the record that Horsey made an on-record objection to the judge's failure to include the mandated questions.[8] Therefore, the court held that Horsey's failure to preserve the issue for review constituted a waiver.[9] The court did review the issue under the plain error standard and held that the failure to ask three required questions did not "constitute a manifest injustice sufficient to establish plain error."[10]

2) Silence when called upon to respond to a judge's statement that all requested *voir dire* subjects have been covered.

2. 602 F.2d 1044 (2d Cir.1979), cert. denied 444 U.S. 950, 100 S.Ct. 421, 62 L.Ed.2d 319 (1979).

3. 526 F.2d 1019, 1025 (10th Cir.1975), cert. denied 425 U.S. 940, 96 S.Ct. 1676, 48 L.Ed.2d 182 (1976).

4. 492 N.E.2d 303, 304 (Ind.1986), appeal after remand 542 N.E.2d 544 (Ind. 1989).

5. 882 F.2d 844 (3d Cir.1989).

6. *Horsey v. Mack,* 882 F.2d at 848 n. 37.

7. 347 F.2d 775 (3d Cir.1965).

8. 882 F.2d at 849.

9. *Id.*

10. *Id.*

In *United States v. Blosvern,*[11] the court found that the defendant who remained silent during the trial judge's *voir dire* after being instructed to make objections immediately waived the issue of *voir dire* errors.

3) Failure to ensure that a court reporter records the *voir dire* examination.

According to Rules 10(b) and 11(a) of the Federal Rules of Appellate Procedure, it is the appellant's responsibility to ensure that all materials on which he relies are part of the record. The rule is upheld in *United States v. Ross,*[12] where the court ruled that lack of a record precludes raising the *voir dire* issue that the judge refused to ask questions proposed by the defendant; and in *United States v. Gerald,*[13] where the court would not consider an objection to the *voir dire* that was not included in the record. The standard extends to objections made off the record. The court stated in *Hicks v. Mickelson*[14]: "We do not know nor may we consider" off-the-record discussions of *voir dire* issues. In *Hicks* the court refused to consider counsel's affidavit regarding an off-record trial conference, relying on *Stearns v. Hertz Corp.,*[15] which stated that the "appeal is to be determined upon the record below."

On the other hand, in *Emmons v. State,* [16] where the trial court denied the defendant's request that *voir dire* questions be recorded, the mere fact that the defendant accepted the jury as selected did not waive an appellate review of prejudicial pre-trial publicity. The *Emmons* court also found the trial court's denial of several requests to record *voir dire* an abuse of judicial discretion.

Barefield v. Texas,[17] addresses the timeliness of the objection. The court found the following objection to be "sufficiently timely to preserve this issue for review," though the state argued that the objection was waived because the defense did not object before the trial court sustained the state's challenge for cause:

(Prosecutor): *We present him for cause, Your Honor.*

(Defense): *For the record, go ahead I'm sorry. I was jumping the gun.*

(Court): *I'll sustain the challenge.*

11. 514 F.2d 387, 398 (9th Cir.1975).

12. 477 F.2d 551, 552–553 (6th Cir. 1973), cert. denied 414 U.S. 912, 94 S.Ct. 252, 38 L.Ed.2d 150 (1973).

13. 624 F.2d 1291, 1295–96 (5th Cir. 1980), rehearing denied 629 F.2d 1350 (5th Cir.1980).

14. 835 F.2d 721, 724 (8th Cir.1987).

15. 326 F.2d 405, 408 (8th Cir.1964), cert. denied 377 U.S. 934, 84 S.Ct. 1338, 12 L.Ed.2d 298 (1964).

16. 492 N.E.2d 303 (Ind.1986), appeal after remand 542 N.E.2d 544 (Ind.1989).

17. 784 S.W.2d 38, 41 (Tex.Crim.App. 1989), cert. denied ___ U.S. ___, 110 S.Ct. 3256, 111 L.Ed.2d 766 (1990).

(Defense): *Would you note the defendant's objections for the challenge for the excusing for cause, Your Honor.*

(Court): *Very well. Bring in [the next venire member].*

4) Failure to review and file objections to transcripts within a reasonable time after trial.

In *United States v. Renton,* [18] for example, the court declined to remand the case based on counsel's failure to review and file objections to reconstructed transcripts. The court found the absence of objections "significant, ... compounded by counsel's inability to indicate one specific error committed during the portions of trial not included in the record."

5) Failure to exhaust peremptory strikes.

A party may not later object that a juror should have been stricken for cause. The following cases are exemplary: *Maine v. Superior Court of Mendocino County,* [19] where the court recognized the need for a change of venue on the grounds that the potential failure of the defense to exhaust peremptory challenges in an antagonistic atmosphere would waive the right to claim on appeal, without a specific showing of prejudice, that the jury was not impartial; *People v. Goldberg,* [20] where the trial court's erroneous denial of a challenge for cause is harmless if the defendant does not use all peremptories; *Kotler v. American Tobacco Co.,*[21] where the failure of the record to show that the jury was not satisfactory to appellant or that appellant would have used another peremptory challenge waives the issue as ground for reversal; *Goldstein v. Kelleher,* [22] which found that "[i]n the absence of any indication that the jury selected was unsatisfactory to plaintiff *at the time chosen,* we are unwilling to reverse the verdict of a jury that to all appearances was disinterested, competent, and suitable." (*Emphasis added.*)

Any disputes concerning the number of peremptory challenges and court rules governing the use of peremptory challenges must be made during the *voir dire.* In *Righi v. People,* [23] the court found that the defendant's failure to object to additional peremptories being granted to both sides constitutes waiver of the right to demand that the prosecution peremptories not exceed the statutory number.

6) Failure to use reasonable diligence to discover any legal objections to a juror.

18. 700 F.2d 154, 158–159 (5th Cir. 1983).

19. 68 Cal.2d 375, 66 Cal.Rptr. 724, 438 P.2d 372 (1968).

20. 110 Cal.App.2d 17, 242 P.2d 116, 120–121 (1952).

21. 926 F.2d 1217, 1227 (1st Cir.1990), cert. granted and judgment vacated ___ U.S. ___, 112 S.Ct. 3019, 120 L.Ed.2d 891 (1992).

22. 728 F.2d 32, 38 (1st Cir.1984), cert. denied 469 U.S. 852, 105 S.Ct. 172, 83 L.Ed.2d 107 (1984).

23. 145 Colo. 457, 359 P.2d 656 (1961).

For instance, in *Parkinson v. Hudson,*[24] the court ruled that failure to ask prospective jurors about matters that might disqualify them waives the right to a new trial; in *Law v. State,*[25] the court ruled that the post-trial discovery that a juror had been a rape victim is not a ground for new trial if counsel did not ask during *voir dire* whether any of the jurors had been raped; and in *Peters v. State,*[26] the court ruled that matters affecting a juror's qualifications that would have been disclosed by reasonable diligence during *voir dire* cannot later be made grounds to attack the verdict.

The failure to test potential jurors by making adequate inquiry, using specific questions, and the failure to disclose any objections as soon as they are discovered later, waive the right to raise an objection on appeal. *Cleveland, C., C. & St. L. Ry. Co. v. Osgood*[27] is a case in point, where counsel's failure to inform the trial court until after the verdict that a juror disclosed three and a half hours before the verdict that he was also a party to a lawsuit waived the right to object to the presence of the juror.

7) In a criminal trial, absence of an in-custody defendant without a personal waiver.

Rule 43(a) of the Federal Rules of Criminal Procedure gives a defendant the explicit right to be present "at every stage of the trial including the impaneling of the jury." The rule underlies the decisions in *United States v. Crutcher,*[28] where the Court ruled that "the right to be present at one's trial is a personal right that may be waived by a defendant"; *United States v. Camacho,*[29] where the Court ruled that the defendant's complete absence from *voir dire* is not harmless error beyond a reasonable doubt; and *United States v. Gordon,*[30] where the Court ruled that the judge should hold an on-the-record hearing to advise the defendant of his right to be present during *voir dire* and obtain a personal waiver. *United States v. Gordon* also distinguishes *custodial* and *non-custodial* defendants, citing dictum from *Diaz v. United States,*[31] that a defendant in custody does not have the power to waive his right to be present "because his presence or absence is not within his own control." In contrast, *Taylor v. United States*[32] recognizes that a non-custodial defendant can waive his right to be present by voluntarily absenting himself.

24. 265 Ala. 4, 88 So.2d 793, 797 (1956).

25. 407 So.2d 572, 575 (Ala.Crim.App. 1981).

26. 712 P.2d 799, 801 (Okl.Crim.1986).

27. 36 Ind.App. 34, 73 N.E. 285, 287 (1905).

28. 405 F.2d 239, 243 (2d Cir.1968), cert. denied 394 U.S. 908, 89 S.Ct. 1018, 22 L.Ed.2d 219 (1969).

29. 955 F.2d 950 (4th Cir.1992).

30. 829 F.2d 119 (D.C.Cir.1987).

31. 223 U.S. 442, 445, 32 S.Ct. 250, 251, 56 L.Ed. 500 (U.S.Phil. Islands 1912).

32. 414 U.S. 17, 20, 94 S.Ct. 194, 196, 38 L.Ed.2d 174 (1973).

A court should therefore hold an "on-the-record hearing" to advise an in-custody defendant of his right to be present during *voir dire* and obtain a knowing waiver. His absence during part of the *voir dire*, however, does not require a knowing on-the-record waiver. In *United States v. Washington*,[33] for instance, the court did not find error in the exclusion of the defendant from a sidebar examination of prospective jurors because the defendant was present and conferred with counsel about juror's responses at the bench. Likewise, in *United States v. Bascaro*,[34] the court found no error when the defendant remained in the courtroom while counsel left briefly to confer during the peremptory challenge phase of jury selection. On the state level, *People v. Bean*[35] makes a critical distinction. The *Bean* court ruled that even without prejudice to the defendant, "*in camera voir dire* without the defendant's presence and without the defendant's express waiver is improper and, in some cases, will inevitably result in the denial of a defendant's fundamental rights to a fair trial by an impartial jury." The right to be present, however, is not absolute, and the court found in this case that the defendant's due process right of presence was not violated.[36]

8) Failure to make a *Batson* challenge during *voir dire*.

As articulated in the following cases, a challenge to the composition of the jury, based on *Batson v. Kentucky*, [37] is waived if the objection is not made during *voir dire*: *United States v. Cashwell*,[38] which found the *Batson* claim "inextricably linked to defense counsel's 'timely objection'," and *Government of Virgin Islands v. Forte*,[39] which held that failure to raise a *Batson* objection at *voir dire* bars raising it later, absent plain error. In *United States v. Cashwell*, however, the appellate court allowed the parties to reconstruct the *voir dire* record in order to ascertain whether the defendant preserved a *Batson* objection for review. The court noted that the district court's failure "to require the recording of *voir dire* proceedings will mandate reversal only if the absence of this proceeding is a substantial and significant omission from the record which cannot be adequately reconstructed." Once reconstructed, if the record shows that the defendant failed to preserve the issue for appeal, the reviewing court will likely deny the *Batson* challenge on appeal, as held in *United States v. Cashwell*. On the other hand, in *People v. McDonald*,[40] when the defense requested leave of the court to establish on the record the race of the jurors at the conclusion of *voir dire* and before the jury was sworn, the prosecution prevailed in

33. 705 F.2d 489, 497–499 (D.C.Cir. 1983).

34. 742 F.2d 1335, 1349–1350 (11th Cir. 1984).

35. 137 Ill.2d 65, 147 Ill.Dec. 891, 560 N.E.2d 258 (1990), cert. denied ___ U.S. ___, 111 S.Ct. 1338, 113 L.Ed.2d 270 (1991).

36. *Id.* at 268, 147 Ill.Dec. at 901.

37. 476 U.S. 79, 106 S.Ct. 1712, 90 L.Ed.2d 69 (1986).

38. 950 F.2d 699, 704 (11th Cir.1992).

39. 806 F.2d 73, 76 (3d Cir.1986).

40. 125 Ill.2d 182, 125 Ill.Dec. 781, 786–787, 530 N.E.2d 1351, 1356–1357 (1988).

its objection to the defense attempt to substantiate its *Batson* claim. The court ruled that the prosecution could not later contend the issue is waived because of a deficient record.

9) Failure to object on the record to preserve other *voir dire* issues for appeal, including: reliance on a juror questionnaire containing a false answer; court-imposed time limits; and off-record conversations between trial judges and prospective jurors.

In *Shamburger v. Behrens,*[41] the court ruled that since reliance on a juror's answers to the Court questionnaire is reasonable, counsel's failure to question the juror about prior felony convictions not disclosed on the questionnaire does not operate as a waiver of the contention that the juror was disqualified as a convicted felon whose civil rights had not been restored. Likewise in *Horsey v. Mack Trucks, supra,* failure to object on the record to court-imposed time restraints on *voir dire* questioning waives the issue for review. Off-record communications between the judge and jurors is "expressly disapproved" in *State v. Tate,*[42] for instance, but the court found that the defendant's failure to object constituted a waiver.

An attorney must be aware that failure to preserve *voir dire* errors will restrict an appellate review to the issue of whether there was "plain error," as in *People v. Bean,*[43] where the defendant did not object in trial or post-trial to the defendant's absence from *in camera voir dire.* Other cases of note are: *United States v. Lookretis,*[44] where the court ruled that the "allegation on appeal that the trial judge improperly conducted *voir dire* ... will not be heard now, where no objection was made below, in the absence of plain error"; *United States v. Flores–Elias,*[45] where the court found that since neither party submitted additional *voir dire* questions or objected to the scope of the *voir dire,* the *voir dire* will be reviewed only to determine whether there was plain error; and *United States v. de Leon Davis,*[46] where the court ruled that counsel's failure to object to a modified *Allen* charge on the third day of trial requires the defendant to show under the plain error standard that the judge's instruction undermined the fairness of the trial and contributed to a miscarriage of justice. *United States v. Stoppelman,*[47] even ruled out the plain error standard; the judge's refusal to ask proposed questions could not be considered under the plain error rule, since no objection was made. Overwhelmingly, the

41. 418 N.W.2d 299, 302 (S.D.1988).

42. 294 N.C. 189, 239 S.E.2d 821, 827 (1978).

43. 137 Ill.2d 65, 147 Ill.Dec. 891, 560 N.E.2d 258 (1990).

44. 422 F.2d 647, 651 (7th Cir.1970), cert. denied 398 U.S. 904, 90 S.Ct. 1693, 26 L.Ed.2d 63 (1970).

45. 650 F.2d 1149, 1151 (9th Cir.1981), cert. denied 454 U.S. 904, 102 S.Ct. 412, 70 L.Ed.2d 223 (1981).

46. 914 F.2d 340, 343–344 (1st Cir.1990).

47. 406 F.2d 127, 133 (1st Cir.1969), cert. denied 395 U.S. 981, 89 S.Ct. 2141, 23 L.Ed.2d 769 (1969).

case law leads to the conclusion that a reviewing court, lacking a *voir dire* record containing specific objections, will either refuse to review the issue or will apply the plain error rule and uphold the trial judge's discretion in conducting the *voir dire.*

It has been argued in some state courts that an attorney's failure to preserve *voir dire* objections for appeal is equivalent to ineffective assistance of counsel, but the argument is rarely successful. In *Klinekole v. Oklahoma,*[48] counsel's failure to object to improper *voir dire* comments was deemed part of trial strategy and, therefore, not ineffective assistance of counsel. The Court in *Montana v. Madera,*[49] noted that failure of defense counsel to ensure a *voir dire* record was cause for concern, but does not rise to the level of ineffective assistance of counsel where other factors show counsel adequately represented defendant and defendant was guilty beyond a reasonable doubt.

§ 7.33 Waiver of *Voir Dire*—Supreme Court Review

The United States Supreme Court has been very reluctant to find a constitutional basis for requiring any specific *voir dire* procedures. In *Rosales–Lopez v. United States*[1] the Court did find that the Constitution requires questioning prospective jurors about racial and ethnic prejudices in "special circumstances." These special circumstances exist only when racial issues are "inextricably bound up with the conduct of the trial and there are substantial indications of the likelihood of racial or ethnic prejudice affecting the jurors in the particular case."[2] Otherwise *Rosales–Lopez* makes the Court's position clear: The obligation to impanel an impartial jury rests with the federal trial judge who has ample discretion in conducting *voir dire* and where *voir dire* inquiries are not constitutionally mandated, even if the defendant requests *voir dire* questions regarding racial or ethnic prejudice, it is not reversible error unless there is a "reasonable possibility" that the jury was influenced by prejudice.

While recognizing that a trial court's *voir dire* must "cover the subject" of potential racial bias, the Court has carefully refrained from requiring any precise "content" questions. In *Mu'Min v. Virginia,*[3] the Court addressed the issue of whether a defendant has the constitutional right to ask prospective jurors about the content of pre-trial publicity to which they have been exposed. The Court admitted that precise inquiries might be useful to a defendant in exercising peremptory

48. 705 P.2d 179, 185 (Okl.Crim.1985).

49. 206 Mont. 140, 670 P.2d 552, 565 (1983).

§ 7.33

1. 451 U.S. 182, 189, 101 S.Ct. 1629, 1634, 68 L.Ed.2d 22 (1981).

2. *See also Ristaino v. Ross,* 424 U.S. 589, 96 S.Ct. 1017, 47 L.Ed.2d 258 (1976) and *Ham v. South Carolina,* 409 U.S. 524, 93 S.Ct. 848, 35 L.Ed.2d 46 (1973).

3. 111 S.Ct. 1899, 114 L.Ed.2d 493 (1991), rehearing denied ___ U.S. ___, 112 S.Ct. 13, 115 L.Ed.2d 1097 (1991).

challenges; however, the Constitution only requires a trial court to "cover the subject." In defense of his right to an impartial jury, a defendant may ask whether a prospective juror has been exposed to any pre-trial publicity but the defendant is not constitutionally entitled to ask what the juror has heard or read. Also, failure to request that a potential juror, exposed to pre-trial publicity, be questioned individually during *voir dire* waives any later objection.[4]

The *Mu'Min* decision reiterated that content questions are constitutionally compelled *only* if the trial court's failure to ask them renders the trial fundamentally unfair.[5] Where content questions have been required, the federal courts have not based that requirement on constitutional grounds. For example, in *Turner v. Murray*[6] the Court stated that a defendant cannot complain that the venire was not questioned regarding racial prejudice unless the defendant specifically asks for this type of questioning. The Court draws a fine line at the constitutional right to cover the subject in "special circumstances" such as interracial capital crime cases. Under *Mu'Min,* a capital defendant accused of an interracial crime is constitutionally "entitled to have prospective jurors informed of the race of the victim and questioned on the issue of racial bias." Such a defendant is not entitled, however, to demand that *voir dire* questions contain any specific language or phrasing in order to uncover racial bias.

In the limited situations where a constitutional right to pursue an area of questioning exists, the reviewing court must still find reversible error before it will grant a new trial. An attorney should be prepared to meet the burden of proving that the trial court's refusal to allow particular content questions rendered the defendant's trial "fundamentally unfair." To meet this burden, an attorney must develop specific questions aimed at uncovering juror bias and prejudice, submit the questions to the trial judge, object if the questions are not asked and ensure that the questions are on the *voir dire* record for later review.

A defendant may also waive their constitutional right to have an Article III federal judge preside at the *voir dire.* Failure to object to the absence of an Article III judge fulfills the requirement of "consent" to the substitution of a magistrate. In *Peretz v. United States*[7] the Court found consent because defendant Peretz never asked the district court to review the rulings of the magistrate and raised no objection regarding jury selection at trial. Although the "additional duties"

4. *See United States v. Cook,* 432 F.2d 1093 (7th Cir.1970), cert. denied 401 U.S. 996, 91 S.Ct. 1224, 28 L.Ed.2d 535 (1971), and *United States v. Bryant,* 471 F.2d 1040 (D.C.Cir.1972), cert. denied 409 U.S. 1112, 93 S.Ct. 923, 34 L.Ed.2d 693 (1973).

5. *See Mu'Min v. Virginia,* ___ U.S. ___, 111 S.Ct. 1899, 114 L.Ed.2d 493 (1991), rehearing denied ___ U.S. ___, 112 S.Ct. 13, 115 L.Ed.2d 1097 (1991).

6. 476 U.S. 28, 106 S.Ct. 1683, 90 L.Ed.2d 27 (1986).

7. ___ U.S. ___, 111 S.Ct. 2661, 115 L.Ed.2d 808 (1991).

clause of the Federal Magistrates Act permits a magistrate to preside over *voir dire* if a defendant "consents," it does not provide for *de novo* review of the magistrate's decisions during *voir dire.* (*See also* Section 11.3, *infra,* for discussion of the pros and cons of magistrate *voir dire.*)

There is only one *voir dire* situation where the Supreme Court has mandated that a waiver requires affirmative consent in the trial record—where, as discussed above, an in-custody defendant is absent from more than a minimal portion of the *voir dire.*

Since the Supreme Court has refused to provide a concrete framework for *voir dire,* even in situations implicitly protected by the Constitution, it is crucial to recognize *voir dire* errors and preserve the errors for appeal. The trial court has such great discretion in determining the scope and form of the *voir dire* that a reviewing court will usually abstain from considering whether the trial court erred in denying a party's request for specific questions unless the proposed questions appear in the record. Absent a trial record of *voir dire,* which should contain the proposed questions and a specific objection to the judge's refusal to ask the question or questions, as well as the judge's ruling on the objection, the reviewing court will consider the error waived.[8]

8. *See,* for example, *United States v. Stoppelman,* 406 F.2d 127 (1st Cir.1969), cert. denied 395 U.S. 981, 89 S.Ct. 2141, 23 L.Ed.2d 769 (1969) (refusal to ask questions regarding conscientious objector status on the *voir dire* was waived when not objected to); *United States v. Rojas,* 502 F.2d 1042 (5th Cir.1974), (trial court's refusal to ask counsel's questions on *voir dire* was waived when no request was made to include the questions in the record and counsel did not object); *United States v. Bear Runner,* 502 F.2d 908 (8th Cir.1974) (failure to submit *voir dire* questions regarding pre-trial publicity constitutes waiver of the issue on appeal).

Chapter 8

QUESTIONNAIRES

Table of Sections

---

§ 8.1 Overview

Courts regularly require prospective jurors to fill out a questionnaire at the time they are empaneled. The questionnaires vary by jurisdiction but generally ask the following information: name, occupation and employer, name of spouse, spouse's occupation and employer, length of residency in the jurisdiction, involvement in litigation, insurance or law enforcement connections, prior jury experience, education, religious or organizational affiliations and physical impairments. (*See*

Appendix 8A for a sample district court questionnaire from the First Judicial District of New Mexico.)

In most instances, counsel receives the questionnaires of the assigned jury panel along with the juror list prior to trial. Obviously, the court questionnaire will not address many issues relevant to your case. It is therefore helpful to request a supplemental questionnaire not only with case-specific questions, but with other relevant questions that will shed light on the jurors' background, experience and perceptions. Supplemental questionnaires are extremely helpful in getting information from jurors. Jurors will many times say one thing in court and another thing on a questionnaire. Having the opportunity to compare several sides of a juror's personality is valuable in itself, and also allows you to use your limited *voir dire* time to ask the necessary questions.

§ 8.2 Length of Questionnaire

Questionnaires can be a variety of lengths depending on the court's openness to the questionnaire and the amount of time that you have to review the data. (*See* Appendices 8B through 8II for sample questionnaires used in criminal and civil cases. The names of some clients and judges have been deleted because the content of the questionnaire was more important than disclosing the parties involved.) If the questionnaire is going to be filled out the morning of trial and you will only be able to analyze the information as the juror enters the box, you will want a shorter questionnaire that can be easily scanned.

In a jurisdiction where the court acknowledges the value of a questionnaire and allows the questionnaire to be disseminated earlier in the day, the evening before or through the mail, you should have as lengthy a questionnaire as the court will permit. A five- to ten- to twenty-page questionnaire will give you a real feel for how the juror responds to a variety of issues.

The advent of computers has made the design of questionnaires more skillful. Use your space to its utmost. You can put your computer on compressed print and get twice the number of questions on a page. If you then cut and paste two pages of questions and reduce them on your copying machine, you will have a four-page questionnaire in one. A hesitant judge is more apt to grant a questionnaire if it is only one-page long. If permissible, put it on a legal-size page for maximum readability. Be sure to advise jurors at the bottom of the questionnaire that they can use the back for additional information, if needed.

§ 8.3 Kinds of Questions to Ask

All questionnaires should have some basic background questions such as vocation, education and marital status. The background questions are important because these are the questions the jurors should feel comfortable answering honestly.

You will also want to include in all questionnaires at least four or five open-ended, case-specific questions. It is important that the questions be open-ended to give the jurors a chance to be more honest about what they think and feel. In the privacy of their living room, the jury room or courtroom, out of the public's hearing, many people are more apt to be candid. The questionnaire is therefore a tremendous vehicle to encourage openness where there are sensitive issues such as contract disputes, rape, drugs, molestation, banking problems or other matters a person may be uncomfortable discussing in front of fellow jurors. Also, it gives you time to evaluate the jurors' responses to sensitive issues to determine appropriate follow-up questions in court.

You can further use the feedback from a questionnaire to substantiate a request for individual sequestered *voir dire* on sensitive issues. Even obstinate judges will find that it is important to get information on these matters in a way that encourages jurors to be honest, and will often grant your request.

§ 8.4 Advance Mail–Out Questionnaires

A mail-out questionnaire can be extremely helpful because it gives you time to analyze and organize the data for follow-up. Many judges realize that it will also save court time, because after the questionnaires are returned, they can be reproduced and distributed so that the parties have an adequate chance to digest the responses. This advance review of the questionnaires not only gives counsel time to prepare follow-up questions and find agreement with opposing counsel on some hardships and cause challenges, but diminishes time spent perusing the questionnaires in court. You should make a point of the time saved when requesting a mail-out questionnaire.

The easier the processing of the questionnaire, the more quickly you are apt to receive your copy from the clerk. Once the questionnaire has been returned, you can offer to assist in the reproduction and take some of the burden off the court staff. Remember, you always want to be on good terms with the court staff, if at all possible.

The mail-out questionnaire should include a cover letter from the judge stating that the questionnaire is being sent out by the court to save court time and requesting the jurors to be honest in their responses, which will be kept confidential. (*See* Appendices 8D, 8E, 8G, 8I, 8K, 8L, 8M, 8S, 8Z, 8AA and 8CC for sample cover letters, with an explanation of their use.) Receiving the judge's letter will make the juror more open to answering the questionnaire and can only help to draw out more accurate information.

With the mail-out questionnaire you will also have time to feed the responses into your computer for comparative analysis, if you have run a jury selection survey, and to analyze the significance of answers that jurors have given. Also, the more advance time you have, the better you can draft follow-up questions for *voir dire,* which can be organized in a three-ring binder for easy access.

§ 8.5 In-Court Questionnaires—Generally

The in-court questionnaire can also be extremely useful if the judge refuses to mail it out. The logistics are a bit more complicated but are still worth the effort. Some information is always better than no information, even when there is less time for analysis.

It is helpful to have an additional person in the courtroom—like a secretary, another lawyer, or a jury and trial consultant—whose only responsibility is to handle the questionnaires. When a juror hits the box or is being examined, the person would pull out the juror's questionnaire for the lawyer to have at hand, along with any follow-up questions that are indicated for the juror. The follow-up questions should be put on a sheet of paper attached to the questionnaire or written on a Post-it™, if there are only a few. Whatever method is used, it is vital that the questionnaires be made readily available in the course of *voir dire.*

Some lawyers feel that the usefulness of a questionnaire is diminished when distributed immediately before *voir dire.* This is simply not true. A questionnaire can give the answers to 20 to 25 questions you may not otherwise have time to get answered or where it is not to your advantage to ask the juror directly for this information.

§ 8.6 In-Court Questionnaires—Logistics

When the court has instructed that the questionnaire be filled out right before jury selection, the logistics become important. You must be organized to make the process simple—simple for each juror to answer the questionnaire and simple for you to glean the most information in the time allotted.

You will want to have the jurors fill out the questionnaire in the jury room, hall or courtroom. It is easier if they do it outside of the courtroom so that the time can be used to take care of other pre-trial matters. This way the judge does not feel that any time is being wasted.

Different jurors use different approaches to completing the questionnaire. Some are rapid and do not take much time; others have a sense of the instrument's importance and go into great detail to make sure that they give complete answers. You will want to give the jurors as much time as possible. If the court is in a hurry, request at least 30 minutes to an hour. In that time the jurors can fill out a one- to two-page questionnaire, and the staff can make and distribute copies to the judge and counsel.

Be sure to provide each juror with a pen so that the court staff is not left with yet another responsibility.

After the questionnaires have been returned, there are two ways to make sure that everyone has a copy. One is to have a member of your staff volunteer to assist in taking the questionnaires to a quick copy service or to assist the court staff in reproduction. The other possibility is to use colored carbon forms so that copies of the questionnaire are made automatically when it is filled out. Again, you want to do all you can to relieve the court staff of extra duties, and stay on their good side.

§ 8.7 When to Request a Questionnaire

A questionnaire will always be helpful in any kind of case that you try. It saves you and the court time, and gives you a wealth of information. In any case with a short *voir dire,* you should request the questionnaire so that background questions can be asked on the questionnaire, and the limited court time that the judge will allow can be used for follow-up questions suggested by answers on the questionnaire and the important case-specific questions. Where a lengthy *voir dire* has been granted, the questionnaire will consolidate vital information on the juror so that court time can be spent on in-depth questioning to elicit latent biases or clarify a juror's thoughts.

A jury and trial consultant or assistant can help you in determining the best use of each questionnaire. Under all circumstances, you should have someone in court to assist you in analyzing the data so that you can focus on the correct follow-up questions to ask.

§ 8.8 Renewing the Request

If the court has definitely ruled out a questionnaire, you may decide not to repeat your request. The authors feel, however, that even if you think you are going to be denied, you should always ask again because many judges have changed their mind. Once again, this is a judgment call that only the lawyer can make. To maximize your chances, make sure that you are armed with the applicable law when filing a motion for a questionnaire. (*See* Appendix 8JJ for a sample motion and memorandum of law in support of a motion to submit a jury questionnaire in a securities fraud case and Appendix 8KK for a sample motion with proposed questionnaire in a death penalty case.)

§ 8.9 In the Face of Opposition—Generally

Sometimes you will get resistance from opposing counsel or from the judge. It is your job to show that the questionnaire is an efficient and helpful mechanism for all concerned. If possible, give the court examples of other cases where questionnaires have been used and other judges who find questionnaires helpful.

§ 8.10 In the Face of Opposition—Judicial Economy

Many courts respond well to the words *judicial economy.* A questionnaire in its completed form can save the court a lot of time and effort asking background questions. Many courts recognize the advantage. You can encourage this viewpoint by presenting affidavits from former judges who found the questionnaires helpful, as well as transcripts of proceedings where the judge commended the process.

Covering background questions by questionnaire also diminishes the tedium of *voir dire*—which is of value to opposing counsel as well.

§ 8.11 In the Face of Opposition—A Sensitive Way to Handle Personal Matters

Most Americans are accustomed to filling out applications for employment. In essence, a questionnaire is just that. It is a job application, which should include the kinds of questions that jurors are accustomed to answering on forms, as well as some sensitive matters that you fear the jurors will hesitate discussing in court. The questionnaire is obviously no safeguard against the juror who intentionally wants to deceive the court. It is, however, a helpful way to elicit personal information from shy or easily embarrassed jurors.

§ 8.12 In the Face of Opposition—In lieu of Individual Sequestered *Voir Dire*

Examining jurors individually in a sequestered setting is the most informative method of jury selection, especially for sensitive matters. If the court refuses individual sequestered *voir dire,* however, you have grounds to ask for a questionnaire instead. Many judges will see granting the questionnaire as a chance for them to give your side something without appearing to take a side. If you appeal to the judge's sense of fairness, you may find yourself with a questionnaire.

The questionnaire offers a window into the juror's thoughts and feelings. Once you have a window, it is easier to pry it wide open in court. At that point, the court may consider the wisdom of your request for individual sequestered *voir dire* to protect the juror from undue embarrassment on sensitive issues like rape, foreclosure, or problems with the IRS.

§ 8.13 In the Face of Opposition—A Benefit to Both Sides

One of the main selling points of a questionnaire is that it is equally beneficial to all parties. It is not something that is slanted to help one side or the other. It should be presented in a fair, impartial and open-ended way so that both sides have equal access to the information they want for jury selection.

§ 8.14 Negotiating the Content

Negotiate with your adversary ahead of time concerning the questions that will be included in the questionnaire. Show them the questionnaire that you propose and ask them which questions they like and do not like and why. You should also ask them what they would like to see included in the questionnaire. You will find that if you are initially willing to include their questions, they are more apt to leave the questionnaire as it stands, with their additions. This will cut down on their antagonism toward questions you want answered.

Compromise on issues that are easy to give up, but by all means stand your ground if there is something you think should really be in the body of the questionnaire. For instance, if law enforcement is a big part of your case, you should insist on such questions as: "What kind of negative or positive contact have you had with a law enforcement officer?" This is not a topic of compromise for you. On the other hand, if standing your ground means losing the questionnaire totally, then it *is* worth the compromise.

§ 8.15 Alternative Questionnaires

You should always ask for the questionnaire that you want. If you want a lengthy questionnaire, you should ask for a lengthy questionnaire. Be ready, however, to settle for a shorter questionnaire. Some courts that will not grant a long questionnaire feel comfortable with shorter versions. This means that you should design two instruments, with the hope of getting the more lengthy one but the willingness to use the shorter one. It is important that both versions be designed ahead of time so as not to miss a beat in the hearing on the questionnaire.

§ 8.16 The Hearing

As mentioned, many judges understand the judicial economy in granting the use of a questionnaire. Before a hesitant judge, however, you will want to request a full-fledged hearing with your motion for a questionnaire. This would include having a jury and trial consultant testify or file an affidavit, stating experience with the use of questionnaires, the courts in which the questionnaires have been granted, the kinds of cases in which they have been used, and their value for this particular case. Again, you should also have affidavits from other lawyers, judges or professionals who see the value of questionnaires, and transcripts from courts where questionnaires were granted. After pressure from counsel, state and federal courts across the country have been persuaded that supplemental questionnaires can be of assistance in obtaining juror information in an expeditious manner.

You should, of course, be ready with the necessary law that will convince the court that this will be helpful and important to the jury selection process. (*See* Appendix 8JJ for a sample motion and memorandum of law in support of a request for a supplemental questionnaire.)

Questionnaires are becoming routine in some states and acceptable in others. It is your job to make sure that questionnaires become more the norm in your community than not.

§ 8.17 Obtaining Transcripts From Other Courts

When a court grants a questionnaire, you should ask the judge to comment on the questionnaire, so that it becomes part of the record. You should also ask other lawyers for instances where a judge responded favorably on record to the questionnaire. Make a point of compiling court-certified transcripts of these positive judicial rulings, which can definitely be helpful in the future when you want a questionnaire and are in a difficult or obstinate jurisdiction.

§ 8.18 Analyzing Questionnaire Data

Analyzing a questionnaire should be at least a two-step process. The first time the questionnaire should be read thoroughly and carefully to get a feel for how the juror answers questions. You should also take note of what kinds of questions the juror was open to answer and when there seemed to be hesitancy. This will alert you to the areas that you need to probe thoroughly once the juror is in the box. Highlight the information that seems to stand out the most.

On the second reading, analyze the responses for what are important follow-up questions and to make sure that in your first reading you did not miss something. You will be surprised when you review a questionnaire several times at the different perceptions you get of a juror and the different ideas for follow-up questions that arise.

The follow-up questions should be carefully noted and attached to each questionnaire. On the front of the questionnaire you should also write the important things that you picked up about the juror from his or her responses. A glance should remind you who the person is, and what more you need to know.

It is always necessary to have a second person review the questionnaires because other eyes and hearts may perceive something different than you did. Use the questionnaire to its fullest.

You will find that the questionnaire will give you a feel for the jurors before you even begin jury selection. You will also be better armed to fight for hardship and cause challenges before the *voir dire* begins. A mail-out questionnaire can also help you decide whether or not to settle pre-trial. There have been instances where the questionnaire indicated that it would be best to settle the case rather than go to trial. The questionnaires showed the majority of the panel to be negative toward one of the parties. This is ultimately a strategy decision, of course, but the questionnaire can be a helpful guide.

§ 8.19 Following Up the Questionnaire—Generally

It is important to analyze the questionnaire carefully to determine the most important questions to ask each juror during *voir dire*. Remember, it is a selling point to convince the judge of the relevance of the questionnaire, as well as its value as a time-saving device.

You may draft questions for each juror on a separate sheet of paper, so that you can proceed without wasting a lot of time flipping through the questionnaire. If you use a separate sheet, you need to flag each question so that you know to say: I noticed in your questionnaire that you said the following, and then ask the follow-up question. Some lawyers choose to highlight the areas of the questionnaire that they think need follow-up and attach the appropriate follow-up questions on a Post-it™.

The follow-up question should be limited to the areas that are case-specific and important to pursue. Do not waste the court's time with folksy questions like, "I see you've got four children. Which is your favorite kid?" The judge can easily curtail the *voir dire* and take away the benefit of the questionnaire follow-up process. Use your time judiciously so that meaningful answers in the questionnaire can be thoroughly explored.

§ 8.20 Following Up the Questionnaire—Background Questions

The obvious selling point of a questionnaire is that it will eliminate repetitive background questions. If, however, there is something unclear about a background question, you should not hesitate to repeat the question for clarification. For example, in a contract dispute case, if a juror says on *voir dire* that he or she has not been involved in any contract dispute, and you notice that the juror's questionnaire indicates he or she was a real estate agent ten years ago, then it would be appropriate to ask whether or not as a real estate agent he or she was ever involved in any contract disputes.

You should go into the background questions only if the person's prior work experience, family situation or other connections indicate any special knowledge about the case that could be either helpful or harmful. You then should feel free to ask questions about that information. If the court has given you unlimited time, ask all the questions you desire to ask.

In the old days the advice was to ask each and every juror questions about themselves and their background, in order to build rapport. In this day and age, with severe time limitations placed on attorneys by many judges, you do not have the luxury of establishing rapport with superfluous, superficial questions. Instead, the bond needs to be made on important probing and significant questions. Unless you are before a judge who will give you unlimited time to conduct the *voir dire,* you should generally replace specific background questions with open-ended juror-specific questions such as, "Please tell me about yourself." This type of question directs you to a juror's self-perception and self-evaluation and gives you guidance on further juror specific questions. You should then ask case-specific questions that further distinguish whether this is the right or wrong juror for your case.

§ 8.21 Following Up the Questionnaire—Clarifying Juror Answers Without Repeating the Question

You can use a questionnaire as a stepping-stone to encourage the juror to open up even more during *voir dire.* Thank the juror for an honest answer on a sensitive issue and ask for any further thoughts and feelings about the issue without asking the same question asked in the questionnaire. For example:

1) In a banking case, when asked on a questionnaire, "What is your opinion of banks?" a juror responded: "You have to watch what they are doing." An appropriate follow-up would be: "I note from your questionnaire that you have some doubts about banks. Please tell me some more about that."
2) In a medical malpractice suit, when asked on the questionnaire about experiences with doctors, a juror answered: "I don't know how we would get by without them." An appropriate follow-up, without repeating the question, would be: "I note from your questionnaire that you have very positive feelings about doctors. Please tell me about that."
3) In a death penalty case, when asked on the questionnaire, "What are your thoughts about the death penalty?" a juror answered: "Sometimes I am in favor of it and sometimes I am against." An appropriate follow-up would be: "You indicated in your questionnaire that you have mixed feelings about the death penalty. Please help me understand what those feelings are."

The point is that when an answer on the questionnaire indicates strong feelings about a concept or idea, it can be critical to have the juror explain the reason for that feeling or opinion. Similarly, when a juror equivocates or attempts to straddle an issue or question, you can ask the juror to explain the answer. For example, if a juror says on the questionnaire that the testimony of an expert may have more bearing or influence than the testimony of a lay witness, you may want to ask the juror for an example of when that would be true. Such a follow-up question acknowledges that you respect the answer given by the juror but more importantly, it gives you vital information about the thinking process of that particular juror.

Another way to urge further disclosure by a juror is to state a position on an issue and get the juror to react to it. For example, "Many people believe oil companies only care about their profit. You said on the questionnaire you believe oil companies are basically honest. What do you think about others saying oil companies only care about profit?" This kind of question will help you analyze if the juror really believes oil companies are honest or just gave a socially acceptable answer.

§ 8.22 Following Up the Questionnaire—When to Re-ask a Question in Court

You will find that jurors answer questions differently in court than on the questionnaire. It is your job to determine when to re-ask the question so as not to inflame either the jurors or the judge. If jurors have left a question blank, then you should re-ask the question in court. This is obvious. If jurors have answered a question in part, then you should ask what else they wanted to say in answer to the particular question. You should also re-ask any question that is of particular importance to the case. You will find that jurors answer questions differently in court than they did in written form. This is noticeably true on emotional questions or questions that elicit biases.

For example, in response to the question on the questionnaire, "What's the first thing that comes into your mind when you hear the words *criminal defense lawyer?*" a juror once answered: "They feed off the blood of people's miseries." When asked the same question in court, the same juror answered: "You're here to preserve the Constitution." This, of course, sent up red flags as to what the juror was really thinking and paved the way to explore the juror's concepts about the roles of different lawyers in the courtroom.

Another set of questions worth repeating relate to the witnesses and parties: "Do you know anyone on the witness list? Do you know any of the parties or their counsel? How do you know them?" Sometimes on the questionnaire jurors will answer no to knowing someone but when they hear the name said, it sends off a signal that reminds them of someone that they may know or have heard of.

You should re-ask as many of the questions as the court will tolerate. Having the two responses to the same question can be extremely valuable. It will tell you a lot about the different faces of the jurors and their different viewpoints on the case.

§ 8.23 Following Up the Questionnaire—Testing the Veracity of the Answers

Jurors should be probed in-depth on case-specific questions on the questionnaire because some people are oral responders and others respond better in writing. You should ask what they think about such issues as the death penalty, tort reform, drugs, the stock market, or any other issues you believe will elicit relevant prejudices or biases. Racism and attitudes toward big business are two other areas worth testing. If jurors say on the questionnaire that they have no feelings about African Americans, for instance, or no opinion of a local industry, you should ask for an example of a situation where they dealt with African Americans and how they felt about that, or for an experience they have had with big business and how that experience affected them. Ask them to give you a positive and negative experience for any issue that you think will shed light on their attitudes toward your case.

The best way to test the jurors' answers is to ask the question in a different way than it was phrased on the questionnaire. The jurors will be less irritated and the court will be less likely to object to the repetition. Most judges realize that certain questions warrant being re-asked if they are of relevance to the case.

§ 8.24 Identifying Potential Hardship, Challenges for Cause and Peremptory Strikes

One of the best uses of a questionnaire is in determining which jurors may be excused for hardship or challenged for cause or peremptorily struck. While the questionnaire may indicate that a juror should be excused for hardship, you may want to keep the juror based on other responses in the questionnaire or during the jury selection. It is important to know this information ahead of time so that you can determine how to save that juror.

You might, on the other hand, determine from the answers on the questionnaire or in court that the person should not be on the jury. A reading of the questionnaire may lead you to a reason he or she should be excused for hardship. You can, for example, remind the juror of a medical problem mentioned on the questionnaire and the potential difficulty of serving in a long trial. To establish a foundation for hardship, it is best to quote the juror's response: "You say you may not be able to keep total attention on a lengthy case." When the response is less definitive, you can suggest, "Is it not possible that your medical problem may make it difficult to sit on the case?"

Look for juror attitudes, based on the choice of words that they use in the questionnaire. If you see a pattern, it may be appropriate to alert the court and suggest that the juror be questioned in more depth in order to develop a challenge for cause. A goal of *voir dire* is to develop grounds for as many challenges for cause as possible. The more challenges for cause you develop, the more argument you have to increase your number of peremptory challenges and thus reinforce your client's right to a fair and impartial jury.

Upon conclusion of the *voir dire,* counsel is left with three areas of information about each juror: the responses in court which have been noted on the jury selection chart; the juror questionnaire; and the lawyer's instinctual feelings and reaction to the jury. Some lawyers also rely on their client's reaction to the prospective jurors. In a close decision of which juror to strike, counsel will often place tremendous emphasis on the written answers in the juror's questionnaire. The lawyer should thoroughly review the questionnaires of the grey or questionable jurors—and not just the answers to case-specific questions. The question, "Is there anything else we should know about you?" is often overlooked, yet contains valuable information when exercising precious peremptory challenges. On many occasions, questionnaires have saved a lawyer from putting a bad juror on the case.

§ 8.25 Organizing Questionnaire Data

If the judge has allowed your questionnaire to be submitted to the jurors in advance of trial, you are in the ideal position for thoroughly organizing and analyzing the data you received. Preferably, the questionnaire has been sent out at least thirty days in advance of trial with a return date of two weeks to ten days prior to the start of the case.

Your relationship with the clerk's office again becomes important because they are the link between the information you need and the individuals providing that information. Regular contact should be kept with the clerk's office to determine the number of questionnaires that have been returned and who has responsibility for duplicating the returns. The preferred method is that counsel pick up a copy as the questionnaires come in and begin assimilating the information. Alternatively, counsel can wait until all the questionnaires or the bulk of the questionnaires have been turned in. The problem with this method is that it tends to create overload, and a mountain of information to be compiled, generally with very little time left. If counsel can obtain completed questionnaires every day or every other day, the task will not be anywhere near as exhausting, overwhelming or hastily organized.

Clearly, if the only option is to receive the returns in one batch, you still want to request a questionnaire. Your goal is to get the information under the best conditions, but short of the ideal, there is no doubt that what you want is the information in whatever way you can get it.

Once the questionnaires begin to trickle in, counsel needs to subdivide the information into a variety of categories. As a general rule, the most important information will come from case-specific questions, but that is only a start. Do not overlook other critical information contained in the questionnaires. For example, if you are trying a criminal case, there should be various portions of the questionnaire pertaining to law enforcement experience or relatives in law enforcement. The fact that a juror has experience or contact with the profession should not in and of itself lead to a conclusion but should raise a red flag warranting a follow-up question, as discussed in Section 8.22 above.

Another category to isolate is what we call juror self-perceptions. Questions such as, "Do you consider yourself a leader or a follower, and why?" tend to elicit answers that shed a lot of light on the jurors' self-image. Other questions pertaining to supervisory experience can also give some indication of how the jurors perceive themselves. Ideally, the questionnaire should be organized into three or four sub-topics which will allow counsel to make a quick analysis, whether it is one page or ten pages long.

If the court has agreed to give counsel the night to review the questionnaires before starting jury selection the next morning, you are still well ahead of 99% of the lawyers who are trying lawsuits. You do not have the time to scrutinize and analyze the questionnaires as you would if they were sent out in advance of jury selection, but you do have an opportunity to get at least a feel for each and every juror. Again, as in the questionnaire submitted in advance of trial, the questions should be arranged by category so that with the help of support staff, you can go through and organize the data. You will have only a limited amount of time to draft follow-up questions, depending on the size of your panel, and you will not be able to organize the information as well as you would like. The key is to look for the areas you need to address, and make sure they are flagged for follow-up in court.

The advantage is diminished when the questionnaire is not filled out until right before *voir dire* and you are trying the lawsuit without an assistant. It is impossible for you to listen to the *voir dire* of opposing counsel, observe the jury and read questionnaires simultaneously. In all jury trials, but particularly those where a questionnaire is distributed prior to *voir dire,* the lone trial lawyer should have someone there to assist in jury selection. The assistant should highlight one or two categories and attempt to write at least one follow-up question for each juror. Generally, the questionnaire should be viewed first for the case-specific questions, then case-related issues; then counsel should scan it to determine if any other red flags have been raised by the responses.

§ 8.26 Computerizing Information

Computers have come to play an integral part not only in general law office maintenance but in jury selection as well. The computer-literate attorney can analyze a tremendous amount of information from the questionnaires in a relatively short period of time. The case-specific questions, case-relevant questions, and juror-self image questions can be programmed into the computer by category and each juror's response input under the appropriate topic.

Potentially, computers with optical character readers can eliminate the need for support staff to manually input the data. To date, however, optical scanners and word processing software have been unable to pick up handwritten responses. Technology is on the cutting edge of solving this problem and new software currently available on the market has had some success with handwriting. Obviously, the benefits of an optical character reader depend on the quality and quantity of handwriting, but rapid technological advances should erase these limitations.

In large cities it is often possible to link up your computer terminals with records maintained at the district court clerk's office. For example, through computer checks, you can discover civil lawsuits where a juror has been either a plaintiff or defendant. Ready retrieval of information can be particularly valuable in civil lawsuits when deciding which precious peremptory strike to make.

If you have run a survey, you will want to correlate the questionnaires with the survey data. This is easily done through a simple program that a computer programmer can design. A comparison of the questionnaire responses with the survey responses to case-specific and case-related questions can help predict a particular juror's reaction to your case theory and decide whether or not to choose that juror in a close call.

§ 8.27 Pre-jury Selection Challenges

A questionnaire opens the opportunity for a pre-jury selection discussion with the court and opposing counsel. During this discussion, you can suggest exercising some challenges for cause prior to jury selection. It is sometimes quite clear from the questionnaire who should be excused. Some jurors will express such a strong impression, feeling or thought about an issue that even if they say they could put it out of their mind, it is obvious to everyone that it would be unfair for them to sit on the case. With pre-jury selection challenges, you alert the court to cause challenges of this nature and, of course, make your record on this issue without the jury having to be present. It is another chance to educate the judge and build your record on jury selection matters.

If the court has already denied your motion for additional peremptory challenges and is being strict about challenges for cause prior to jury selection, the questionnaire can underscore your argument for several additional peremptory challenges. Right there in black and white the jurors have said things that would lead you to believe that they could not be fair in this case. If the court will not excuse them with challenges for cause, then you should be allowed additional peremptory challenges.

If the court refuses to grant you additional peremptory strikes, you should push for individual sequestered *voir dire* of those jurors who have given equivocal or questionable answers. This encourages the court to allow you more leeway and, if granted, allows you to question the jurors about their questionnaire responses. This can be very helpful because, as everyone knows, jurors are more apt to be honest in the individual sequestered session.

§ 8.28 Handwriting Analysis

A final clue from the questionnaire is the writing—whether the responses are handwritten or typed, the handwriting itself, and the choice of words. A typed questionnaire can indicate someone who likes an orderly appearance, is accustomed to typing documents, or has a spouse in clerical work. Shaky handwriting could mean the person has a physical ailment or drug-related problem. Very small writing can indicate a person who needs to keep things in a very confined, orderly fashion. Large writing, the slant of the writing and various embellishments may also be keys to personality traits. With time and resources available, it may be worth your while to hire an expert to review the questionnaires for added insights into the jury panel.

Examining the jurors' handwriting may give you a second sense of them as people. Examining how they phrase their answers will also tell you something about their flair for the English language, or lack thereof, and possibly, how creatively they think. Handwriting analysis is obviously a luxury, but there are those cases where you cannot afford to leave any stone unturned.

Chapter 9

JURY INVESTIGATION

Table of Sections

§ 9.1 Overview

You must realize that you see people in a cocoon when they enter a courtroom. Some people dress up in order to look professional, when in reality they live a more humble lifestyle. Others, who live extravagantly, will wear blue jeans and an old beat-up shirt. Without a drive-by to see where a juror lives, or other background investigation, you may get a totally opposite impression of the person in the jury box.

Consider conducting jury investigation in any case where you have the staff and resources to do so. There are many creative approaches that will help complete your image of a juror. Viewing the juror's home and surrounding neighborhood can put the juror in context. Checking voter registration and court records of civil proceedings, where available, can be relevant to case-specific issues. Observing jurors during jury selection and conducting investigation in the community can identify questions that warrant follow-up. The following are some approaches that have been used successfully with the help of competent staff.

§ 9.2 Drive-bys—Generally

How does a juror's house compare with other houses in the neighborhood? A drive-by can be extremely helpful in providing information about the juror's lifestyle and character. It means something if the rest of the yards in the neighborhood are overgrown and unkept, and the juror's house is newly painted with a trimmed lawn. That juror believes in himself and has a lot of pride, wishes to present an orderly image or cannot stand anything out of place. On the other hand, if the rest of the neighborhood is well kept and the juror's home is run down, that tells you something as well. The juror could be someone who likes being different, has been out of town a lot, does not live there on a regular basis, or has had financial problems. Whatever you find, you should factor this information into what you have learned about the juror, to uncover obvious patterns and deviations from the obvious.

Pay particular attention to the kinds of vehicles parked in and around the neighborhood and in front of the juror's home, as well as bumper stickers displayed on vehicles. Such things as the kind of toys or pets in the yard further reflect the juror's lifestyle. Check for political placards during election time and for other stickers and signs that provide insight into the juror's frame of mind or the environment in which he or she lives. Neighborhood Watch signs and signs for individual security systems will tell you something about the juror's desire for safety, which can be relevant, depending on the kind of case you are trying.

There are things to note in specific cases. For instance, in cases where motorcycle gangs are involved, it would be helpful for the drive-by staff to note where motorcycles are located in relation to a juror's home. In cases where racial issues are involved, it would be helpful to figure out which jurors live in mixed neighborhoods and which do not. In cases involving foreclosures, it would be helpful to see which neighborhoods have an abundance of foreclosure signs in front of the houses. In cases involving bank failures, it would be important to find out which jurors live near troubled banks.

Another important aspect of drive-bys is that it tells you which jurors are neighbors or live near members of either trial team or the witnesses. The fact that one juror lives close to another is information which would probably not come out in *voir dire* and could be important in the jury's group dynamics. It means that one juror has something in common with another, that they may know each other or get to know each other during the trial and could directly or indirectly influence each other in deliberations.

Drive-bys can be extremely helpful in cases where the lawyers are from another part of the state or from another state altogether. The drive-by observations will give the lawyer insight into what it means to live in certain neighborhoods and on certain streets. The lawyer will also have more of an understanding of the design of the community and the particular choices or circumstances of each juror in the context of that community.

§ 9.3 Drive-bys—Training Drive-by Staff

Carefully train drive-by staff in order to insure that everybody knows the proper way to proceed. At least two meetings should be held to teach the drive-by staff their role. You will find that drive-by teams take their responsibilities to heart and will do their jobs conscientiously if adequately instructed.

The staff should understand that it is never their duty to decide what is important information. They should take down everything that they see and leave nothing out. What may be irrelevant to a drive-by staff person could be quite relevant to the trial attorney. They should be given a drive-by checklist that gives them examples of what they should note about each house, neighborhood and surrounding area. (*See* Appendix 9A for a typical Drive-by Checklist.)

The drive-by staff should also be given examples from other cases that show the value of the information they will be collecting. They should be aware that their input in the trial of this case will be extremely important. As with any tedious task, knowing its relevance will keep the staff involved and on their toes.

It is of vital importance that the drive-by staff have *absolutely no contact in any way* with any juror, juror's family members or neighbors.

They should be instructed merely to drive by the house taking into account everything they see, and once they get out of the neighborhood, stop the car and dictate or write down their observations. Having a second person in the automobile is helpful so that one can drive and the other can either write or dictate what both have observed.

If the drive-by staff needs directions or gets lost, they should go to a gas station. Never stop on a juror's street or in the juror's specific neighborhood to ask for directions. This is only inviting unnecessary detection. If they need to make a second pass by the house, they should do so, but preferably at a later time. It is best not to drive by a juror's house more than once in any given day, to avoid the appearance of impropriety.

The trial lawyer should personally speak to the drive-by staff, informing them of their importance in the jury selection process and briefing them on the "dos and don'ts" of their job. Their role is not in any way to invade the juror's privacy but to see a neighborhood as anyone else driving by that particular house may see it. The lawyer should also reinforce that they should have absolutely no contact whatsoever with any juror, juror's family member or neighbor. It is the trial lawyer's responsibility to make sure the instructions are heard loud and clear.

§ 9.4 Drive-bys—Who Should Do It

When choosing the drive-by staff, look for people who are responsible, dependable and intelligent. You need hard workers with good perceptions and good observation skills and not thrill-seekers or risk-takers or people who will overstep their bounds. Law students, psychology students, or other people who have an interest in the case and would like to help would be the best drive-by volunteers.

No one who will be appearing in court should conduct a drive-by. If a juror remembers a face and puts two and two together and realizes that this was the person who cruised the neighborhood, it could create undue suspicion or bias that would adversely affect your client. While there is nothing illegal or immoral about drive-bys, people by nature do not like the idea of being inspected.

Organizers should be sensitive to neighborhood ethnic and racial makeup when assigning drive-by teams. In order to avoid problems, it would probably be best when going into a predominately white upper-class neighborhood, that a white driver do the drive-by. Likewise, a drive-by staff person going into a predominately African American or Hispanic neighborhood should be African American or Hispanic. These kinds of accommodations can make a big difference in terms of getting the work done without disturbing anyone's peace of mind or sense of order. The point is to obtain the information in the least conspicuous and invasive manner.

After the staff training, if there is anyone in the group whose personality does not seem suited to conducting drive-bys, he or she should be given another task. Do not run risks of having people you do not trust do this sensitive work in the community, given its potential impact on the jury selection process.

§ 9.5 Drive-bys—When to Do It

It is best to conduct drive-bys during the daytime because the staff can observe a variety of things about the house and neighborhood that would be hard to see in the evening. During an evening drive-by, however, there is the advantage of catching vehicles that may be gone during work hours. A weekend drive-by accomplishes the same purpose, but there is the risk that a juror will be in the front yard or driveway when the drive-by is being done. Drive-by staff should be instructed that if they see a person outside the house, they should not slow down or stare but keep driving until they are out of the neighborhood.

§ 9.6 Drive-bys—Drive-by Equipment

Drive-by staff should have a pad and pen to take notes on anything that they see. They should be well supplied so they do not run out while en route. They may also want to bring a tape recorder or dictating machine and have the tapes transcribed at a later date. If they have numerous drive-bys to do, they can spend their time dictating while driving to the next neighborhood. It can also be helpful to do drive-bys in pairs; one can dictate while the other drives, and they have the benefit of collaborating on their observations of the neighborhood, the house and the cars.

Cameras may be called for when the trial lawyer wants photographs of the jurors' homes. Photographs should be taken in the rare case, and only by people who are properly trained so no question is raised about invading the juror's privacy. The photographs can be helpful to the lawyer in amplifying drive-by comments, since the lawyer will not see the neighborhood firsthand, but care should be taken that the photographs are literally snapshots, as you drive by.

§ 9.7 Drive-bys—Organizing the Drive-bys

The drive-by staff should be divided into teams, under a team leader, to cover the jurors' neighborhoods in the most expeditious manner. A large wall map should be posted in the drive-by staff room with each route plotted out. Separate maps should be given to each staff person, indicating the location of the homes of specific jurors on his or her route. In this way people will not be driving all over a county or a district wasting time, gasoline or energy.

Drive-by time can also be saved if there is a likelihood that the judge will excuse jurors living beyond a certain number of miles from the courthouse. This is the practice in some jurisdictions, although some judges are more lenient than others in allowing this hardship excuse. The lawyer should find out from local attorneys or from the judge's clerk or the court clerk how the judge tends to handle this issue, and apportion the investigative time accordingly.

§ 9.8 Drive-bys—The Juror Map

Mapping the jurors facilitates a drive-by plan but also reveals other key information that would affect jury selection. If the jury panel is all from one county, get a large county map. On a federal panel, you will need to get the several county maps that comprise the district and find a large enough wall to display them according to their respective locations. Another helpful way of mapping the jurisdiction is to get Key maps, available from any good map store. You can lay out the maps by key number or zip code, corresponding with the areas from which jurors are drawn. They can then be plotted by juror number on the map, either with small different-colored circular tabs or with stick pins.

The map immediately reveals which jurors are neighbors or live on the same route to the courthouse. Over the course of a long trial, jurors could potentially car pool to get to and from court. Friendships could develop, which may prove problematic if you have not thought beforehand about who might influence whom during deliberations.

Once the jurors are plotted, important locations related to the case should also be plotted, to see who may have some feeling about the case because of their proximity to a relevant incident. If a juror lives a block from where a major accident occurred, this could be important information in determining whether or not you would like to strike or keep this juror in your personal injury case. All information is valuable. Use your creativity to decide how to make maximum use of the juror map.

Key witnesses, the legal teams, and other participants in the trial should also be located on the map. Relative locations can be important to the case. A juror, for instance, could see a witness or lawyer leaving home for court, and feel a kinship that the juror may not have otherwise felt. These connections, however subtle, may influence the juror. You should have this information to follow up in *voir dire* and to factor into challenges for cause and peremptory challenges.

§ 9.9 Drive-bys—What Not to Do

The "don'ts" of drive-bys are important to emphasize. The staff should never have any contact with any juror, neighbor or member of a juror's family. They should know that it is their job to record everything they see, and never edit the information. It is the trial lawyer's and consultant's job to determine what is the important information. The drive-by staff should also be informed that they should not be driving an easily noticeable vehicle. A flashy, high-priced car, a jacked-up pickup, a bomber with a loose muffler or a car papered in bumper stickers may all draw unnecessary attention to the drive-by in progress. Standard run-of-the-mill cars are best. If the budget allows, it may be worthwhile to rent vehicles for the drive-by staff.

Again, the staff should be instructed never to stop and ask for directions in a juror's neighborhood. They should properly map out their route beforehand so this will be unnecessary. If they do get lost, they should drive out of the vicinity of the jurors' neighborhood and stop at some inconspicuous place to get their bearings.

§ 9.10 Drive-bys—In Case of a Problem

Drive-by staff should be instructed that if any problems arise during a drive-by, they should immediately contact their team leader and report what has occurred. It is the team leader's job to notify the trial lawyer to discuss what should be done.

Several scenarios qualify as a "problem":

1) If the juror somehow initiates contact.

2) If a juror's family member initiates contact.

3) If a neighbor asks questions.

In each situation the drive-by staff should leave courteously without any discussion with the person and call the team leader.

It can also be a "problem" if the drive-by staff is stopped by a law enforcement officer or some watch group representative who wants to know their purpose in the neighborhood. Drive-by staff has no obligation to explain that they are conducting a pre-trial investigation. Should they be pressed for information, they should ask to make a phone call and immediately call the trial lawyer.

§ 9.11 Record Checks—Generally

There are numerous public records that can be searched to determine valuable information on the jury panel. This is a labor-intensive project but can give insight into jurors that you would not otherwise have. Most of the information will be available at the courthouses within the jurisdiction, including: voter registration, civil and criminal proceedings; and property holdings. Jury investigation teams should be divided up to cover the various information sources.

§ 9.12 Record Checks—Voter Registration

Choice of political party obviously tells you something about a person. In some jurisdictions the voter registration card will indicate a change in political party, and the year of the change. If the juror changed political affiliation for a particular election, this will indicate the influence of certain candidates or the issues or interests they represent.

In one Los Angeles case, a juror was found to have been a member of the conservative American Independent Party (George Wallace's party), and then to have switched to the progressive Americans for a Democratic Society (Tom Hayden's group). This was considered valuable information about the juror's political mood swings, and fed into other perceptions of the juror in open court.

In some jurisdictions, the voter registration card also shows which primaries or elections the jurors voted in. Research of those primaries will give you additional information about issues that were important enough for the juror to take time to vote.

The investigators reviewing voter registration cards should be instructed to take down all information on the card such as, occupation, address, date and place of birth, Social Security number, and date of original registration. All this data may be helpful in learning about the juror.

§ 9.13 Record Checks—Civil Proceedings

It is quite common that people get involved in some kind of litigation in their lives. The most common litigation, of course, is divorce. Other suits that you will find in a search of civil court records include financial losses, property disputes and bankruptcies. The case at issue and whether the juror was a plaintiff or defendant in the lawsuit will give you a feel about any predisposition the juror may have toward your client.

In some jurisdictions, as discussed in Chapter 8 on questionnaires, the court questionnaire asks jurors if they have been a party to a lawsuit, the nature of the lawsuit and whether they were a plaintiff or defendant. When that information is not required on the court form, you may turn to the court files. The court file will indicate whether the litigation is still pending or how the matter was resolved. Again, the disposition of the juror's case and the juror's potential reaction, as plaintiff or defendant, may have bearing on his or her impartiality in your case.

If trying a federal case, a records check of this kind can take an inordinate amount of time because the jury panel is drawn from a number of counties that comprise the federal jurisdiction. Plot where the bulk of the jurors live, and if there are limited resources, confine the records check to that area.

The research, though labor-intensive, will usually prove fruitful. In one case, a juror who worked for the state government, and who in every other way appeared to be very conservative and peace-loving, was found through the court records to have been involved in a fistfight at his place of business. The altercation led to a civil suit in which he was the named defendant because he had attacked another employee. The fact that this person would resort to violence in certain situations turned out to be critical since the case he was to sit on involved an allegation of violence.

§ 9.14 Record Checks—Property Taxes

The county assessor's office and the state property tax division are sources of public information about a juror's property holdings and mineral rights. Normally the records can tell you the pieces of property listed under a certain name, the current worth of that property and the taxes paid annually. This information may be relevant in determining a juror's wealth, and more particularly, whether he or she would have any financial interests that would bear on your case.

§ 9.15 Investigation in the Community—Generally

Where time allows, it inevitably proves helpful to circulate the jury list to see if anyone you know knows any of the prospective jurors. "Knowing" the jurors can mean any background information at all, but should especially include any knowledge the juror may have of your case, any experience that may affect the juror's impartiality, whether the juror is a leader or a follower, and the context in which your informant knows the juror. You can do a systematic background investigation in the community by categorizing the jurors according to neighborhood, workplace, church, club, and where applicable, college or university. In smaller communities, there will often be several jurors on a panel who work, for instance, at the local hospital or in the public school system or for a large manufacturer. The jury investigation team should make a point of finding a contact person in these key places who will be willing to provide information and whose perceptions can be trusted and kept confidential.

The larger the group in which you circulate the jury list, the more information you are likely to collect. There are logical sources of information, people who know a broad range of people in the community or know numbers of people in their social or professional circle. These are the sources to cultivate in order to find out more about your jurors than what is public record.

§ 9.16 Investigation in the Community—Lawyers

Individual lawyers can be a fountain of knowledge of local legal disputes and jury panelists, whom they may know personally or professionally. They may have encountered a particular juror during *voir dire* in their own case, or represented a juror in the course of their law practice. Juror questionnaires will generally indicate if the juror has been a party to a lawsuit and who provided representation. The lawyer, in turn, can tell you the strengths and weaknesses of that juror as a client, and how experience with the legal system may affect his or her impartiality in your case. Often the most prolific sources of juror information are public defenders and district attorneys, who are more likely to take their cases to trial and therefore have more contact with the jury panels.

Remember to gauge a lawyer's knowledge of the jury, based on his or her personality and perspective on your case. Realize that just because this lawyer thinks someone can be a fair juror does not mean the juror will relate to you and your client. Probe deeply as to why that lawyer thinks someone would be a good or bad juror and what life experiences have shaped that opinion. Many years of jury work have taught us that it is not necessarily who someone knows that makes the difference but how he or she perceives a situation. Be careful of accepting or rejecting a juror based on another lawyer's say-so.

§ 9.17 Investigation in the Community—Tax Assessors

In small communities tax assessors know everybody, at least every property owner. They also know a lot about their personal background and the money issues in their life. Should you make the acquaintance of the tax assessor through local contacts, he or she may be willing to sit informally over a cup of coffee and go through the jury list with you.

§ 9.18 Investigation in the Community—Postal Employees

The post office is the main contact with residents in a small town. In many instances the postal clerk will be open to reviewing the jury list on a volunteer basis or for payment after work. Rural mail carriers are a tremendous resource; they know everybody on their route on some level. This can be extremely helpful when the jury panel includes rural segments of the judicial district.

§ 9.19 Investigation in the Community—Politicians

Politicians obviously get to know many people in order to win the support of their electorate. They can offer substantial help in jury selection because they cover a broad base of the community. Once again, you should judge their observations based on their political slant, knowledge of the person, and duration of that relationship. You should ask politicians what they know about how the person has voted in the past and in what kinds of campaigns they have taken an active part. This will give you insight into their political leanings and the depth of their commitment to particular issues.

§ 9.20 Investigation in the Community—Shopkeepers

Shopping is a context for observing social behavior. Shopkeepers often note how individuals interact with other members of the community, as well as how they make decisions and allocate their resources.

§ 9.21 Investigation in the Community—Active Community People

You would be surprised at the help you can receive from leaders of community clubs and organizations. Not only may they know individuals on the jury list but they may be willing to organize their members to assist with further juror investigation, mock trials, pre-trial publicity surveys and in-court juror observation. Since some clubs thrive on local gossip, it will probably be easy to organize a coffee hour, which can yield much more interesting and colorful information than you might receive from other sources.

Membership in clubs—whether social societies, fraternal organizations or ethnic community centers—not only says something about a juror but about the person commenting on any member of the jury panel. Remember to take the informant's perspective into account. Also, remember to caution the community person not to discuss the inquiry or anything else related to the case.

§ 9.22 Investigation in the Community—Restaurant/Cafe Managers

Eating has always been a social part of people's lives. In small communities, talking with the managers and owners of restaurants and cafes can give you an insight into people who frequent their establishments. You should, of course, talk to the waiters and waitresses as well, because they have the most direct contact with patrons. Through them, you can find out whether the jurors come in often, are easy to get along with, leave good tips, are outgoing or introverted, fraternize with any particular group of people or have publicly expressed any controversial views that may have bearing on your case. You might even want to find out what kind of food they are most interested in eating. All information is valuable. As with all other groups, your contact should be a closed-mouthed, trusted person.

§ 9.23 Investigation in the Community—Bartenders and Waitresses

It is a fact that people talk about themselves more freely in bars than almost any other place. Cocktail waitresses and bartenders wind up doing more counseling than any psychotherapist would ever hope to. They are a key opportunity to find out about the drinkers on the jury panel. In smaller communities you should also talk to bar customers to find out what they know about the jurors. Ask whether or not they are big spenders or penny-pinchers, what they drink, who they drink with, what they talk about after they have a couple of drinks under their belt. For the cost of a drink or two, you may uncover information you would never have known. As always, consider your source in assessing the value of the information.

§ 9.24 Investigation in the Community—Clergy

Deacons, rabbis, preachers, priests, nuns, and other people who work in or around churches can help you with your jury list. Always approach such people with discretion, emphasizing your search for justice. Be clear that you are not interested in prying into anyone's personal life, and do not want to violate the preacher-parishioner privilege. Your concern is assuring that your client gets a fair trial.

Members of the clergy can also be very helpful in court during jury selection. Have them sit in the spectator section of the courtroom and approach you at breaks and at lunch so that it is clear you are associated. Their intuition and understanding of human nature will no doubt be valuable in your final choice of jurors, and their presence will put you in a favorable light with the jury panel.

§ 9.25 Investigation in the Community—Police Officers

In civil cases, police officers can provide insight into the jury panel from the perspective of where the jurors live. In jurisdictions where community riders are allowed, try to arrange with the police department to accompany a police officer on the Friday or Saturday graveyard shift. You will see the town after hours and get a chance to chat with the police officer about what it means to live in different neighborhoods and learn about the different establishments located in those neighborhoods. This could be your chance at a free education on your jury's community life. Obviously in criminal cases, this is a questionable method of obtaining information due to the officer's inherent conflict of interest. If you are not required to state verbally or in writing your purpose in taking the community ride, this potential conflict may not arise.

§ 9.26 Investigation in the Community—Taxi Drivers

Taxi drivers are another source of information about neighborhoods. For a fee most taxi drivers will talk as long as you like about their business in the different neighborhoods where jurors live. They have a very interesting perspective because they are on the street day and night, and fares they pick up tend to talk in the back seat of the taxi as if the driver were not there or share with the driver personal information and ideas.

If you are an out-of-state attorney, you should always ask the taxi driver questions about your case when you are coming to and from the airport. They have a lot of knowledge about community attitudes and are a good sounding board for your preconceptions. Remember, all information is helpful information.

§ 9.27 Investigation in the Community—Senior Citizens

Since more and more senior citizens are called to jury duty, you should include senior citizens in your review of the jury list and in the jury selection process. Go to retirement clubs and homes and see if anyone there knows any of the prospective jurors and what they know about them. Have one or two senior citizens assist you in court during jury selection. They are generally more than happy to volunteer or to work for a small fee. The important thing is that they be included, not only out of respect for their established place in the community but because their experience and input can be extremely valuable.

§ 9.28 Investigation in the Community—Former Clients

Former trusted clients may know some prospective jurors and should be asked to review the jury list. They will be more than willing to help a lawyer who has helped them. They may also know things about the jury panel that you would never have suspected.

§ 9.29 Investigation in the Community—Office Staff

Your office staff should always review the jury list and on occasion should be invited to assist you in jury selection. This accomplishes a number of things: It provides them with a better understanding of your work, and involvement in the process. It gives them a chance to observe the jury members and to give you feedback on what they know about any particular juror or juror's family.

§ 9.30 Investigation in the Community—Family, Friends and Neighbors

The people closest to you are at least curious about your professional life. Jury selection is an opportunity to actually assist you, and you will find that many family members, friends and neighbors will gladly offer to help for the experience of working with you. They will know different segments of the community that you do not know, and will know things about people that you would never imagine.

§ 9.31 In-Court Observation—Generally

In-court observations are critical to your knowledge of the jury panel. This is your opportunity to see the jurors face to face and analyze their public demeanor. Use these observations as a backdrop for information from out-of-court investigations. If your observations about the jurors in court totally contradict what you have learned through public records or a neighborhood check, this should alert you to look further into this person's true self.

§ 9.32 In-Court Observation—What to Observe

The courtroom observer should note the appearance and demeanor of each juror, as well as the interaction between jurors. Also of import are reactions to *voir dire* questions, the client, the lawyers and the judge, and any change in demeanor as the jury selection progresses. A juror, for example, may be friendly at first and then turn hostile after a particular line of questioning or for no apparent reason.

Observers should meet with the attorney at least once before trial to be briefed on what to look for, what to do and not to do, and how to coordinate the information. Subsequent meetings are also advisable with the rest of the jury investigation team to compare notes and to follow up or discover new information about members of the panel who remain a mystery.

Observations made of each juror during court sessions should be compiled in individual reports, so that the information is not lost on various scribbled notes. Reports should be combined in a three-ring binder under each juror's name or number, with the drive-by and background information collected by the investigative team.

§ 9.33 In-Court Observation—Where and How to Observe

In-court observers should divide up the territory. Assign specific observation points, such as who will cover which part of the courtroom and who will cover which part of the hallway. This will make maximum use of the in-court observers and avoid their being conspicuously clustered in one area. Outside the courtroom observers should sit or stand reading a book or doing a crossword puzzle. *Under no circumstances should the observer bring a newspaper into the courthouse.* The idea is to set a silent stage from which to be observant. From this vantage point, the observer should view and listen to all activity. All information about the jurors will be helpful, but there are particular things to look for:

1) Who is in a position of leadership?

2) Who do the other jurors seem to consider funny?

3) Who is polite to other members of the panel?

4) Who are the smokers?

5) Who seems offended by smoking?

6) Which jurors are grouped together?

7) Who are the loners?

8) What are panel members reading?

9) Is anyone reading a newspaper?
10) Who seems to be continually making phone calls?
11) Who is complaining?
12) Who seems to be enjoying jury duty?
13) Which jurors seem nervous or agitated for some reason?
14) What jewelry are jurors wearing?
15) What is noteworthy about any of the jurors' clothing?
16) Are any panel members socializing with the bailiff or other court staff? If so, do they appear to be acquainted with each other or are they just conversing?
17) Which jurors keep looking at their watch?
18) Who has a briefcase or notepad?
19) Who looks tired or sleepy?
20) Who has a loud, demanding voice? Who has a soft, congenial voice? (Describe the jurors' specific tone of voice.)
21) How do jurors sit, stand, walk? (Note any distinguishing characteristics.)

This is a partial list of court-observation techniques. Once again, information is always valuable. Observers should be instructed not to edit what they see or hear and give you or your consultant all input for analysis.

It is crucial that in-court observers never have any direct or indirect contact with the jurors. If approached by a juror, they should say that they cannot talk with the juror because the juror is on jury duty. As in a drive-by contact, they should move away from the juror immediately but in a courteous way. In a situation where the juror continues talking after the observer has made it clear he or she cannot talk to the juror, the observer should notify the team leader so the trial attorney can decide whether this should be brought to the attention of the court. Likewise, in the unusual occurrence that a juror knows an observer, or if there is any other unexpected encounter, the team leader should be immediately informed. It is the team leader's responsibility to bring this information to the lawyer's attention.

§ 9.34 In-Court Observation—Flexibility of Hours

It is helpful to organize morning and afternoon shifts of in-court observers. This allows you to involve more people where schedules might otherwise conflict. The goal is to have as many people observing for as much time as possible.

You may also find that with a very talkative jury panel, it is best to change observers every day or two to lower the risk of any kind of contact with a panel member and to make sure the observers remain observant.

§ 9.35 In-Court Observation—Who Are Good Observers?

The people most helpful in jury selection are people who understand other human beings. Many times they have no formal training but they are sensitive to others' feelings, perceptions and issues. Some of the best are family members, friends and neighbors who are good listeners with good instincts, who always seem to know what is going on, and with whom others want to talk about their personal problems. Not only are they a great asset in selecting the jury, but informing the panel that your assistant is a relative, friend or neighbor gives a warm "family" feeling to the courtroom. Some lawyers feel it may look unprofessional to have a family member or friend helping. Post-trial interviews of jurors have indicated otherwise. Jurors have said they appreciated a family member supporting the lawyer's belief in his client.

People on religious, spiritual or metaphysical paths can also be very helpful observers. They are adept at keying into a juror's personality, and their keen intuition can assist you in listening to what the jurors are really saying during *voir dire.* Some of their input may seem far out, but if a juror is a total enigma, incorporating other people's perceptions can facilitate decision making.

Again, senior citizens, former clients and office staff should not be forgotten. They may recognize faces of jurors whose names did not ring a bell on the jury list, and what they observe "people-watching" may be decisive in determining whether a juror can be fair and impartial in your case.

§ 9.36 Team Leaders

When a number of assistants are doing jury investigation, team leaders should be selected to oversee each of the investigative projects. This division of labor makes someone ultimately responsible for the tasks at hand and helps assure that everything gets done. As the data begins to flow, this kind of organization is essential.

§ 9.37 Paid Versus Volunteer Investigators

A low budget should not deter you from launching a jury investigation. Some of the most helpful people have been volunteers, depending on the people and their dedication. Paying people, however, keeps their attention. Unless they have a personal commitment to you or your client, and especially if you are going to need them for more than one or two days, you are more apt to get follow-through with paid participants. Do what you can to get the best information you can; the information will be invaluable in selecting a jury.

§ 9.38 Discoverability

Jury investigation should be considered work product. However, before embarking on an intensive investigation, it is advisable to research the current law on discoverability in your jurisdiction. You do not want to wind up doing the legwork for opposing counsel, if you can avoid doing so. Check and see if the law distinguishes between information in the public domain or of public record and information accessible to only one side, such as jurors' criminal records that only the prosecution can obtain.

The U.S. government through its vast and wide-reaching investigative and information-gathering resources may compile data on prospective jurors regarding verdicts actually returned during prior jury service in criminal cases as well as any arrests and/or convictions appearing on their "rap sheets." This information is retrieved through computers and other government sources and made available to federal prosecutors. Similar information may be available at the state level, but in neither case can you expect the prosecution to share that information voluntarily. It has been successfully argued that the nonreciprocal nature of the government's resources in compiling data on prospective jurors violates the mandate of the Equal Protection clause that a state not permit a defendant to be deprived of "... the basic tools of an adequate defense" by reason of his poverty.[1] This practice creates an unfair imbalance favoring the prosecution, and the Due Process clause of the Fifth Amendment made applicable to the states by the Fourteenth Amendment "... does speak to the balance of forces between the accused and his accuser." [2]

Practices such as the gathering of information regarding prospective jurors through means available only to the government provides "nonreciprocal benefits to the state" with regard to the investigation and preparation of its case. As the Supreme Court noted in *Wardius,* "... when the lack of reciprocity interferes with the defendant's ability to secure a fair trial," such a practice constitutes a violation of the defendant's constitutionally protected right to due process. In *Wardius,* the court found:

> *[t]he State's inherent information gathering advantages suggest that if there is to be imbalance in discovery rights, it should work in the defendant's favor.*[3]

While there is not universal recognition of a defendant's right to discover juror information compiled by the prosecution for use in jury selection, neither has the defendant been arbitrarily denied access. In

§ 9.38

1. *Britt v. North Carolina,* 404 U.S. 226, 227, 92 S.Ct. 431, 433, 30 L.Ed.2d 400 (1971).

2. *Wardius v. Oregon,* 412 U.S. 470, 474, 93 S.Ct. 2208, 2211, 37 L.Ed.2d 82 (1973).

3. 412 U.S. at 476 n. 9, 93 S.Ct. at 2213 n. 9.

Losavio v. Mayber,[4] the court held that the defendant was entitled to discover the police records of prospective jurors in the possession of the prosecution.

You should take an aggressive stance to get all juror information possible. If it means sharing information with the prosecution, it will then be a judgment call to what extent you wish to expose the fruits of your investigation. In the end, we would argue that sharing the information on jurors is better than having no information, or too little information to pick the best jury possible.

See Appendix 9B for a sample Motion to Compel Disclosure of U.S. Attorney's Jury Selection Data and memorandum of law in support, and Appendix 9C for a sample Motion for Defense Access to Prosecution Juror Records filed in state court. *See also* Section 5.52, *supra,* for discussion of the work-product doctrine and its application to mock trial materials.

§ 9.39 Right to Juror Tax Information in Federal Tax Cases

If you are trying a case in Federal Court that involves a tax court, counsel should be aware of 26 U.S.C.A. § 6103(h)(5). This statute states, in pertinent part:

> "In connection with *any judicial proceeding* described in paragraph (4) *to which the United States is a party, the Secretary [of the Treasury] shall respond to a written inquiry from an attorney of the Department of Justice* (including a United States Attorney) involved in such proceeding *or any person (or his legal representative who is a party to such prospective juror in such a proceeding has or has not been the subject of any audit or other tax investigation by the Internal Revenue Service.* The Secretary shall limit such response to an affirmative or negative reply to such inquiry."

Although this provision was enacted as part of the Tax Reform Act of 1976, no appellate court had reviewed this statute until 1989 when the Ninth Circuit had the opportunity in *United States v. Hashimoto.*[1] The Court held that a party to such a proceeding has an absolute right to find out whether any of the prospective jurors have been the subject of any audit or other tax investigation. The key to making a § 6103(h)(9) claim is to make the request immediately. A Motion for Early Release of the Jury List should be filed along with a copy of the statute and the *Hashimoto* case. If the motion is granted, counsel should prepare a letter to the Secretary of the Treasury in Washington, D.C. requesting the tax investigation information on each juror. Once

4. 178 Colo. 184, 496 P.2d 1032, 1034 (1972).

§ 9.39

1. 878 F.2d 1126 (9th Cir.1989).

the list of jurors is obtained, counsel should mail to the Secretary the order from the Court a copy of the statute and the juror list.

Two of the stumbling blocks that counsel may encounter are: (1) the Secretary of the Treasury does not respond in a timely manner; and (2) simply providing names without other identifying information is insufficient data for the Secretary of the Treasury. Each of these can be remedied if counsel anticipates these problems and addresses them in the motion. The Motion for Early Release of the Jury List should request the name, address, date of birth or other identifying information to assist the Secretary of the Treasury. Secondly, the order should specify a period of time in which the Secretary of the Treasury has to comply with the court order.

Chapter 10
JUROR ORIENTATION

Table of Sections

---

§ 10.1 Overview

Prospective jurors are assembled by panel prior to jury selection for an assigned case, or several assigned cases, and are briefed on trial procedure and their role as jurors. It is crucial to discover what goes on during the orientation of the jury panel prior to trial. You will want to know who presides over the jury assembly room and what information is conveyed to the panel. In some jurisdictions the county attorney gives the orientation; in others, it is the judge, the judge's clerk, or the jury commissioner. You may be surprised at what jurors are told at that time and dismayed at the exposure you would prefer they not have.

§ 10.2 The Jury Assembly Room—Generally

The climate of the jury assembly room and the format of the orientation vary from jurisdiction to jurisdiction, with varying effect on the jurors. Many jurisdictions have designed their own film or video presentation. One jurisdiction runs clips from the film "Twelve Angry Men" and then begins to take excuses for hardship from the jurors. Some have a clerk or judge give an oral overview. Others hand out jury orientation booklets and ask the jurors to orient themselves. There are obvious problems with all of these procedures. Whatever format, you or a representative should be present to observe the process.

§ 10.3 The Jury Assembly Room—What Jurors Need to Know

Jurors' most common complaint is that no one has taken the time to inform them of the trial process. Jury orientation is the appropriate forum to prepare jurors for what will happen, and their role in the process. Jurors should first be told how jury selection works, that the attorneys or judge will ask them questions about their experiences and opinions. They should be informed that this is the time when they should be totally honest about anything they have heard or read, believe or feel about a situation. They should understand that the only good juror is the open and honest one, regardless of whether or not they are chosen for that particular case.

Once the jury is sworn, they should be prepared to hear opening statements, followed by the plaintiff's or prosecution's case. They should understand that the defense is entitled to cross-examine each plaintiff or prosecution witness and to object to any evidence, and the defense can choose or not choose to put on evidence of its own. In a criminal case, the defense has an absolute right not to present a case. It should be clear that the subsequent closing arguments are not part of the evidence and the evidence should be considered only in light of the instructions of the court. They should also be told to expect interruptions in the trial when the lawyers take up matters with the court.

In addition to the facets of the trial process, the jurors should have logistical issues clarified. Jurors are generally worried about small things like where to park their car, where to eat lunch, where to get coffee or a soft drink, where the restrooms are and other things that can help them feel more familiar in a unfamiliar environment. The fewer fears with which jurors approach *voir dire,* the more responsive they are apt to be to the questioning. You may suggest to the person conducting orientation that these simple explanations can make a big difference in how jurors feel about their experience. You should also make sure that a question and answer period is allowed after the orientation so that jurors can follow up with any questions that remain on their minds.

§ 10.4 The Jury Assembly Room—Who Should Do the Orientation?

An orientation given by a court representative has the potential for bias. Nevertheless, the best person to do the orientation is a judge, a judge's clerk or a jury commissioner—someone who appears impartial to both sides and whose sole motivation is to help the jurors to understand and be comfortable with the process and their role in it.

§ 10.5 The Jury Assembly Room—Orientation Films

Film clips may show the aggravation and antagonism that can develop in deliberations, or a biased view of trial procedures, leaving the impression that this is a duty jurors may want to avoid. As a result, jurors may be more inclined to seek hardship excuses rather than accommodate the court. The fact that the excuses are made outside the attorneys' hearing denies the attorneys information that could be important in determining a juror's state of mind and fitness for the case.

On the other hand, a film specially designed for orientation could be helpful. You should look at some of the films that other jurisdictions are using and decide if this form of orientation may be of value, given the particulars of your case and the trial venue. One good thing generally about a film presentation is that jurors are accustomed to watching television and are more apt to relax when oriented in this manner. Ideally, the film would be followed by a question and answer session to dispel any confusion or misunderstanding.

§ 10.6 The Jury Assembly Room—The Pros and Cons of Orientation Booklets

Orientation books run the gamut from excellent to very poor. Some accurately describe the jurors' job: to listen to information and determine what they believe from the facts. Others tell the jurors that they should have no opinions or thoughts, giving the impression that during *voir dire* it is wrong for them to disclose information or express an opinion. Such indoctrination, written and verbal, inhibits free-flowing conversation with the jurors during jury selection.

Some booklets say that they have been prepared by the county attorney's office and overseen by the district attorney's office. This gives the impression that the party most interested in a fair and impartial proceeding is the prosecution, which is a handicap for the defense in a criminal case. (*See* Appendix 10A for a sample juror orientation booklet.)

If your jurisdiction uses a booklet that is incomplete or in any way biased in its presentation, or discourages jurors from being open and honest about their thoughts and feelings during jury selection, the legal community should organize to get the booklet rewritten. There is, of course, the added problem with orientation booklets: Where jurors are left to orient themselves, the better reader will be better informed than those with reading difficulties.

§ 10.7 The Jury Assembly Room—Monitoring the Orientation

You should always have a representative at the juror orientation or outside the jury assembly room to hear how the orientation is being conducted. This person should carefully observe what the jurors are being told and if there is any specific mention of your case. Note should also be made of the jury panel during the orientation. Do people already appear to know each other or some member of the court staff? Are they already beginning to socialize or are they more comfortable sitting alone? Who has brought something to read, and who is reading newspapers that could affect their impartiality, if yours is a publicized case?

Another reason to have someone present is to find out what areas have not been covered in the orientation and where jurors still appear to be confused. This will alert you to the matters that should be discussed further during *voir dire.* You can be helpful, as the information giver, if you are aware of what they need to know.

§ 10.8 The Jury Assembly Room—Who Else Is Present?

You will also want to observe the presence of others in the room who are not jurors. Often the district attorney or assistant U.S. attorney or opposing counsel will make an appearance. This is important if they are given any kind of acknowledgment by the people conducting the orientation or if they are positioned at the front of the room, prematurely giving them credibility. You should privately, but on the record, object to their presence if they are at the front of the room unless you are also allowed to be there.

§ 10.9 The Jury Assembly Room—Who Is Excused?

Some jurors will ask to be excused during the orientation or will arrive early and ask to be excused. It is important that you know who the clerks are allowing to leave without first being questioned by or in the presence of the attorneys. In a civil case, for example, where you may want to seat more educated or self-employed jurors, you do not want them being excused before you have a chance to object. If you are not able to have a representative at the jury orientation, you should request, before trial, a list of the people excused by the clerk, with the nature of their excuse. If you find that excuses have been granted for circumstances that are not statutorily covered, you should object on the record, stating that the clerk has improperly excused an otherwise qualified juror and as a result has interfered with your ability to obtain a fair cross-section of the community.

§ 10.10 The Jury Assembly Room—Juror Questionnaires

If you have requested and been granted a juror questionnaire, the orientation may be the perfect time for the jurors to fill out the questionnaire. This is a time when they are assembled in one place, and invariably, given court schedules, have extra time on their hands. The court clerk can then easily collect the questionnaires and have them reproduced while you are in the court taking care of other pretrial matters.

§ 10.11 The Courtroom—Generally

You will want to know what the jury panel has seen in the courtroom before jury selection begins. Some jurisdictions put the jurors in the courtroom when there are other matters taking place. You should have a representative there to find out what they have been exposed to before you begin your *voir dire.*

§ 10.12 The Courtroom—What Has the Panel Observed?

Jury panels who are seated in the courtroom prior to *voir dire* may observe clients and others coming out of the holding cell. In a criminal case, you may not want the jury panel to know that your client is in custody. They may observe another case in trial or defendants plead guilty. They may witness settlements being made in civil cases, or the conduct of other lawyers that could have a negative impact on how they see you.

Someone should be on the scene from the very beginning to monitor what is happening in and around the jury panel and to determine what could become an issue for the jurors. If, for example, they have seen the settlement of a civil claim, and the issues are similar to the case that you will be conducting, the jurors have already been exposed to some information that you may want to follow up on *voir dire.* If a plea of guilty has been taken in front of the panel, you may want to question the jurors to determine their reactions or impressions, and how that may affect your criminal case.

The best way to avoid this problem of exposure is to have the jury panel remain in the jury assembly room until *voir dire* is to begin in your case. The less they are exposed to extraneous information, the better it will be for your client.

§ 10.13 The Courtroom—Interaction Between Jurors and Court Personnel

Before jury selection begins, you or your observer may notice that jurors know people who work in the judge's office or the courtroom personnel. You should be on the alert for any tangential connections to any aspect of your case and how it may affect your client. For example, if you know you and the judge will be disagreeing on a number of issues and have learned that a juror knows the judge's secretary, this could become a potential problem because of the juror's identification with the judge through the judge's employee. If you feel there could be any possible adverse effects, raise this issue with the judge prior to the commencement of the trial. You may want to ask for the juror to be immediately excused, or if there is a connection to courtroom staff, that the staff person be excused until the conclusion of the case and told not to have any discussion with any panel member. If the problem is not resolved to your satisfaction, put this issue on the record and discuss it with the juror, preferably at the bench during *voir dire.*

§ 10.14 The Courtroom—Introduction by the Court

You will want the judge to give a thorough introduction that encourages the jury panel to be open and honest in *voir dire.* You will also want the judge to tell the jurors that if there is anything they do not want to discuss in open court or in front of other jurors, they have the option to go back in chambers or come to the bench. You should request to have input into what the judge says and how it is said, emphasizing the judge's influence over the jury. (*See* Chapter 11 for further discussion of the judge's impact on the jury.)

§ 10.15 The Courtroom—Introduction by Counsel

As you know, first impressions can be important. The first things you say to the jury should convey that you are a person who cares about what they think and feel and are sensitive to the discomforts of being in the jury box. Introduce yourself and your client, and do whatever you would do in other social situations to create a cordial atmosphere. None of us would think of hosting a gathering and not introducing the people in the room. It should be no different in the courtroom. You should use jury selection as an opportunity to be the master of ceremonies by introducing the judge's clerk, court reporter, secretary, bailiff, opposing counsel and clients, if the court or your opponent has not done so already. This is important because it gives the appearance not only that you are in charge, but that you are a warm, friendly person.

Be careful, however, when introducing opposing counsel, that you do not say, "That's my good friend Joe." Do not leave jurors with the impression that the war in the courtroom is a sham. Merely say, "I would like you to know everyone who will be working in the courtroom," and introduce opposing counsel along with the rest of the judge's staff.

Assure the jurors that you understand that they are uncomfortable and nervous, and acknowledge the inconvenience of getting to the courthouse and being on jury duty. Take time to outline what will be happening during jury selection and throughout the trial. Knowledge is power. By putting information in the jurors' hands, you become a person of power in their eyes. (*See* Chapter 12, "Voir Dire Strategy," for further discussion on counsel introductions.)

Chapter 11

THE JUDGE AND THE JURY

Table of Sections

---

§ 11.1 Overview

Judges, as we all know, have a powerful impact on jurors and their willingness to be open during jury selection. It is therefore important to remind the judge of his or her role in setting the stage for *voir dire.* Jurors want to please the judge and if the judge tells them to be open and honest, they are more apt to be open and honest.

It is also useful to analyze what the judge says to the jurors before the questioning begins. There are ways to convey that the court sincerely wants to hear what the jurors have to say and that there are no right or wrong answers. There are other ways that can give jurors the impression that the court is not interested in their responses. (*See* Appendix 11A for a motion and memorandum of law for proposed introductory remarks, citing the introduction of Chief Judge Robert Peckham in a highly publicized case.)

A judge's demeanor can affect jurors, too. If the judge is relaxed in introducing the *voir dire,* it conveys a whole different tone than if the introduction is rushed and delivered in a loud, curt or disinterested tone of voice. Likewise, the judge can react non-verbally to the attorneys' questions or the jurors' responses in a way that expresses disapproval or disbelief, or discourages dialogue, (e.g., turning away from the lawyer, talking with court staff or other lawyers, tapping fingers or a pen). The attorney, if possible, must reassure the jurors of the importance of the *voir dire* questions, and may need to make a record of the judge's negative influence on the jury.

§ 11.2 Court–Conducted *Voir Dire*—Generally

There are pros and cons to the court participating in *voir dire.* The traditional wisdom is that lawyers should do all the questioning, and this continues to be the preferred approach. It can be positive, however, for the court to ask some jurors some of the potentially embarrassing questions such as prior convictions, health, ability to read and write, level of education, or religious affiliation. Also, in jurisdictions where statute or case law automatically disqualifies certain individuals from serving on jury duty, you may want to consider having the judge ask the automatic disqualification questions so as not to appear to be picking on certain segments of the panel. For example, in most jurisdictions, those who have been convicted of an offense and have not had their civil rights restored are not eligible for jury service. Because the judge is cloaked with the air of authority, jurors are less likely to be offended if the judge asks these generic questions.

On the other hand, you do not want the judge to ask the questions in which you know nine times out of ten you will do a better job. The typical racism question a judge will ask, for instance, is, "Is anyone going to hold it against the defendant because he comes from a minority group?" This is a meaningless question and provides no information; it exemplifies why judges should not participate in this line of inquiry. It is also not helpful for the court to ask case-specific questions, such as whether or not jurors or any member of their family have ever been involved in a sexual molestation, been sued or foreclosed on, or had an experience pertinent to your case. The problem with the court conducting the substantive *voir dire* is that the court is not fully versed with both sides of the case, the facts or the unique issues. It is important, if the court conducts part of the *voir dire,* that it be carefully structured so the court asks just a few questions to break the ice and then allows the lawyer to take over.

§ 11.3 Court–Conducted *Voir Dire*—Defining the Judge's Role

On the record, you should discuss with the judge and opposing counsel prior to *voir dire* who will do what and when during jury selection. Make clear your desire that the attorneys ask most of the questions and that if there are any areas where you would like the court to assist, you will ask at that time. Ironing out logistics beforehand can save a lot of difficulties in the long run.

A recent Supreme Court case, *Peretz v. United States,* [1] warns of another possible concern. The Federal Magistrates Act [2] grants district courts the authority to assign magistrates certain "additional duties as are not inconsistent with the Constitution and laws of the United States."

In *Gomez v. United States* [3], the Supreme Court held that those "additional duties" do not include the selection of a jury in a felony trial without the defendant's consent. In *Peretz,* however, the Supreme Court, upholding an earlier decision in *United States v. Musacchia,* [4] found that if the defendant, through counsel, consents to magistrate jury selection prior to trial and does not object to the magistrate conducting the *voir dire* at trial, she waives any subsequent challenge to the jury selection process on those grounds, if convicted. If a magistrate has been assigned to your case, be sure to find out as much as possible about her beforehand so that you can determine whether the magistrate or the trial judge will grant a more thorough opportunity to question the jury panel. Many federal magistrates are inclined to spend more time on jury selection and many will allow attorney participation because their calendars are not so busy as those of a federal district judge.

§ 11.4 Court-Conducted *Voir Dire*—Following up on the Judge's Questions

Make it clear that if the judge is going to ask questions that are boilerplate, you will request the right to ask follow-up questions where appropriate. It is appropriate, for example, to say to a juror who just told the judge that he or she has three children in law enforcement, "Tell me how you feel about what they do for a living?" This would be a logical and useful follow-up to the judge's question of whether a juror or any family members or friends have ever been in law enforcement. Appropriate follow-up questions convey to the jurors that you and the judge are working together to learn about the jurors.

§ 11.5 Court-Conducted *Voir Dire*—Sensitive Questions for the Judge to Ask

If the court has ruled against individual sequestered *voir dire* on sensitive issues, you should prepare a list of three or four questions and

§ 11.3

1. ___ U.S. ___, 111 S.Ct. 2661, 115 L.Ed.2d 808 (1991).

2. Pub.L. 90–578, 82 Stat. 1108, as amended, 28 U.S.C.A. § 636(b)(3).

3. 490 U.S. 858, 871–872, 109 S.Ct. 2237, 2245–2246, 104 L.Ed.2d 923 (1989).

4. 900 F.2d 493 (2d Cir.1990), cert. denied ___ U.S. ___, 111 S.Ct. 2887, 115 L.Ed.2d 1052 (1991).

ask the court to introduce them by telling the panel members they can approach the bench and discuss these matters with the judge and counsel in private. For example, in a bankruptcy fraud case, these questions would include:

1) Have you ever been audited by the IRS?

2) Have you ever filed for bankruptcy?

3) Have you ever had a foreclosure on a home?

Convince the judge that it is best to take each juror who responds back into chambers or into the jury room. So as not to suggest the right answer, the judge should introduce these sensitive questions in the following format:

Many people have had the experience of (describe experience). *It would not be unusual if you have had this experience or if someone you know has had this experience. All I want to know is yes or no as to whether you or anyone you know has ever had this kind of experience.*

When a hand is raised and the person answers yes, the judge should ask the person to come to the bench or go into chambers.

§ 11.6 Court-Conducted *Voir Dire*—Convincing the Judge to Bring Jurors to the Bench

It is important to encourage the judge to bring a juror to the bench whenever it is clear that the juror is equivocating or uncomfortable answering a question in open court. The judge should be continually reminded that speaking in public is the jurors' number one fear and that they are embarrassed to talk about sensitive matters in front of people from the community. Judges generally respond well to this argument and are more apt to call a juror up to the bench when they understand the rationale. Likewise, jurors are more apt to be candid when their privacy is respected.

To push the judge to allow the juror to approach the bench, you can ask the juror if he or she would be more comfortable discussing the matter at the bench. The judge would probably not contest. After all, the judge would appear as less than sensitive and leave you looking like the good guy.

You might approach the bench and say, "Judge, I think it would be more sensitive to Ms. Jones if we spoke about this at the bench. Can we please ask Ms. Jones to come up here?" Generally judges will allow jurors to approach the bench if it is requested in this delicate manner.

§ 11.7 Educating the Judge—Generally

Encouraging judges to be sensitive during *voir dire* can be quite a task. Many are initially very uncomfortable asking questions in an open-ended manner. Through effective record making and education by lawyers, expert testimony and other information, however, judges have been convinced that there are better ways to ask questions than their customary procedure.

To encourage the court to ask a question in a different way, the attorney should make a record after each juror has been questioned. Or, the attorney may write down the exact phrasing of a question and request that the court ask the question in this manner because it does not suggest the answer. Each piece of paper with a proposed question should be marked as an exhibit and put into the record.

In addition to affidavits to expand *voir dire,* as discussed in Chapter 7, affidavits should also be filed pre-trial to educate the court on the importance of asking *voir dire* questions as they are framed by the attorney. If the judge agrees to a hearing on the issue, the affidavits, as well as expert in-court testimony, should address the effect of tone of voice, non-verbal language and other aspects of judicial demeanor. The important thing to remember is that judges can be open if they are given enough information to warrant changing their style. Some of the most rigid judges in this country, when properly educated and presented with well-made records, have modified the way they have conducted *voir dire.* This took tenacious lawyers fighting for what they believed was the crux of their case—effective jury selection.

§ 11.8 Educating the Judge—How Not to Embarrass the Judge

Judges have feelings like the rest of us. To suggest that the court ask a question in a different way or open up the style of questioning may be challenging the way the judge has always done things. You must be sensitive to the judge's ego and slowly encourage the changes you seek. You are less apt to embarrass the judge if you preface your suggestions in a way that defers to the judge's authority but does not concede your point. You may say, for instance,

> *As the court well knows, your thoughts and feelings are conveyed to this jury panel because of the power you hold in this courtroom. Because I know the powerful position you hold in jurors' eyes, I would like to request that the court ask this question in a slightly different way.*

You might also say, in explaining what information you would like to elicit,

> *Judge, I know you were asking that question to find out* (describe intent of question), *however, I believe that if you were to change the wording just slightly, we would get more of the information that you and counsel feel is necessary in order to determine which jurors truly can be fair and impartial on this case.*

Some lawyers are hesitant to cajole a judge, for fear of losing rapport with the judge. This generally happens when a lawyer is discourteous to the court, not when strongly asserting a client's rights. There is a way to persist and keep your credibility with the court. When asserting your client's rights, it is important to say, "Respectfully, I must make a record," and go on to express exactly what you are feeling: "I'm sorry you and I seem to be at odds here. That is not my intention. My intention is to make a record for my client, and I am doing the best I know how. I mean no disrespect."

§ 11.9 Educating the Judge—How to Apologize and Not Give up Error

It is wise to be courteous and respectful of the court and to apologize when an apology is due, but that does not mean ignoring potential error. You can say to the judge that you did not mean in any way to be discourteous; you are simply protecting your client's rights. You may want to say that you did something in a way you did not intend and that you will do better in the future. Or you can say, though you are sorry about making the court unhappy, you feel that you must still push ahead in your quest for a fair and impartial jury in this case. Do not say, "Judge, I am sorry for what I did and I won't do that anymore." This undermines your record making, unless you are apologizing for something that has nothing to do with the record. Then a full and open apology is appropriate.

People are generally afraid to apologize, for fear of losing ground. Lawyers, particularly, forget it is okay to apologize. An apology can be made simply by saying, "I found it important that you understand (*explain your action*), and though I do not apologize for wanting you to understand, I meant no disrespect and I apologize if I offended you, Judge." This approach can also be taken in court. What is wrong with attorneys saying that they are sorry or concerned about something, if that is truly what they feel? Why do lawyers resist being real in the courtroom? Consistently being yourself in interactions with the judge, the jury, witnesses and your client, will make you a more credible human being in the jurors' eyes and no doubt put your case in a better light.

§ 11.10 Educating the Judge—How to Diffuse the Judge's Anger at You

If you have been pushing courteously to have certain questions asked in a certain way, and the court becomes unhappy or wants to rush things along, then you know you probably have been doing your job. It means, however, that you must defuse the judge's anger without losing ground and make the motions necessary to persuade the judge to ask better questions. This can be credibly done at the bench in the presence of the court reporter, by saying:

Judge, I am in no way interested in disrupting this proceeding or making the court uncomfortable, I am only interested in finding out what these jurors truly think and feel. They are the most important people in my client's world right now, and I need the information to make an intelligent choice as to who can truly be fair and impartial in this case.

Before making any record, it is advisable first to talk to the judge in chambers off the record and express your concerns about the court's *voir dire* as well as your hope that this can be worked out so that the proceedings can go smoothly. If the court continues to give you a hard time in front of the jury, you should again approach the bench with the court reporter and put on the record that the court is making you nervous and uncomfortable and you feel it is affecting your ability to render your client effective assistance of counsel. If that argument does not sway the court, it is important to continue making a record, stating that you want to be fair to the court and at the same time you need answers to certain questions in order to be able to make intelligent decisions in this jury selection.

At this point the judge may agree that you should ask the question, but if you are not allowed to ask the question you want to ask, then in front of the jury you should say:

Judge, I am just trying to find out what these good people think and feel, and I don't know any other way to do that other than asking good open-ended questions. I am sorry I have upset the court but I am just trying to do my job in representing (name of client) *in this case. Judge, I'll do my best to move this along, but I must ask these questions to find out what the jurors think and feel.*

You should realize that some judges will continue to be angry with you, but if you are doing your best to make peace and still represent your client, then that is all you can do. A couple of hours, or if you are lucky, a couple of days down the road you may want to request a conference with the judge in the presence of opposing counsel and say that you hope he or she agrees that everyone is getting along better now. Assure the judge that you are doing your best to honor the judge's wishes and do your job.

§ 11.11 Handling Objections in Front of the Jury—Generally

Most lawyers have had the occasional experience of feeling that there were two opposing sides in the case, opposing counsel and the court. It can be very uncomfortable when every time you ask a question, opposing counsel objects and the judge sustains. There are various ways of dealing with this opposition. One is to make a record at the bench with the court reporter present. Another is to respond in front of the jury, saying: "These are important questions, and I don't understand why important issues are being suppressed or stepped on by opposing counsel." Still another is to re-ask the question in a different way.

Opposing counsel have a tendency to "make a speech" when objecting to a question. You should have previously filed a motion in limine, limiting objections to legal argument. In the unlikely event that motion is denied and opposing counsel objects *ad nauseam,* you may want to tell the court in front of the jury that you object to opposing counsel testifying in front of the jury. You should say that it is not proper for opposing counsel to impose his or her opinions on the jurors, and that if there is an objection, counsel should merely say, "I object," and the objection should be discussed outside the presence of the jury. As much as possible, objections should be dealt with out of the presence of the jury, because even though they know it is appropriate to object, jurors still feel that if you continue to object and approach the bench, you are hiding something.

Judges will sometimes say, "You set yourself up, counsel." In turn, you should tell the court that you feel that you are doing your job and asking a good question, and interrupting was opposing counsel's way of trying to prevent a juror from speaking his or her mind. Argue that opposing counsel knows this question is an appropriate question to get to the bottom of the issue and is trying to prevent the truth from being heard. If the jury is present, they will likely conclude, to your advantage, that opposing counsel is trying to hide something and silence the truth.

The important thing to remember is to always remain courteous, forthright and determined in seeking the truth from the jury panel. This is the first time that you have been showcased in front of the jury and if they perceive you as a strong, open and sensitive person, this first impression can hold you in good stead throughout the trial. Being courteous, however, does not mean allowing an objection to stand on a question that you feel is imperative to your case. Jurors respect lawyers who fight for their clients in a respectful way.

In that spirit, when you choose to object to opposing counsel's questions, you should not only say, "I object," but raise specific objections, like opposing counsel trying to put words into a juror's mouth, twisting the facts, suggesting information that is not a part of the case.

§ 11.12 Handling Objections in Front of the Jury—When the Court Objects for Opposing Counsel

Often during jury selection the judge will raise an objection on behalf of opposing counsel. When the judge interrupts and says that the lawyer is out of line in pursuing a particular line of questioning, it gives the impression that the lawyer has done something improper.

This can be very difficult because the judge carries so much weight with the jury.

If you are interrupted by the court, you should approach the bench and put on the record that the court has in essence imposed objections for the other side and that you are trying your best to ask good questions that have to do with the case issues. If the court continues to interrupt, it is important to tell the court in front of the jury that you are asking only the questions that you feel are appropriate. Be prepared to be told that the court does not find your questions proper and in turn, to tell the court in front of the jury why these questions are proper. Many times jurors will understand why you are asking a question, despite the judge's interruption, if you explain the necessity of asking the question in this kind of case. You should remember that even the jurors who resent a lawyer during *voir dire* generally change their opinion once they are sworn in.

§ 11.13 Handling the Court's Non-verbal Responses

Judges can influence jurors non-verbally both in jury selection and during trial. It is important that the non-verbal language of the court be put on the record so the jurors do not misread the judge's behavior or infer that the judge is for or against a particular party. Judges have been known to tap a pen on the side of the bench in apparent frustration or shake their heads in disbelief. It is appropriate to approach the bench and tell the judge that these actions are not only distracting counsel during *voir dire* but are leaving an impression with the jurors that the judge in the first instance, is frustrated and irritated with the questioning, or in the second instance, does not believe what is being said.

Any and all non-verbal language that you feel is negatively influencing the jury should be put on the record. It helps bring the record alive in case of an appeal and encourages judges in the trial proper to be more conscious of their demeanor. Even difficult judges have modified their demeanor so the record will not reflect non-verbal responses or voice inflections that could be interpreted as bias toward one side or the other.

It is possible to jump to the wrong conclusion about a judge's conduct, but this should not deter you from protecting your client's interests on the record. One judge was seen rolling his eyes in response to a question and looking at the ceiling. When the lawyer approached the bench and told the judge that by rolling his eyes and looking at the ceiling, he was giving the impression that he did not believe what was being said, the judge contested that what he was doing was looking away from the open window that was blinding him. That judge did not realize that his non-verbal language would be interpreted in another way. Once it was brought to his attention, the judge corrected his behavior and informed the jury that he was very much interested in what the person speaking had to say, but had turned away only because of the sunlight in his eyes. The lawyer's assertiveness put aside any negative inferences and changed the mood of the courtroom.

§ 11.14 Time Limitations

Lawyers have found that more and more courts are imposing time limitations on *voir dire.* The most dramatic example of taking away this valuable right was passage of California's Proposition 115, which follows the discretionary rule governing the federal court system. The reason, generally, for courts' limiting lawyers is that lawyers spend most of their time lecturing to the jury instead of asking good questions.

Most judges will extend time limitations if they feel that lawyers are asking relevant and case-specific questions. If you spend the time asking the three or four most important questions relating to your case—rather than making mundane or inflammatory inquiries or asking pure background questions—you will get the information you need to determine challenges for cause and intelligently exercise peremptory strikes, and the court will generally be more lenient. As "guardian" of the jurors, the court will appreciate the need for more time if the jurors are participants, not merely spectators, in the jury selection process.

When you find yourself before a judge that wants to adhere to time limitations, we suggest bartering with the judge. For example, we have agreed to reduce our time for argument or examination of witnesses in exchange for additional time to conduct a meaningful *voir dire.* Tell the judge that you will raise only three or four specific areas of inquiry, each of which is central to your lawsuit. The judge will more often than not give you the necessary latitude if aware of the finite areas you intend to cover.

Of course, the court can grant more time, but not enough time to conduct a proper *voir dire.* If the court allows an unreasonably short period of time, thirty minutes or less, counsel must choose between seeking limited information from each juror and lecturing on as many issues as possible. We recommend the former option. Asking each juror to share his or her feelings or opinions on the most important case-specific issue is generally more fruitful. It at least opens the door to a challenge for cause and provides some information on which to base a peremptory strike.

To prevent limits on your time, it is important to make a record before *voir dire* as to the need for latitude to ask case-specific questions. As mentioned, you can cut *voir dire* by eliminating background questions, but you should not relinquish the time needed for case-specific questions that go right to the heart of the matter. If the court then cuts you off, you should say, "Judge, if you had given me time, here are the questions that I would have asked," and present a list of closed-ended questions that would be considered appropriate in any case.

Examples of appropriate case-specific questions would be:

(In a self-defense case): *If you were in a situation where you had to defend yourself, would you, and how would you defend yourself?*

(In a drug case): *What do you think about the war on drugs?*

(In a contract dispute): *Have you or any member of your family ever been involved in any kind of contract dispute and if so, what happened?*

(In a patent case): *Have you or any member of your family ever invented anything or had an idea that you would like to have laid claim to? What happened with that?*

These are the kinds of questions that you should ask if your time is limited. Save questions dealing with legal issues and the more innocuous background questions for the record you make at the end of jury selection. If the court will not allow you to make the record at the bench, object and submit in writing all the questions you would have asked, to be marked as an exhibit and put into the court record.

§ 11.15 When and Why to Submit Questions

If you are in a jurisdiction where the judge is limiting *voir dire,* a good tactic is to propose a set of ten questions to be asked. Tell the court that if you are allowed to ask these ten, you will stick to this limit, unless an obvious follow-up question is indicated. This is a fair and reasonable proposal and many times is acceptable to the court.

Some judges expect to have two hundred questions submitted ahead of time, from which they will pick and choose. It is then at the court's discretion to determine what are the important questions. This can be a real problem when some issues are deemed important and others are not, given that the judge does not understand what the important facts of your case are.

Whenever possible, avoid submitting your questions early so the court and opposing counsel cannot spend a lot of time picking apart your important questions. By all means, do not volunteer any questions in advance unless the court demands them.

§ 11.16 'Move Along, Counselor'

Judges are taught to keep a pace in the courtroom by saying these irksome words, "Move along, Counselor." This can be like a cattle prod in your back when you are attempting to get jurors to open up in a sensitive and caring way. Calmly tell the judge that you are moving along as quickly as you can and that you will try to keep up a good pace and at the same time ask the questions that need to be asked. This may at times upset the judge; however, if you keep your tone calm and continue to move along without forgoing your *voir dire,* most judges will allow you to complete your questioning.

§ 11.17 Keeping Your Rhythm

The key to *voir dire* is not only to cover the questions you want asked but to maintain a rhythm that keeps the jurors' attention. It is helpful to have before you one page that has the ten most important areas you want to ask the jury panel. If the court interrupts you or in some way disturbs your rhythm, you will have that sheet of buzz words to get you back on track.

You may want to prepare for *voir dire* by writing out 50 to 100 questions, but once you are in the courtroom, it is easy to lose your place. Having a clear idea of the ten most important areas you want to broach with the jury panel will smooth the way for an effective *voir dire.*

You should use the same sheet of paper to keep you focused if opposing counsel tries to disrupt your flow. Remember what you are discussing with that particular juror and forget about opposing counsel's attempts to throw you off balance.

§ 11.18 When a Judge Begins Interrogating Jurors

There have been occasions where a juror has acted inappropriately, prompting the judge to bring in each juror for interrogation on what he or she knows or has heard another juror say. It is important to get this information, but the manner in which it is obtained can make the difference between jurors being honest about another's impropriety and the entire panel clamming up for fear that they will be the next object of a witch hunt. Do what you can to temper the inquiry, if that is in the client's interest, but remember that juror impropriety can not only "ruin" jury selection, it can also be grounds for mistrial. (*See* Section 12.33, "Polluting the Panel," and Section 12.40, "Making a Case Regarding Jury Misconduct," for discussion of potential grounds for mistrial.)

Request that the court allow counsel to question the jurors and make sure that the questioning is done without creating a chain reaction of fear of reprisal. You can allay jurors' fears simply by saying:

> *It has come to our attention that another juror has done or said* (describe the act or statement). *We would like to know your impression and what you have heard, understanding that we all respect the fact that you have been totally honest and we desire that you continue to do so.*

If the court will not allow counsel to ask the questions during this process, then it is your job to write out the specific questions you want the court to ask and why. You must emphasize to the court that if the questioning is done in a way that leaves the impression of being an interrogation, the jurors will likely be closed and not be forthright about other issues they will be questioned on.

This process should be delicately handled, and avoided altogether if it appears it will disrupt the proceedings. There are other ways to make your record. After the jury is sworn, in jurisdictions where it is allowed, you can get affidavits from jurors that have been released, or you may request after the jury has been empaneled that they be called back and questioned. Try your best to get the information at the time of the incident, always keeping in mind that your first concern is obtaining important information from the jurors. If you believe there is a basis for mistrial, you should request a hearing where you would introduce the testimony of jurors, or in the alternative, juror affidavits stating what they heard. By law, jurors cannot assess the impact of what they have heard on their decision making but they are also to be free from extraneous or prejudicial input. (*See* Appendix 11B for a sample motion for a new trial or mistrial with attached affidavits based on unauthorized communication by jurors and Appendix 11C for sample juror affidavits filed with the affidavit of the jury consultant in another case involving the influence of pre-trial publicity.)

§ 11.19 How to Win the Judge's Attention and Respect

Judges see many lawyers during any given month and, under the pressure of normal court calendars, do not always give lawyers their due. It is your responsibility to make yourself different from other lawyers that the judge sees on a daily basis. You are most apt to win the judge's respect by trying first to establish a rapport. If you are having problems, you should attempt to talk to the court off the record with opposing counsel present. Many judges will appreciate your effort and make changes.

You can impress the judge by timely filing motions and preparing memoranda of law so that the court understands that you do not consider your request to be frivolous. Always be warm and cordial to the court staff and courteous to the judge, and where possible, learn something about the judge so that you can communicate on a more personal basis. If you frame your arguments with the judge in mind, the judge is more likely to listen to what you have to say and to grant your motions and proposed modifications of the jury selection process.

§ 11.20 Building a Record

When judges remain intractable, despite your efforts, the only recourse is to begin making a record. You must properly think through how to build your record. If the court is being unduly unfair, invite other lawyers and people from the community to come in and observe the judge's demeanor and write affidavits that you can incorporate as part of the record. Some lawyers have requested hearings, where they present witnesses who discuss their impressions of the court's attitude toward counsel. Jury and trial consultants have also been called to give their expert opinion. Although this testimony generally makes the judge uncomfortable, it definitely creates a record for appeal.

To establish the grounds for changes in the traditional jury selection process will probably require a hearing. File the following motions, requesting an evidentiary hearing: a) motion for attorney-conducted *voir dire;* b) motion for individual sequestered *voir dire;* c) motion for questionnaire; d) motion for additional time to conduct *voir dire;* e) motion for additional peremptory challenges; f) motion to employ the Arizona Struck System. Also prepare memoranda of law in support of these motions to convince the court that there is precedent and value in granting the changes you request. (*See* Chapter 7, "Improving *Voir Dire* Conditions," for further discussion on approaches to expand the traditional *voir dire* system.) At the hearing, present expert testimony regarding the importance of adequate time to conduct *voir dire,* individual sequestered *voir dire* on sensitive issues, the value of a questionnaire, the need for attorney-conducted *voir dire* and the differences between attorney-conducted and judge-conducted *voir dire.*

Additional preparation is necessary to qualify jurors for a death penalty case, and another complete battery of experts may be called to build a record. (*See* Chapter 18 for what evidence you need to begin making a record in a death penalty case.)

As jury selection progresses and it becomes evident why your requests should have been granted, you should approach the bench and continue to make a record. If a juror seems to equivocate on information, you should ask that this juror be questioned individually in a sequestered setting to overcome the juror's discomfort with speaking publicly. In a highly publicized case, if only a few people indicate that they have heard anything about the case, renew your request for individual sequestered *voir dire* on publicity. The few people who raise their hands indicate that other members of the jury panel, out of discomfort with talking in groups or for some other reason, must be hesitant to respond.

You should always be looking for creative ways to make your record. Judges tend to respond well to conscientious efforts to build a record and to give you more than what you had expected if you stand strong and vigilant.

Appendix 11D, the case of *Wheatfall v. State,* 746 S.W.2d 8 (Tex. App.—Houston 1988), contains an excellent example of how a record should be made, at least in Texas, when the trial court places time limitations on *voir dire*. Regardless of the jurisdiction, the record must contain, at a bare minimum, the questions you would have asked if given the time and the fact that one or more jurors who actually served were not examined because of the time limitations. Such a showing is necessary to demonstrate the harm caused by the time limitations.

A successful challenge must also demonstrate that in the entire *voir dire* examination, counsel did not lecture but instead asked meaningful and relevant questions. You must further show that the questions you would have asked, but for the time limitations imposed, were likewise meaningful, relevant and proper. Making such a record is equally vital in civil and criminal cases.

§ 11.21 Judge Trials—Generally

Judge trials are like any other trial; you must play to your audience. Learn as much as you can about the judge before you enter the courtroom. Understand what upsets him, what he is open to, what his likes and dislikes are on and off the bench. You should never think of presenting a case without thinking about who is in the jury box. Likewise, lawyers should not disregard the person judging their client at the bench.

Learn from other lawyers what the court has granted or not granted in the past. Just because someone else has been limited by a lack of creativity should not discourage you. Judges have been known to grant all kinds of issues to lawyers who have tried new approaches. Be creative, use your thinking cap and always be yourself in front of the judge. Combining ingenuity and genuineness is a good way to get judges to listen to you. If they believe you, believe in your client and case, they are more apt to follow your lead.

§ 11.22 Judge Trials—Juvenile Court

Judges have been known to have pet peeves about certain kinds of juvenile offenses. It is important, since they are the judge of the facts as well as the law, that they be asked questions on issues you think may cloud their ability to be fair and impartial. In discussing pre-trial matters in your case, you should respectfully request time to *voir dire* the judge if you have any doubt about his or her impartiality. Similarly, if the proceeding is to go before a hearing examiner, you will want to explore his or her prior employment and any issues that may be a negative influence. You may meet some resistance to your challenging the judgment of the court in this manner, but you should courteously persist in protecting your client's right to a fair trial. At the least you should file a motion to *voir dire* the court, and make it part of the record in order to preserve the potential error.

Chapter 12

VOIR DIRE STRATEGY

Table of Sections

§ 12.1 Overview

We believe that you must prepare your case backwards. That is, you must know what instructions you want given to the jury. Once the instructions are prepared, you will have a foundation for your closing argument, direct and cross-examinations, opening statement, and of course, *voir dire*. It is critically important that you tie your case theory to your anticipated instructions and *voir dire*.

Voir dire should have a theme like any other effective communication. It should be coherent and tied into the rest of your case. It must divulge your case theory and diffuse the theory of the other side. In the course of *voir dire*, you should identify your good jurors and through them, educate the rest of the panel, while ferreting out those who should be struck. Use this opportunity to humanize yourself, your client and your case strategy, to capture the jurors' interest. Above all, listen to what the jurors have to say and always follow their lead.

§ 12.2 Tying *Voir Dire* to Case Strategy

Even before you begin to design your *voir dire* questions, you must think through your case strategy and the instructions that will be given to the jurors to frame their deliberations. You can then test jurors' reactions to determine who will understand and be open-minded to the issues and witnesses in your case. You may have a juror who would be perfect in every other kind of case because of his or her liberal or conservative views, but not be a good juror given the particulars of your case.

You must also consider how you want the jury to perceive your client during *voir dire*. For example, if you are defending an oil company in an oil spill case, you will want to discover who the jurors think is responsible for cleaning up an oil spill. If it will be brought out in evidence that your client has been in a mental institution, you will want to find out what jurors think about people who have had a mental breakdown. If you will be vigorously cross-examining the expert for the other side, you will want to find out what jurors think about holding experts to the highest of standards when they present what they call expert testimony. If you are alleging that there has been a conspiracy by the other side to implicate your client, then you will need to ask if jurors believe that people would come together and conspire to set someone up.

You must, in other words, think through the facts of your case and the theory you will use to interpret those facts, then carefully design, and ask, questions that focus on these elements. Should the judge try to prevent you from going into any of these areas, you must actively resist being shut down. Unless jurors are educated to be open-minded about particulars in a case, they frequently cannot be fair.

§ 12.3 Format—Generally

There is a natural order to the *voir dire,* once you determine the case strategy. Routinely, the judge and counsel will make formal introductions before the questioning begins. The questions should go from simple background queries, if time permits, to more complex case-specific issues that provoke thought and evoke feeling. Judge and lawyer both should create an atmosphere of openness that encourages jurors to be candid with comfort.

§ 12.4 Format—Introduction by the Court

Customarily, the judge introduces the *voir dire,* as discussed in Chapter 11, "The Judge and the Jury." The judge should explain to the jurors that this is their time to speak the truth and that they should tell the court and the lawyers everything they think and feel about the issues raised. The role of the judge at this stage is primarily to encourage the jurors to be open and honest with the lawyers.

You may also decide that you want the judge to ask a few succinct questions on sensitive issues that may embarrass or even disqualify a juror. (Again, *see* Section 11.2.) These areas should be determined beforehand, and the questions submitted in writing, so that the *voir dire* is carefully structured and you remain in control of the courtroom. The questions should be submitted in the language you want the questions asked, language that will not discourage the jurors from being honest. For instance, having the judge ask, "Have you ever had a negative experience with an African American person?" is likely to have a chilling effect that can be avoided by asking instead, "What has been your experience with African American people?" Explain to the judge the difference between these questions, and the responses they will elicit; that it is obviously more comfortable for a juror to dismiss the first question with a no, rather than open up to describe the experiences he or she has had.

It cannot be emphasized enough how essential it is for you to convince the judge to set the tone of the *voir dire* by encouraging the jury panel that honest answers are much more important than "right" answers.

§ 12.5 Format—Introduction by Counsel

The old saying that first impressions are lasting impressions applies in jury selection as well. The first take jurors get on counsel normally sticks. This is why being a warm, real person in the beginning of *voir dire* is important. At the same time you should appear self-assured, that you are the teacher and guide through this process. You should reassure your pupils—the jurors—that it is all right to be open. Remember, as students, the best teachers that any of us had were those who encouraged us to think for ourselves and probe our own perceptions, thoughts, feelings, reactions and actions. They were the ones who were interested in what we had to say as opposed to always doing the talking.

You want to tell the jurors that they are the most important people in the courtroom and invite them to share their thoughts and feelings with you. They must understand that all you want to know is what they think and feel and that though you may not like some of their answers, you want to know their answers at any cost. Assure them that if there is anything they do not want to discuss in the courtroom, they can either go back into the judge's chambers or they can approach the bench with you and opposing counsel. You should also pay attention to your non-verbal language, to encourage jurors to feel comfortable.

Part of making jurors comfortable is to familiarize them with their surroundings, including the people in the courtroom. You should take the responsibility to introduce not only the people at counsel table but opposing counsel and court staff. As lead attorney, you should make a point of putting co-counsel on equal footing. If you are a male, you should refer to your female co-counsel as "co-counsel," not simply as "the lawyer who will be assisting me." In fact, when you are trying a case with co-counsel, always refer to the team as "we" or "us," never "I" or "me." Be very careful, regardless of the jurisdiction, not to demean the role or importance of any member of your team. Even an unintentional or subtle slight of a woman or a minority person could be offensive to members of the jury panel. It is also important that you introduce the non-lawyers at the table and very briefly describe their role, so the jurors are not left to speculate.

When introducing your client, you should let the jury know that you care about this person, whether he or she is a corporate officer or someone accused of first-degree murder. You can make this clear by walking over and putting your hand on your client's shoulder and looking at your client and then looking at the jurors. You can say, "I have the pleasure of representing today (*name of client*)." In turn, the client should stand up and say, "Good morning" or "Good afternoon," nod and make eye contact with the jury panel members. In the same way that it is important for the client to show interest in the jurors during jury selection, you should continue to show your personal concern for your client throughout the trial. (*See* Section 13.9 for further discussion of the value of lawyer-client interaction in court.)

As discussed in Section 10.15, you will want to introduce the court staff and explain to the jury panel what each member of the staff does. By explaining everyone's role to the jury, you again appear to be the party most concerned about telling the jurors everything about the case and courtroom.

When introducing opposing counsel, do so succinctly and impersonally. It is not your role to make them the "nice guy" in the courtroom. If you are a criminal defense lawyer, it is particularly important that you not appear too chummy with the prosecutor. You are best served in court by referring to the prosecutor as "the prosecutor," rather than the government lawyer or the U.S. Attorney or the District Attorney. Similarly, if you are the prosecutor, you should refer to opposing counsel as the defendant's lawyer.

Defense counsel should also make a point of countering the routine prosecutor claim, "I represent the State of Texas," or "This is a case of The People v. John Doe." Tell the jury panel that you also represent the people of Texas and that you are equally serving justice. This is important so that jurors do not identify with the prosecutor as being their lawyer, or give more power to the government's case. You may ask the judge for an instruction on this issue during *voir dire* so that the jurors realize that both sides are upholding the Constitution.

You should never use the prosecutor's name or relate on personal terms. Fraternizing at breaks and at lunch is inappropriate. You want to keep the line drawn, to reinforce that you are not playing a game.

Before you begin the questions, you may want to add a few things about yourself, such as your history in the community and whether or not you are married or have children. This self-disclosure will make you appear more familiar and more like the jury panel. Telling them, on the other hand, that you are chief of the litigation department of a 180–person law firm will probably not make you someone that is more like the jurors. If you want the jurors to talk to you, find some common ground at the start.

§ 12.6 Format—Background Questions

As in any social situation when meeting someone for the first time, it is important to ask questions that the person finds comfortable to answer. You should open *voir dire* with questions about what the jurors do for a living, what their job responsibilities are, how they would describe themselves or how others would describe them.

§ 12.7 Format—Background Questions—Job

A job tells a lot about how people have chosen to live their lives. It gives an indication of what they enjoy doing with their minds and with their bodies. In many instances, it tells you whether they are more physically oriented or more intellectually oriented. You should not, however, presume that someone who is in a physical line of work does not have intellectual acumen. Some of the most intelligent jurors have proven to be laborers.

You will want to listen to how the people talk and compare that to what you know about their job. Ask them about their job, how they see it, what they would be doing if they were not in this line of work, what they like best about their job, what they like least about it. You should ask how long they have been doing this work, and what other jobs they have held in the past. You should ask about their job responsibilities, and note whether they define their job in human terms or object terms. For example, there is a big difference between someone saying that she supervises 22 hourly wage earners and someone else saying that his job is to help everybody enjoy the work more. One is object-oriented, the other is people-oriented.

§ 12.8 Format—Background Questions—Family

You will want to ask jurors to describe their family and probe how they feel about their family. You might then ask what he likes best and least about being married or about being a father. Or, you might ask her to describe her spouse and how she thinks her spouse would describe her. These are all questions to help you see the juror in context.

§ 12.9 Format—Background Questions—Etc.

You, of course, will want to explore each juror's education, hobbies, leisure activities, and other matters that tell you about the personal life of the juror. The goal is to check your intuition against what you can find out about this juror. The more information you have, the more intelligent decisions you are apt to make in selecting the jury.

Only in those circumstances where the court has imposed the strictest of time limitations should counsel forgo the warm-up period. For example, in federal court many judges invoke the powers of Rule 24A of the Federal Rules of Criminal Procedure and Rule 48A of the Federal Rules of Civil Procedure and allow counsel to participate in *voir dire* on only a limited basis. In those situations counsel should tell the panel that his or her time is severely limited or otherwise more time would be spent getting to know the jurors. Counsel should then proceed immediately into one of the designated areas of inquiry, starting with the least controversial or least sensitive topic.

§ 12.10 Format—Case-Specific Questions

Once you have passed the "getting to know you" period of the jury selection and you have a sense that you and the jury have mutually shared some of yourselves, you can then go on to the case-specific questions. Remember, if you are under time constraints, you should very promptly move into the case-specific questions, rather than spending a lot of time on background questions or making speeches.

Many lawyers have a tendency to try to explain or even persuade the jurors to take their side of the case during *voir dire.* This approach is ineffective, and judges in many jurisdictions now prohibit lawyers from using the time to try the case instead of asking questions of the jurors. It is an imperative in rendering effective assistance of counsel, whether you are representing an indigent citizen or a Fortune 500 company, that jury selection be spent asking questions and listening to answers rather than giving speeches. Besides, jurors are more inclined to listen to your side of the story after you have taken the time to allow them to express their feelings and thoughts.

Case-specific questions do just that. They are questions that both reveal the case themes and explore the jurors' thoughts and feelings about what concerns you most about your case. They should encompass the major issues in your case. For example, if you are the plaintiff in a personal injury claim involving a rear-end collision, one of the questions to ask is whether or not the juror, a family member or a close friend has been accused of or sued for a rear-end collision. If the answer is yes, you should ask the juror to discuss the incident in front of the entire panel or, if it is more comfortable, in private at the bench with the judge. In the same case, if you are the defendant, you should ask each juror whether or not the juror, a family member or a close friend has ever been injured in a rear-end collision or sued someone who caused a rear-end collision. Again, if the answer is yes, you want to give the juror the opportunity to speak in public or in private, however he or she feels more comfortable.

§ 12.11 Civil Claims—Generally

In addition to fact-specific questions, there are two lines of inquiry in civil cases that demand attention in *voir dire.* One important issue is how jurors feel about money damages. Some jurors may be strong on liability but will not award large money damages. They may consider, for example, a $50,000 award to be appropriate when you feel this is a million dollar case. Find out as quickly as possible which jurors are resistant to awarding the amount of money you think your case is worth. The following questions will help:

1) *Some people feel that it is not right to award a large money verdict. What do you think?*

2) *What would you feel about awarding $20 million dollars in this lawsuit? Why would you feel that way?*

3) *What verdict have you read about that you felt was too high? Why did you feel that way?*

After exploring how jurors feel about money awards, you should then proceed to questions about insurance or where states do not allow discussion of insurance, questions about claims.

§ 12.12 Civil Claims—The Insurance Question

The issue of insurance can come into play when asking questions about claims. Frequent questions are:

1) *What is your experience with insurance companies?*

2) *Have you or a family member or friend ever worked with claims in any way?*

3) *Some people believe that the rise in insurance premiums is a direct consequence of lawyers bringing lawsuits. Others believe premiums are increasing because insurance companies are greedy. What do you think?*

The plaintiff's right to an unbiased jury entitles her to discover whether any prospective juror has an interest in, or connection with, any insurance company. Similarly, the defendant is entitled to a jury verdict that is based on the merits of his case, rather than a jury's belief that the insurance company will ultimately pay any judgment. Simply stated, the problem is to discover whether potential jurors are biased because of a connection with the insurance industry without suggesting or revealing that the defendant is insured.[1]

Not all jurisdictions, however, permit *voir dire* questions about insurance. In a state that prohibits mention of the word *insurance,* a plaintiff's lawyer might ask about claims after asking about money damages to imply to the jurors that the claim will be covered by insurance. Another way to develop insurance as an issue in the case is to ask about a verdict that the jurors felt was out of line with what they knew about the facts?

1) *In what instances do you think it is appropriate to bring a lawsuit?*

2) *Who do you think is responsible for the large ad campaign against lawsuits? What do you think is their purpose?*

3) *Have you ever campaigned for tort reform?*

4) *Have your insurance premiums gone up or down since the promotion of tort reform? Why? Who do you think is responsible for this?*

Among the courts that have considered the impact of insurance advertising on jurors, a few have allowed attorneys to question poten-

§ 12.12

1. *See generally,* Annotation, Admissibility of evidence, and propriety and effect of questions, statements, comments, etc., tending to show that defendant in personal injury or death action carries liability insurance, 4 A.L.R. 761 (1949).

tial jurors about their overall attitudes, both favorable and unfavorable, toward the insurance industry. Most courts, however, are suspect of this line of questioning. As the issue gains prominence, it is likely that judges will demand a preliminary showing that such an inquiry is relevant.[2]

If you are a defense lawyer in a civil case, you might try asking the jurors if they would consider not awarding large sums of money, and follow up with the question "What kinds of things could happen to a company that is required to pay a large money judgment?" to leave the impression that people will be paying the claim as opposed to an insurance company. Other tactics to diffuse the issue of insurance in the case are to ask the jurors:

1) *Have you ever been called upon to pay for something that you felt you shouldn't have to pay for? How did you feel about that?*

2) *Have you ever felt that someone was trying to get something for nothing, or trying to get more than what he or she had a right to get from you? Please tell me about that.*

3) *Have you ever had someone try to bring a claim against you that you felt you shouldn't have to pay? What happened?*

As mentioned above, the courts at the federal and state level are divided on the question of whether a trial judge must allow *voir dire* questions relating to a prospective juror's association with the insurance industry. In some federal jurisdictions a trial judge must allow an attorney to obtain information regarding a prospective juror's insurance associations or prejudices, while in other jurisdictions this line of questioning is at the trial judge's discretion. In *Kiernan v. Van Schaik*[3], the court held that a plaintiff in an accident case may reasonably inquire whether prospective jurors "are or have been connected with the business of investigating or paying accident claims, either as employees, agents or stockholders of insurance companies or claims agencies without suggesting the existence of insurance in the case." The court stated that this rule was necessary to allow the plaintiff "to exercise intelligently his limited number of peremptory challenges and to determine whether ground exists for challenge for cause." The trial judge's refusal to ask submitted insurance-related questions was deemed prejudicial error. The *Kiernan* court also stated that the judge should adequately caution the jury that *voir dire* questions regarding a juror's connection with the insurance industry does "not imply either the defendant is insured or that the matter of

2. *See Fuller v. Johnson,* 301 Ark. 14, 781 S.W.2d 463, 466 (1989), where the court ruled that questions concerning the effect of jury verdicts on insurance premiums must be supported by proper foundation.

3. 347 F.2d 775, 782 (3d Cir.1965).

insurance or lack of insurance is to be considered in reaching a verdict."

The court in *Langley v. Turner's Express, Inc.*,[4] was not so permissive. The court rejected *Kiernan* and held that there was no prejudicial error where a trial judge refused to allow insurance-related questions during *voir dire.*[5] The court ruled at 297:

> *We must strike a balance between the probability of danger to plaintiffs that someone sympathetic to insurance companies may remain on the jury and the danger to defendant that the jury may award damages without fault if aware that there is insurance coverage to pay the verdict. We think the latter danger is greater than the former, and are not persuaded by Kiernan v. Van Schaik....*

Some commentators suggest that these courts reached contrary conclusions because of the circumstances of the cases. It may be that federal courts have reached contrary conclusions because in balancing the plaintiff's interest in an unbiased jury and the defendant's interest in obtaining a jury verdict uninfluenced by insurance considerations, they weighed these disparate interests differently. In those jurisdictions which adopt the *Kiernan* decision, there is no need for a court to apply a balancing test.

Hinkle v. Hampton[6] rejects *Kiernan* on more general grounds. It believed that the *Kiernan* decision had the effect of abolishing judicial discretion during *voir dire* questioning.

At the state level, rules governing *voir dire* questions about insurance interests vary greatly among jurisdictions. The majority of jurisdictions have adopted the rule that, "provided counsel acts in good faith, he may, in one form or another, question prospective jurors during the *voir dire* respecting their interest in, or connection with, liability insurance companies for the purpose of exercising peremptory or for cause challenges." Within those jurisdictions adopting the majority rule, however, individual courts have added their own directions to ensure that the interests of both the plaintiff and defendant are protected. For example, the New Mexico Supreme Court in *Canter v. Lowrey,*[7] stated:

> *We do wish to observe the practice which has developed in many jurisdictions of advising the trial court, in the absence of the jury, of the questions proposed to be asked, the purpose thereof, and making of a showing of good faith ....*[8]

4. 375 F.2d 296 (4th Cir.1967).
5. *Id.* at 298.
6. 388 F.2d 141, 144 (10th Cir.1968).
7. 69 N.M. 81, 364 P.2d 140, 143 (1961).
8. *Canter v. Lowrey, supra,* at p. 140.

Missouri allows insurance questions on *voir dire* but "the insurance question should be sandwiched between other general questions so as not to give it undue emphasis."[9] Maine requires "extraordinary special circumstances" before counsel may pose insurance questions to prospective jurors. In *Duguay v. Pomerleau,*[10] the court, citing from *Deschaine v. Deschaine,*[11] explained:

> *... in cases where the wealth or poverty of a party is not a proper issue in the case, references by counsel to these matters ... [is] improper.... The impropriety of mentioning insurance or the lack of it in such cases has its origin in that rule ....*[12]

Virtually all jurisdictions adopting the majority rule allow the trial court considerable discretion in prescribing the specific form of *voir dire* interrogation. In jurisdictions that require a good faith basis for insurance questions, it is largely at the judge's discretion to determine whether a good faith basis exists and to limit the extent of the questioning. The Nevada Supreme Court set "good faith" guidelines in *Silver State Disposal Co. v. Shelley:*[13]

> *By "good faith" we mean questioning for the purpose of ascertaining qualifications of prospective jurors and for ferreting out bias and prejudice, and not for the purpose of informing them that there is insurance in the case.*[14]

To ensure the good faith of a *voir dire* examination, some courts require attorneys to obtain prior approval of any insurance-related questions. Others insist that insurance-related questions be "couched" between other, less prejudicial questions and still others limit the right to ask insurance questions to the entire jury panel, but not to each juror individually. It is ultimately the trial court's responsibility to guarantee the good faith basis of counsel's questions. Evidence that an attorney's injection of insurance issues was in bad faith may constitute reversible error. In *Potter v. Trent,*[15] the court condemned artful *voir dire* questioning aimed primarily at informing the jury that a party had insurance. The *Potter* court reversed the judgment because counsel's questions were not a good faith attempt to expose juror bias. In *Commonwealth, Dept. of Highways v. Swift,*[16] the court held that even an admonishment of counsel did not remove the prejudicial effect of an opening statement telling the jury the amount of the commissioner's award. *Kenney v. Grice,*[17] however, citing an earlier ruling in *Johns v.*

9. *Vaeth v. Gegg,* 486 S.W.2d 625, 629 (Mo.1972).

10. 299 A.2d 914 (Me.1973).

11. 153 Me. 401, 140 A.2d 746 (1958).

12. *Duguay v. Pomerleau, supra,* at p. 914.

13. 105 Nev. 309, 774 P.2d 1044, 1047 (1989).

14. *Silver State Disposal v. Shelley, supra,* at p. 1044.

15. 262 S.W.2d 186, 187 (Ky.1953).

16. 375 S.W.2d 691, 693 (Ky.1964).

17. 171 Colo. 185, 465 P.2d 401 (1970).

Shinall,[18] found that information that the defendant had insurance, whether conveyed intentionally or inadvertently, should be handled by the trial court like any other inadmissible testimony; on motion it should be stricken and the jury told to disregard it.

In *Hunt v. Regents of University of Minnesota,*[19] the court went so far as to say that failure to permit any inquiry regarding potential jurors' connection with the insurance industry was an abuse of judicial discretion, but, given the fact that plaintiff was allowed to question jurors about their places of employment and that of their children and spouses, the court would not find grounds for reversal as a matter of law.

It is wise to research the findings in your jurisdiction but we would not discourage you to try to break new ground in this critical area of *voir dire* examination.

(*See also* Sections 16.17 and 16.18, *infra,* for discussion on how to handle "power brokers" on the panel with insurance and claims experience.)

§ 12.13 Civil Claims—A Civil Jury of Six or Twelve?

Effective December 1, 1991, Rule 48 of the Federal Rules of Civil Procedure was amended. The amendment reads:

> *The court shall seat a jury of not fewer than six and not more than twelve members and all jurors shall participate in the verdict unless excused from service by the court.... Unless the parties otherwise stipulate (1) the verdict shall be unanimous and (2) no verdict shall be taken from a jury reduced to fewer than six members.*

This amendment may have a major impact on litigation in civil cases. Prior to this change, civil juries consisted of twelve people unless the parties agreed to a reduced number. Furthermore, the verdict had to be unanimous unless the parties consented to a majority verdict. Under the old rule, a mistrial could be declared if one of the jurors got ill and there were no alternates. Many federal districts got around this problem by adopting local rules establishing six-person juries. Thus, the national pattern in civil cases was to have six-person juries.

Under the amendment, it is anticipated that civil juries will now be comprised of nine to twelve members, without designating jurors from alternates. Under this scheme, jurors may be excused for illness, hardship or impropriety without the threat of mistrial as a result of diminishing the jury to not less than the required six members.

18. 103 Colo. 381, 86 P.2d 605, 609 (1939).

19. 460 N.W.2d 28, 33–34 (Minn.1990).

Since the dynamic is decidedly different when the jury is twelve people instead of six, the parties and the court should establish, prior to jury selection, the number of jurors that will decide the case. With the larger jury, the collective IQ and the number of power brokers will substantially increase. Counsel must strategically evaluate who will control the jury deliberations, with whom must he communicate, and most importantly, whom must he strike from the panel to be assured the most favorable jury.

The critical question is: What should counsel do if twelve jurors are chosen and all twelve remain at the end of the trial? Should counsel remove some jurors or keep the entire panel, if the court offers that option? We generally prefer smart juries, collectively or individually. We would therefore recommend a larger jury. On the other hand, if counsel seeks a rapid verdict or is willing to entrust the verdict to one or two individuals, a smaller jury is advisable. Clearly, the implementation of amended Rule 48 will have a substantial impact on *voir dire* strategy in federal civil cases.

§ 12.14 Sensitive Issues—Generally

Once introductions have been made, backgrounds covered, and case-specific questions explored, you should then dive into sensitive issues. There should always be an introduction to each sensitive issue that makes it clear that some questions may or may not be considered sensitive or invasive to one or more of the jury panel. Continually emphasize during this part of the *voir dire* that any juror may discuss an answer in chambers or at the bench, if so desired. It is important to give the jurors the option to be open with you but not have to embarrass themselves in front of the rest of the panel.

Most cases include one or more sensitive issues, be it a misdemeanor or a corporate dispute. Sensitive issues worthy of exploration are:

- **Unwanted sexual contact**
  1. Rape
  2. Child molestation
  3. Date rape
  4. Fondling
  5. Incest
  6. Bad experience with a gynecologist
- **Racism**
  1. African American
  2. Hispanic
  3. Native American
  4. Asian

5. Middle Eastern

- **Religion**
- **Financial matters**
  1. Wealth
  2. Poverty
  3. Foreclosures
  4. Bankruptcies
  5. Denial of a loan
- **Sexual preference**
  1. Homosexuality
  2. Bi-sexuality
- **Contracts**
  1. Broken contract
  2. Had someone doubt your word
- **Injuries**
  1. Being accused of hurting someone on the job or otherwise
  2. Physical problem resulting from an injury that is embarrassing to discuss
- **Medical problems**
  1. Anorexia
  2. Bulimia
  3. Alcoholism
  4. Drug addiction
- **Mental problems**
  1. Psychiatric assistance
  2. Manic-depressive
  3. Schizophrenia
  4. Other mental problems
- **Domestic Issues**
  1. Contest of a will
  2. Violence in the home
  3. Problems with children
  4. Bad relationship with siblings or parents
  5. Nasty divorce

This is a partial list of sensitive areas, for which you could request individual sequestered *voir dire.* There may also be sensitive issues particular to your case. If required to question the jury panel *en masse,* tell the jurors, "I realize these matters are difficult to talk about in a big group of strangers. Please understand I must ask you these questions so we, you and I, can figure out whether or not this is the right case for you. I must make sure that (*first name of client*) gets a fair trial."

When introducing sensitive issues, if you yourself feel uncomfortable or embarrassed, then it is important for you to disclose that fact to the jurors. Saying that this topic makes you feel uncomfortable or nervous sends a clear signal to the panel that you find it acceptable for them to feel the same way. Sensitive issues require expressing highly personal opinions. Sometimes, when a sensitive issue is raised, jurors find themselves asked to call upon an experience that they have repressed for years, if not decades. It can evolve into an emotional or angry scene but it is a necessary exercise in *voir dire.*

If you detect that a juror is upset or otherwise uncomfortable, you should consciously acknowledge the juror's feeling and make every effort to comfort that person. If, for instance, you have given a juror an opportunity to speak privately about a sensitive topic and the juror declines, then becomes emotional during the answer, you might say softly to the juror, "If you want to stop or to talk privately with the judge, please know that it is okay." Such a demonstration of sensitivity on your part will be effective with that juror and will convey a sense of caring to the rest of the panel as well. Sensitive issues are not easy to discuss but the answers could hold the key to jury selection.

§ 12.15 Sensitive Issues—Law

As a general rule, people will not disagree with the law because, since the earliest days of their schooling they have been taught to follow the rules. Thus, when the judge instructs the jury as to what the law is regarding burden of proof or the necessary quantum of evidence, human instinct is to want to follow the law, even if the jurors do not understand it. Only those persons who have had a negative experience with the legal system or who are willing to question authority will honestly voice their objection to the law.

You should therefore cover legal issues last. Starting out your *voir dire* by talking about the law encourages people to say what they are told and not what they feel. This is a dangerous entry into jury selection since it does not foster an air of honesty or openness. You are suggesting to the jurors that they should not have any thoughts or feelings and should be silent when questioned on sensitive matters. Questioning jurors about such concepts as presumption of innocence and preponderance of evidence should be done at the end of jury selection so that jurors think through these issues only after they have explored their true thoughts and feelings about the specific issues of the case.

An additional benefit to discussing legalities last is that you have already established a rapport with the jury and if your definition of the law deviates from that of your opponent, the jury will be more inclined to believe you since you are the lawyer who cared enough to find out their thoughts and opinions on a variety of important topics.

One final note with respect to the law: You should include the law in your *voir dire* only in those circumstances where you are relying on a particular law. If you have to choose between a sensitive issue or a case-specific issue and how a juror feels on a legal issue, you should forgo the legal issue. Jurors do not measure verdicts by legal instructions; they use the instructions that they understand to justify the decision they have already made with their head or their heart. The law is a sword or shield only when the jury chooses to use it as such.

§ 12.16 Sensitive Issues—Closure

You should close your *voir dire* by thanking the jurors for their honesty in saying what they thought and felt during the questioning. You should ask them whether or not there is anything else, now that they have had time to think about it, that they would like to tell you about themselves or an experience they may have had. You might also want to inquire if there is a question that you should have asked that you did not. You might be surprised at some of the questions that jurors raise, and at their responses; both will likely have bearing on your final choice of jurors. Again thank them for their time and tell them that if later in the day something comes to mind that they feel that you should know, they should not hesitate to contact the bailiff or U.S. Marshal, or raise their hands so that information can get to the judge.

§ 12.17 Sharing *Voir Dire* With Co-counsel—Generally

When two lawyers are trying a case it is important that there be some division of the *voir dire* if at all possible, so that each lawyer will have a relationship with the jury. One of the hurdles to overcome is persuading the judge. First, however, you should confer with opposing counsel as well as the court reporter to make sure neither party has any objection. When presenting the request to the judge, you should explain that a split *voir dire* enables counsel to divide up the case by relevant issues and that for consistency it is critical, and more effective, if each lawyer is allowed to present the issue that he or she has prepared from beginning to end. It should also be made clear to the judge that only one lawyer will be doing the objecting and only one lawyer will be questioning jurors on a given topic. If the judge is inclined to grant your request, assure the judge that you do not see splitting the *voir dire* as an opportunity to make speeches or lectures or to repeat questions that have already been asked by co-counsel.

§ 12.18 Sharing *Voir Dire* With Co-counsel—Dividing the Panel by Alternating Jurors

Division of the *voir dire* is essential in any case, civil or criminal, and especially for a lengthy *voir dire.* The key to dividing the panel is devising a procedure that will be most helpful to counsel and most likely to be approved by the court.

One way is to divide the panel so that every other juror is questioned by one of the lawyers. This process works especially well with individually sequestered *voir dire,* as well as in a death penalty case where *voir dire* can last for many hours, if not many days or weeks. In this way, each lawyer can recover his or her balance from the taxing experience of questioning jurors and be fresh and ready for the next round.

§ 12.19 Sharing *Voir Dire* With Co-counsel—Division by Groups

Dividing the panel by groups is a practical solution. The courtroom can be dissected, leaving one lawyer to question the right side of the courtroom and the other, the left side.

§ 12.20 Sharing *Voir Dire* With Co-counsel—Division by Row

One effective technique for jury selection is dividing the panel by rows. State District Judge Pat Priest of San Antonio often has the lawyers question the jurors row by row. When using the method of alternating rows, counsel should reserve the right to go back to a prior row if new information has been injected into the *voir dire.*

§ 12.21 Sharing *Voir Dire* With Co-counsel—Division by Age

If one of the lawyers seems to have a better rapport with a particular age group, it may be advantageous in certain circumstances to divide the panel by age. Caution should be taken that the young good-looking male lawyer does not always interview the young female jurors. This can leave the impression with all the jurors that the lawyers believe they can win their case by seduction or manipulation. It is better to have the older lawyer or female co-counsel do the questioning rather than foster this misperception. On the other hand, some lawyers relate better than others to the elderly. They project warm, loving feelings for aging people that impress a jury panel.

Whether or not to divide the panel by age should also be considered in terms of the theory of the case and the principal contributors to the case. For example, in a criminal case, if co-counsel or any defendant is older and part of the defense deals with old-time values, it might make more sense for the older lawyer to *voir dire* jurors in his or her age group since those are the individuals he will be counting on to educate the other members of the panel. By the same token, if the defense is one of immaturity or lack of knowledge, then it may be wise to have the younger lawyer *voir dire* the older jurors, to reinforce the factor of youth.

§ 12.22 Sharing *Voir Dire* With Co-counsel—Division by Race

If you have a racially mixed legal team, you should avoid having the minority lawyer question all minority jurors. Instead, a healthy rapport with all members of the community should be established by each member of the team taking turns examining the jury panel.

Obviously, should one team member convey a lack of rapport with minority jurors, then this should be discussed and dealt with by the team before the damage is irreparable.

§ 12.23 Sharing *Voir Dire* With Co-counsel—Division by Sex

It is a false assumption that a female lawyer should examine the women jurors. Except perhaps on a sensitive matter like rape, this tack should be avoided at the risk of appearing patronizing. The questioning should be divided in a more intelligent way, by issue or section of the courtroom.

§ 12.24 Sharing *Voir Dire* With Co-counsel—Division by Occupation

You and co-counsel may be familiar with different occupations. You might have experience in construction, for example, and find that you feel comfortable relating to people who work with their hands. Likewise, your co-counsel may have studied engineering and find it easier to talk with jurors with a scientific background. Your husband being a teacher at the local high school may put you at ease questioning people in education, while your co-counsel, whose brother-in-law is out of work, may have better rapport with someone who is unemployed.

Lawyers are always trying to find things in common with jurors to make the questioning process more relaxed. Think through each juror's circumstances to decide who should question which juror.

§ 12.25 Sharing *Voir Dire* With Co-counsel—Division by Issue

If your case has a number of important issues, an easy way to divide the *voir dire* is by issue. Counsel should carefully confer on the ways to approach the key issues and then divide the *voir dire* according to which lawyer will be covering which issue during the trial. For example, if you will be cross-examining opposing counsel's expert, then you should probably ask the questions regarding expert witnesses. If you are going to be the lawyer questioning the client, then you may want to talk to the jury about the client's right to testify or not testify in a criminal case. It is wise to think through who will be handling which witnesses and what are the important case issues that will be revealed through these witnesses; then divide the issues accordingly.

§ 12.26 Sharing *Voir Dire* With Co-counsel—Division by Who Has More Energy

Voir dire is the most rewarding part of any trial because you accomplish the most. You build rapport, get information and help the jurors in their analysis of issues specific to the case. Notwithstanding, *voir dire* is a tiring and often anxiety-producing experience for the trial team. This can be lightened when lawyers divide the *voir dire* based on who has the most energy and who is on a roll with the jurors. If the jurors are answering the questions and information is flowing, the lawyer should stay on course and continue to elicit information. When that lawyer runs out of steam, co-counsel should take over. The transition should be made when it is clear that you are no longer eliciting the kind of information that you want; either you are not responding to the jury panel in the way that you think you should or the questioning has begun to drag. Again, when co-counsel loses energy, you should pick back up. You should see it as a piece of legal choreography where timing and inspiration are closely in tune. If you do not have the assistance of a jury and trial consultant, then the lawyer who is not questioning the panel should be taking careful notes. As a rule, the lawyer conducting *voir dire* should never take notes.

The problem with conducting *voir dire* when you are tired is that you may misperceive what a juror is saying or brush over an important statement. Do not hesitate to accept notes from co-counsel so as not to miss appropriate follow-up. Notes can easily be passed on Post-its™. The Post-it™ should be large enough so that a full question can be written in handwriting that is easily read by the lawyer conducting the *voir dire*. To cover any awkwardness, the lawyer should say to the jury panel,

> *My co-counsel may have some questions for you as well. He will either ask them directly or I will pass on his questions as I receive them. So, if you see me walk over to counsel table and pick up a note, you will know my co-counsel is helping to make sure that I ask good questions.*

§ 12.27 Getting the Total Picture

How do you go about getting to the bottom of an answer? The first answer rarely tells you everything you want to know about a juror. You must approach an issue from four or five different angles to get the total picture. You must find out what people have heard or think or feel about a particular event, the *happening.* You need to find out what they thought, their *perception,* when they read or heard about the event. You must find out what they felt, their *emotional response,* to their perception. And then you must learn what kind of *action* or *reaction* they had as a result. This is important because you may initially like someone's perception but when you hear what they feel or how they might have reacted, it may totally change your opinion. For example:

> The news media talks extensively about one large oil company suing another large oil company. This is the *happening.* The juror's perception is "that business will be business." His feeling is one of dismay, but he reacts in anger that the big company was putting the little company out of business.

You can see, if you are representing the big company, how stopping your examination at the answer "business will be business" could have led you to think that this juror would be good for your case. Once you delve further into the juror's feeling and reaction, however, you are left with a quite different perception. As another example:

> A major political figure is charged with child abuse. The story has been given big play in the newspapers. When asked her perception on reading the news coverage, the juror, who is a teacher, said she was shocked and astounded to read something like this about such an important person in the community. She *felt* uncomfortable, however, that these kinds of allegations were being made and reacted with a sense that she needed to be careful so as not to be falsely accused while teaching her classes.

Once again, had the questioning stopped at what the juror's perception was, the lawyer could have believed that the juror automatically presumed guilt. Delving into the juror's action or reaction revealed that the juror was identifying with the accused.

Still another example would be a self-defense case involving a barroom brawl where one person pulled a knife on another. You should explain the facts to the jurors and ask what they think about self-defense in such a situation. A juror may respond, "If someone pulled a knife on me, I would defend myself." You would then ask his perception of the people in that situation. The response could be, "If they weren't in that type of bar, this kind of thing wouldn't happen." When asked about his feelings, the juror could say, "This makes me angry." His reaction may be that bars where people are hurting each other need to be cleaned up. Because there is a discrepancy between what he thought about the situation and his perception, feeling and reaction, a lawyer must seriously think about this juror and the meaning behind the discrepancy. Follow-up may be necessary to figure out where this juror stands in relation to the case.

§ 12.28 Peeling the Onion

Feelings are layered in life. If people say they are angry about a situation and you probe deeper, you may find out that really they are scared. This is because anger is generally a reaction to fear or a sense of lack of control. Fear is often a reaction to a prior or perceived hurt or that which is unknown. It is important to get to the root of that hurt. For example, if you asked a juror what she thought about street gangs and she said, "they scare me," on asking why, you might find that she was attacked as a child and this makes her afraid some other innocent person could fall victim to gang violence.

In another instance, when asked, "Why do you feel angry about businesses that fire employees who claim a violation of their civil rights?" a juror might respond, "I was discriminated against on a job that I had and still carry the frustration of that experience."

These are just a few examples of how feelings can be a reaction to other feelings. It is important to continue to probe and "peel the onion" until you get down to the core.

§ 12.29 Following the Juror's Lead

You should follow a juror's lead whenever possible. This means that you listen to what the juror is interested in talking about and ask numerous follow-up questions in response. Most lawyers want to lead, even in *voir dire*. They are so busy being out front that they do not listen, which can cost them a good juror or an opportunity to educate the rest of the panel.

§ 12.30 Subtle Messages

Devise ways to convey subtle messages to the jury panel that you want them to receive. Think of how to ask questions that will get at jurors' thoughts and feelings about the case issues without asking outright. For example, if you want to know about negative experiences with doctors, one way to uncover bias is to ask what jurors have heard, read or experienced that gave them a less than favorable impression of the medical profession. If you need to explore jurors' associations with large corporations, ask what they feel about free enterprise or what big companies have done to help or hurt the local community.

§ 12.31 Hiding the Good Juror

Many lawyers feel that they can play what is called "hide the ball from your opponent." Sometimes this can work, but in many instances it backfires. The result is that the lawyers prematurely stop questioning a juror, only to find out in the post-trial interview that there were one or two questions they should have asked that would have told them this was not the favorable juror they thought. It is important to ask enough questions to enable you to understand who this juror truly is.

Once you have determined that this is a favorable juror and you are certain you are not using your own stereotypes to color your perception, then you should try hiding the juror from your opponent. There are a couple of ways to do this. One is to make sure that all jurors have given enough information about themselves that opposing counsel can become confused as to who is good and who is not. For example, in a contract dispute case, if you are the defendant claiming that breaking the contract was an appropriate thing to do, you might ask the jury panel,

> *How many of you have ever felt that if you could have, you would have broken a contract—you would have gotten out of a lease, stopped payment on a lemon car, or returned an appliance that wasn't working properly?*

In response to that kind of question there will probably be numerous jurors who say yes. You will then want to delve into each of the responses. What you will uncover are many more people potentially unfavorable to the plaintiff than what plaintiff's counsel once thought. The key is to think of questions in your particular case that could elicit enough responses to confuse the opponent about which jurors to strike.

Another way to hide the favorable jurors is to ask questions that would make them look negative for you, and thus confuse the opponent as to which side the jurors would be on. For example, in a drug case, if a juror's responses have left you with the opinion that overall this is an open, flexible and sensitive person, you may want to ask what he or she believes should be done to remedy the problem of drugs in our country. You can feign concern about the answer, leaving the impression with the other side that you no longer like this juror. Your non-verbal language can say as much as any verbal reply, but avoid being too much of a ham; you do not want to foul the play. A mere look of concern will often be all that is necessary. Remember also to listen to the answer; you could discover a clue that the juror is less favorable than you initially thought.

§ 12.32 Identifying Adversaries on the Jury

Case-specific questions are the path to adversarial jurors. Make sure that each juror is asked four or five case-specific questions so you can determine which jurors are not going to start out open-minded. These questions will help you determine who is open to you and your case and who is not. When you have uncovered the people with strong prejudices against you, you can then begin developing challenges for cause. (*See* Section 12.34, "Polluting the Panel—Challenges for Cause.")

§ 12.33 Polluting the Panel—Generally

There is always the risk, when asking case-specific questions, of what is called "polluting the panel." Many lawyers are hesitant to ask such open-ended questions or case-specific questions because they are afraid that if a juror gives an honest answer that is unfavorable, it will persuade the rest of the panel to think the same way. Research shows, however, that you cannot pollute a panel that is already tainted. If jurors have attitudes similar to the juror who speaks out, you would rather know that fact now than when the jury goes back to deliberate. (*See* Section 13.35, *infra,* for discussion on "reinforcing honesty, even if it hurts.") The point is that open-ended questions often yield bad answers *and* good answers. You must learn to deal with the bad answers and make the most of the good answers.

It is also our experience that by allowing potential jurors to express their true, though unfavorable, opinions about your client or key issues in your case, you create an opportunity for the jurors to release the venom they conceal. Venting those opinions often neutralizes the "poison," and gives the jurors space to be open to your client's view.

In ruling on juror statements made in the presence of the rest of the panel, courts have focused not on whether the juror who made the statement should be excused—in most cases he or she is excused—but on whether the rest of the panel has been tainted by hearing the statement. Questionable statements would concern possible bias of that juror, some form of outside or extraneous information, or an opinion of the defendant's guilt.

In *People v. Frantz* [1] a prospective juror repeatedly indicated that he could not be fair and impartial because of his past employment as a police officer and because of his association with defense counsel and with the officers who were expected to testify. The statements were heard by the other members of the panel. At the close of *voir dire,* defendant moved for a mistrial. The appellate court held that the denial of the motion was not error because the court had carefully questioned the other members of the venire about whether they could be fair and impartial and they responded that they could.

In *People v. Del Vecchio,*[2] a prospective juror stated on *voir dire* that she had read about and discussed the case and, based on what she had read, commented: "I think the guy shouldn't be out walking the streets." The judge excused the juror who made the statement, as well as other jurors who had heard or read about the case. He would not excuse the remaining jurors who had heard the statement but not otherwise heard about the case. Nor did the judge instruct the remaining jurors to disregard the statement. The Illinois Supreme Court held that there was no abuse of discretion. "We are unable to say that

§ 12.33

1. 150 Ill.App.3d 296, 103 Ill.Dec. 649, 654, 501 N.E.2d 966, 971 (1986).

2. 105 Ill.2d 414, 86 Ill.Dec. 461, 468, 475 N.E.2d 840, 847 (Ill.1985).

because of this single, isolated comment the jurors were unable to reach a verdict based solely on the evidence." [3]

In *Commonwealth v. Frazier,*[4] two jurors stated in the presence of the rest of the panel that they had formed an opinion that the defendant was guilty. Those jurors were immediately excused. The appellate court stated that it was not an abuse of discretion to deny a motion for mistrial because the judge thoroughly questioned all jurors as to whether they could be impartial and they responded that they could. The court also stated that there was no evidence that the comments prejudiced the defendant. "Not every unwise or irrelevant remark made in the presence of the jury compels a new trial. The comment must be of such a nature or made in such a manner as to deprive the defendant of a fair and impartial trial." [5]

In *Worton v. State,*[6] a prosecution for passing a worthless check with intent to defraud, a prospective juror stated that he might know the defendant because he may have given him a check. This juror was dismissed and the panel was instructed to disregard the statement. The appellate court found that the denial of a motion for mistrial was not error because of the judge's instructions.

The panel can also be "polluted" when prospective jurors discuss the case among themselves, but whether that constitutes juror misconduct is another question. At issue is the effect of what was said in the jury room.

In *Commonwealth v. Brantner,*[7] three prospective jurors indicated on *voir dire* that the case had been discussed by other members of the panel in the jury room. Defendant's motion for a mistrial was denied. The Pennsylvania Supreme Court rejected a per se rule that would mandate a mistrial whenever it is discovered that members of the jury panel have previously discussed the case. Instead, the court stated that the question is whether the jury selected will be fair and impartial. Therefore, there was no error in the denial of the motion for mistrial where the judge thoroughly questioned the jurors about whether they had formed an opinion of defendant's guilt or innocence based on what was said in the jury room and the jurors stated that they had not.

Case law supports excusing the jurors for cause who have prejudicial views. Do not be afraid of polluting the panel. They are already "polluted." They already have these opinions and biases, which need to be uncovered during jury selection so that you can save peremptory challenges when possible.

3. *Id.* at 847.

4. 269 Pa.Super. 527, 410 A.2d 826, 831 (1979).

5. 410 A.2d at 831, quoting *Commonwealth v. Whitman,* 252 Pa.Super. 66, 380 A.2d 1284 (1977).

6. 492 S.W.2d 519, 521 (Tex.Crim.App. 1973).

7. 486 Pa. 518, 406 A.2d 1011, 1014–1015 (1979).

(*See also* Section 12.40, "Making a Case Regarding Juror Misconduct," *infra*, for further discussion of court review of juror misconduct.)

§ 12.34 Polluting the Panel—Challenges for Cause

Developing cause challenges is a skill. You first need to get people to talk about their perceptions, thoughts, feelings and actions or reactions to a situation. This means that you must first develop what they think and feel in an open-ended manner and remain non-judgmental about the answers. Verbal and non-verbal responses—nodding and repeatedly saying "uh huh, uh huh" in response to what they are saying—should keep them talking. As they divulge information that you know may disqualify them, you can also say,

> *I am interested in what you have to say. Please tell me more. What else do you think about that? What are your reactions to that? What are your feelings about that? What does it make you want to do?*

You must continue in every way possible to encourage that juror to divulge more information that will establish bias. Nod your head, motion with your hands as if to say "please give me more," reach out your hand and pull it back towards your abdominal area—these are all non-verbal responses that can keep the juror talking.

Once the juror has given you the information, then you can switch to your closed-ended response, saying to the juror,

> *Earlier you told me* (repeat what the juror said). *This tells me that you may have some feelings on this subject, that you are skeptical about being able to be as fair in this case as you would like to be. Given all this, do you mind if I ask the judge to excuse you in this case?*

The juror may say yes or no; however, you should persist in pinning down a challenge for cause. To follow up, you might say respectfully,

> *While I believe you could be fair in every other case, your answers indicate that something in your background or life experience may cause you not to be as fair in this case as you'd like to be. Don't you agree with me?*

Wait for the juror to react or respond; gather all the information you can to convince the court of the grounds for your challenge.

One way to develop a challenge for cause is to suggest to the judge before *voir dire* that challenges for cause be handled at the conclusion of the *voir dire*. If you use this method, someone at the table should take careful notes of who needs to be challenged for cause and why, and the grounds established for the challenge. Again, you should make sure that the judge will give you time to go back and develop any further challenges for cause that he or she feels has not been properly developed during the questioning. Should the court not allow you to develop all your challenges for cause at the end of *voir dire,* you again need to remind the jurors that while they might be excellent for every other case being tried in the courthouse, they may not be right for this particular one. To that end, you may want to say to the juror in question,

> *Ms. Smith, given all you have told me, do you think you may want to ask the judge to excuse you from this case so that you may be able to serve on another one.*

This is a delicate way to handle a potentially disastrous situation.

Another way is to thank the juror for being so candid about her thoughts and feelings and assure her she is the epitome of a great juror because she has been so honest. You should hold in high esteem the jurors who say negative things as much as those that say positive things for your client. This will create an atmosphere of openness and jurors will believe they will be positively reinforced if they say exactly what they feel. Lawyers have been known to develop 75% to 100% more challenges for cause using this method. Once again, integrity and honesty win the day.

There is one particular factor that jurors dismiss as an influence, but experience shows can be a serious threat to an impartial jury. This is prior jury service. As a rule of thumb you should file a motion to disclose prior jury service in similar cases. (*See* Appendix 12A for a sample motion and memorandum in support.) Case law in several jurisdictions supports the presumption of bias from the fact of interim jury service but not necessarily from undergoing *voir dire* in a similar case or performing prior service. The Fifth Circuit has established the rule that when jurors who in the interim after their selection in one criminal case serve as jurors in a similar case that ends in conviction, the bias of those jurors in the second case will be inferred and the jurors may be challenged for cause. An example of a "similar case" is a case with the same witnesses for the prosecution. The four cases establishing the rule are: *United States v. Brown;*[1] *United States v. Mobley;*[2] *United States v. Jefferson;*[3] and *United States v. Mutchler.*[4] The Tenth Circuit has adopted a similar standard. Other jurisdictions have modified the standard to require that jurors be excused only upon a showing of *actual* bias or prejudice resulting from the interim service.[5]

§ 12.34

1. 699 F.2d 704, 707–708 (5th Cir.1983).
2. 656 F.2d 988, 989 (5th Cir.1981).
3. 569 F.2d 260, 262 (5th Cir.1978).
4. 559 F.2d 955, 959–960 (5th Cir.1977), modified 566 F.2d 1044 (5th Cir.1978).
5. *United States v. Dempsey,* 733 F.2d 392, 397 (6th Cir.1984), cert. denied 469 U.S. 983, 105 S.Ct. 389, 83 L.Ed.2d 323 (1984); *United States v. Carranza,* 583 F.2d 25, 28 (1st Cir.1978), and cases cited therein.

The presumption of bias is founded on the premise that, having convicted a defendant in one case, jurors preselected to serve on a second similar case will be unable to come to that second trial with an open mind. As stated by the *Brown* court:

> *Having passed upon the credibility of witnesses in a similar case, and having rendered a verdict on their oaths, it is improbable that these jurors can sit without their previous opinion and verdict influencing them. This is the "interim jury service" prohibited by these cases.*[6]

The cases make clear that the defendant does not have to keep track of each juror's record of service to assert an objection to interim service. The defendant need only object to the *possibility* that some jurors performed interim service. The objection must be made before testimony begins in order not to waive his right to object. The court is then obligated to conduct supplemental *voir dire* to determine if any juror did serve on a similar case in the interim.[7]

If the judge does not grant all your cause challenges by the close of *voir dire,* you may want to file a formal motion for renewed challenges for cause, stating the basis for challenging each juror and the transcript cite of the juror's prejudicial responses. (*See* Appendix 12B for a sample motion for renewed challenges for cause used in a death penalty case, but adaptable to any *voir dire.*)

§ 12.35 Weighing Workers Under Pressure—Generally

There is the option of having jurors excused for hardship. Sometimes you will want to encourage a juror to remain on the panel, despite the hardship it would create. Other times you will be glad that the juror has a viable way out. You should carefully examine the jurors under pressure to determine how well they can put aside their priorities and pay attention to your case. To obtain a tactical advantage in peremptory strikes, get opposing counsel to use a strike on a juror you would like to keep, rather than let that juror go for hardship.

§ 12.36 Weighing Workers Under Pressure—Shift Workers

People who work shifts are constantly having their biological clock rearranged. Should they have been on the night shift before going on jury duty, it will probably take several days, even a week, before their biological clock adjusts. This means that there will be a time when they will not be functioning on all eight cylinders and their attention span will be shorter than that of other jurors.

6. 699 F.2d at 708.

7. *United States v. Franklin,* 700 F.2d 1241, 1242 (10th Cir.1983) and *United States v. Capua,* 656 F.2d 1033, 1036 (5th Cir.1981).

If you have a shift worker on the panel whose answers to case-specific questions have left you uncomfortable, you may want to approach the bench and discuss this juror's potential sleep deprivation problem as a reason that he or she should be excused for hardship. The court will probably require that you interview the juror, which you should do in the following manner to maximize the chances for a challenge for cause:

1) *Ms. Smith, you told us that you do shift work and have recently been working nights. I am concerned that you may be somewhat sleepy the first few days of the trial. What do you think about my concern?*

2) *Mr. Jones, you look tired today and you told us you have been working the night shift. Don't you think that may make you feel a little sleepy and less attentive than what you would like to be if you were to serve on a jury? Tell me about that.*

§ 12.37 Weighing Workers Under Pressure—Work After Court or on Weekends

The juror who works after court or on weekends may also be eligible for a hardship excuse. If you feel that this work schedule could detract from the juror's attention to the trial and you are leery of the juror anyway, you will want to develop how the desire to continue working after court or on weekends during jury duty reflects a concern about risking the job, getting behind in work or losing some financial remuneration. On the other hand, should you like the juror and not want the other side to have this juror excused for cause, you will want to develop how the juror will likely be able to overcome the pressures of work. The following questions will assist with those jurors you want to have excused:

1) *Ms. Smith, you said that you will be working after court and on weekends during the course of this trial. I am concerned that this is because you are afraid that this may affect your job if you were to serve on this long jury. What do you feel about my concern?*

2) *Do you think it may be better, Ms. Smith, if we asked the court to excuse you from this case and allow you to sit on a shorter case when you won't feel so concerned about your employment? Tell me about that.*

The following questions will assist with those jurors you want to keep on the jury:

1) *Ms. Smith, I am sure that you take your responsibility quite heavily to assure that a cross-section of the community serves on this jury. I trust that despite the fact that you have*

business concerns, you will not let that distract you from your responsibility as a juror. Am I correct?

2) Many people have jobs that they feel they will have to keep up with during the course of this trial. I am sure that you will not allow your work to interfere with your duty as a juror. Please tell me how you will not allow it to interfere with your duty.

§ 12.38 Weighing Workers Under Pressure—Tax Season

Accountants, bookkeepers and support staff, among others in the tax field, go into a tailspin as tax season approaches. For many of them there is no way to get around the fact that their clients all have deadlines, and that they are responsible for getting the work in on time. Unless you truly like a juror, it is better to allow jurors in the tax field to seek a hardship excuse during tax season.

If, however, there is a juror in the tax field whom you consider to be the best or one of the best jurors on the panel, you will want to fight to retain that person, with the hope that at the very least you can make the other side use a peremptory challenge. The following questions will assist you with jurors under the pressure of tax season:

1) Mr. Jones, you seem to have a conflict between wanting to do your civic duty and your responsibilities at work. I know being at work right now is important to you, but aren't there other people who could help you out for the few days it will take to try this case? Some of the pressure would be lifted if you could call your office at breaks, over lunch, after court and on weekends so you would be available to serve as a juror.

2) Mr. Smith, I understand that you are under a lot of pressure right now due to tax season; however, other jurors also are under a lot of pressure. Isn't it true that despite the pressure you are under, you would be able to put that aside and do your duty as a juror?

§ 12.39 Weighing Workers Under Pressure—End of School Year

Teachers can be extremely good or extremely bad jurors, depending on your case and their philosophy of life. (*See* Section 16.12, *infra,* for an in-depth discussion of teachers as power brokers on the jury.) At the end of the school year, however, when teachers are faced with preparing tests, grading papers and evaluating projects, the pressure may be so great that jury duty would be a hardship. As with other professionals under pressure, you must decide whether to try to keep the teacher on the jury or allow the court to grant an excuse for hardship. Should you want to keep the teacher and risk the year-end distractions of the job, the following question will assist:

> *Ms. Smith, I understand that this is a tough time for you because it is the end of the school year. However many of the other jurors also have problems regarding their job and I am sure if called upon to serve on the jury, you can put your job aside and do your duty. What do you think?*

§ 12.40 Making a Case Regarding Juror Misconduct

Sometimes, no matter how they are encouraged to be open and honest, jurors do not tell the truth. The implications for the jury selection process are profound: If a juror does not answer *voir dire* questions honestly, counsel may not uncover information relevant to the juror's bias to establish the necessary grounds for a challenge for cause or intelligently exercise a peremptory challenge. Whether intentional or unintentional, the juror's failure to respond truthfully may constitute juror misconduct.

States have addressed this problem in different ways. Some of the pertinent considerations are:

1) What did the juror conceal?

2) When was the falsity discovered?

3) Was an alternate juror available?

4) Was the juror biased?

5) Did the party waive any objection?

In *People v. Diaz,*[1] a prospective juror concealed that she had been the victim of a crime substantially similar to that which the defendant was accused of committing. The record does not reflect whether this was intentional. The truth was discovered during the last day of a four-day trial. The juror stated that the incident would not affect her impartiality. Defense counsel moved to dismiss this juror but would not agree to proceed with eleven jurors. The trial court denied the defendant's motion to dismiss the juror. The appellate court held that it was error not to dismiss this juror: "A juror's misconduct is good cause which ... may permit the court to replace him or her with an alternate, or if there is no alternate, discharge the jury, impanel a new one, and retry the cause."[2] The court stated that because there was no alternate available, the entire jury should have been discharged and a new trial should have been granted.

The court also stated that where

§ 12.40

1. 152 Cal.App.3d 926, 200 Cal.Rptr. 77 (1984).

2. *Id.* at 82.

a prospective juror in a criminal case fails to respond to a relevant, direct and unambiguous question presented by defense counsel in voir dire, although having knowledge of the information sought to be elicited, the trial court should, upon motion for a new trial, determine whether the question was (1) relevant to the voir dire; (2) whether it was unambiguous; and (3) whether the juror had substantial knowledge of the information sought to be elicited. If the trial court's determination of these inquiries is in the affirmative, the court should then determine if prejudice to the defendant in selecting the jury reasonably could be inferred from the juror's failure to respond. If prejudice reasonably could be inferred, then a new trial should be ordered.[3]

The court went so far as to say that "a presumption of prejudice arises from any juror misconduct."

In *Petteway v. State*,[4] the court held that "[i]t is an abuse of discretion to refuse to grant an accused a new trial where a biased juror is selected without fault or lack of diligence by defense counsel." Here, the juror withheld information that he knew the defendant and was biased against him, that he knew of the events in issue, and that he had been a defendant in a criminal case. The court stated:

There are two categories of cases where the information withheld has been found to be material, thus requiring reversal: (1) where a juror withholds information that he had personal knowledge about or was in some way acquainted with either the complainant or the defendant; and (2) where a juror by reason of past personal experience had the potential to be biased or prejudiced.[5]

The court granted a new trial based on the juror's concealment of material facts which reflected on his impartiality.

In *State v. Tresvant*,[6] the court held that it was not error to replace a juror with an alternate after it was discovered that the juror had lied about whether she had been arrested numerous times. The court stated that if there was no alternate available, a mistrial would have been warranted.

In *Minnis v. Jackson*,[7] the court reversed the trial judge and granted a new trial on the issue of damages because the jury foreman falsely stated on *voir dire* that no member of his family had been injured in an accident. It was subsequently discovered that the foreman's daughter had been injured on a county bus the previous year.

3. *Id.* at 83, quoting *Odom v. State*, 355 So.2d 1381, 1383 (Miss.1978).

4. 758 S.W.2d 861, 865 (Tex.App.—Houston 1988).

5. *Id.*

6. 359 So.2d 524, 526 (Fla.App.1978), cert. denied 368 So.2d 1375 (Fla.1979).

7. 330 So.2d 847, 848 (Fla.App.1976).

This fact was critical because plaintiff Jackson was suing the county and the bus driver for injuries sustained while riding on a county bus. Although the foreman denied he had played an active role in the jury discussions leading to the verdict, post-trial interviews with the remaining jurors disclosed that the foreman had recommended the verdict be high enough to allow the plaintiff to pay her attorney.

In *People v. Borrelli,*[8] a new trial was ordered after it was discovered that a juror had lied about whether she was a patient of a psychiatrist. A year after the trial, information was obtained that the juror had been treated by a psychiatrist for a serious personality disorder for the last eight years.

(*See* Appendix 12C for an evidentiary summary and memorandum of law in support of a motion for a new trial that may be used as a guide if jury misconduct becomes an issue in your case.)

A new trial has not been a remedy where the court found that the juror's misstatement was not intentional or the juror was seated by an omission of counsel. Whether the defendant would suffer any prejudice as a result of the juror's service may be, but is not always, a deciding factor. You should be alert to cover all questions with all jurors, so that there are no surprise connections, and when information is uncovered about a juror that may prejudice your case—no matter at what point in trial—you should register your objection on the record and move for a mistrial. Experience shows that failure to promptly point out a juror's misstatements can forever lose your client's claim to a fair jury.

In *Decker v. State,*[9] a prospective juror responded on *voir dire* that he did not know the complainant. After being selected, empaneled and sworn, however, he acknowledged at a hearing prior to trial that he "recognized" the complainant as a co-worker. He testified that he knew nothing about the case and his acquaintance with the complainant would not affect his duties as a juror. His false answer during *voir dire* was found unintentional and counsel's objection and motion for mistrial summarily overruled. In objecting, counsel stated that he did not believe the juror's acquaintance warranted a challenge for cause but, if known, would have been reason to strike the juror peremptorily. The appellate court found that the defendant was entitled to a new trial, but, on rehearing, the court reversed its finding. The crucial question for the court was whether the misstatement on *voir dire* was intentional. Since it was not, the court found that the defendant failed to show that he suffered any prejudice as a result of this juror's inclusion on the panel and was not entitled to a new trial.[10]

8. 624 P.2d 900, 903 (Colo.App.1980).

9. 717 S.W.2d 903, 904–905 (Tex.Crim. App.1983).

10. *Decker v. State* at 907–908.

In *People v. Childers,*[11] one of the jurors told the trial judge on the second full day of trial that he was an auxiliary policeman. No questions regarding any connection to law enforcement had been posed to him during *voir dire* and he did not volunteer the information. The judge had an extensive discussion with the juror and, as the principal question at trial was the defendant's sanity, determined that the juror was not biased. Defendant's motion to dismiss that juror and replace him with an alternate was denied. In affirming the denial, the appellate court stated that "[d]efendant here has failed to demonstrate any prejudice, especially since no false answers were involved."

In *Cisneros v. State,*[12] one of the jurors failed to reveal that he was a first cousin of two state witnesses. The truth was discovered by the defendants sometime during the trial but they made no motion for mistrial at any time nor objected in any way. The court held that the failure to object or to move for a mistrial when the defendants learned that a juror had possibly made false statements during *voir dire* waived the issue.

In *Dueitt v. State,*[13] it was discovered by the defendant on the second day of trial that one of the jurors knew the defendant and may have known of his attempted escape. The court again held that defense counsel's failure to bring this matter promptly and timely to the attention of the trial judge prior to deliberations waived the issue after announcement of the verdict.

(*See also* Section 12.33, *supra,* "Polluting the Panel," for further examples of juror misconduct reviewed by the courts.)

§ 12.41 How to Make Biased Jurors Better Jurors

The mere process of asking questions in an open-ended manner and truly listening to the jurors' responses can convert unfavorable jurors to positive, helpful forces on the panel. In revealing their thoughts and emotions, many jurors become self-aware in a way that they had never been before. It is your job to help them hear what they truly think and feel so that they can open up in ways that they may not have been open. For example, in a case where there will be testimony from an informant and a juror has already stated his approval of informants in order to catch criminals, it is appropriate to ask how the juror would feel if someone he considers to be a friend or loved one had made up things about him. How would that make him feel about himself and about that other person?

11. 94 Ill.App.3d 104, 49 Ill.Dec. 939, 945, 418 N.E.2d 959, 965 (1981), cert. denied 455 U.S. 947, 102 S.Ct. 1448, 71 L.Ed.2d 661 (1982), rehearing denied 456 U.S. 939, 102 S.Ct. 1998, 72 L.Ed.2d 460 (1982).

12. 747 S.W.2d 946, 947–949 (Tex. App.—San Antonio 1988).

13. 491 So.2d 1258, 1259 (Fla.App.1986).

In a case involving a wealthy client, you may want to talk about your own feelings of jealousy toward people who have more than you and ask the jurors to talk about instances of feeling envious of someone who had something that they did not have. You may get an answer that "rich people can buy their way out of anything and hire the best lawyers." You can, however, turn the question around by asking if any jurors have ever been in a situation where someone was envious of them and how did they feel about that.

You must always look for ways to open up the jurors' minds. There is always a way to get the jurors to think about the subject matter in a different light. At the same time you must avoid trying to brainwash a juror by asking a series of leading questions or by giving a lecture. This may make the lawyer feel powerful but makes the juror resentful. The lawyer's job is to ask questions that capture the jurors' imagination and make them explore parts of themselves that they have never seen before, to own up to who they are. The most useful information emerges when the juror reaches the same conclusion as the lawyer.

§ 12.42 Having Jurors Take Notes or Not Take Notes—Generally

If the judge has indicated that this is a case where he is considering allowing the jurors to take notes, request that either the judge ask some questions or preferably, that you be able to ask some questions in this regard. It is important to find out what the jurors think about the idea of taking notes and who on the jury will become the power brokers as a result. (*See* Chapter 16, "Power Brokers and Followers," for information on how to identify and cultivate people who can influence the jury deliberations.)

You should note which jurors are anxious or hesitant about the prospect. This could indicate which jurors will be taking a lot of notes and which will not. You might want to ask why they think it would be a good idea or a bad idea to take notes, and whether or not they think it may interfere with their ability to listen to what a witness is saying. In the process, you may learn something more about which jurors would be positive for your case. There are things you can tell about jurors from their stand on taking notes; for instance, whether they are more oriented toward written or oral evidence. Willingness to take notes may say something about their overall interest or commitment to being a juror.

§ 12.43 Having Jurors Take Notes or Not Take Notes—Beware the Note Takers and Speed Writers

Post-trial interviews show that people who take the best notes tend to have a very powerful position on the jury. For that reason alone, you want to identify the people who tend to take a lot of notes because of their current job or a job they held in the past. You should thoroughly probe the jurors' experience, or if the court will be conducting the *voir dire,* request that the judge carefully question whether or not the jurors take notes in their line of work or have ever been responsible for note taking at a job or in a club.

You also want to find the fast writers. They are usually proud to let you know. You or the judge should query each juror whether he or she is a fast writer or a slow writer. If you are doing the questioning, of course you can ask this question in a more probing, thorough way. A very important question is whether or not any juror has ever taken shorthand or any speed-writing course. Ask if there are any club secretaries on the panel. They are comfortable taking notes and will often volunteer their skills in the jury room or leave the impression that their notes are more reliable. This once again gives them an edge with other jurors and should be weighed along with all the other information on that juror. This may in fact influence your thoughts on a juror you considered to be more of a follower. The mere fact that the judge allows notes to be taken may transform that follower into a leader on your jury.

§ 12.44 Having Jurors Take Notes or Not Take Notes—The Pros and Cons of Note Taking

If you have a very technical case, you may see a benefit in jurors taking notes on charts and other technical evidence. You will want to weigh this benefit against the particular jurors you have identified as note takers during jury selection. It may be wise to request that the judge reserve his decision about whether or not the jurors will be able to take notes until after the jury selection has been concluded. This way you can determine how many strong note takers you have and how many opposing counsel has, and make your arguments based on whom you would like to see taking notes or whom you would not.

Once it is decided that the jury may take notes, be alert for opportunities to offer some guidance on important points. On direct or cross-examination you can say to the jury, "This may be something you may want to particularly note," and gesture toward their pad and pencil.

The problem with note taking is that many jurors get more caught up in the sound of their pens on paper than in what the witness is actually saying. They miss the nuances of the testimony and the body language that gives new meaning to the words. It is an obvious problem when a juror bypasses pertinent information while busily trying to remember what was said earlier in the testimony. The juror goes back to the jury room and deliberates from notes based on fragments of information rather than the whole presentation of the witness.

One consideration is that jurors may take copious notes at the beginning of a trial and taper off as the case comes to a close. If you are the plaintiff, this could be helpful but if you are a defendant, it could be dangerous. Of course, there are just as many examples where jurors continue to take notes conscientiously throughout the trial. Whether to argue for or against note taking is ultimately a judgment call best made on a case-by-case basis.

Chapter 13
RELATING TO JURORS

Table of Sections

§ 13.1 Overview

Jury selection not only involves the mechanics of a good *voir dire*—what questions to ask and when to ask them—but also the dynamics between the people asking and answering the questions. Both lawyer and juror enter the courtroom with a hesitation, if not a fear, of being human that hinders communicating with each other and defeats the object of jury selection—disclosure. Discovering who a juror is requires meeting halfway and relating person-to-person.

§ 13.2 Names, Not Numbers

Many lawyers overlook the importance of making an effort to call jurors by name, rather than the impersonal "Juror # 1" or the clumsy "Juror in the second row, third seat from the left." It is easy to keep track of juror names by making a chart in the order in which the jurors are seated in the courtroom. If *voir dire* begins before you have time to make a complete chart, it is imperative that you get co-counsel or an assistant to do so for you and hand you the chart as soon as it is completed.

It is worth emphasizing that this chart should be used simply as a reference point for interviewing the jurors, not as another ploy for taking notes. Your attention should stay on the jurors. You do not want to break the flow of communication. As we continue to advocate, you should have someone assisting you during jury selection to write down juror responses so that you do not lose contact with the jurors.

Should you mispronounce a name or misplace a juror in your seating chart, apologize for having mis-spoken the name and tell the juror you will do better. One of the authors, Robert Hirschhorn, when he mispronounces a juror's name, generally makes the comment, "With a name like Hirschhorn, I should know better." Some people are quite sensitive about their names being mispronounced; others find it humorous. If you have an unusual-sounding name or even if you do not, you may want to use yourself as the object of levity to lighten the moment.

Lawyers may also take courses in memory that teach mnemonics and other association techniques. For instance, a lawyer can remember a juror's last name by something about the person: The juror's name is Bloomstein and she is wearing a blue dress. If you have the kind of mind that can use memory games, you may develop your own techniques or take a memory course that will assist you in quickly memorizing names.

In the end, the important point is to make an effort to call jurors by their names, as one more way to show your interest in them as individuals. They do not expect you to be perfect and remember everyone's name. The eye contact you make, the close attention you pay to what they have to say, and how you express verbally and non-verbally that they are the most important people in the courtroom is what matters. Remembering their names is the final touch.

§ 13.3 The Three E's—Generally

Jury selection has three purposes: self-educating the panel, eliciting information and establishing rapport.

§ 13.4 The Three E's—Self-Educating the Panel

From the moment that jurors are subpoenaed into the courtroom, they become a peer group, though they may come from a variety of backgrounds and socio-economic levels. This means that they value what each other has to say, over and above what a lawyer has to say. Remember, you are the advocate and the panel expects you to argue your case, whereas if a disinterested juror makes your point, other jurors are more apt to listen. Of course, jurors can educate each other for better or for worse.

Self-education is in essence the process of jurors defusing the hard issues in your case and persuading their peer group to your side. The collective wisdom is thinking of a pool of jurors as a congregation or constituency. By that we mean the group may look to one or two essential figures as the leader, but within the group dynamic, individuals will learn and form their opinions from each other.

For example, assume in a criminal case that the essential defense theory is self-defense. Counsel can stand up and explain the concept of self-defense, can elaborate on the anticipated court's charge on self-defense or even belligerently tell the jury that if they find the accused was acting in self-defense, they should acquit. Such a technique provides absolutely no information about how the jurors view the critical issue of self-defense. To be more effective, to be more persuasive and to be able to intelligently exercise peremptory and cause challenges, counsel should handle the issue of self-defense along the following lines:

(Addressing juror # 1) "Have you, a family member or close friend ever felt threatened?" If the answer is yes, the follow-up is: "Would you mind sharing that experience with us? If it is too personal, I know the judge will allow us to talk in private." If the answer is no, the next question is: "Have you ever heard of a situation where a person was acting in self-defense?" If the juror answers yes, again ask the juror to share the example. If the juror says no, you should follow with, "What does self-defense mean to you?"

After the juror answers, ask the juror to relate a situation where he or she might act in self-defense. Then ask the juror to describe some situations where she would defend herself to the point of using deadly force.

Once the juror answers one or more of those questions, you have laid out the theory of the case for the panel to consider. What is important is that it was not done in your words but by one of the members of the panel. After the juror has given you satisfactory answers, move on to find out the next juror's view of the first juror's answers by asking juror # 2 directly what he or she thought of juror # 1's answers, or by asking juror # 2 the same questions as juror # 1. This achieves self-education.

§ 13.5 The Three E's—Eliciting Information

The next important ingredient in relating to jurors is to get the jurors to give you as much information as possible about themselves. Information-gathering is the cornerstone of effective jury selection. If you are getting jurors to talk about themselves as opposed to you doing the talking, the judge is more apt to allow you to continue with your *voir dire.* To get information you must do all the things discussed earlier with regard to conducting an effective interview. (*See* Chapter 2, "Client Interview.")

Jurors will never "self-educate" unless you create an atmosphere that encourages them to speak openly. Eliciting information in a courtroom can often be difficult, if not extremely limiting. This has nothing to do with the jurors; the fault lies with the lawyers. In almost every instance, lawyers unintentionally shut the jury down either by the type of question they have asked, the language and the lawyer words they have used or worse yet, by their verbal or non-verbal response to a juror who has been brave enough to speak. To elicit information you must be willing to ask solid concrete questions and be willing to accept the answer, be it good or bad. Think of jury selection as a conversation with a loved one, a potential employee or even a client, where it is essential for you to receive honest and accurate information. Saying that you will accept the answer, no matter what, will make the juror more willing to respond freely, even in the courtroom.

The authors were hired in a civil case after the first trial resulted in a mistrial. Upon review of the case, we requested to see the defense lawyer's *voir dire.* The entire two-hour *voir dire* consisted of the lawyer asking a total of fifteen questions. Each question was at least fifty words long, contained numerous lawyer words and was confusing. It came as no surprise when the transcript read "no response by the jury."

A typical wordy question is: "Does everyone agree that the plaintiff should have the burden of proof and therefore must present the preponderance of evidence in order to win this case?" This is obviously a compound question with a number of legal terms, which makes it easy to answer no because the juror does not understand the question. The question should be broken down and asked in lay language in order to get a thoughtful response.

Another way to get no response is to ask jurors if they can consider awarding 50 million dollars. No one will speak up, whether out of fear of public speaking, misunderstanding of "punitive damages," or because it is easier to say no when asked that kind of closed-ended question. It is better to ask each juror questions such as:

1) *What is the purpose of punitive damages?*

2) *Why do you agree or disagree that the purpose of punitive damages is to punish a company?*

3) *Under what circumstances would you award punitive damages or under what circumstances would you not award punitive damages in the amount of, say, 30 million dollars?*

These open-ended questions will elicit information and indirectly get the jurors to educate one another about the importance of holding corporations responsible. Giving lectures and then asking wordy, compound and oblique questions will never help counsel pick a good jury or win cases.

§ 13.6 The Three E's—Establishing Rapport

The third E in effective *voir dire* is establishing rapport with the jury panel. When people like other people they want to please them. In the trial context, this means if you win the juror's acceptance, you are more apt to win your case. To establish good rapport, you need good interview skills. It means you must practice being sensitive and being yourself. It means that you must listen effectively. It means you must observe what is going on around you so that you can appropriately respond, rather than try to make a juror think like you think. You can never convince someone to think like you. You can only listen to what they have to say and feel and how they perceive a situation, and decide how that fits into your case scenario and whether or not they are appropriate jurors for your case.

Establishing rapport with jurors should be the easiest part of jury selection but lawyers often make it the hardest. If you acknowledge to the jury that you have thoughts, feelings and fears just like they do, you will begin to break down the socio-economic and educational barriers that exist between you. If the jury sees you as one of them they will want to be cooperative and helpful. If, on the other hand, they feel that you are demeaning, condescending or egotistical, they have no reason to want to assist you. Building a rapport can be as simple as admitting to the jurors in the beginning that you are feeling a little nervous and that you always feel this way when you start jury selection. This simple disclosure can put jurors at ease because they, too, feel nervous. Through the process of disclosing your own feelings and vulnerabilities and encouraging jurors to do the same, you can in many instances transform a biased juror into a much more open minded one.

In the process of building rapport, be aware that there may be some jurors who either have had a bad experience with a lawyer or simply do not like lawyers. These jurors will never be helpful to you, no matter how hard you try to build a rapport. Many lawyers will ignore this juror or, worse, get into a verbal brawl with the juror. This is not an advisable tactic since you invariably look like a bully. A better approach is simply to say to the juror, "Have I done or said something that angered or upset you?" Again, the juror may not help you, but the other jurors will see that you are genuinely trying to establish a rapport with this juror, that you have done nothing wrong and that in all likelihood the problem lies with the juror and not the lawyer. The other benefit to this approach is that it enhances your position with the rest of the panel, which obviously is to your and your client's benefit when it comes down to a verdict.

§ 13.7 Humanizing Yourself and Your Client—Generally

Being one of the crowd can be a very appealing way to humanize yourself and your client. This, once again, requires that both of you are real and show a real interest in the jurors. It means you must express your feelings and weave in situations from your life and your client's life that identify with the jurors' experience. Create a sense of commonality. You do not want to wind up mimicking the panel; however, occasionally making contact with a juror when it is an authentic contact can make a big difference. If your client has been in the military, for instance, and there is a military person on the jury panel, saying that your client served in Saudi Arabia or Vietnam or Korea or World War II cannot hurt. If you are talking to a mother of three and you are a parent, mentioning your own child can make a connection that will open the lines of communication and hopefully sow seeds of compassion for your client.

§ 13.8 Humanizing Yourself and Your Client—Personalizing a Corporation

You will also want to think of ways to humanize the corporation you are representing if you are a corporate lawyer. This can be done by asking questions about the CEO or other people who are the movers and shakers in the corporation. Ask jurors if they have ever known anyone who was the head of a corporation. If they say yes, ask what they thought about the person, and what the corporate executive said about his job. Ask what is similar about running a corporation and the juror's job. These questions will help jurors relate to the corporate executive.

You should have at least one respected corporate representative whom you can periodically stand behind with your hand on his or her shoulder when referring to the corporation in *voir dire.* You should promote the image of an upstanding corporate citizen and remind the jurors of the good things the corporation has done in the community, such as charitable donations, blood drives and civic sponsorships. Ask the jurors whether or not they have read anything about these contributions or participated at any level. Caution should be taken not to over-dramatize these philanthropic efforts. If the corporation is a manufacturer, you should ask the jurors what their experiences have been with that company's products.

At the earliest possible time in the trial, put into evidence documents that illustrate something positive about your client, the more personal, the better to humanize a corporate entity. You should identify the kinds of documents that will interest the jurors you think are leaders. For example, awards the corporation has received could be entered into evidence to show its interest in the community. This tactic is equally effective when representing individual clients.

If you find it hard to humanize or personalize a large corporation such as Exxon or a person charged with capital murder, we are confident that a jury will find it easy to award large sums of money against Exxon or convict and sentence your client to death.

§ 13.9 Humanizing Yourself and Your Client—Interacting With Your Client

Remember that you are always center stage in the courtroom. One thing jurors will be watching is how you relate to your client. They will notice whether you seem to like your client or not; whether you pay attention to your client or ignore him or her. Many lawyers spend a lot of time showing the jury that they do not identify with their client. This can create a negative reaction. If you do not seem to like your client, jurors will rightfully question how can you expect them to.

This means you should interact with your client. Sit next to him or her, and ask for input, especially during jury selection. The client should have a pad and a pen in hand to take notes and write down ideas, and should make a point of facing the jury with interest and concern. You and your staff should touch the client on the shoulder in conversation and make him or her an obvious part of the legal team. This should not be overdone.

In a criminal case it can be helpful to have your client take an active part in the trial. Some lawyers have had their client give part of the opening statement or participate in *voir dire.*

In military court the accused can assist and ask questions. This can do more to humanize your client than any five days of testimony. In the right case with the right client you should consider this approach. Involving the client in the process will not only make him or her easier to work with during trial, but it will create an opportunity for the client to "converse" with the jurors and show that he is a human being held in high regard.

In a Hell's Angel case, when polled as to why they found the defendant not guilty, the jurors responded that it was clear that the client was well regarded by the lawyer and his staff and that since they liked the lawyer and his staff, the accused Hell's Angel must have some redeeming qualities. This was enough to give them a reason to doubt the government's case. Needless to say, a tremendous stereotype was overcome by client identification, leaving the jury panel with positive feelings, not only about the defense team, but about the person they were defending.

One caveat: If a juror questionnaire was distributed prior to trial, your client should not look at the questionnaire in front of the panel. In post-trial interviews, jurors have said they resented the client being allowed to see where they lived and were made to feel uncomfortable and fearful as a result. Jurors want their privacy respected and do not appreciate the client having access to personal data they gave in trust. Only you should look at the questionnaires during *voir dire.* This is a good rule of thumb in both civil and criminal cases.

§ 13.10 Breaking Down the Barriers—Generally

Barriers between lawyers and jurors are numerous. Negative publicity and public sentiment have created an atmosphere that makes it acceptable to "lawyer bash." Some obstacles that must be overcome are the social distance between lawyers and jurors; lawyer language; physical barriers in the courtroom and dress.

§ 13.11 Breaking Down the Barriers—Social Distance

The fact that you went to law school, and most of your jurors did not, creates a huge social distance. You should, therefore, find common ground so that you can discuss things that matter. Generally, the feeling aspects of your case are what you have in common with your jury panel, and should be emphasized in *voir dire.* If, for instance, your client does something in good faith, ask the jurors what it means to do something "in good faith." This is a concept that you and your client have in common with the jury panel. If your client did something out of fear, then you should ask the jurors about fear because this is a feeling they will all understand. Exploring the feeling tones of your case will help break down the social barriers.

§ 13.12 Breaking Down the Barriers—Lawyer Language

Avoiding "legalese" will do more to decrease the social barriers than almost anything else. The following is a partial list of lawyer words that you should avoid in jury selection and throughout the case. They do nothing but inhibit open discussion between you and the jury panel members and cloud understanding of the issues.

1) Credibility
2) Subsequent
3) Disposition
4) Deposition
5) Alibi
6) Allegations
7) Preponderance of evidence
8) *Voir dire*
9) Subordinate
10) Subpoena
11) Fraudulent
12) Compounded
13) Estoppel
14) Collateral
15) Quid Pro Quo

§ 13.13 Breaking Down the Barriers—Physical Barriers

You should not conduct *voir dire* behind a podium. If you are in a jurisdiction where a judge requires you to question jurors from a podium, file a motion in opposition and request a hearing. Talk to the judge about how you feel trapped behind the podium and how it inhibits your ability to relate to the panel. The fact is that the podium reminds jurors of school teachers who make them feel stupid or preachers who talk down to them or other people who have all the marbles in their circle. You should come from behind counsel table whenever possible and talk to the jurors with nothing separating you. The less between you and the jurors, the more apt they are to see you as an open person willing to meet them on their own ground.

§ 13.14 Breaking Down the Barriers—Dress

Casual clothing is more appropriate during *voir dire* because you are trying to project an open image that will encourage jurors to speak openly. A male attorney should wear a sport jacket and slacks of neutral color and comfortable material. A female attorney should wear a dress or a blouse and skirt. The exception would be when *voir dire* will be done on the same day as the opening statement. You should then sport your finery. Otherwise, save those three-piece suits for the days when you want to cut an authoritative figure, when you are cross-examining the other side's expert or client. How a lawyer dresses should be dictated by the situation, not by tradition.

A certain segment of legal eagles feel, "If I am a professional, I must dress the part." They wear a three-piece suit or their finest attire during all parts of the case to convey that they are in charge. It is important always to dress professionally; however, during *voir dire* dressing more like the jurors will minimize the distance between you.

If you insist on pin-stripes or three-piece suits during jury selection, our suggestion would be that you simply say to the jury, "Some lawyers like to dress in slacks and a jacket during voir dire and others like myself are more comfortable wearing a suit." The benefit of this is that you have minimized the barrier by explaining one of the most obvious differences between yourself and the jurors.

You will want your client to dress in a way that is socially acceptable to the rest of the people in the courtroom. During the cooler seasons he could wear a sweater over a shirt and tie. In warmer weather he could substitute a sport jacket. If you are representing a corporation, the corporate representatives should dress in a suit and tie. In instances where your client is a working man, you may want him to wear a nice shirt with slacks. Think about what will make your client most acceptable to the jurors during jury selection.

If your client is wealthy, advise your client to dress tastefully and conservatively and not wear flashy or expensive clothing or jewelry. During a fairly lengthy trial, the client should wear only a few suits and a few sport jackets. You do not want the jury to judge your clients by their wardrobe.

For female clients or female witnesses, it is imperative that they not wear anything that is too short, too tight, too bright or too flashy.

§ 13.15 Winning the Jurors' Acceptance

You must always work at winning the jurors' acceptance. This begins with feeling acceptable to yourself. If you have some kind of physical condition that concerns you and makes you feel uncomfortable in groups, you should seek out professional assistance to deal with the problem or its underlying cause. Most problems attorneys have are stress-related and can be remedied by learning some kind of relaxation technique.

Once you have your ego in check and a good sense of yourself, you are ready to engage the jury panel. The jurors will like you all the more if you are real. This means you, with all of your flaws, inconsistencies and eccentricities. Make them aware that you know you are not perfect.

Lawyers may also be imperfect in the jurors' eyes by choice. They may have long hair, a ponytail, a beard or wear bow ties—physical traits that are neither fashionable nor socially acceptable in the mainstream community where they practice. In that situation, lawyers have been known to deliberately call attention to their difference. One lawyer defending American Indian Movement activists charged in connection with the 1973 occupation of Wounded Knee asked, during *voir dire,* what the jurors thought of long hair and if his having long hair would in any way color the jurors' view of his clients. Acknowledging that there is an issue which could stand in the way of communicating with the jurors is often the first step to eliminating the issue.

§ 13.16 Self-Disclosure—Generally

You should be as open with jurors as you would be with your client. Disclose your human side. Talk to the jurors about your true feelings. Tell them when you are nervous, sad, happy, distracted or have other thoughts and feelings. This will enable them to feel comfortable doing the same with you. When you express on the outside what you are feeling inside, you become an integrated human being. This *congruence*—expressing on the outside what you are feeling inside—makes you more respectable, believable and approachable. The more real you are and the more approachable you become, the more the jurors are apt to accept you and listen to you.

It is also a common reaction that the more human a person becomes, the more people want to help them. Being vulnerable does not mean that you become less than powerful. This is simply a false fear. It is okay for a lawyer to be vulnerable before the jury panel. This is a true sign of power—not to be afraid to disclose who you are.

§ 13.17 Self-Disclosure—Admitting Fears

One thing we all have in common is that we are afraid of something, even the most self-contained and self-controlled of us. If you can admit your fears and tell the jurors what concerns you, it makes you more like them. You should tell them, for example, that you fear that they will have thoughts and feelings about issues and will not feel that it is okay to express them. Or, that they may have had a relevant life experience that is embarrassing and to avoid drawing attention to themselves, they will not raise their hand and say, "Judge, can we talk about this in chambers?" Tell them you are afraid of not being able to communicate as well as you would like so that they can understand your client's perspective. Acknowledge that lawyers are not very well liked in our society and you are afraid that this may in some way impact on your client. You are limited on this topic only by your imagination. The main point is that it is okay to talk about fears because it makes you more like the jurors and once again reduces the social distance.

§ 13.18 Self-Disclosure—Admitting Mistakes

What is our natural inclination when we make a mistake? Many people try to gloss it over and pretend it did not happen. Others may simply try to correct it without alluding to the fact that a mistake has been made. Still others will feel embarrassed or lose their train of thought. While all these reactions are predictable, they are not the most effective with the jury. When your children or staff make a mistake, you expect them to acknowledge their error. To be consistent, you should expect the jury to hold you to a similar standard. Admitting the mistakes you make during *voir dire* makes you genuine in the jurors' eyes and more like the people who will be judging your client. Moreover, the ability to laugh at one's mistakes can win valuable allies in the courtroom.

§ 13.19 Self-Disclosure—Admitting Bias and Prejudice

Admit your biases to the jury to make them more comfortable in admitting theirs. If you have been burglarized, for example, you may want to say to the jurors that you would be a good juror in every kind of case except a burglary case because of your particular experience. Similarly, if a family member has been involved in an automobile accident, you may want to say that you could not be fair in that kind of personal injury case.

Can we realistically expect the jurors to admit bias and prejudice if we do not set an example and "cop" to our own? Since no one wants to admit to having such feelings, it is preferable not to use words such as *bias* and *prejudice*. Instead, you should refer to feelings and thoughts that are the result of our life experiences. John Davis, a trial lawyer in Houston, Texas, refers to this as a person's "attitude and latitude" and describes jury selection as "the process of determining the latitude of your attitude." Such a catchy description really does summarize the concept of bias and prejudice. By setting the example and illustrating the latitude of your attitude, jurors are then primed to share their own experiences.

§ 13.20 Empathy

You should empathize with what the jurors think and feel in the same way you would empathize with your client. Empathy does not mean sympathy, but it does mean that you try to walk a mile in the jurors' moccasins. You may not know what it feels like to drive a truck for an oil company, but you can talk to the jurors about what it feels like to work long hours. You may not know what it feels like to have a child die in an automobile accident, but you can talk with the jurors about what it feels like to have a great loss. You may not know what it feels like to have a friend of yours assaulted, but you can talk about what it would feel like to have someone frighten or injure a loved one.

The goal is to express empathy with the jurors' life experience. Though you may not have actually had that particular experience, you can communicate to the juror that you understand what it feels like to have been there. The common ground once again are the emotions of the situation.

§ 13.21 Respect

Respect is the underpinning of the better part of humanity. If you show people respect, they will feel more inclined to do what you want them to do. In jury selection, respect will bring you more thorough and honest answers.

You show respect for your jury panel both verbally and non-verbally. This can be done by conveying to your panel that you hear what they are saying and respect their point of view and want to hear more. This is done by open body language, by tone of voice, by not turning your back to a juror when he or she is answering a question. It is done by making direct eye contact and nodding your head as the juror answers your question. Your entire body, voice intonation and choice of words should convey to the jurors that "you mean something to me, you are important to me and I respect you."

§ 13.22 Courtesy

Courtesy is another important key to acceptance. You must apologize when it is appropriate to apologize to a juror or to the judge; yet you must stand your ground to be a good advocate. You should always project a strong image. At the same time it is important not to browbeat a juror simply because you do not like what he says or how she looks. You can legitimately confront a juror without being combative, merely by saying, "I heard you say earlier (*repeat the juror's words*). This concerns me, what did you mean?" Remember, like anyone else seeking approval, jurors are more apt to accept a person who is not on a pedestal.

If you have hurt a juror's feelings in the process, you should express your honest concern that you have done so. It is okay in the courtroom to admit that you have done something inappropriate. This will make you ten feet tall in the eyes of the other jurors, not to mention the person you have affronted.

§ 13.23 Warmth

Being warm can make a big difference in someone's willingness to give you information. Many lawyers feel that they leave their heart behind when they walk into a courtroom. This is simply ludicrous. Trials are nothing more than heart brought to life. The more warmth you show toward your client, the more apt you are to win. You must be careful not to appear manipulative, however. The warmth should be a genuine expression of the human being that you are. It is your job to disprove the impression that lawyers do not have warmth and do not have hearts.

§ 13.24 *Voir Dire* on Opinions of Lawyers—Generally

Some lawyers would like to think that lawsuits are about their clients and the events that transpired. In reality, the lawsuit is about the lawyers and how they portray what happened and who was wronged. Jurors will often make up their mind on the basis of which lawyer they trust and which version they believe. The role of the lawyer, therefore, is not a conveyor, but a player. By that we mean the jury will be looking at the lawyer as closely as they will the facts and witnesses and invariably form opinions, in some instances strong opinions, about the lawyers themselves. Your *voir dire* should anticipate this scrutiny and open the door to the issues you will raise by virtue of your role as a lawyer and by your personal appearance.

§ 13.25 *Voir Dire* on Opinions of Lawyers—Facial Hair

Facial hair is tolerable on male attorneys depending on how it is kept and the type of case they are trying. For example, if counsel is representing a motorcycle gang, his wearing a beard might make the accused more acceptable. As a general rule, however, people believe that beards, especially unkempt beards, are a signal that the lawyer has something to hide. Unique mustaches might be distracting to a jury in a short trial and that may be just the result the lawyer desires. However, since our general philosophy is that we seek smart jurors, a temporary distraction can be just that and the ultimate wisdom of the jury may well result in a bad verdict for counsel. We would recommend that counsel consider the potential effect of a beard or a mustache and at the very least keep it neat and trimmed.

If you decide to shave your beard prior to trial, make sure you do so far enough in advance that your skin has a chance to tan evenly. If you are inclined not to remove or trim your beard, then we would strongly recommend some self-disclosure during *voir dire.* Ask a question along these lines: "Some people like a man with a beard and others think that a man who wears a beard has something to hide. What do you think?" Another way to deal with this would be for the lawyer to say to the jury: "I have had a beard for years. I know that some people like men with beards and some don't. I could have shaved my beard, but that would have been dishonest to myself and to you. Instead, I chose to keep my beard and I want to know how you feel about men with beards?" Counsel could also ask the jury whether or not they have a close family member or friend that had a beard, how would they feel if a loved one had a beard and why do they think it is that some people dislike people with beards.

The benefit to the discussion is that it is a natural lead into more sensitive issues like racism. People with beards are often unduly labeled; looking at labeling for what it is can easily open the way for probing into racial prejudice.

§ 13.26 *Voir Dire* on Opinions of Lawyers—Weight

Whether we admit it or not, our society has a prejudice against people who are overweight. With all the money that people spend on dieting and health, it is not surprising that portly people are frowned upon by large segments of our society. If the lawyer, or for that matter the client or key witnesses, have a problem with weight, this issue must be dealt with during *voir dire.* This is especially true when the lawyer is in a jurisdiction where he can approach the jury box during either *voir dire,* opening statement, witness examination or closing argument.

If the lawyer is large, whether male or female, it may be advisable to address the issue head on. Ask whether or not the jurors know anyone with a weight problem, and if so, to tell you about that person. Counsel should also inquire into whether or not the jurors or anyone the jurors know have ever had a bad experience with someone who was large, or whether they have witnessed a situation where a large person was discriminated against at a job or for a date or in some other circumstance. The point of this exercise is twofold. First, to acknowledge that you are a large person and you are aware there is a social stigma against being overweight. Second, by self-disclosing and showing the sensitive side of the issue, you are again encouraging the jurors to disclose personal matters about themselves or their life that would be important in jury selection.

§ 13.27 *Voir Dire* on Opinions of Lawyers—Hair

Your hair style is an excellent avenue for self-disclosure. For example, a male attorney who wears his hair longer can say to jurors, "Some people have distinct thoughts and opinions about men who have long hair. What are yours? I have heard almost everything imaginable so I'd be curious what you think about men with long hair." You might also want to ask the jurors if your long hair will in any way affect the jurors' attitude toward your client. At the same time, if your client has refused to cut his hair, you can ask jurors, while standing behind your client, "What do you think about my client because he chooses to wear his hair long?"

If you are a man who has lost his hair earlier than what you would have liked, then you can use this as a chance to interject some humor with the jury. You can say, "Some people, including my wife, have thoughts and feelings about bald people. What are yours? Don't worry, I have heard every joke imaginable, so just tell me what your thoughts are about people who are bald."

If you are a woman who chooses to wear her hair long, you can discuss this with the jury. You can say, "I'd like to know what you think about women with long hair. My mother always tells me I should get it cut; however, I find it easier to manage when it is long. I can put it up or put it in a ponytail or wear it in a braid. What do you think about long hair?"

If you have red hair you can say, "Some people have opinions about people with red hair. What are yours?" Or if you are a woman with blonde hair you can say, "Some people have opinions about blonds. What are yours?"

Hair is a springboard into issues of prejudice. You can point out, for example, the stereotype that blonds are dumb or redheads have fiery tempers as just another form of prejudice. That can lead you into a discussion of race or sex discrimination. Pick out a juror and say, "Ms. Smith, what were some of the things that happened to you as a young kid growing up. For example, what were some of the derogatory remarks that people said to you regarding your red hair?" You should always mention that the juror's hair is attractive.

You can also use hair to introduce the issue of misidentification. You might ask jurors if hair length or hair style is one of the first things that they notice about someone. This is especially educational if a witness in the case has identified someone with hair that is different from your client's.

§ 13.28 *Voir Dire* on Opinions of Lawyers—Race

If you are a minority lawyer, then it is always appropriate to *voir dire* on your race. Some lawyers hesitate about this because they feel it may create a new barrier. We believe that people already have feelings about race and it is more important to try to expose them during *voir dire* rather than get the bad news in the post-trial interviews. You may broach the topic by saying, "I realize that I am an African American lawyer and that people have different opinions about race, so it is important for me to ask you what kind of experiences you have had with African American people." (The same line of inquiry can obviously be used for Hispanic, Native American, Asian or other minorities.) You will also want to ask what kind of experiences, if any, they have had with African American lawyers and how they would feel about having a minority lawyer represent them. Urge the jurors to be honest with you. If they had their choice between hiring a white lawyer or an African American lawyer, whom would they choose? And why?

§ 13.29 *Voir Dire* on Opinions of Lawyers—Sex

Even in this day and age people have feelings about women being lawyers. Though this particular prejudice has declined, it still exists in some parts of the country and in the minds of some jurors. Therefore, it should be explored during *voir dire.* As a female lawyer, you should ask jurors what they think about women going to law school and representing clients. Ask if they had their choice between hiring a man or a woman, whom would they hire and why. (*See* Section 15.3, "Jurors' Perceptions of Female Lawyers" and Section 15.4, "Female Lawyer to Female Juror", *infra,* for further discussion of how to handle the "gender gap" in jury selection.)

§ 13.30 *Voir Dire* on Opinions of Lawyers—Hard of Hearing

Some lawyers have a hearing loss and hesitate to discuss this with jurors during *voir dire.* The lawyer may wind up yelling at the jurors and leave the jurors thinking that the lawyer is a jerk rather than hearing impaired. Admit the hearing problem and explain that sometimes it causes you to speak louder than you should. Like your family members, who often say to you, "Hey dad, stop yelling," they should feel free to say to you, "Hey Mr. Jones, you're yelling," and you will soften your voice. This will endear you to the jurors rather than irritate them, and ease the way for them to make what might otherwise be an embarrassing admission.

Experience has taught that this is a more critical issue than appears on the surface. It was not until the post-trial interviews that lawyers on the 1980 prison riot defense team in Santa Fe, New Mexico learned that one juror who sat on two different cases was hard of hearing. When asked what was the significant evidence that led him to acquit in the first case and convict in the second, the juror replied, "I don't know. I couldn't hear the evidence." Though not hearing the evidence may work in your favor, it is not a risk you want to take.

To pursue the issue further, you may want to ask the jurors if they or any family member have ever suffered a hearing loss and how that has affected them, if at all.

§ 13.31 *Voir Dire* on Opinions of Lawyers—Speech Impediments

People have many kinds of speech impediments. If you stutter or slur your words or have some other speech problem, you should ask the jurors how that may affect them in listening to you during trial. Ask the jurors to please be honest. Explain that you have lived with this all your life and that you have done your best to get assistance, but it is something that you have to work with on a daily basis to overcome. Again this is a way to humanize yourself. It can become your best asset rather than a disadvantage.

It can also open discussion about how people sometimes stutter or slur their speech when they are nervous or scared. This can help jurors to identify with your client, should your client stutter or mumble during trial. Self-disclosure here again can be a way to defuse what could be an otherwise damaging factor in your trial.

§ 13.32 *Voir Dire* on Opinions of Lawyers—Accents

America is teeming with a myriad of prejudices, including prejudice against people with different regional accents. For example, if you are a southern lawyer practicing in a northeastern community, you may find yourself the object of prejudice because of your drawl. You can ask jurors what they think about how people from Mississippi talk. You can ask them how many people from the South they have known and what they have thought about their accents. You can also insert humor here by saying that when you go to visit your relatives in the South, they think that you speak with a northeastern accent now. Humor at this juncture may be the best entree into the sometimes delicate situation of getting jurors to talk about their regional prejudices.

The concern here is that if you are an out-of-town lawyer, jurors will side with the local counsel simply because of your accent. You might talk about the hometown advantage and how that may or may not affect each juror. Another issue may be that you have lived in that community or in that state for a number of years but still have your native accent. You should make it clear to the jurors that you are proud to be a member of their community or citizen of their state; you just have not lost all of your accent.

§ 13.33 *Voir Dire* on Opinions of Lawyers—Speed of Speech

Some lawyers are criticized for speaking slowly; others get criticism for speaking too rapidly. If you know you have a tendency to speak at a slow pace, say to the jury panel, "I understand that I speak slowly. That's just how I speak. How do you think that may affect you?" If you tend to speak rapidly, tell the jurors that you understand that sometimes when you become involved in a matter close to your heart, you speak rapidly. The jurors should know that it is okay for them to raise their hand and tell you to slow down the same way your family does, because you want them to understand and follow everything you are trying to communicate.

§ 13.34 Do Not Deny Jurors' Feelings

If jurors say they feel a certain way about a situation, it is not your role to tell them that they should not feel that way. You should respect their perspective, and be empathetic and warm. For example, when jurors express their nervousness, you should say, in turn, "I understand you feel nervous and we're going to get through this together because I also feel nervous." If jurors say they feel stupid about these kind of things, do not say you shouldn't feel stupid. Rather, you should say, "Tell me what makes you feel that way. I am interested."

Denying feelings has never done anything but put a bandage over what people truly feel. A lot of times lawyers hear things from jurors that they would prefer not to hear. It is easier to deny the feelings and move on to the next juror. The courageous lawyer will listen to what the juror says, encourage the juror to express more about that subject and then follow up on what the juror says in response.

§ 13.35 Reinforce Honesty, Even if It Hurts

Many times jurors will say things in the courtroom that you wished that they had not said. They may say that your client is guilty or that your client did something that they feel was wrong or deceptive. Merely thank the jurors for their honesty and tell them to continue talking about that. The more honest the jurors are and the more reinforced they are for their honesty, the more apt you are to get people excused for cause. You not only have to stand strong and take the blows, as it were, but continue to encourage jurors to divulge more and more information, no matter how painful. After one adverse remark, you may want to say, "Who else agrees with this juror?" Then ask who disagrees with this juror, and who falls in between. The more information you have the more intelligent choice of jurors you will make. It is very important to keep the ball rolling. You can keep the ball rolling only by reinforcing honest responses.

§ 13.36 'Get the Lawyer' Game

Any lawyer who has tried a few cases will tell you that when *voir dire* becomes either personal or lengthy, there will generally be at least one juror who plays the "get the lawyer" game. This is the juror who tries to make the lawyer look like a jerk in front of the rest of the panel. The juror will try to attack you or criticize your questioning process. The normal instinct is to ignore this juror and reserve a peremptory challenge, and not draw attention to criticism of your *voir dire.* This is not only the coward's approach to the situation, but it signals to the rest of the jury panel that you really do not want to hear what they have to say, that all your encouragement to be open and honest are empty words.

You need to address the juror's difficulty with your *voir dire* in an honest manner. This is easily done by saying to the juror, "Mr. Jones, it seems that I am doing something to make you feel uncomfortable during *voir dire.* Please tell me what it is." You should be prepared for, and accept, what he has to say and encourage him to tell you more. You need to tell the jurors that they are the most important people in your client's life and that if you are making one of them uncomfortable, this does not help your client.

Through this process you have done several things: You have told the juror that it is okay to be honest and have kept your pact with the jurors that every answer is acceptable. You have signaled to the rest of the jurors that you are a stand-up person and you will accept whatever any juror has to say to you. You have also defused the agitator and made yourself a bigger person. Additionally, you have signaled to this person that you really are accepting their thoughts and opinions. In many instances this juror may realize that this is not appropriate behavior and will accept your explanation as to why you are asking all these probing questions. Even if the juror does not understand your process, you will generally find that the rest of the panel appreciates your honesty and courage. In many trials throughout the United States, when lawyers have employed this method, they have turned a potentially bad situation into a very fruitful one.

§ 13.37 Concreteness

If you explain to the jury panel where you are going with the questioning, they are more apt to go along. This means you should prepare the jury to move from one subject to another with a topic sentence such as, "I am now going to ask you some questions about," and then tell them what you are going ask them about and the reason for asking. This is especially important in sensitive areas like child molestation, drugs, contract breaches, foreclosures, money matters, wrongful death, divorce, battering relationships or anything that you deem could be sensitive to one or several of the panel members. Explaining to the jurors why you must ask these sensitive questions will make them willing to answer. This is called *concreteness,* because you are being clear about what you want them to answer and the reasons why.

§ 13.38 Beware of Liking a Juror, but Not Being Objective

Lawyers make the mistake of liking a juror based on how he or she looks or things a juror has in common, thinking a juror likes them or being reminded of a good juror in the past. Though having a warm feeling about a juror can be a helpful indicator, it should not cloud your objectivity. Many times lawyers will like a juror and therefore not ask the necessary questions to find out who the juror really is. This is another reason for having assistance in selecting a jury, to be sure your objectivity remains in tact and you do not make a choice you should have made otherwise.

§ 13.39 The Pros and Cons of Promises

Will all of you promise that if the state does not prove each and every element beyond a reasonable doubt that you will find the defendant not guilty?

Juror Smith, will you give me your word that you will set aside any bias or prejudice you may have and decide the case solely on the evidence and testimony presented?

Extracting such promises is not an effective tactic for *voir dire.* Many lawyers used to believe that soliciting a promise from individual jurors or the jury panel as a whole creates a bond. In reality, nothing can be farther from the truth. First, we must remember the adage that "promises were meant to be broken." Second, extracting a promise does not assist the lawyer in obtaining sufficient information on how the jurors feel about the particular topic at hand. Third, some jurors may accede to the promise only to keep the lawyer from asking them any meaningful questions. Fourth, and most obvious, a person who intends to get on the jury for whatever reason knows he must make that promise.

Breaking promises is a part of our daily lives. Promises are broken by our spouses, our children, our peers and employees. Why should *voir dire* be any different? Even the simplest promise may be broken by the jurors. For example, the promise to maintain an open mind or the promise not to make a decision until all the facts are presented is inconsistent with human nature. It is impossible to sustain an open mind when a person has a predisposed opinion and it is equally unlikely that a person will not formulate some opinion, if only an initial opinion, until all the facts are in. Therefore, we strongly suggest that counsel not extract promises from the jurors. Cases are won and lost on the basis of how counsel relates to the jury, prepares and presents the case. Jurors' decisions are never based on a promise that they made in jury selection.

There are certain exceptions. It is okay to solicit certain promises from the jurors: 1) to give honest answers, no matter how harsh they may be; 2) to share their thoughts and feelings, even if they know the lawyer will not agree with them; and 3) if the lawyer does anything that angers, upsets or disturbs a juror, to share that information with the lawyer. These promises foster an environment of honesty and encourage the jurors' truthfulness, in contrast to the traditional request for a promise that inhibits truthful answers, is often perceived as condescending and renders little or no aid in the intelligent use of cause challenges and peremptory strikes.

Just as we generally reject the notion of soliciting promises from the jurors, we strongly recommend that counsel make certain promises to the jurors. The promises should be meaningful and not hollow. By that we mean you can use the promise as one of the sub-themes in your case and give the jury something to be looking for throughout the trial. Once the promise has been kept, the jurors' belief in counsel, and thus in his or her client, is reinforced and there is good reason for the jury to want to side with you.

We must caution you that the promise must not be subject to interpretation. If opposing counsel can argue that you made a promise and can give the jury a plausible theory for why that promise was broken, you have lost a valuable tool. Thus, if you promise that you will present evidence that shows the actual cause of the rear-end collision is inconsistent with the theory advanced by opposing counsel, you must deliver on that promise or else the jury could well reject you and your case.

Nor is it beneficial if you promise the jury that throughout the trial you will be seeking the truth, and then try to exclude evidence in the presence and hearing of the jury. If your motion in limine is denied in the middle of trial and some damaging evidence comes in that you had not dealt with during *voir dire,* you must either take it apart and show that it has no value or you must be honest with the jury and tell them that the evidence is damaging but not irreparable. If you make a promise to the jury, make it clear, convincing, unequivocal and not subject to interpretation.

§ 13.40 Taking Care of the Jurors' Needs

It is your job to take care of the jury at all times. The jurors feel that they are the forgotten people in the courtroom. Showing sensitivity to their needs will work to your benefit. During *voir dire* and again once the jury has been chosen, you should ask the judge if the jurors can have a glass of water if they so desire. Even if the judge says no, you look like a person concerned about others. You should also never drink water at the podium or at the counsel table unless water has been provided for the jurors. Chicago lawyer Tom Decker tells about a bailiff who overheard one juror say to other jurors about the lawyer who was drinking water while they had none, "What does he think we are—a bunch of dogs over here."

When the *voir dire* or case presentation has gone on for more than an hour and a half, you may rest assured that there is at least one juror who needs to use the restroom. You should make it clear during *voir dire* that if any juror needs to use the restroom at any time, all he or she need do is raise a hand and get the judge's permission. This is important because many people have bladder problems and they cannot pay attention if they are thinking about their personal discomfort.

Taking care of the jury also means recognizing that people have very short attention spans. Jurors often tire out because the terms are so technical and the arena is so unfamiliar. It is your job to note when you see a tired juror and say, "Judge, I think it might be appropriate for us to take a break and for everyone to stand up and stretch for a moment." Even if the judge says no, once again you have set yourself up as the concerned party in the courtroom.

Often, despite their pledges to the contrary, jurors can become distracted by concerns about work and family they have left behind. The concern may be merely an economic one—how to make up for lost wages or how to pay for child care. In one Georgia death penalty case, counsel anticipated jurors' inattention, if not excusal for hardship, because of these real, day-to-day problems and filed a motion to compensate wage earners at current wages and reimburse caregivers for day care costs. (*See* Appendix 13A for the sample motion.) A motion with similar intent, requesting a questionnaire for jurors facing potential economic hardship, was filed in a California death penalty case to support a subsequent motion for augmented juror fees. (*See* Appendix 13B.)

You should always be a jury-centered lawyer and keep the jurors in mind. Some lawyers might find this burdensome, but they are the same lawyers who do not understand why they get bad verdicts.

Chapter 14

VOICE INFLECTION/BODY LANGUAGE/NON-VERBAL COMMUNICATION

Table of Sections

§ 14.1 Overview

It is a psychological fact that people's non-verbal language tells us more about them than what they say verbally. Often, when you do not believe what someone is saying, it is because his non-verbal communication is giving him away. Body posture, facial expression, voice intonation or eye contact are telling you that the person means something different from what his words are saying. To that end, you must carefully observe jurors at a multitude of levels in order to get a true picture of what they are trying to say.

The following is a representative list of non-verbal juror traits that you should be noting during *voir dire* and having your jury and trial consultant observe throughout the trial. Keep in mind that these are signals only, and that you should not make an assumption about a juror until all the information is in. Contrast any trait with all other non-verbal and verbal indications of who the person is.

§ 14.2 Talks to Fill Silence

Many people, when they are nervous, talk to fill the silence. They are afraid that unless they keep talking they will appear stupid or unprepared. Lawyers tend to be some of the worst culprits in this regard, but some jurors also have this problem. When someone tends to talk a lot, you should evaluate whether this is a sign of shyness or leadership. Often it indicates insecurity as opposed to having a sense of one's self. Some people talk to fill the silence because they want to give the impression that they know more than they actually do. They believe that people think smart people talk a lot. In truth, more intelligent people tend to listen before they speak.

Watch for jurors who seem to have an awful lot to say about a subject and ramble rather than answer succinctly. Explore a range of topics with them to see if they respond differently. It is also helpful to have spotters during the breaks to observe how these jurors act in other situations, whether or not they communicate the same way with other people.

§ 14.3 Slow to Talk

Some people are hesitant or slow to talk. This can mean a variety of things: 1) the person is extremely intelligent and wants to think through the question or idea before commenting; 2) the person is introverted and tends to go inside, consider all the options and then express an opinion or feeling; 3) the person is insecure and afraid to speak; 4) the person is trying to hide something. Once again observe how the person acts in other situations or explore a variety of topics with the person before concluding why there is a hesitance to answer.

§ 14.4 Pace of Speech

Listen for how people pace their speech. If they speak with a slow deliberate cadence, this tells you that they are thinking through their answer. This can mean, among other things, that they do not want to make a mistake, they are trying to camouflage what they truly think, or they are hesitant by nature. If they speak rapidly, this can be their way of dealing with nervousness, an attempt to change the subject, a reflection of their natural aggressiveness or assertiveness, or something else altogether.

If people begin talking in one rhythm and then slow down or speed up, this can indicate that they are trying either to gloss over some information or to suppress or repress something that could be very important to your case. This should be your signal to follow up and say to the juror, "Let's go back to what we were just talking about because I felt that there was something else that you wanted to tell me." Any change in a juror's demeanor could mean that there is some information that you need to dig deeper to uncover in order to understand what the juror really thinks and feels.

§ 14.5 Stutters

As discussed in the prior chapter, stutterers feel extremely uncomfortable talking in big groups. You should be sensitive to the stutterers' feelings and allow them to speak at their own pace. Remember, they have probably had this problem all of their lives and this is not the first situation in which they have had to deal with it. Your inclination may be to finish their sentences for them, but you will make them more uncomfortable and maybe even resentful toward you if you try to put words in their mouth.

Do not cut this juror short. His speech impediment may have taught him the valuable lesson of taking time to listen and hear what is being said.

§ 14.6 Intonation

You should observe if people are soft-spoken or very loud. This can tell you a lot about how people see themselves in the world. Do they find that in a soft tone of voice they can make their point, or do they feel that they have to raise their voice to be heard?

You or your consultant should also take note of any subtle change in the pitch of a person's voice. If a juror suddenly lowers his voice, this may mean that there is something he either wants to hide or is uncomfortable discussing. It can also mean that the person has been talking for a long time and is losing his voice. Again you should say to the juror, "Let's back up and let me ask you some more questions about that area."

If the juror has been talking in a steady monotone, then raises her voice in answer to a particular question, this can indicate feelings of either a conscious or subconscious nature. You should follow up what the person is saying to you by asking, "What else would you like to tell me about that subject, Ms. Smith?"

A lack of affect may indicate someone who is either naturally subdued or on some kind of medication. You should pay attention to this to determine whether or not this is the kind of person that you want on your jury. It may be appropriate, if the affect is very flat, to approach the bench and request that the judge privately ask if the juror is taking any kind of medication. Hopefully, the juror questionnaire would have made you aware of the medication beforehand to assure that the matter is handled sensitively.

§ 14.7 Choice of Words—Generally

A juror's choice of words can tell you a lot symbolically about how the juror sees a situation. For example, in talking about publicity, if a juror says, "I really don't pay a lot of attention to what the local newspapers have to say," this may indicate that she pays more attention to the national news. As another example, when you are asking about contracts and a juror says, "I don't put a lot of stock in a written contract," he could be communicating that a person's word means more to him than something in writing. Listen to the jurors' choice of words for indicators of other messages they may be communicating. The adjectives and adverbs a juror uses in response are often flags for the true meaning of an answer.

§ 14.8 Choice of Words—Qualifiers

You should pay attention to what qualifiers, if any, a juror uses in response to your questions. Many lawyers brush over qualifying statements and do not realize the importance of the message inherent in the qualification. The following are some frequently used qualifiers:

1) *I think so.* This means "I'm not sure."

2) *I believe I can.* This means "I'm not certain if I can."

3) *I don't think so.* This means "I have some doubt."

4) *Not really.* This can mean "Yes, but I don't want to tell you what I think or feel."

5) *I don't know if I can and I won't know until I hear the evidence.* This means "I don't want to tell you what I am thinking about that right now because I don't want to commit myself."

These are a few of the qualifiers that you will hear jurors say on a regular basis. You and your consultant must make sure that you ask the appropriate follow-up questions. You should follow up any "I think so" response by saying, "You sound as if you have some hesitation about that, Ms. Smith. Please tell me about that." If the juror says, "I believe so," you should follow up with, "Mr. Smith, I know you believe you can do that. I need to know whether or not you are sure you can. Please discuss that with me." You might also ask:

1) What else do you feel about that?

2) What do you mean by that?

3) What are your thoughts and ideas about this issue?

4) What are your opinions about this? Please tell me more.

Remember, it is okay to question what a juror is saying to you; it is all in the way in which you do it.

§ 14.9 Choice of Words—'Yes, But'

When someone says "yes, but" and then goes on to say something totally different, she has just wiped out what she said before the "but." It is a well-known fact among interviewers that people who respond "yes, but" are saying yes because they think that is what the interviewer wants to hear them say; however, they really feel differently. There is another school of thought that believes when someone says "yes, but," he is really saying "I believe that, but I believe something else as well." You should not take one stand or another in response to what a juror says, but listen carefully to these kinds of comments as an indicator that you need to carefully explore the juror's thinking on the issue because the juror himself has not made up his mind.

§ 14.10 Choice of Words—'Okay, Okay, Right'

When a juror says something like "okay, okay," he is telling you he does not want to talk anymore about the issue. He is saying, "I have heard enough and said enough about this and I would appreciate if you would move on to something else." He can also be saying, "Okay, I get your point and finally agree with what you are trying to communicate."

Jurors can send the same message by saying "right." This can be their way of saying, "Okay, I understand what you are saying. Now let's move on." Or it can mean, "You're right. I give up," or "You are right. I agree with you." Once again you will want your observer to help you analyze what is really being communicated.

§ 14.11 Choice of Words—Feeling Words

You will also want to listen for which jurors use feeling words and which jurors use thinking words. If a juror says, "I have a warm place in my heart for corporations in our community because they provide jobs," you can assume this is more of a feeling person, as compared with someone who says, "I think that corporations have their place in our society." Depending upon your case, you will be looking for either feelers or thinkers. Pay attention to the words jurors use that indicate where they fall.

Jurors who speak in feeling tones relate more comfortably on an emotional level. In many instances they are more in touch with their feelings and tend to use feeling words to express themselves, even when addressing unemotional issues. These are some examples of jurors speaking in feeling tones:

1) When asked to describe herself, a juror responds: *I am a person who has lots of love for other people. I care what other people feel. I am sad when others are not happy.*

2) When asked how he feels about the death penalty, a juror says: *I am angered by the amount of crime in this country. It saddens me that people hurt other people and I would have to think long and hard before I made a decision in this matter.*

3) When asked what he thinks about insurance companies in a lawsuit against an insurance company, the juror responds: *I feel happy with my insurance company. They always seem to help me and care about my situation. I like my agent very much because she is such a warm person and I feel good when I call her on the phone.*

When you discover jurors who speak in feeling tones, you should realize that they tend to see the world that way. You will most likely tie into them if in your *voir dire* and opening and closing arguments you use feeling words. Feeling words are words that deal with emotions such as *happy, sad, angry, resentful, guilty, fearful,* and *joyful.* In *voir dire* you should include the following follow-up questions to elicit a feeling response:

1) How do you feel about that?

2) What do you feel when you think about that situation?

3) What emotions came up in you when you heard what kind of case this was?

Because these people tend to respond first from an emotional place, in many instances they will understand human emotions and how they motivate people. Whether that is to your advantage or disadvantage will depend on the case and the juror's experience.

§ 14.12 Choice of Words—Thinking Words

Jurors who speak in thinking tones use such words as "I think," "I perceive," "I believe." They will respond to your *voir dire* questions and arguments more fully if you use words that tie into thinking as opposed to feeling or action. The following are sample responses that indicate jurors who are thinking-oriented people:

1) When asked how she would describe herself, a juror says: *I think I am a good person who likes other people. I see myself as being a hard worker.*

2) When asked about the death penalty, a juror says: *I think it is a good way to teach people not to hurt other people.*

3) When asked about insurance companies, a juror says: *I believe insurance companies aren't there when you need them and yet they always want to get their premiums on time.*

When examining thinking jurors, you will want to ask questions in the following manner:

1) What do you think about yourself?

2) How would you describe yourself?

3) What are your thoughts about tort reform?

4) What do you believe a juror's main job responsibilities are?

Also, remember to talk directly to the thinking jurors when making arguments that relate to how people think. Use words that deal with their thinking process. They will be more apt to listen and absorb what you are saying.

As with the feeling and action-oriented juror, you will want to listen to the totality of what the thinking juror has to say. Do not put any of them in a box, based on their first response. It should be noted that all people have a combination of these ways of seeing the world. The question is which one or two ways of seeing will dominate how they listen and what conclusion they will reach.

§ 14.13 Choice of Words—Action Words

A juror who speaks in action tones sees events from the perspective of what has happened and what people did to make this occur. Some examples of the action or reaction-centered juror would be:

1) When asked to describe herself, the juror says: *I behave in ways that require me to put myself to the test. I like myself best when I am doing things.*

2) When asked about the death penalty, the juror responds: *I think that a person should be held responsible for his own actions.*

3) When asked what he thinks about his insurance company, the juror says: *They generally do a good job, but on occasion you realize that you can't live with them and you can't live without them.*

You will want to listen to everything a juror says during *voir dire* to determine whether or not he or she is an action-oriented person. One statement taken in isolation is not a sufficient indicator. It is the totality of what they communicate to you that will convey whether or not jurors fall into this category. If they do, they will pay closer attention to your case when you speak in action tones, using verbs and motion words in your descriptions during opening and closing argument. They will also be more attentive to demonstrative aids that show movement or, better, when the lawyer actively uses the demonstrative aids or acts out what the demonstrative aids explain.

Your assistant during jury selection should take down the jurors' feeling, thinking and action words so that in opening and closing argument you can use what a juror has said to make a point. Using the jurors' words, rather than your own, brings alive the *voir dire* and best drives home the point of your argument.

§ 14.14 Blurts Out Thoughts

Many times, when you have the jury panel really talking, jurors will blurt out a thought before they have had a chance to really think it through. When this happens, know that you are doing your job well. This means that jurors are feeling free to express themselves. The first thing that comes to mind is exactly what you are looking for to grasp their true thoughts and opinions.

To set up this dynamic, you might ask each juror, "What's the first thing that comes into your mind when you hear the following," and give a specific of your case. Encourage the jurors to speak rapidly by saying, "Okay, how about you, Ms. Smith? How about you, Mr. Jones?" Move quickly through the panel so jurors do not have time to think through their thoughts.

§ 14.15 Censors Talk

When a juror answers as if she is censoring her own discussion with you, it is your obligation to say, "I think there is something else that you want to tell me about that matter." You can assume the juror is withholding something if she is fidgeting in her seat as she talks or saying "and that's really about all I have to say about that." If a juror covers his mouth with his hand or looks away from you when answering a question, many times there is something he does not want to say or he has just said something he wished he had not said. You should follow that up with a question like, "Was there something else that you wanted to tell me, Mr. Jones?" or "Was there something that you wish you hadn't said? I noted that you seemed uncomfortable then."

This issue of censoring will be discussed further in the chapter, in illustrating non-verbal language.

§ 14.16 Reverses Words

Sometimes when people are nervous they reverse words. You should note this only as an indication that they are uncomfortable either in answering the question or talking in groups. This generally means that their mind is racing ahead of their tongue. If a person continues to reverse words on a regular basis, you may want to consult a mental health specialist whether this person could have some kind of brain dysfunction.

If you think nervousness is what is causing the juror to reverse words, you might say, "I can imagine that you are feeling a little nervous, as I am. I know we are going to get through this together." Remember, you always want the jurors to realize that you care what they are feeling during this most uncomfortable process.

§ 14.17 Big Vocabulary/Small Vocabulary

You will want to listen to the size of the words that a person uses and match the vocabulary with what you know about his or her educational background and occupation. A large vocabulary can tell you that jurors are highly educated or have read a lot on their own. This can be an index of a self-starter or someone who is self-motivated.

Some people, however, use big words to distance themselves from other people. If the way in which they communicate their thoughts and their choice of multi-syllable words suggest that they think they are better than other people, you should take that into account in measuring whether or not that attitude would be appropriate for your particular case. This can be a positive or a negative quality.

Some people have the grace to use smaller words, knowing that it helps to communicate with more people. Once again you should compare their occupation and education with their vocabulary to determine whether they use smaller words to facilitate communication or because that is the extent of their vocabulary.

§ 14.18 Laughter

It is a well-known phenomenon that people who are nervous sometimes laugh inappropriately. If, for instance, a juror laughs at the mention of someone's pain, discomfort or nervousness, it is okay to say to the juror, "You seem nervous about this line of questioning. Please tell me about that." Many people cover up nervousness by laughter. Rather than humiliating jurors about their laughter, it is best to ask them what is making them so nervous. You will not want to make comments too often heard in the courtroom, like, "Do you find something funny in what we are talking about?" It is never okay to insult a juror who is uncomfortable or nervous.

Jurors may also laugh after saying something they realize reveals what they are truly thinking or feeling. This "self-aware laugh" illustrates a juror who can laugh at himself or analyze herself in a probing manner. This is a good sign.

Then there are those jurors who laugh in a way that you know is mocking what you are saying. You do not want to leave this stone unturned. You should say to the juror, "I have a sense that you find what I'm doing amusing or it is in some way upsetting. What do you think about what I just said?" Once again, you should pay particular attention not to offend the juror. It is permissible to be confrontational but do not become overly aggressive.

Of course, there is genuine laughter that comes from the belly. This is the laughter that tells you the juror finds what you have just said to be humorous in a positive way. Some people have a free-flowing laugh; their entire body communicates, "I'm really enjoying what's going on here." Other people have a shy introverted kind of laugh; they hold back some of their emotions or feelings. How people laugh can tell you a lot about who they are.

§ 14.19 Crying

If you have put a juror under a lot of pressure, sometimes she will cry to relieve stress. You need to be very sensitive and respond in a loving, caring way so that the juror does not feel she has done something wrong in expressing her emotions. Generally, the juror will feel quite embarrassed after crying in public. You need to tell the juror that it is okay to cry and that crying is a natural response to emotional situations. You should ask the juror whether or not she would like a break or would like a tissue or a glass of water. You want to come across as the sensitive party that pays attention to the juror's emotional needs.

Some lawyers overreact to crying and see the juror as an overly emotional person. This may or may not be true. It could simply mean that the subject matter is sensitive and has brought up old feelings. Follow up in a soft, compassionate voice and ask what brought on the tears.

Research indicates that emotional tears reflect different hormonal levels in a person's body. Women tend to cry more often than men because they have 60% more prolactin in their blood. This does not mean that women are more emotional; it just means that women have hormones that make their bodies more responsive to their emotions than men.

On the other hand, if a juror seems to cry at everything you say, something is amiss; she is having a bad day, physically ill, deeply troubled by the subject matter or has an emotional problem that needs to be explored. You may want to approach the bench and ask the court if this juror can be interviewed out of the presence of the other jurors in order to avoid further embarrassment.

§ 14.20 Facial Expressions

You should watch people's faces to determine what they are saying to you. When scanning facial expressions, it helps to have someone trained in non-verbal communication to decipher the signals. If a juror is squinting, this can denote that he is confused about what you are saying, questioning what you are saying, or left his reading glasses at home. Whatever the squinting indicates, always follow up with a question that allows the juror an opportunity to explain his facial expression. You might say, "You seem to have something to say about this question, Mr. Smith. Please tell me what that is."

You should pay particular attention to someone's mouth. A downturned mouth can indicate fear, anger, nervousness or a variety of other emotions. As we age, all of our mouths tend to turn down. You want to look for the person whose mouth seems to be turned down in an aggressive fashion and ask what he or she is feeling, so that you can figure out what the expression may be indicating in this particular instance.

People's faces are a road map to how they have lived their lives. You should take note of how the lines in each face have developed. It can be helpful to sketch the faces; the lines will tell you something in addition to the words out of the jurors' mouths and their demeanor in the courtroom.

§ 14.21 Eye Contact

It is true that the eyes are the mirrors of the soul. You can often see happiness, pain, sadness, confusion and other emotions in someone's eyes. If a juror sends you a message, as it were, follow up your instinct and ask about the juror's feelings at the time, to ascertain if they could impact on your case.

You will also want to pay attention to jurors' eye contact during the questioning process. Do they look you in the eye? Do they make eye contact with your client, with opposing counsel, with the opposing client? This will tell you their comfort level in communicating with members of each trial team as well as their comfort level in talking in groups in general. If a juror will not look at you, this indicates he is shy, irritated with you, or thinking. You should follow up to find out what the resistance to making eye contact actually means.

There is often a juror who tries to stare you down. This can indicate either a very strong, assertive personality who is comfortable making eye contact or one who is feeling aggressive with you at the moment. Once again, you should follow up with the juror by saying, "I feel that you are having some strong feelings right now. Please tell me what they are."

People in supervisory positions and people accustomed to speaking in groups know the importance of having good eye contact. Many times they will maintain eye contact out of habit rather than any true interest in what you are saying. You will want to pay particular attention to whether these people are sincerely listening or are just trained communicators.

§ 14.22 Where Do They Look When Speaking?

If you ask a question and the juror turns to opposing counsel to answer, that tells you the juror is probably more comfortable with opposing counsel and looking for his approval. It can also mean, however, that the juror is afraid that opposing counsel may not like what he or she is saying and is looking for signals. Once again, you must look at the totality of what the juror is communicating to you.

If you are asking a very important question and the juror looks at the judge for help or assistance, that tells you that this person is generally apt to follow authority. It also tells you that he thinks the judge is not on your side and that he regards the judge as his protector as opposed to an impartial party in this proceeding. Depending upon the juror, you may want to ask why the juror looked at the judge when answering that particular question. It is very important when you ask this kind of confrontational question that you ask it in a caring manner so that the juror does not feel offended or challenged.

§ 14.23 Use of Hands—Generally

We all know people who cannot talk without using their hands. Generally, these people are much more expressive than the rest of us. You will want to look for ways in which they use their hands to accentuate different statements or opinions. Sometimes people use their hands almost as if they are speaking in sign language. A trained observer can help you figure out what they are saying with their hands and how that relates to or detracts from what they are saying with their words.

You should watch for jurors who answer questions with a closed fist as opposed to an open hand. Closed fists can indicate tension or anger. Follow up gently by saying, "You seem a little frustrated right now. Tell me what's going on, please." In contrast, an open hand generally indicates the juror is more flexible and open to what you are saying.

§ 14.24 Use of Hands—'Steepling'

When jurors put the tips of their fingers of each hand together, this can mean a number of things. It can indicate that they are deeply considering the question and what their comments should be. It can mean that they are trying to ground themselves and make sure they properly communicate what they are trying to express. It can also mean that they are uncertain about what they are saying and that they are questioning whether or not they are saying it in the way they would like to say it. You should pay particular attention when a juror "steeples" and make sure you follow up with some questions to decode the message. You might ask:

1) *Mr. Jones, you seem to be contemplating my question. Tell me what's on your mind.*

2) *I feel there is something else I need to know about your thoughts and feelings about this issue. Please tell me what that might be.*

Jurors have commented that seeing a lawyer steeple made them think the lawyer was trying to deceive them or not telling them the whole truth. It may just have been the lawyer's way to get centered or concentrate on the communication at that moment, but the gesture raises suspicion. Jurors do not always know why they are picking up on a non-verbal response or, in turn, what they are communicating with their own. Yet, it is such an important part of our way of giving each other information that we cannot discount it. In *voir dire* it needs to be closely analyzed.

§ 14.25 Use of Hands—Hands on Neck, Throat, Mouth, Chest

When jurors put their hands on their neck, throat, mouth, or chest, they can be telling you that there is something that they are trying to cover up or something they are uncomfortable about. Once again this is a sign to explore this issue carefully with the juror. You should follow up especially if the juror has been responding with open hands and open body language and then begins to cover his neck, throat, mouth or chest in response to a specific question.

§ 14.26 Use of Full Body—Generally

Some people move their entire body when they are talking. Many times this indicates a very emotional, feeling person or an emotional response to a specific issue. Note how they move their body and respond with their body to different questions. For example, they may be telling you that they are open to your theory of the case and meanwhile their arms are closed and their legs crossed. This can mean merely that the courtroom is chilly; you should not automatically presume that they are closed to your theory of the case. It is a red flag, however, that you need to follow up. Say to the juror something like, "You appear to have some hesitation, Ms. Jones, about what I am saying to you. Please tell me what that is." Your trial consultant can help you decipher what this non-verbal language truly means.

§ 14.27 Use of Full Body—Body as Barrier

There are times when a juror seems to be having a healthy conversation with you, with arms open, leaning toward you and listening. Then you move into a new area of inquiry, and he turns sideways with his legs at an angle as if to set up a barrier between you. This is your signal to ask once again if you have touched on something that has made him uncomfortable or if there is some other thing that he needs to tell you. Another movement of the body as barrier is when a juror crosses her arms and turns sideways from the waist up. This can tell you once again that you need to follow up and ask what the juror might be thinking about the issue in question that you have not asked.

§ 14.28 Chin

How people hold their chin can tell you what they are thinking or feeling at the time. For example, a person who juts his chin forward at you may be saying he is proud of his position and daring you to challenge his thoughts. On the other hand, he may just be a stoic, proud person who was taught in military service or on his high school drill team to hold his chin out straight. Once again you will want to measure this non-verbal response with the totality of what you know of this person.

If people hold their chin close to their neck, this can indicate that they are trying either to hide something or to cover up something. Dogs often protect their necks when they are about to get into a fight. Human beings do the same thing. You should examine whether or not something about the nature of the question or the manner in which it was asked may have intimidated a juror or struck a sensitive chord. You will want to explore this area delicately and ask, "What else would you like to share with me about that, Ms. Smith?" Holding the chin close to the neck is also a sign of a person who is shy and afraid of not measuring up to his peers. You will want to handle this juror carefully and with the aid of your jury consultant, decipher what the juror is trying to say. You will also want to note these non-verbal messages once the jurors are seated, to see when they are responding and what subjects they find uncomfortable.

When you see jurors slightly cocking their chin from side to side, this can indicate that they are carefully listening to what you are saying and deciding their thoughts on the matter. You will want to ask them what they are thinking about and what else is running through their mind regarding the issue.

§ 14.29 Ankles and Feet

If you can see the jurors' ankles and feet, you can get a sense of their comfort or discomfort with the *voir dire* process. If someone is tapping the floor, this can indicate that the juror is irritated or in a hurry. You should follow up this non-verbal cue by saying, "You seem somewhat frustrated at the moment. Tell me what is happening for you."

Women raised in traditional society are taught that a "real lady" always crosses her ankles underneath or in front of her chair. If a woman has her legs firmly planted in front of her, that tells you she is not particularly tradition bound and will be comfortable standing her own ground and making her point known. This is not just a female trait. Men who answer your questions with their feet firmly on the floor are probably firmly grounded in what they are saying.

Jurors who place one foot in front of the other may be taking a slightly aggressive stance. Watch for other indications that give you the feeling they are being aggressive with you or with opposing counsel. Once again, it is important to have an observer sit at the side of the jury box or the side of the courtroom during *voir dire* to be able to see the jurors' non-verbal language from the waist down.

§ 14.30 Purse, Book, Briefcase

You will want to note the people with purses, books or briefcases and where they place them during *voir dire.* Some people will put their purse or briefcase or book in their lap, indicating that they would like to leave as quickly as possible. If the jurors seem to be holding on for dear life, they are no doubt using that purse, book or briefcase as a barrier between you and them. They are uncomfortable with what is going on and are using the next best thing to a teddy bear to put themselves at ease. Sometimes, as the *voir dire* progresses, they put down the "barrier," indicating that they are becoming more comfortable with you. This is a good sign.

§ 14.31 Toucher–Feelers

If your case is steeped in feeling issues, look for jurors who make physical contact or show signs of affection toward others on the jury panel. You may see jurors during breaks touch someone in conversation or slap someone on the back. During *voir dire,* if a juror appears comfortable sitting shoulder to shoulder with another juror, you can presume that juror is comfortable with other people and potentially a strong social leader.

Social leaders can be the most controlling people in the deliberation room because they are well liked for paying attention to people's feelings and desires. (*See* Sections 16.26 and 16.54 for a more detailed description of the social leader and the effect on the jury.) You should therefore take particular note of their expressions of affection, and the other jurors' response, to analyze if this particular social leader is someone that you want or do not want on your jury.

§ 14.32 Fear of Physical Contact

If a juror pulls away when another juror leans toward him or puts a hand on his shoulder, this tells you that either the juror does not like that person or is generally uncomfortable with physical contact. If your case involves emotional issues, be careful about people who shy away from physical affection. These could be folks that make up their minds on their own and choose not to deliberate with other jurors when the time comes to share their opinions at the conclusion of the case. They could, however, merely have been raised in an environment where physical affection was not expressed. They may have a big heart but never had an opportunity to show it. Once again, you must look at the jurors in the total context of everything that they have said or done during the *voir dire* process.

§ 14.33 Scared To Death

Being scared is a normal reaction for everyone during *voir dire,* including the lawyers. There are certain jurors, however, who are extremely intimidated by the process, and this tells you something about their personality. If they feel overwhelmed by this situation, you can just imagine what a heated deliberation will do to their psyche. Take note of which jurors appear overwhelmed and what may be causing this tremendous fear within the juror. It is your job to ask why they are feeling so uncomfortable and uncover the root of their fear.

Because fear can translate into anger, you do not want a juror who will become so uncomfortable during the deliberations that she either refuses to deliberate with the rest of the jury or takes it out on the other jurors so that they wind up trying to get everything over with just to be rid of this person. You want to carefully explore if the juror is just a very shy person who is easily intimidated by having to speak in public or if this is someone whose extreme fear could disrupt the deliberations for the rest of the jury.

§ 14.34 Admiring of Power

Some people are prone to put others on a pedestal, whether they are deserving or not. Look for the jurors who lean forward to pay particular attention to other jurors they perceive as powerful or to members of either trial team they seem to revere. You can tell by the look of adoration in their eyes or by their forward body movement as they hang on to every word the person is saying. They may nod their head or move their hand in a forward motion indicating, "Yes, I agree with what you are saying. Give me more information."

This selective attention will be a clue to who will be a potential influence during the trial. It is your job to determine whether or not that is going to be of help to you or the other side. It will also help you determine whether or not this juror will be teaming up with other jurors that you like or do not like.

§ 14.35 The Sleeping Juror

When you see a juror nodding off, this could mean any number of things. It could mean that he has worked a night shift and is very tired, that the process is boring, that he is on medication or has some kind of sleeping disorder. The sleeper becomes a particular concern if this is the juror you have decided to rely on to pull weight for your client. In short, you cannot count on this juror to do anything to help you in deliberations unless you uncover the cause of the sleepiness.

If you see a juror sleeping whom you do not like, you may be able to have this juror excused for cause or for hardship as opposed to wasting a peremptory challenge. Again, an observer is helpful in this instance to make sure that these subtle things that happen during the course of an active *voir dire* are noted and used to your best advantage.

§ 14.36 Nurturers

Some people like to nurture other people. You can see this during *voir dire* in how they relate to you, opposing counsel or other jurors. Should you have a case that involves emotional issues, find out as much as you can about the nurturers, to see if you want them on your jury or not.

Nurturers are generally liked by other members of the panel because they make a point of taking care of people. On the other hand, if they take it to the extreme where they are constantly nurturing everyone around them, this can become irritating to jurors who do not particularly like to be taken care of. Note which jurors seem to like or not like the nurturance of a particular juror, and consider whether he or she could become a social leader on the jury.

§ 14.37 Dress

Many jurors dress up for jury duty as if they are going to church. This is not uncommon. What you will want to note is if in a jury selection that goes on for more than one day, there are jurors who start dressing up or dressing down as the days go by. If jurors start dressing up, they may be vying for power and esteem among the jury panel. If jurors begin to dress casually, they are probably feeling more comfortable and in control and do not care what they wear because they know they can stand on their personal traits as opposed to what they have on their back.

Note if jurors who are in a highly educated profession tend to dress inconsistently with their occupation. This tells you that they feel comfortable being who they are in the courtroom and feel that they do not need a coat and tie in order to make a statement. They may also be the ones to take power in the deliberation room. On the other hand, if a juror is in a line of work that normally does not dress up and comes to court dressed very meticulously, this tells you that she wants to take power and does not want to be judged by what she does for a living or her socio-economic status.

Also note the quality of a person's clothing and jewelry. You may have concluded from the questionnaire or what the person has said about what he or his spouse does for a living that he comes from a particular socio-economic group, though his attire conveys something very different. This can tell you that he either has money from another source or is downplaying his socio-economic station. If, however, he is not wearing the finery you expected, he may have fallen on hard times or just simply chosen not to dress in a manner that is in line with what people expect.

Using these cues, check out your intuition about jurors. Remember to follow up the gray areas as much as possible and to look at the whole picture each juror paints before making a decision to select or strike.

Chapter 15

BASIC BIASES: GENDER, RACE, RELIGION, AGE, SOCIAL–ECONOMIC STATUS

Table of Sections

---

§ 15.1 Overview

Bias permeates our society and, unfortunately, floods the courtroom with programming and life experiences which must be met head-on to create a fair environment. This chapter looks at some of the more common prejudices and ways to explore them in *voir dire,* to lessen their impact on your client.

§ 15.2 Gender—Generally

Like men, women appreciate respect. Many women are managers, supervisors, directors or leaders in their everyday lives and are accustomed to receiving the respect that comes with that position. Others, no matter what their occupation or social status, expect and value being treated as an equal. During *voir dire,* you should thoughtfully ask the women on the jury whether they would prefer to be called Miss, Ms. or Mrs. If they say Ms., do not make an issue of it. Women throughout the United States prefer this title. It is not a strong indicator of a woman's view of women in society. On the other hand, it does reflect a woman's awareness that women should be seen on an equal footing with men.

You should also avoid terms of endearment like "honey," "sweetie," "dear" that may not be intended as an insult but many female jurors would consider insulting, from a man they do not know. You may believe it is the woman's problem for taking offense, if you have been raised to think so otherwise. It is important to remember, however, that some men do use such terms because they see women as unequal or subordinate, and there is strong sentiment that these are terms that have suppressed women through the ages. While reactions may differ, depending on the venue, it is better not to run the risk of offending a woman in the courtroom.

In this day and age, it is also well to remember that female and male jurors can be feminists; they both can believe in the equality of the sexes and be sensitive to the discrimination and harassment women face. They will generally be more aware of others' prejudices. Male lawyers should take this into account and never treat a woman any differently than a man in the courtroom. They should communicate with all jurors equally during the course of the trial. Similarly, female lawyers should make every effort to bridge the gender gap so that the judge's or jurors' bias does not impinge on their client.

Should your case involve women's issues, questions on feminism become quite important. For example, if your client is a female executive or there is a charge of battery or rape, you most certainly want to discuss the treatment of women in our society. The following questions will help you determine a juror's feelings on feminist issues:

1) *In your mind, what is the most important women's issue in the country today?*

2) *Have you or any family member ever taken a stand on women's issues? How did you feel about the result?*

3) *What do you think about women's organizations like the National Organization of Women, or NOW, Pro–Choice, Pro–Life? Have you or any family member ever belonged to such organizations?*

4) *What do you think about women in the workplace today?*

5) *How do you think women are treated in society?*

§ 15.3 Gender—Jurors' Perceptions of Female Lawyers

Being honest with jurors that you are concerned about how they view female lawyers is very important because it sets the tone for the rest of the trial. Honest lawyers will always be accorded more credibility than lawyers who do not deal up front with tension that builds in the jury box. The tension may arise from jurors' accurate and inaccurate perceptions of female lawyers. To get to the core of the problem, ask the jurors if they have ever known a woman lawyer and how they would feel about hiring a woman lawyer should they ever need legal services. Discuss whether any female member of the family or female friend has ever wanted to go into law or whether they have ever personally known a woman who was in the field of law. Ask how they felt about that woman becoming a lawyer and how she felt about being in the field of law. Should you encounter resistance from a particular juror, you may also want to discuss the special and unique problems that face a woman in the law. Ask what, in their opinion, are the advantages and disadvantages of being a woman in the field of law and what they have heard from female friends or relatives about the advantages and disadvantages. On a more fanciful note, you might ask what movies or television shows they have seen about women in the law and how did they feel about the women portrayed in those shows. Who was their favorite woman lawyer among those portrayals?

§ 15.4 Gender—Female Lawyer to Female Juror

Many women lawyers experience particular problems relating to female jurors. They fear that because they are functioning in a "traditional" male role in the courtroom, jurors may be resentful or feel they have overstepped their bounds. While there may be a few women jurors who feel this way as a result of restrictions in their own lives, most have been found to admire women who have achieved professional status. The following kind of questions will uncover whether or not being a female lawyer will be a problem:

1) *Some people feel that a woman should not be a lawyer and others feel that a woman should be whatever she is motivated to be. What do you think?*

2) *What are your thoughts about women becoming lawyers?*

3) *Some feel that it is not appropriate for a woman to be a lawyer. What do you think?*

Should you find a woman on the panel who makes you uncomfortable, determine whether your discomfort relates to her feeling that it is inappropriate for you to be a lawyer or if there is something else making her stand-offish. It could be she is uncomfortable with you because of an issue in your case, or because she has had a run-in with one of your family members or with someone in your office. The following questions will help you determine if it is more of a personal problem or a case-specific issue, as opposed to a gender conflict:

1) *Ms. Smith, you seem uncomfortable about something. Can you tell me what that is?*

2) *Ms. Jones, do you know anyone I work with or any of my family members? Please tell me how you know them.*

3) *Ms. Jones, tell me what you feel about what I have been discussing with regard to this case?*

§ 15.5 Gender—Female Judge and Female Lawyer

Some female lawyers fear discrimination from female judges. This generally is not founded in fact, but the fear persists. It is important to treat a female judge the same as you would treat a male judge and to realize that any conflict that arises may have to do with your interaction and not a woman-to-woman issue. As in any instance when you are having problems communicating with the judge, it is important that you discuss the conflict either on the record or in chambers with opposing counsel present. It would be best to broach the discussion by saying,

> *Judge, I fear that we are having a problem communicating here and it concerns me. Please tell me what's going on so that I can focus on representing my client rather than the discomfort of feeling that I am doing something to offend the court.*

You will obviously want to take the soft, direct approach first and put matters on the record only if the court continues to be offensive to you in front of the jury. You should resort to making a record only after attempting direct and open-minded communication off the record.

§ 15.6 Gender—Male Judge and Female Lawyer

Most male judges tend to treat female and male lawyers with equal respect. Occasionally, however, a male judge will have problems with women. The judge who feels that women are inferior to men should be confronted directly. If the judge makes jokes, offensive remarks, or in some other way is demeaning in front of the jury or in chambers, the female lawyer should tell the court that his statements and behavior are making her uncomfortable and could negatively reflect on her client. As with a female judge, it is advisable first to try talking to the judge off the record to help keep his ego intact. Should the judge not be receptive to the criticism and understand that his behavior is inappropriate, the lawyer may then want to make a record of his behavior or comments and also state her concern that his behavior is adversely affecting her ability to represent her client by its impact on the jurors, as well as the client. Be prepared for the court's anger at being confronted; yet if you consistently maintain a record, most judges will desist so as not to appear prejudiced to an appellate court.

§ 15.7 Gender—Sexual Dynamics in the Courtroom

Male and female lawyers have flirted with jurors in the courtroom only to realize that this turned out to be a major problem during deliberations. If you are aware of sexual innuendos between yourself and a juror, no doubt other jurors will sense it as well. A well-known civil rights lawyer tells a story about making eyes with an attractive female juror in a death penalty case who was told by the other members of the jury that because of this, they were going to elect her foreperson to lead the way to the death verdict. She was overcome by the peer pressure and the desire to fit in, and though she was attracted to the male lawyer, she felt it was important that she identify with the jury. She became a strong advocate for the death penalty to win the approval of other members of the community. This is a sad story about how sexual dynamics in the courtroom can hurt a client to the *nth* degree.

When making eye contact with jurors, it is best that you make eye contact with all jurors so that no one feels slighted or gets the impression that there is some kind of flirting going on when there may not be. Remember, in a courtroom there is a lot of time when people are sitting around bored and have nothing better to do than flirt. This flirting is best done among jurors, rather than between counsel and a juror. You should especially shy away from paying too much attention to a juror of the opposite sex. You can easily leave the impression that you are interested in sexual pursuits, and not the important case matters at hand. Rather, you want jurors to see you as putting your client's problems first and foremost.

§ 15.8 Gender—The Battered Woman Case

Jurors usually do not know or are unwilling to admit that they have any prejudice toward women as parties in a criminal or civil proceeding involving abuse. Counsel must therefore sensitize the panel, first to sexual bias in general, then to the specifics of the Battered Woman Syndrome, and finally to the fact that the battered woman who defends herself is acting in self-defense. These issues can be intimidating. The more delicate approach of asking jurors to say how they feel about these issues will lessen the threat, encourage more open responses and elicit more information. To begin, you might ask these kinds of questions:

1) *What do you think are a woman's rights in a marriage or relationship?*

2) *What do you believe* (name of client) *did to put her on trial?*

3) *Do you think women are treated more leniently than men on trial? Why?*

4) *Do you think women overreact in many situations? Why?*

5) *Do you feel women are too emotional? Why?*

6) *Why do you think* (name of client) *did not call the police or a family member?*

7) *Why do you think* (name of client) *did not leave?*

A battered woman knows the pressures and sense of helplessness she experiences all too well. She knows the fear of staying and the fear of what might happen if she leaves the relationship. Her life is filled with moment after moment of terror that no matter what she does she cannot stop the time bomb. Physical helplessness and emotional torture are her daily treatments from a man she once loved or still does love.

There are some people who think she brought this on herself and those who do not understand why she did not leave. Misunderstanding plagues this dynamic and the mystery of it all must be deciphered for the jury. The deciphering begins during jury selection. Questions to be asked of jurors are:

1) *Who has heard of the Battered Woman Syndrome? What does it mean to you?*

2) *Most people have read or seen a television show about the Battered Woman Syndrome. Ms. Jones, what have you read or seen about battered wives or children?*

3) *Who saw the television show, "The Burning Bed," with Farrah Fawcett? What did you feel about that show? How did you feel about how she was treated in the judicial system? How did you feel about the final result in that case?*

4) *Who feels that a battered wife means someone who is abused emotionally or physically or both? Tell me about that.*

5) *Some people feel that being emotionally battered is not as bad as being physically battered. Who feels that way? Tell me about that.*

6) *The defense will present a witness, Dr. Lenore Walker, who will testify about the Battered Woman Syndrome. Who would want to hear from Dr. Walker? Please tell me what you would like to know.*

7) *Many people know someone who is battered. Please tell me about that situation. What happened in that family? What did the battered woman do?* (Let the jurors know that they can discuss these matters in private.)

8) (Name of client) *killed her husband in self-defense. She is one of the women Dr. Walker will describe as being a battered woman. Who feels that a battered wife could kill her husband in self-defense? For those who feel it is self-defense, tell me about that. Those who do not feel this, tell me why.*

The answers to these questions will alert you to who will and will not listen to the defense's case. The questions also will give you the opportunity to educate the jurors on issues about which they are closed-minded or have little information, including: domestic violence, marital problems, guns and self-defense.

§ 15.9 Gender—The Battered Woman Case—Domestic Violence

Emotional versus physical battery is a repeating conflict in jurors' perceptions of violence. Many feel that domestic violence only means physical episodes and that a woman loses her claim of violence if it was psychological in nature. These findings are based on numerous jury selections and thousands of post-trial interviews of jurors. Addressing this conflict during *voir dire* and through your client's testimony creates a bridge between each juror's private world and the world of your client.

Everyone has experienced violence to varying degrees. The magnitude of the damage and turmoil is the real crux of the problem. If jurors are afraid of their own feelings about having been battered, then perhaps they will not be open to your client's feelings. Some jurors will have battered someone themselves and will struggle to justify their own actions. Asking jurors to talk about their own experiences with domestic violence is most difficult. Questioning should be done in private, if possible, to elicit honest answers. The questions that need to be asked during the client interview and again during jury selection are:

1) *What does family violence mean to you?*

2) *What experiences in your life have affected you in a significant way?*

3) *Tell me about books and magazine articles you have read or television shows you have seen regarding violence in the family.*

4) *In what ways do you believe that emotional violence and physical violence are alike?*

5) *Have you, any family member, neighbor or co-worker ever been the victim of any crime involving violence? Please tell me about the experience.* (Let the jurors know that they can approach the bench to discuss this experience privately).

6) *What organizations do you or your family belong to?* ✓

7) *What do you think is the # 1 cause of divorce?*

8) *What is the main cause of domestic violence?*

§ 15.10 Gender—The Battered Woman Case—Marital Problems

An equally sensitive issue in battered women cases is marital problems that, again, are best discussed in individual sequestered *voir dire.*

Personal experiences with marital problems will affect jurors' emotions in a trial, causing them to second-guess the woman's actions. Often-heard remarks are: "I had problems in my marriage, but we worked it out." "I've gotten angry with my husband but I never tried to kill him." "Why didn't she leave if she was afraid?" "She should have gotten out if it was that bad." "Why didn't she call the police? I did." Such remarks are indicative of the lack of empathy confronting your client. Extra effort is necessary to break down this barrier as well as the general inhibition to discuss problems in marriages and relationships. The following questions are best asked in private:

1) *What are the causes of problems in marriage?*
2) *What should a woman do if she has marital difficulties?*
3) *What might be some reasons why a woman would not tell anyone about her marital difficulties?*
4) *I feel uncomfortable asking this, but I must know who has gone through the break-up of a relationship, a separation or a divorce? Tell me about this experience. What are your feelings about that? Did you hire a lawyer to help deal with this? What was the result? We can discuss this privately, if you desire.*
5) *Has anyone in your family or any friend ever been through such an experience? Please tell me about what happened. Did they hire a lawyer? What was the result?*

§ 15.11 Gender—The Battered Woman Case—Fear

For many jurors it is a big leap, if not an implausible one, from marital problems to prosecution for murder. Fear is the link. Fear is a common denominator among emotions. All other emotions are reactions in one way or another to this basic feeling. Effectively describing this dynamic brings the jurors into the battered woman's environment. People prefer to ignore our limitations as human beings that are brought to the surface when fear grips us. The lawyer must ask questions about fear, experts must testify about it, and your client must learn to explain how it affected her. Questions for the jury panel include:

1) *How does fear affect people?*
2) *Tell me about an experience where you were afraid. How did it affect you?*
3) *Tell me the difference between how you behave when you are afraid as opposed to not afraid.*
4) *Have you ever been in fear for your life? Tell me about that.*
5) *Some people feel that fear makes people do things they normally would not do. What do you think about that?*

§ 15.12 Gender—The Battered Woman Case—Self-Defense

Self-defense is a concept that means many things to many people. Frequently the discussion takes some moral turns. A portion of our population believes in "turning the other cheek"; others feel that a person should be entitled to "stand her ground" and that using deadly force can be necessary, if dictated by fear. Because some feel that self-defense does not mean protecting one's own life or one's loved ones, this value must be explored in jury selection. First, however, lawyers must deal with their client's feelings, since it is often the case that even a battered spouse has difficulties dealing with her own self-protective instincts.

Some jurors say that they can understand when a person could shoot another in self-defense, when, for example, an intruder enters someone's home or a passenger like Bernard Goetz is in fear of being mugged on the New York subway. In the same breath, many of these jurors do not give the same rights to a woman who is threatened or intimidated in her own home by her own spouse or lover. The old argument arises: "Why didn't she call the police or leave if things were so bad?" Once again, the jurors' values must be discussed. A juror who does not feel a woman should defend herself, use deadly force or stand her own ground in a domestic situation, should not sit on the jury. To find out how jurors feel about domestic situations, you should ask:

1) *What does self-defense mean to you?*

2) *Have you ever felt trapped? How did you respond? How did that make you feel?*

3) *Have you ever felt terrified? How did that make you feel?*

4) *Have you ever been in a situation where you felt you needed to defend yourself, emotionally or physically? Tell me about that.*

5) *Some feel that defending oneself only extends to street muggers or someone who breaks into your home. What are some other instances where you feel you should defend yourself?*

6) *If someone attacked you or you feared they might, what would you do?*

7) *Some people feel that if their life was in danger they would not defend themselves because it meant hurting someone else. Who feels that way? If you do, it is okay; many folks agree with that feeling.*

8) *If a woman was in fear of being hurt, who feels she should defend herself against her husband? Why or why not?*

9) *If a woman fears her husband will harm her, under what circumstances would she be justified in using deadly force?*

10) *Who feels that being emotionally battered warrants the same self-protective measures as being physically attacked? Tell me what makes you feel that way.*

11) *Who feels that the emotionally or psychologically injured person should not be entitled to defend herself? Why? Why not?*

12) Who would use deadly force if you felt endangered, emotionally or physically? Why or why not?

13) Who feels that under no circumstances would he or she kill another person? It is okay if you feel that way. Please tell me about those feelings.

§ 15.13 Gender—The Battered Woman Case—Guns

There are some people who will convict someone simply because a gun was used in the incident. There is a growing belief that guns should not be in the home and that a person committed an offense with premeditation because he or she purchased a gun or allowed one to remain in the home. Where a gun was used in a battered woman case, jurors should be asked about their pro- or anti-gun feelings. Suggested questions are:

1) What are your feelings about guns?

2) Do you or any family member own a gun?

3) What purpose is served by owning a gun?

4) Have you or any family member ever owned a gun in the past?

5) Can you share with me a bad experience you or someone you know has had with a gun?

6) Have you or anyone you know ever been the victim of a crime where a weapon was used or exhibited? How has this experience affected you?

7) Do you or anyone you know belong to the N.R.A., a gun club or any anti-gun organization?

8) If you no longer have a gun, why did you or the family member get rid of the weapon?

9) Who feels that handguns should be available to the general public? Who feels they should not be available to the general public? Please explain.

10) Some people are anti-gun. Who would say they are opposed to guns, in general? To handguns?

11) Have you ever shot a gun? Tell me about that.

12) What would you feel if a woman used a gun to protect herself from her husband (boyfriend)?

Of course these questions may be adapted to other cases involving use of a firearm.

§ 15.14 Gender—The Battered Woman Case—Psychological Experts

Case law has established in most jurisdictions that the subject of battered women is beyond the knowledge of most people and therefore expert testimony is proper. Jurors have been seriously jaded about expert witnesses since John Hinkley's temporary insanity defense in the shooting of then-President Ronald Reagan. Proper *voir dire* procedures must question jurors' feelings about psychology and sociology. Jurors' personal experiences with people in the helping professions need additional exploration. Sensitizing jurors to psychological issues is the lawyer's responsibility. Questions to be asked are:

1) The fields of psychology and sociology are ones in which many of us have an interest. Who has taken any courses in psychology or sociology? Please describe.

2) Who has ever known or used anyone in the psychology or sociology professions? Please describe your experience.

3) How helpful did you find that person to be? If not helpful, tell me about that.

4) Who has a family member or friend who has known or used anyone in the psychology or sociology professions? Please describe that person's experience.

5) How did you, your friend or family member feel about the professionals? Helpful? Not helpful? Why?

6) What are your feelings about psychologists? Psychiatrists? Social workers? Counselors?

7) If someone were to testify about psychological pressures on my client, how open might you be to that kind of testimony?

8) (Name of client) *was a Battered Wife. Dr. Walker, who is an expert on the Battered Wife Syndrome, will testify in this regard. What would make you feel open to Dr. Walker's testimony?*

Experience confirms that battered women cases are as complex as the principles that govern our relationships. Careful examination of jurors' feelings about these sensitive issues is paramount to tearing down the walls that lay people attempt to hide behind in the courtroom. An effective *voir dire* mandates asking sensitive questions. There have been many convictions and lost civil claims because of the questions that were not asked during jury selection. Equally important, an attorney must be prepared for any answer and respond sensitively. Some of the questions may be difficult to ask, and it is certain that some of the responses will not be liked. However, it is better to use that unwelcome information to exercise a peremptory challenge rather than discover the answer during a post-trial interview.

§ 15.15 Gender—Homosexuality

Our society is distinctly biased against people whose sexual preference is other than heterosexual. Gay people are the butt of jokes and the victims of violence. Especially with today's fears about AIDS and other sexually transmitted diseases, gay-bashing is on the rise and there is a genuine concern, if not paranoia, about the right of homosexuals to hold certain jobs and to raise children, let alone to enjoy "life, liberty and the pursuit of happiness." Among women, there is resentment that lesbians are usurping the agenda of the women's movement. On the other hand, the greater visibility of the gay movement has brought greater understanding of gay people.

Should your case in any way involve homosexuality, you must *voir dire* the panel on this controversial, complex and sensitive issue. Obviously people will be uncomfortable discussing the topic, as they are discussing any sexual issues. Some jurors may feel anger; others, embarrassment. You should politely acknowledge the sensitivity of your questions, but explain that you must pursue the answers for the sake of your client. Continue, despite the jurors' hesitancy to answer. At the same time, always maintain your sensitivity about the issue so that you never communicate any sexual or homosexual bias you may have. Some questions you might ask the jurors to bring out homophobic feelings or latent fears, are:

1) *Have you ever known a homosexual? In what context?*
2) *What words do you use to refer to a homosexual?*
3) *Do you believe people have the right to be different from mainstream society? Why? Why not?*
4) *In what ways do you think homosexuals are different?*
5) *Knowing that someone is homosexual, would you treat that person differently than you would a heterosexual person? How?*
6) *Why do you think someone is homosexual?*
7) *How would you feel if your son or daughter were gay?*
8) *Do you think homosexuals are oppressed or discriminated against in this society? How?*
9) *Do you think they are justified in feeling that way? What makes you think that?*
10) *If otherwise qualified, are there any jobs homosexuals should not hold? What jobs? Why?*
11) *If otherwise qualified, do you think homosexuals should be teachers? If not, why not?*
12) *Do you have any concerns about homosexuals parenting a child? Being foster parents? What are your concerns?*
13) *If a homosexual and a heterosexual were to testify in this case, would you believe one more than the other? Why?*
14) *Do you believe homosexuals should hide their homosexuality, or try to be as heterosexual as they can?*

15) *Is there anything in your religion that says homosexuality is immoral? Could you be impartial toward homosexuals in a court of law when your religion teaches that homosexuality is wrong?*

You should particularly note if there are gay members of the panel. As discussed below with regard to minority jurors, you should not make any assumptions about their attitudes. Give them equal attention, and carefully weigh their potential strengths and weaknesses for your case—including how they will interact with other jurors.

§ 15.16 Race—Generally

Yes, racism is a difficult and sometimes disconcerting issue to deal with in a group. Yet, it is one of those sensitive issues that must be dealt with, and in a delicate though forthright way. It is necessary to tell jurors that you feel uncomfortable having to talk about this issue but it would not be fair to the juror or your client if you bypass this issue so that everyone could feel comfortable. Many lawyers have found it helpful to discuss their own biases and prejudices to provide an opening for the jurors to discuss theirs. It would be the unusual person who has not had some kind of experience in his lifetime that would make him a little less open to people of different races. Making it a comfortable subject to discuss during *voir dire* is the lawyer's task.

§ 15.17 Race—Individual Sequestered *Voir Dire*

Always push for individual sequestered *voir dire* when including questions on race. (*See* Section 7.2, *supra,* for an introduction to the use of individual sequestered *voir dire* for sensitive issues.) Jurors are much more apt to discuss their feelings of bias and prejudice one-on-one, outside the presence of the other jurors. This is especially true should the case involve a racial incident that has been in the public eye or is a matter of controversy in the community.

Even if the court has refused to grant individual sequestered *voir dire,* write down four or five questions that you would ask. As jury selection proceeds in open court and you encounter a juror who is hesitant to discuss these matters in public, you may want to say to the juror, "I'm sure this is a little uncomfortable. Do you feel it would be easier if we talk about this at the bench with the judge?" Should you get one or two jurors who agree that they are uncomfortable discussing this subject in open court, then even if they do not want to come to the bench, you should make a record at the bench that jurors are uncomfortable discussing their feelings in open court and, once again, renew your motion for individual sequestered *voir dire.*

§ 15.18 Race—*Voir Dire* on Interracial Issues

Many lawyers tend to avoid asking questions about race for fear that they may alienate one group or another. This is problematic because to ignore that race is a factor when you have a minority client or people of different races involved in a lawsuit is to believe that there is no racism or ethnic bias in this country. We all know that racism unfortunately is alive and well in America and that subtle forms of racism such as a credibility gap, lack of contact, or an isolated negative experience can play a role in how jurors perceive witnesses and clients. It is best to address the issue head-on to uncover problem areas and build a rapport with the jurors that sensitizes them to the importance of not allowing these attitudes to enter into the deliberations.

The first Supreme Court case dealing with the right to question jurors as to racial prejudice was *Aldridge v. United States,*[1] in which the Court stated that, "it would be far more injurious to permit it to be thought that persons entertaining a disqualifying prejudice were allowed to serve as jurors and that inquiries designed to elicit the fact of disqualification were barred." The petitioner in Aldridge was an African American man convicted of first degree murder of a white police officer and sentenced to death. The Court reversed the petitioner's conviction, holding that he was entitled to have the jurors asked whether they had any racial prejudice, by reason of the fact that the defendant was an African American man and the deceased was a white man, which would prevent their giving a fair and impartial verdict.

The *Aldridge* Court, relying on several state court decisions, found that "the practice of permitting questions as to racial prejudice is not confined to any section of the country, and this fact attests to the widespread sentiment that fairness demands that such inquiries be allowed." Furthermore, "[t]he right to examine jurors on the *voir dire* as to the existence of a disqualifying state of mind, has been upheld with respect to other races than the black race, and in relation to religious and other prejudices of a serious character." [2] Finally, the risk of barring inquiries to jurors' potential prejudices becomes most grave when, as in *Aldridge,* the issue was one of life or death.

Aldridge has barely withstood the test of time. In *Ham v. South Carolina,*[3] a trial of an African American civil rights worker charged with possession of marijuana, the judge refused to ask jurors specific questions, requested by defense counsel, aimed at eliciting any possible prejudice against the defendant because of his race. The defendant was convicted and appealed. The Supreme Court agreed with the defendant's reasoning that, "[s]ince one of the purposes of the Due Process Clause of the Fourteenth Amendment is to insure [the] 'essential demands of fairness,' ... and since a principal purpose of the adoption of the Fourteenth Amendment was to prohibit the States from invidiously discriminating on the basis of race, ... we think that the

§ 15.18

1. 283 U.S. 308, 315, 51 S.Ct. 470, 473, 75 L.Ed. 1054 (1931).

2. *Id.* at 313, 51 S.Ct. at 472.

3. 409 U.S. 524, 93 S.Ct. 848, 35 L.Ed.2d 46 (1973).

Fourteenth Amendment required the judge in this case to interrogate the jurors upon the subject racial prejudice." [4]

In *Ristaino v. Ross,*[5] the Court explained the limits of its decision in *Ham.* In *Ristaino,* the defendant was charged, with two other African American men, for various non-capital felonies resulting from an attack on a white Boston University security guard. The defendant argued that he should have been permitted to question prospective jurors concerning their possible racial prejudice. The Court affirmed defendant's conviction by distinguishing his situation from the petitioner in *Ham.* Ham's reputation as a civil rights activist, which, if not already known, would have been inevitably revealed to the jurors during the course of the trial, and the defense he was going to interpose, would have been "likely to intensify any prejudice that individual jurors might harbor." Accordingly, racial issues "were inextricably bound up with the conduct of the trial."[6] The *Ristaino* Court focused on the unique facts in *Ham* to limit a party's right to question on possible racial prejudice.

The Court further limited *Ham*'s application in *Rosales–Lopez v. United States.*[7] In *Rosales–Lopez,* the petitioner was of Mexican descent and charged with participating in the smuggling of illegal aliens into this country. The district court refused to question potential jurors concerning possible racial or ethnic prejudice since the alleged victims were of the same racial or ethnic group. The Supreme Court affirmed, reasoning that "[t]here may be other circumstances that suggest the need for such an inquiry, but the decision as to whether the total circumstances suggest a reasonable possibility that racial or ethnic prejudice will affect the jury remains primarily with the trial court, subject to case-by-case review by the appellate courts." [8] Lower courts have similarly given wide discretion in formulating or denying *voir dire* questions as to racial prejudice. Cases of note are: *United States v. Givens,*[9] in which the court ruled that *voir dire* with respect to racial attitudes was sufficient where the trial judge asked two general questions on the topic of prejudice instead of defendant's proposed five specific questions; and *United States v. Kibler,*[10] in which the court ruled that a trial judge is not required to question prospective jurors individually on racial prejudice where race is not a central aspect of the case.

4. *Id.* at 526–527, 93 S.Ct. at 850.

5. 424 U.S. 589, 96 S.Ct. 1017, 47 L.Ed.2d 258 (1976).

6. *Id.* at 597, 96 S.Ct. at 1022.

7. 451 U.S. 182, 101 S.Ct. 1629, 68 L.Ed.2d 22 (1981).

8. *Id.* at 192, 101 S.Ct. at 1636.

9. 712 F.2d 1298, 1301 (8th Cir.1983), cert. denied 465 U.S. 1009, 104 S.Ct. 1005, 79 L.Ed.2d 237 (1984).

10. 667 F.2d 452, 455 (4th Cir.1982), cert. denied 456 U.S. 961, 102 S.Ct. 2037, 72 L.Ed.2d 485 (1982).

Although subsequent decisions seem to have narrowed *Aldridge* and its progeny to cases where race is a central issue, the Supreme Court has reaffirmed the *Aldridge* principle for capital offenses. In *Turner v. Murray,*[11] an African American man was charged with the capital offense of murder for fatally shooting a white jewelry store owner in the course of a robbery. After the trial judge refused to question prospective jurors on the issue of racial prejudice, the jury convicted the defendant and, in a separate sentencing hearing, sentenced him to death. The Supreme Court affirmed defendant's conviction but reversed the sentence of death, citing *Caldwell v. Mississippi.*[12] The Court reasoned that since "the crime charged involved interracial violence, the broad discretion given the jury at the death-penalty hearing, and the special seriousness of the risk of improper sentencing in a capital case," involve "highly subjective, 'unique individualized judgment regarding the punishment that a particular person deserves.' "[13] Accordingly, the Court announced a bright line rule holding "that a capital defendant accused of an interracial crime is entitled to have prospective jurors informed of the race of the victim and questioned on the issue of racial bias."[14] Thus, in a capital interracial prosecution or where the crime charged or defense raised is inextricably bound to race or ancestry, a defendant has the right to question prospective jurors on the issue of prejudice.

§ 15.19 Race—Bringing Out Biases

Getting jurors to talk about their biases and prejudices requires a lawyer to be honest about biases and prejudices he or she may have. As discussed in Section 13.6, self-disclosure is key to effective *voir dire,* especially on sensitive issues like race. To get jurors to see that biases inhibit their ability to open up to people whom they could otherwise respect and appreciate, it is helpful to use an example from your own life. You may, for instance, have been raised in an environment that nurtured some feeling which you have had to work to overcome or had an experience that pushed aside a prejudice of your own. Jurors should understand that everybody has had these experiences and that it is not the fact of having the experiences, but how they have dealt with them that is important. First, however, you must find out what experiences, if any, the juror has had and how the juror feels about them; only then should you ask how the juror has since dealt with them. Dealing with one's bias can take years or a single, powerful experience. The following are some examples of what jurors have said:

11. 476 U.S. 28, 106 S.Ct. 1683, 90 L.Ed.2d 27 (1986).

12. 472 U.S. 320, 340, 105 S.Ct. 2633, 2645, 86 L.Ed.2d 231 (1985), on remand 481 So.2d 850 (Miss.1985).

13. 476 U.S. at 33–34, 37, 106 S.Ct. at 1687, 1689.

14. *Id.* at 36–37, 106 S.Ct. at 1688–1689.

1) *I've never felt this experience affected me.* (The lawyer should follow-up on this kind of answer and ask: "That was a difficult experience, how did you not get affected by it?")

2) *I vented my anger and worked through it.* (Ask: "How did you work through it?")

3) *My life has given me the opportunity to learn that my upbringing was not the way to treat people.* (Say: "Please tell me more.")

§ 15.20 Race—General Questions on Race

Questions about "labeling" will help tap into empathy and determine if a juror can put aside any prejudices that may interfere with hearing the case. For example, you might ask:

1) Have you or any family member or friend ever felt labeled? If so, please tell me about that.

2) Labeling is nothing more than prejudging someone. This is prejudice. What does prejudice mean to you?

§ 15.21 Race—Experience With Different Races

It is particularly important to have jurors talk about their experiences with the ethnic group to which your client belongs. The examples they use and the types of experiences they recount will reveal a lot about them. Asking open-ended questions that allow the jurors to talk about their experiences, rather than suggesting possible scenarios, is the best method. The following questions will lay the groundwork:

1) Please tell me what kind of relationships you have had with African American people?

2) You say that you knew Native American people when you were growing up. Please tell me how you have known them and what your relationships were like?

3) Please describe what it is like to work with Asian people at your place of work?

4) Most of us have known someone who is Hispanic. Please tell me in what way you have known Hispanic people?

5) What good and bad experiences have you had with African Americans?

6) Please tell me about the African American person you know best.

7) Please describe for me the qualities that you admire most in the Hispanic person that you say is a good friend of yours.

How jurors describe their experiences with people of another race or ethnic group will tell you whether they harbor positive or negative feelings toward that group of people. Jurors can give pat answers such as, "There are good and bad people in every race or I don't have anything against African American people." Such generalizations are usually more negative than neutral. Or, jurors can describe real interactions which reflect a genuine respect for people different than themselves. Each juror should be asked to develop his or her experiences with the ethnic group in question.

All of us, whether we like it or not, carry with us experiences from childhood that either make us open-minded and loving toward people who are different from us or in some way shut down our natural ability to relate. Because what we have heard growing up has a definite effect on our later attitudes, it is often helpful to find out from jurors how their parents felt about different races and whether they agreed or disagreed with their parents. This is a marker of the impact of those childhood experiences. The following questions will assist:

1) *Please describe how your parents felt about people who were African American.*

2) *Did you agree or disagree with them? Why?*

3) *Do you think your views about people who are Hispanic are similar or dissimilar from your parents?*

4) *Do you and your parents ever get into disagreements about people from different races? If yes, please tell me the side they take and where you stand on the issues?*

§ 15.22 Race—Confrontational Questions

Some lawyers go so far as to confront jurors regarding their experiences with a particular ethnic group. They feel that putting the juror on the spot will expose the depth of any bias the juror may have. Some of the questions lawyers ask are:

1) *If your daughter wanted to marry an African American man, how would you feel?*

2) *If you had the choice between your daughter marrying a white man or Hispanic man, which would you choose?*

3) *How often have you invited African American people to your house for dinner?*

4) *How many Hispanic neighbors do you have?*

5) *Would you say that your neighborhood is predominantly African American or predominantly white?*

6) *Why did you choose to live in a predominantly white neighborhood?*

7) *You say that most of your friends are African American. My client is white and that makes me wonder whether or not*

you would choose not to affiliate or associate with white people, if you could avoid it?

These questions can prove fruitful with the difficult juror who seems not to be responding to open-ended questions—the juror who continues to deny any bias but who you feel in your gut is not telling the truth. Many jurors take a longer period of time to express their biases and sometimes these confrontational questions can jar their honesty.

A problem with confrontational questions is that sometimes they can make you sound as if you are accusing someone of prejudice who is not overtly, or even inadvertently, prejudiced and make an enemy of someone who may have been one of your best jurors. The authors feel that the extremely confrontational questions should be reserved for only the exceptional juror who you feel is definitely not telling the truth. You do not want to create enemies. Some people are reluctant and embarrassed to talk about bias. They should first be approached with open-ended questions before you begin slamming them with direct questions. Out-and-out racist questions, like "How do you feel about the word *nigger?*" can be helpful to jar jurors into talking about their discomfort with the word or to open up a conversation about how that kind of word is an embarrassment to us all. It can also be helpful, when open-ended questions have not prompted disclosure, to get the jurors to talk about such racial slurs as "wop," "kike," "wetback," or, as mentioned above, to ask jurors whether or not they would allow their child to marry someone from a different race or have a minority person over for dinner. Once again, do not create an antagonistic atmosphere if you can avoid it. Go slow and easy on this subject and only get heavy-handed if your open-ended questions have not succeeded in opening the conversation or if you feel the juror has not been telling you the truth.

§ 15.23 Race—Violence and Racial Prejudice

Many people believe that African American, Hispanic, Asian and Native American people are more prone to violence than Anglos. They feel that these cultures are more apt to express feelings toward one another and toward others through violent means.

Prejudice is ugly anywhere, but especially so when it permeates the trial of a woman who stands accused in an incident of domestic violence. Lawyers representing battered women must examine their own prejudices. They should put themselves through the same thorough questioning they will do in jury selection. They must humanize their client, for themselves as well as the jurors, by spending time getting to know her, by crawling into her world and learning that feelings of sadness, fear and conflict cross all cultural lines. It is these feelings that have to be communicated to the jury panel. The jurors must be made to see and feel how their racial biases prevent them from understanding the client and the context of the charges. Suggested questions are:

1) *What does family violence mean to you?*

2) *Have you ever felt labelled in your life for any reason? Tell me about that.*

3) *What is prejudice?*

4) *Give me an example of a person behaving in a prejudiced way toward another person. How did that make you feel?*

5) *Some people believe that African American (or Hispanic or Asian or Native American) people have more violence in their cultures than do white people. Have you heard this? Tell me what you have heard.*

6) *Other people feel that African American (or Hispanic or Native American) people have more violence in their families than do white people. What you think about that?*

7) *Some people feel that violence toward an African American (or Hispanic or Asian or Native American) woman is more acceptable than toward a white woman. What do you feel?*

8) *Some people say law enforcement officers are hesitant to go into an African American (or Hispanic or Asian or Native American) neighborhood to respond to a domestic violence call. What are your thoughts about that?*

§ 15.24 Race—Special Community Issues

It is always important to research and be aware of special racial issues or incidents that have occurred in the community. For example, should you be representing an African American client in the New York area, ask jurors their view of what went on in Howard Beach. If you are trying a case in Miami or Los Angeles, ask jurors their opinion on the use of force by police in their area. Questions on the Rodney King verdict in Simi Valley or the Lozano verdict in Miami can yield very important information about the jurors. These are just a few vivid examples of local racial issues. In many instances each community will have its own Rodney King, Howard Beach or police brutality case that needs to be explored and used as a stepping-stone to jurors' thoughts and feelings about your client's particular ethnic group.

§ 15.25 Race—The Fallacies of Stereotyping

It is easy for lawyers to fall back on old stereotypes such as African Americans and Hispanics will be better jurors than whites for criminal defense cases or Asians are more likely to convict than other groups. The problem with any stereotype is that it prevents a lawyer from truly listening to what a juror is saying and from grasping the import of experiences that might make this person a good or bad juror for the case. Plaintiff lawyers have often been known to stack a jury with minorities, thinking that they will award bigger verdicts. For the same reason, defense lawyers have been known to strike as many minorities as possible from a civil panel. Both neglect asking enough questions to determine whether this person will truly be favorable or unfavorable to their case. Stereotyping alone will not answer the real question: how jurors think about the case issues.

§ 15.26 Race—Differences Within Ethnic Groups

Within different races and ethnic groups there is as broad a range of attitudes as there is between races. Other factors come into play. For example, should a juror live in a high-crime housing project and have been the victim of crime or have family members or friends who have been crime victims, she may very well be more punitive with someone from her own race who is charged with crime. Likewise, if a minority juror owns a business that has been sued, he could feel as negative about lawsuits as anyone else.

In some communities there is also a need to consider the bias among members of the same race, based on skin pigmentation. It is said that some dark-skin African Americans have a negative feeling about African Americans with light skin and some light-skin African Americans occasionally have negative feelings toward dark-skin African Americans. This may or may not be the case, but you should watch how people of a particular race look at your client and not assume that because they are from the same race that they will automatically relate.

One of the most talked-about differences is among Asian people. When a particular group of Asians moved into a city or community may affect how they are received by other Asians and whether or not they have biases of their own. For example, in the San Francisco Bay area, it is well known that Koreans have been ostracized by the Japanese and Chinese. Similarly, Latin groups are at odds with each other. In the Miami area, for example, it is well known that there is a great deal of bias from Cuban nationals toward people from Colombia and Peru. Some of this has to do with the drug traffic and some with the fact that Cubans as a group were in Miami earlier than the other groups. All of this once again points to the necessity of asking questions and not presuming that because someone comes from a similar ethnic background, he or she will identify with your client and witnesses. Find out what particular racial or ethnic group a juror belongs to and that group's thoughts and feelings about your client's national origin.

It is important to emphasize that you should never jump to conclusions about jurors based on a couple of answers. This is especially true for jurors of the same race or ethnicity as your client. Remember that people are individuals with their own life experiences. Many lawyers have made major mistakes by believing that jurors from the same race as their client would be positive jurors when in fact they were not. All jurors should be questioned in the same manner and any prejudgments about who may be good jurors should be double-checked by the person assisting you with jury selection.

§ 15.27 Race—Do Not Overlook Minority Jurors During *Voir Dire*

A mistake often made during *voir dire* is ignoring the minority jurors. Many lawyers think they should direct the bulk of their questions to the jurors they believe are most likely to control the jury and mistakenly presume that will be the whites on the jury panel. This simply is not true and it can cause you big problems should you fall into this pit. One of the authors, many years ago, made a bad call when time was limited and advised a lawyer not to *voir dire* a quiet African American man in the back of the jury panel. This juror turned out to be a former police officer with whom the rest of the jury had to fight, for over a day and a half, in order to return the appropriate verdict. Had this juror not been on the case, the jury would have imposed an even shorter probationary period.

Pay attention to all members of the jury panel and do not jump to conclusions based on race or demeanor. In post-trial interviews, minority people who were ignored during *voir dire* discuss their resentment toward the lawyer for presuming that they would be either a good or a bad juror based on their race. They felt this was a sign of the lawyer's racism. They admitted they may have been predisposed to assist the lawyer but felt pigeonholed when the lawyer asked them no questions. That was enough to make them look twice at the arguments of opposing counsel, who at least asked them a few questions during the jury selection. Your goal once again is to make as many friends as possible. Acknowledging people for their views, opinions and life experiences is the best place to begin.

§ 15.28 Race—One Minority Person on an All–White Jury

If you fear that racial slurs and comments may surface in the deliberations, try to select as many minority people as possible. Their input will be valuable in a case where race is an issue and their presence tends to curb this kind of talk during the decision making. In high-profile cases, however, having one minority on an all-white jury has been a problem. The other jurors use the minority person as a pawn to get a prejudiced judgment. What has occurred in a number of instances is that the African American, Hispanic or Native American juror has been elected foreperson to give the rest of the jury the appearance of not having made a racial decision. This raises a dilemma. You want to have as many minority jurors on a case involving racial issues, even if it is only the one minority left after the other side has systematically excluded the others. You must look at who this minority is and how you think his or her input will help or hurt you. Once again, you must pick your juries on the basis of the individuals, not their race.

§ 15.29 Race—Trying a Case in a Homogeneous Community

Should you have a minority defendant on trial in a predominantly all-white community, you must confront the issue of race. It is quite important because some people from homogeneous neighborhoods or communities have not had exposure to people from other races and therefore believe all of the negative stereotypes. On the other hand, homogeneous neighborhoods or communities may not have had negative experiences with people of other races and may not subscribe to negative beliefs about other races. Of course, this applies not only to all-white or predominantly white communities but also to predominantly ethnic communities. *Voir dire* should explore jurors' exposure to the racial or ethnic group of your client. You may want to ask some of the following questions:

1) *You are aware that this community is predominantly African American. Because my client is white, I have some fears that he may not get as fair a trial here, as he might get in a community with a variety of ethnic groups. What do you think about my fear?*
2) *As you know, I do not come from this community. I would like you to educate me on whether or not I should be uncomfortable with the fact that my client is African American and most of the citizens here are white. Should I feel uncomfortable or not and why?*
3) *I'm not saying that people in this community are any more prejudiced than people in other communities. I would like you to help me understand why my client will be able to get, or not be able to get, as fair a trial here as in another community?*

Obviously, in asking these kinds of questions, you want to avoid any insinuations that this is a racist community when, in fact, many of your jurors may not bear such prejudices.

§ 15.30 Religion—Generally

Much has been written about how different religions see the world. These points of view invariably find their way into the jury room, notwithstanding the secular tone of the legal process. Religion can encourage someone to be open-minded or it can encourage someone to become immersed in rules. Ask jurors to describe their religious beliefs and how those beliefs have influenced their life. Listen for a softness in their voice as opposed to an edge. Determine whether they are talking in desires, rather than shoulds. Self-righteousness can be a problem on any jury, while tolerant, open-minded people who have taken religious and spiritual concepts to heart and truly believe "thy brother, thyself," can be your very best jurors.

While religious stereotypes abound, the problem with categorizing people by religion is that you can strike jurors from the panel that you should keep and keep jurors you should strike. You need to know not only jurors' religious affiliations, but how they live their religion, what they feel about their religion and what they think their religion stands for.

In a highly publicized death penalty case, for example, the defense lawyers wanted to strike a juror who belonged to a very conservative pentecostal church. They jumped to the conclusion that this person's church affiliation meant that the juror had a stance in favor of the death penalty. Later that day, the juror was seen putting leaflets on all the cars in the parking lot stating that the death penalty was immoral and wrong. In *voir dire,* the juror stated he felt there were many problems with the death penalty. The lawyers kept this juror on the case and the juror voted against the death penalty. This is one among many examples of how religious stereotyping could have hurt the defense if they had not bothered to follow up with additional questions and get a whole picture of the juror.

§ 15.31 Religion—Religious Viewpoints

With the caveat against stereotyping firmly in mind, it is worth noting the research on religious attitudes. People who believe that the person who makes judgments is exercising his moral responsibility are generally going to be more open-minded than those who feel that God has laid down the absolutes in stone. The stricter protestant religions such as Baptist, Methodist, Church of Christ and Assembly of God have proved to be more conservative on law and order issues and plaintiff's claims. Lutherans are also known to view social issues and law and order-related matters conservatively.

Another religion known for its conservative tendencies is the Mormon Church, which is pro-family and pro-business. It is well established that the Mormons believe that you should take care of your own and not look for or offer outside help. If you have a client who is on welfare or has lived off of other people, Mormon jurors could be a problem.

Catholic jurors can run the gamut from very conservative to very liberal, depending upon their parish, priest, and, of course, their attitude toward life. If abortion is an issue or the fact that a client has had an abortion may come into evidence, you will obviously want to address this issue directly in *voir dire,* given the strong sanction by the Pope and the range of opinion of individual Catholics.

Jewish jurors are believed to be more liberal than others. Though this may be true on some social issues, in terms of law and order today, Jewish jurors should not be considered any more liberal than anyone else. They, too, require probing *voir dire* on the specifics of the case to determine if they can be open-minded.

Followers of Eastern religion such as Hindus, Buddhists or Muslims can have a variety of feelings that would affect their ability to hear and deliberate issues at trial. Educate yourself on the views of these religions so you will know their potential impact on your case. It is important to know whether followers of these religions were raised in these religions or switched religions later in life. Changing from one religion to another can tell you as much about a juror as their original religious denomination. For example, someone who was raised in a Southern Baptist church and is now a Muslim could be more political than other jurors. Similarly, a juror raised Catholic who converts to Zen Buddhism could have a more "live and let live" attitude than others. The key is to ask questions about what precipitated the change and its impact on the juror's way of seeing the world.

§ 15.32 Religion—Spiritualism

Though many people who are religious are also spiritual, it does not necessarily go the other way. When asking about religion, go beyond whether or not jurors belong to a traditional church, and include questions on spirituality. Find out if they participate in a meditation group or nondenominational church or have any other spiritual pursuits. The following questions will assist:

1) *Some people feel that they are very religious; others feel they are more spiritual. How do you see yourself?*

2) *I note from your questionnaire that you do not attend church. Many people do not attend church but still feel that they are spiritual people. How do you see yourself?*

3) *Tell me what kinds of books or programs in which you have taken an interest for your religious or spiritual self.*

Someone who seeks spiritual guidance outside the mainstream can be a help or a hindrance, like any other religious people. The question is: Will the person truly listen to your case? You also want to ask these people what role their spiritual practice has in their lives and how they think it has affected them. How they answer should give you a sense of whether they walk in the world with self-righteous certainty or an open mind. People who do not attend church but feel they have a close connection with the Divine can be of two stripes: They will either be more apt to vote their own conscience because they feel they are divinely led or they will feel that there is an absolute right and wrong and have their mind made up from the start.

Those who identify with New Age spiritualism believe in an Ultimate Power as much as people who regularly attend church. Find out how their sense of God will affect them in deliberations. They may have a broad-minded perspective or they may have bought into the New Age as a dogma, which can stifle their thought process as well as any traditional beliefs. It is important to ask enough questions to figure out what kind of spiritual person you are dealing with.

§ 15.33 Religion—Atheism/Agnosticism

A self-proclaimed atheist or agnostic many times has come to this conclusion by rejecting other more socially-approved thought. In a very sensitive way, ask what has led him or her to feel this way. Also ask whether or not, at some time earlier in life, the juror belonged to a religion, and if so, what was the motivating factor to renounce those religious tenets.

Atheists and agnostics have probably spent years trying to defend their position to other people. This could have made them more open-minded to a variety of thought or left them feeling bitter and at odds with the rest of the world. Ask enough questions to distinguish how this person has grown from the experience or has been stifled. People who identify themselves as agnostics or atheists tend to be more liberal about social issues. Again, a word of caution: never presume anyone to be liberal or conservative based on a generally held view.

§ 15.34 Religion—Free Will v. Predetermination

People who believe that everything has been laid out and determined by Spirit can eliminate free choice from the equation. They can feel that if someone has been charged with murder or has been sued, that person should reap the consequences, however harsh. It is God's will that determines whether the accused should receive a life or death sentence or whether the defendant deserves to fork over a lot of money. Once again, *voir dire* will help you determine how much someone believes in free choice—their own and others'—and how much they believe in predetermination.

There are jurors who would shun the term "free will" but who believe that everyone can change. If you have a client who has a past history of unsavory pursuits, a juror who believes in change will obviously be of help to you. Should you be on the other side of such a client, representing a discriminatory employer, for instance, steer clear of people who believe that all can change. What you want to know from those who believe that people do change and those that do not, is how they developed this belief and what role, if any, their spiritual or religious beliefs have played in this understanding. This will give you a better sense of who they are and the influences in their lives that may affect your case. The following questions will assist:

1) Some people believe that people will change and can change. Others believe that the die is cast. What do you think?

2) What role, if any, have your religious or spiritual beliefs played in your feelings regarding this?

You also want to know whether those who talk about God's will are using it as an excuse to justify their punitive thoughts or whether they truly believe that everything is in the hands of the Creator. Is that juror mimicking what he or she has heard at church or affirming a true belief in God's will, and what does that actually mean? The following questions will help:

1) You say, Ms. Smith, that God's will be done. What does that mean to you?

2) What is God's will about how you will view this case?

3) I have a concern that you will believe that God put my client in this situation and she should pay the consequences. What do you think about my fear?

Also keep in mind that "free choicers" and predeterminists do not always think along the lines you might expect. Free choicers can feel that someone chose that walk of life and therefore should be held responsible for all their actions. People who believe things are predetermined could feel that someone needs to grow from this experience and therefore should be given a second chance. The categories are not clear-cut and you should not make any assumptions until you hear what the person says that he or she means.

§ 15.35 Religion—The Juror and the Church

Determine which of the jurors attend church regularly. This can say more about them than their religious affiliation. Ask them if by regular attendance they mean once a month, every week or several times a week. Obviously, the more regularly they attend church, the more apt they are to be in the hierarchy of the church or to define themselves socially and politically in terms of the church.

§ 15.36 Religion—Sunday School Teacher

No doubt a Sunday School teacher will firmly believe that it is important to pass the teachings of the church on to the members of the church. To learn about this person, find out what age group he or she teaches and what sort of fulfillment is derived from this job. Listen closely to the reasons in order to discover if this person is strictly into church doctrine or has a larger humanitarian view, and how this will affect your case.

§ 15.37 Religion—Minister

Ministers can be your best jurors or your worst, for obvious reasons. If they are open-minded, then they can be very influential in helping the jurors stay on track because they see it as their moral obligation to encourage people to speak their own mind and make their own decisions. On the other hand, you may have a minister like one in a recent criminal case who believed it was his responsibility to rescue the jury and guide the decision making on the "right" path. When the jury could not decide which direction to go, the minister asked the other jurors if they would mind praying with him. The jury consented and after the prayer, he, along with a couple of other jurors, convinced the hold-outs to vote for conviction. Ministers can be a strong force on the jury because they are looked to for moral leadership and are comfortable in that role. Again, it is the lawyer's call whether or not this type of leader would be helpful to the case.

§ 15.38 Religion—Minister's Family

There is an old saying that the minister's son or daughter is the wildest kid in school. This can be true on some occasions and totally false on others. You will want to probe thoroughly as to how it feels to have a minister for a father or mother and what kind of influence it has had. You may ask how often the juror disagrees with his or her parents on religious, social or political matters and how they tend to differ. If the juror is generally at odds with his or her parents, you will want to pursue whether this is merely the wild child in rebellion or a reasoned view that may serve your client.

A minister's spouse can be a very strong member of a jury. Some totally agree with their minister's spouse and others feel very differently about issues. Explore areas of agreement and disagreement.

§ 15.39 Religion—Deacon

Someone who has chosen to be a deacon does this for societal approval or out of commitment to serve the church. Ask questions to determine the juror's motivation and how this would influence his or her decision making on the jury. It is likely that the juror will not encourage independent thinking in deliberations if he or she is motivated by a need for approval.

§ 15.40 Religion—Church Secretary

The person who serves as secretary to a clergyman may or may not have embraced the beliefs of the church. Once again, do not jump to conclusions about this person, but probe how job responsibility has influenced his or her thinking. For example, a lawyer could make a mistake about a juror who is the secretary to the minister of the First Methodist Church if he did not find out she is married to an orthodox Jew. This obviously reveals something about the juror's religious views and should be explored.

§ 15.41 Religion—The Church's Stance on Social Issues

Because the church often gives structure to individual lives, it is important to know how the church stands on contemporary issues that may affect your case—issues like the death penalty, abortion, social services and sexuality. *Voir dire* all jurors who are church members or employees, about their church's stance on these matters and how the juror agrees or disagrees with the church.

Should you be trying a death penalty case, which is opposed by almost all the major religions, you might use an educational question to encourage jurors to look at the official position of their church. Ask how their local congregation agrees or disagrees with the church nationally on the matter and how they personally feel.

§ 15.42 Religion—Connections to the Courtroom

Inquire whether or not jurors know anyone in the courtroom through their church—other jurors, opposing counsel, the judge, bailiffs or anyone else. Since religion is such a powerful force in people's lives, they may feel that a person who attends their church or church gatherings is on the side of right. Do not jump to conclusions that this is the case because the juror may not like that person. Once again, you should explore how knowing this person through the church may affect them as jurors. Express your concerns that they may align with the person's position at trial because of their religious ties. Note how the jurors answer and try to read their non-verbal language, as well as what they say.

§ 15.43 Religion—Religious Opposition to Lawsuits

It is well known that many Jehovah's Witnesses are opposed to lawsuits. There may be other churches who also do not believe that disputes should be resolved in the courtroom. Their followers may be loving, caring and compassionate people, but on a jury it will be difficult, if not impossible, for them to reach a verdict. In many states, a twelve-person jury does not have to be unanimous, but why would a lawyer want to lose a juror right off the bat? It is much better to find out if any members of the panel have moral, religious or personal opposition to lawsuits. Allow them to state their opposition without necessarily stating the reason, to avoid polluting the rest of the panel.

There are generally two reasons why jurors have a religious objection to lawsuits: 1) their church has come out against suing other people; or, 2) they feel that it is up to the Lord to right wrongs and that people should not sit in judgment of others. Should you represent the defendant in a civil lawsuit, such opposition may or may not work in your favor, depending on the juror's willingness to participate in deliberations. Should you represent a criminal defendant, do not be hoodwinked into thinking that a person whose religion opposes judging others will automatically be a good juror for you. Likewise, someone with a religious objection to lawsuits is not necessarily a bad juror for plaintiffs or the prosecution. As always, you must ask appropriate questions to determine how these religious scruples will affect the juror's decision making. The following questions will assist:

1) *Do you, your church or religion have any opposition to lawsuits? Please tell me about that.*

2) *Mr. Smith, you say you have a religious objection to lawsuits. Please tell me about that.*

3) *How does your church feel about lawsuits? How do you agree or disagree with your church's stance on this matter?*

4) *Should you sit on this case and be asked to determine whether or not someone did something wrong, how will you feel about making such a decision? What standards would you use to decide if someone is guilty or innocent?*

5) *Some people feel, for religious reasons, that it is okay to sue others; other people do not. What do you think?*

Jurors may also have a religious objection to awarding monetary damages. For instance, if a juror's religious sect requires its members to turn over all, or a portion of, their assets to their religious leaders, it may be very difficult for that juror to award large sums of money to a plaintiff when he realizes that individual will enjoy the bounty of the award, rather than some religious order.

There is also a segment of society that believes it is okay to compensate for physical injury, but not for mental anguish or psychological impairment. They will refuse to award monetary damages, or will give only nominal damages. Their hesitance or unwillingness is rooted in moral, religious or ideological convictions, or in a lack of knowledge. Some jurors morally believe that unless the evidence can show a physical problem, such as a broken arm, paralysis, or retardation, there is no way to compensate monetarily for an injury; they will therefore refuse to award any sum. Such moral convictions are generally found among conservative jurors who would not award large sums of money in any case. Those who have a religious objection to lawsuits may also reject traditional legal methods of restitution. If you represent the plaintiff and do not eliminate jurors bound by these religious tenets, you are in serious danger of losing your case or, at the very least, receiving a dramatically reduced award.

Finally, there are the jurors who refuse to give monetary damages out of ignorance, because they personally have never felt the emotional or psychological trauma the plaintiff is claiming. These are jurors who do not go to psychiatrists and invariably believe psychiatrists are quacks. Or they may have had similar problems that they worked out on their own and did not experience any long-term injury as a result of psychological or emotional trauma. They feel that all of us have bad experiences in life that affect us emotionally and mentally, and it is not appropriate to collect on that. Also, some people feel that many mental injuries are faked or manufactured by the legal team. It is important to ferret out the jurors who look askance at mental anguish. The following kind of questions will assist:

1) *We are asking for money damages for my client's mental anguish. This means that because of the problems he has had as a result of his physical injury, we feel it is appropriate that the other side pay monetary damages. What are your thoughts about awarding money compensation for mental problems caused by physical injury?*

2) *Some people believe you can put a dollar sign on pain and suffering. Others do not. What do you think and why?*

3) *Under what circumstances could you award* (name the sum you are requesting in damages) *for pain and suffering?*

4) *If someone caused you severe emotional or psychological distress and discomfort, would you sue them? Why?*

5) *If mental anguish and psychological suffering is not compensated, how are we going to keep people from hurting others?*

Of course, if you are defense counsel in a civil suit, juror opposition to judging others and to monetary damages may be the ideal situation. By seating those jurors, however, you could be subjecting yourself to a motion for a new trial or, worse yet, reversal.

§ 15.44 Religion—Religious Symbols and Books

Years ago if people wore a cross, it generally indicated that they believed in the Christian religion. With the advent of Madonna, heavy metal music, and other cultural connections to the cross, you cannot categorize the cross with any one belief system. A person's age can indicate if the cross is a religious symbol or a fad, but again, you should not jump to conclusions. Young and old wearing a cross should be *voir dired* as to its symbolism, and enough questions should be asked to get a sense of the whole person.

Should people be carrying a Bible, Book of Mormon, the Koran or some other religious book, find out why. Ask what effect reading religious text has on them in daily life. What passages have they read most recently and how has that influenced them? Do not draw the conclusion, just because you see the Bible or some other religious book in hand, that this makes the person a good or a bad juror.

§ 15.45 Religion—Asking Religious Questions

The ability to *voir dire* about religion varies by state and local custom. Under some circumstances the judge may find it proper, as in a case involving abortion issues or parties who are connected in an obvious way with a religious sect. In other more subtle situations, research the law in your jurisdiction and perhaps outside your jurisdiction, as well as federal case law, to find cases on point. Just because questions on religion have not been asked in your courthouse does not mean you should not try to make a strong stand for the relevance of these questions in your particular case.

§ 15.46 Age—Generally

Age stereotyping should be avoided by lawyers. Lumping jurors into positive or negative categories based solely on age can be as shortsighted as analyzing them based only on gender or race. Though sometimes age indicates length of exposure to life, it does not tell you a juror's specific life experiences. Look for potential problem areas that age can indicate and proceed with questioning to check a juror's age against case issues and strategy.

§ 15.47 Age—Juror Bias Against Clients in the Same Age Bracket

Though this is not a positive quality, most people have the tendency to judge other's actions by their own. In the courtroom, this is exemplified by people of the same age bracket who feel they have been through similar experiences and would have made a different choice. For this reason, carefully observe jurors who are the same age as your client and probe if they have any predisposition against your client because they would have acted differently or cannot accept your theory of the case based on the time in history in which they were raised.

§ 15.48 Age—Beware of Young Jurors

Abbie Hoffman said in the Sixties that you should never trust anyone over 30. In the Nineties, because of the growing trend toward conservatism in this country, it is important to look carefully at jurors who are under 30. Young jurors tend to reflect more of their parents' values. They are striving to get ahead and are intolerant of social ills that lead to crime in the streets. Of course, if you are an insurance defense lawyer or prosecutor, then people under 30 may be more in line with your case than if you are a plaintiff's or criminal defense lawyer. The following questions will assist you in determining whether or not the younger jurors may judge your client adversely because of different experiences or a different mind set or because they feel they would have acted differently in the same situation:

1) *You are a young woman who grew up in a generation that could be described as conservative. What do you think about that description?*

2) *Would you describe yourself as a conservative, moderate or liberal? Why?*

3) *How do you feel about the direction our country has taken in the last ten years?*

4) *What are your hopes and aspirations for yourself as the years go on?*

Trial lawyers have also been wary of jurors under 30 because they think that young jurors will not carry their weight in the jury room. Post-trial interviews have shown the contrary. Many young jurors, because of so much media exposure, family background, or job experience, wind up having strong opinions that make them mature for their age. To determine their influence on the rest of the jury, you should ask them the same questions related to leadership as you would ask of older jurors:

1) *In what kind of situations do you feel that you are a leader? Tell me about that.*

2) *How are you alike and how are you different from people your own age?*

3) *When you are in a group made up of people who are older than yourself, how do you tend to express your opinion?*

There are, however, those jurors who, because of their upbringing, education and professional pursuits, may be young for their years. They may have been sheltered or taken care of in ways that fostered a naive view of the world, or they may behave younger than what you would expect, given their age. Again, this is a time to be careful of stereotypes and quick conclusions. You may have a juror in his late twenties or thirties who, because of his job experience, appears to be appropriately mature but through questioning, you find is really young for his age. These jurors, more often than others, tend to be followers in a group. The following questions will help you gauge a juror's maturity:

1) *Describe your upbringing.*

2) *Describe your work experiences and job responsibilities at each place of employment.*

3) *In what situations do you tend to be a leader? A follower?*

§ 15.49 Age—Child-Like Jurors

A juror who acts with innocence should not be confused with the juror who acts child-like. A naive juror may appear to be child-like but could command tremendous power in deliberations. In contrast, the true child-like juror will have little or nothing to add to the proceedings and will in all likelihood simply want to get this task over with. He or she will have a difficult time sitting quiet for long periods of time, may have a short attention span, and when answering questions, will give responses that are either irrelevant or shallow. This juror does not command respect from other jurors and will generally fall into the category of a follower unless the case involves an issue that he or she believes in strongly. Then the juror may abandon the child-like behavior in order to be heard. Therefore, once again, do not forget to ask case-specific questions.

There are some jurors who have come to believe that if they act in a child-like manner, they will get more attention. In some instances they may be covering up their intelligence or their fear of being intelligent. Once they are on the jury, they can become more powerful than what you originally thought. It could also be their method of dealing with nervousness, and once they become more comfortable they will become more vocal. Ask enough questions and do not jump to conclusions because of their child-like manner.

§ 15.50 Age—Lack of Knowledge of Events

Whether out of youth, naiveté or ignorance, there are inevitably jurors who are unaware of certain events in history that lawyers take for granted. There are jurors, for instance, who are too young to remember the Vietnam War and do not understand what it was about. Should you choose a Vietnam post-traumatic syndrome defense, it is important to find out what the jurors know about the war and to begin using the *voir dire* process to educate them. As discussed under the Three E's in Section 13.4, find jurors who know about the events in question and have them talk at length about their knowledge. Jurors will pay much better attention to their peers than to you, the lawyer, telling them what to think. Of course, these "educators" on the panel will likely be struck by the other side. You probably cannot hide them, but meanwhile, they can be expert witnesses for you during the course of the *voir dire.* Sometimes you have to sacrifice a good juror in order to educate the rest.

§ 15.51 Age—Senior Citizens

Some lawyers are guilty of age discrimination. They presume that the older the juror is, the more conservative. This is not necessarily so. Different people age in different ways; it is therefore important to understand how life has affected senior jurors—whether they have used life to understand that anything is possible or whether they have become more and more unhappy because of a series of hard knocks. The following questions will assist in your evaluation:

1) *Ms. Smith, can you please tell me how you think life has treated you?*

2) *Please tell me what you think has affected you the most in your lifetime.*

3) *How do you think surviving a series of life experiences can help you understand other people's misfortunes?*

Obviously with retired people you need to know what jobs they held in the past, but you also need to know how they are presently spending their time. Many retired people will tell you they are retired when they are actually working part-time or volunteering. Others may be actively involved in hobbies that could influence how they see your case or belong to clubs or organizations that may have knowledge of your witnesses or case issues. Also explore any family connections with the case issues. It is helpful to ask a number of open-ended questions to find out how a senior citizen's current activities may affect your case.

1) *Mr. Smith, now that you are retired, how are you spending your time?*

2) *What kind of part-time work or volunteer work are you doing?*

3) *How is your spouse spending his (or her) spare time?*

4) *What clubs or organizations do you belong to now or have you belonged to in the past?*

5) *Might you know any of the witnesses through your community work or volunteer work?*

6) *What has your family said about the matters we are discussing here?*

§ 15.52 Age—Goals in Life

It is helpful to ask jurors what their goals are, to help figure out how their life experiences have affected what they look forward to. Everyone needs to have something to look forward to and what they look forward to can reveal who the person is. For example, someone whose goal in life is to make a lot of money is different from someone who is looking for contentment and harmony. Obviously this is a distinction between the object-oriented person and the emotionally-oriented person. The nature of the case will suggest who to choose. You may also want to find out how their goals have changed in life. The following questions can assist:

1) *Many of us had one set of goals when we were younger and have a different set now that we are moving up in years. Tell me how you feel your goals have changed?*

2) *How are your goals similar to or different from those you had when you were younger?*

Occupational goals are also a clue. In a celebrated case in the 1970's in Boston, a woman named Susan Saxe was on trial for killing a police officer during a bank robbery. The name recognition of Susan Saxe was higher in Boston at the time she went to trial than that of Attorney General John Mitchell when he went to trial for the Watergate break-in in Washington, D.C. One of the jurors on the Saxe panel was a bank teller. Obviously, in a bank robbery case most lawyers would have stricken this individual automatically. The trial lawyer, Nancy Gertner, proceeded to ask the follow-up question, "What kind of jobs would you like to hold in the future?" The juror said that he planned on working in a low-income housing project as a therapist. He stated that the teller job had always been just a job to make money until he could really do what he cared about and believed in. Susan Saxe was a revolutionary concerned about the treatment of minorities in this country. The juror thus went from being a bad juror to a positive juror and, in fact, turned out to be one of the best jurors for the defense. The jury hung 9–3 for acquittal in a case that included videotapes of the incident in progress.

This dramatizes the reason it is important to find out what kind of jobs jurors want to hold in the future and why they are dissatisfied with their present job and interested in doing something different. People's hopes and dreams are what motivate them and sometimes their present occupation is merely the way to pay the rent and utilities. The following questions will help you discover a juror's potential job hopes:

1) *What jobs would you like to hold in the future?*

2) *Most of us enjoy what we do for a living but some folks would do something else if they could. How about yourself?*

3) *Some jurors probably have future jobs lined up or jobs for which they would like to apply. How about you?*

4) *What interests you about that line of work?*

§ 15.53 Socio–Economic Bias—Generally

Socio-economic bias permeates the justice system. There is discrimination against jurors who are poor or lower middle class because they *may* sympathize with offenders from their socio-economic background, and because of the stereotype that poor people commit more crimes. A defendant's testimony on the stand may be given less weight because they are less well off. On the other hand, a distinct prejudice exists against rich people who are accused of a crime or make a claim.

It is essential during *voir dire* to expose these attitudes that would prevent a juror from seeing beyond the poverty or wealth of the client—or witness—to hear the facts of the case.

§ 15.54 Socio-Economic Bias—'Poor People Commit More Crimes'

Many people hold the bias that poor people are more apt to do something illegal. Should you have a client that might be described as poor or from a lower middle-class environment, ferret out the jurors who make these socio-economic distinctions. The following questions will assist:

1) *Some people feel that people who have less money are more apt to commit crimes. What do you think?*

2) *Have you ever known someone you would describe as poor? Please tell me about that person.*

3) *Why did you feel that person was more or less likely to commit a crime than someone else?*

4) *Some of us have known people who are less financially fortunate than ourselves and have come to realize they are no more likely to commit a crime than any of the rest of us. What do you think about this, Ms. Smith?*

§ 15.55 Socio-Economic Bias—Poor People Excluded From Juries

It is clear that poor people are less apt to serve on a jury than people who are middle class or above. In instances where your client may be poor, it is important to fight to keep jurors from the lower socio-economic brackets. You should be sure to make the point in front of the jury that opposing counsel is striking people from lower socio-economic groups in violation of your client's constitutional right to a jury of his peers. This can be done in the following manner:

1) *Ms. Jones, why do you think it is less likely that people who make less money than others are going to sit on this jury?*

2) *How fair do you think it would be for a poor person to be judged by people who are more well-to-do?*

After the jurors are seated, make a record that opposing counsel blatantly struck jurors on the basis of their socio-economic level. (*See* Sections 15.62 and 17.13, *infra,* for discussion of the use of the *Batson* issue to protest exclusion of cognizable groups of jurors.)

§ 15.56 Socio-Economic Bias—Poor People's Opinions Not Respected

There is a tendency among educated and well-to-do people to devalue people who make less money. You should not allow this bias to enter into jury selection. The same respect should be given to jurors as to clients and witnesses who have less money. Many cases have been decided by the juror who was less well-to-do. They either chose not to make money in their lives or never had the opportunity. Their lack of wealth did not mean they were any less intelligent thinkers than other people. You should therefore never allow socio-economic bias to enter your decisions to exclude a juror or deny that juror the benefit of the doubt.

The only caveat to this, of course, is in representing an upper middle-class or rich client, if you fear that people who make less money could be hostile toward your client. Rather than automatically exclude people who make less money, however, you should ask enough questions to determine whether or not the individual juror has such a bias. The following questions will assist:

1) *My client would be considered by many to be someone who makes a lot of money. I have a fear that some people may have a bias against him because of that. What do you think about my fear?*

2) *Some people feel that wealthy people are discriminated against and others feel that they are not. What is your opinion?*

3) *What have your experiences been with wealthy people?*

4) *What words would you use to describe the wealthy people you know?*

§ 15.57 Socio–Economic Bias—Rich People 'Walk the Line'

Some jurors feel that rich people "walk the line" in their business and personal transactions. There is the belief that because they have more money, the rich are inclined to cut corners, use others to take care of their dirty business or in some way do things that are either illegal or give the appearance of being wrong. Explore this in *voir dire.*

Should you have a wealthy client who is accused of a white collar crime, you must uncover the jurors with this bias. This is especially important to explore while there is so much in the news about insider trading and stock market violations. The following kind of questions will help:

1) *Some people feel that wealthy people are more apt to cut corners in their business activities than others. What do you think?*

2) *What have you read about wealthy people not being as honest as less well-to-do people?*

3) *Some people feel that if someone has money, they are more apt to be dishonest. What do you think?*

4) I have a fear, because my client makes more money than the rest of us or most of us, that some people may say, "Well that person is more apt to do something wrong than I would." What do you think about that fear?

5) Some people think that people who make a lot of money are just as apt to be honest as those who do not. What do you think?

6) Have you ever known someone that you would consider to be wealthy who you felt walked the line or cut corners? Describe that person. How about someone who did not make a lot of money whom you considered to walk the line or cut corners? Describe that person.

7) What do you consider walking the line or cutting corners? Would you ever do that? Why or why not?

§ 15.58 Socio-Economic Bias—'Rich People Get More Breaks'

Some jurors feel that rich people get more breaks in life. Should this be a potential issue, you may want to ask questions about the number of people at your counsel table, the clothing that your client wears, photographs that will indicate your client has a big house or an expensive car or other things that may come into evidence, either visually or through witnesses, that may flaunt your client's well-being. The following questions will assist:

1) Some people feel rich people get more breaks than others. What do you think?

2) Some people feel that people who are wealthy are judged by a harsher standard. What are your thoughts on that?

§ 15.59 Socio-Economic Bias—'Rich People Deserve Punishment'

If a juror surfaces who feels that a rich person should be punished because she has had more breaks in life, you have a problem. Ask jurors whether or not this might be an opportunity to get back at all the rich people who have not been fair to them. The following questions will assist:

1) Some people feel that serving on a jury is their opportunity to punish rich people who have looked down on them or society in general. What do you think about someone who may think like this?

2) Have you ever known anyone who thought like that?

3) Have you ever heard the statement, "All rich people think they are better than other people"? What did you think about that comment?

§ 15.60 Socio-Economic Bias—'Rich People Look Down on Others'

Unfortunately, some people have had wealthy people make them feel inferior because of something they said or did. In many instances this is a group perception, as opposed to an actual experience. You need to find out whether someone has actually been looked down on by wealthy people or whether this is a perception from what the juror has read or heard about people who are rich. The following questions will assist:

1) *Some of us have had the unfortunate experience of having someone who made more money than us make us feel inferior. Have you ever had that experience? If so, please tell me about that.*

2) *Some people feel that wealthy people are more apt to think they are better than others. What do you think about that?*

3) *If I were to tell you that the evidence would be clear that my client saw himself as being no better than anyone else, would you believe that or feel that this is not likely to happen with a wealthy person? Why or why not?*

§ 15.61 Socio-Economic Bias—The Forgotten and Angry Middle Class

The majority of people in this country are middle class and feel they have been forgotten, not only by our government, but by the ruling class. Some feel that the poor and the wealthy get all the breaks; the poor are given handouts and the rich are given loopholes. It is the middle class who are not given any breaks in life. This is important to discuss should you have a client that is either from a poor environment or from a wealthy one. The following questions will help:

1) *Some people feel that poor people get more breaks than middle-class people. What do you think?*

2) *Some people feel that the rich and the poor get all the breaks from our society. What are your thoughts?*

3) *Some people feel that poor people are given handouts and that rich people have loopholes. What are your thoughts about that?*

4) *Some people feel that we are all treated equally in this society and others feel that people from poorer and richer environments are given more opportunities. What do you think?*

§ 15.62 *Batson* Challenge

Anytime you see opposing counsel systematically striking jurors of a particular race, religion, age, gender or other cognizable group, you should raise a *Batson* challenge. This is a very viable opportunity for reversal or to get extra peremptory challenges. (*See* Sections 17.13 through 17.15, *infra,* for further discussion of *Batson v. Kentucky,* 476 U.S. 79, 106 S.Ct. 1712, 90 L.Ed.2d 69 (1986) and subsequent case law establishing the improper use of peremptory challenges in criminal and civil trials.)

It is important to request additional peremptory challenges to make it clear to the court that you feel that your client has not been provided with a fair cross-section of the community due to opposing counsel's systematic exclusion of certain segments represented on the jury panel. (*See* Appendix 7F for a sample motion, with authorities, for additional peremptory challenges.)

Chapter 16

POWER BROKERS AND FOLLOWERS

Table of Sections

---

§ 16.1 Overview

A jury verdict is reached by power brokers and followers. The power brokers are those to whom other jurors will look for knowledge, direction, and leadership. They are the jurors who will determine the slant of the deliberations, the kind of questions that will be asked by the jury and the final outcome. Followers assume an important place on a jury because they are likely to be good listeners, and though they may not take an active role in deliberations, they often will throw out thoughts that the power brokers will catch and make part of the decision-making process. An effective foreperson will transform a follower into an active player.

It is therefore important when looking at the jury composition to distinguish who will be power brokers and who will be followers during the trial. Many lawyers believe power brokers come only from the higher socio-economic bracket but, in fact, they come from different backgrounds and experience. Identifying the follower is a more subjective call. People have so many preconceptions about what a follower is and is not. Lawyers wind up overlooking people with definite follower tendencies and not asking the appropriate questions to determine whether or not a person who is normally a follower may see this as a golden opportunity to emerge a leader. This chapter will assist you in identifying the power brokers and followers and deciding if they are jurors for your side.

§ 16.2 How to Identify a Power Broker

Power brokers come in all shapes, occupations and walks of life. They are often the people who have prior jury service, are skilled in an area relevant to your case, or work in a job that requires them to be leaders. They are careful thinkers and convincing speakers who are quick to respond. People like the way they say things. They are friendly and caring.

The following list is a sample of the kinds of jurors who have been power brokers on various cases.

- A security guard in a case involving guns.
- A mother of four in a case where a mitigating circumstance is that the accused was raised in a home without a mother.
- A juror with jury service three times in the past who becomes the "expert" on what the instructions mean in a civil case.
- A woman who plays the stock market in a case involving securities fraud.
- A father who has a child in day care in a case involving a day care center.
- A humorous, interesting juror who is well liked by other jurors in a case involving drugs.

The list can go on and on. It is important to examine a juror's characteristics with an open mind and determine how life's experiences could affect this person's status on the jury and whether or not this would be a good influence in your particular case.

Because of the broad gamut of things that make a power broker, you must ask questions that will expose how people feel about being influential during jury deliberations. The following questions will assist:

1) *Some people like being leaders and others do not. How about you?*

2) *Because of what you do for a living, you could be an influential person on this jury. How do you feel about that?*

3) *How do you think your prior jury experience will affect you on this case?*

4) *Should other jurors ask you to speak your mind, how would you react?*

5) *There are twelve individual votes on a case. How will you go about making yours heard?*

It is valuable to remember that some leaders, when taken out of their natural setting, become shy and reserved. The juror, for instance, who is a church deacon, may feel out of place in the courtroom and maintain a low profile. To flush out the "hidden leaders," it has proven helpful to ask if any juror knows anyone else on the panel and in what context. Of course, juror investigation also comes in handy.

Also watch for the humble people who, when asked to describe themselves, refrain from calling themselves a leader for fear of being put in that position if seated on the jury. Yet they could end up taking charge. To uncover their leadership potential, you might ask them to describe situations in which they feel comfortable as a leader, or inversely, comfortable as a follower. You will also want to know how others perceive them, whether or not their family, friends and colleagues consider them a leader or a follower.

§ 16.3 'Natural' Power Brokers—Generally

People always look for leaders in a leaderless group like a jury panel, and jurors look for leadership from people they identify as leaders in everyday life. It is not unusual, therefore, that people with higher socio-economic status, more education, managerial experience or political clout are appointed foreperson by their peers. Also among the "naturals" are people with prior jury experience or familiarity with the law, lawyers and the courthouse personnel. Sometimes these people take charge out of a love for power or the inclination to rescue a sinking ship; other times fellow jurors merely fall back on classic stereotypes of who should be the leader.

§ 16.4 'Natural' Power Brokers—High Socio-Economic Status

Someone from a higher socio-economic bracket is more often appointed foreperson in a short case because there is not enough time for less evident leadership qualities to surface among the other jurors. As the lawyer, however, do not be fooled into believing that the better-off person will automatically be the foreperson. He or she may refuse the role and instead operate passive-aggressively, without taking the responsibility of being the presiding juror. This stance in some ways allows for more power than there would be in the classic role of foreperson.

Someone who gets social status from his or her occupation will generally use this social status in a jury situation. Carefully watch for signs among the jurors: assuming leadership in the hallway; waiting for other jurors to go through the door; being the spokesperson for jurors' feelings; feeling the necessity to become a leader on the panel. You will want to ask questions that evaluate whether or not this person will be a positive juror or a potential problem. As always, how the person feels about your case issues is most important in determining how he or she will use the influence that comes with social status. The following questions will help:

1) *Mr. Jones, you seem to view yourself as a leader. How do you think that will come into play if you are on this jury?*

2) *Ms. Smith, in your place of business you are used to decision making and advising other people how to make decisions. How do you think that will affect you if you are on this jury?*

3) *Mr. Jones, I could not help but notice that you were speaking for other jurors. How do you think you will be affected by this feeling that you are the spokesperson, should you end up on the jury?*

§ 16.5 'Natural' Power Brokers—Previous Jury Service

Prior jury service can make leaders of sorts out of jurors who would otherwise not be seen as leaders or who, ironically, consider themselves followers. The reason is simple: They have more knowledge and experience than their fellow jurors. The other jurors will feel that by dint of experience the former jurors know something about the process. They may either be asked for direction or volunteer it. The jurors who are insecure about their jury duty will look to those with "job experience" in deciding the case issues. They, therefore, can be your absolute best jurors or, given the facts and theory of the case, your absolute worst. One way to better the odds is to find the lawyers in the prior cases and glean from them what information you can. If the lawyers conducted post-trial interviews or spoke to the jurors after the verdict, discover what the jurors said.

In *voir dire,* ask the former jurors about their experience on jury duty, the case at issue, whether they were the foreperson and, if you are in a jurisdiction where the question can be asked, what was the result. If they have been a juror more than once, prior jury service becomes an even more significant variable. Ask how they were lucky enough to serve on so many juries and why they think they were picked so often. This is important because it tells you something about their self-concept, which you can contrast with your own perceptions.

Some lawyers believe that someone with a lot of jury experience is automatically a bad juror. This has not been borne out in post-trial interviews. It seems to depend on the juror, the juror's experience and the kind of case at trial. If the juror served on a case that involved similar issues to your case, delve into this in depth. The juror may have heard some of the arguments that you or the other side plan to make and feel that this is just something that lawyers always say in these kinds of cases. On the other hand, if you do some research about that case, you may find out not only about the verdict, but how your case is similar and different. For example, if you are trying a contract dispute and there is a juror who previously sat on a similar case, ask if the earlier case involved an oral or written contract and whether the juror sided with the minority or majority vote. If you are trying a criminal burglary case with fingerprints and eye-witness identification, it could make a critical difference if a juror previously heard a case with only fingerprint evidence. Doing this kind of research before the jury deliberates could pay big dividends in determining how to present your case and what arguments to make to the jury.

§ 16.6 'Natural' Power Brokers—Grand Juror

There is something about being called a "grand" juror that makes other jurors feel this person is special. Those who have sat on a grand jury can become power brokers in a criminal trial because they can talk about what is involved in an indictment. The danger, of course, is if the former grand jurors do not accurately explain the grand jury process, the rest of the panel may believe that if someone has been indicted, that means the person has already been convicted by another jury—a grand jury.

Voir dire people who have served on the grand jury about this experience. Use them as experts to educate the rest of the panel as to how indictment does not equal guilt. The following questions will assist:

1) *Ms. Smith, you say you were a grand juror. Please explain to the jury panel members what it means to be a grand juror.*

2) *Some people believe that all the evidence is presented at a grand jury proceeding. Please explain to the rest of the jury panel how the defense lawyer and the accused are not allowed to present evidence at this proceeding.*

§ 16.7 'Natural' Power Brokers—Civil Juror

Jurors who previously sat on a civil case are potential power brokers in a civil trial. Discuss with them the kind of case they sat on and what were the main issues they recall from that proceeding. You will want them to discuss what *preponderance of the evidence* means and have them distinguish for the rest of the jurors the difference between *guilt beyond a reasonable doubt* and *preponderance of the evidence.* This distinction is important to make because of jurors' exposure to a higher standard from television shows and criminal jury experience. This should be done in a manner that will not embarrass jurors who sat on a civil jury and still do not understand that this is the standard of proof.

For a criminal panel, it is important to have former civil jurors distinguish between *preponderance of the evidence* and *beyond a reasonable doubt.* There could be grave consequences should a juror who sat on a civil case believe that the same burden of proof applies in a criminal case. People have often confused the two standards and because of their prior jury experience, have led a criminal jury quickly to a conviction based on an erroneous assumption about burden of proof. The following questions will help you sort out this matter:

1) *What is the difference between a reasonable doubt and a preponderance of evidence?*

2) *Mr. Smith, you sat on a civil jury before and I am concerned that some people think that the burden of proof in criminal cases is the same as in civil cases. Please tell me the difference, as you understand it, between the two proceedings.*

§ 16.8 'Natural' Power Brokers—Criminal Juror

Jurors who have sat on criminal cases in the past can easily become power brokers in another criminal case. Find out what kind of case it was and if they can recall who the lawyers were. This is important should there be similar issues in your case. It will help to find out what you can about the case to determine whether or not there are overlapping issues. Ideally, you want to learn if arguments you may use in your case were made, or could have been made, in the prior case and if the juror accepted or rejected those arguments. If a juror has already sat on a case involving similar issues where he or she did not agree with your logic, you should carefully weigh the risk of having this juror on your case.

On the other hand, many lawyers believe that the power broker who sat on a criminal jury that convicted will find it easy to convict again. This is simply not borne out by experience. In truth, many times jurors feel that they need to be even more careful the second time around. You must explore how their jury experience affected them, and not jump to conclusions merely because they have had that experience.

Should you be in a civil trial and have a juror with prior criminal jury experience, again, find out that person's understanding of the burden of proof. The following questions will assist you:

1) *Mr. Jones, you previously served as a juror in a criminal case. I am concerned that you may be an influential juror on this case because of that experience. What do you think about my concern?*

2) *How do you think that prior jury service will affect you?*

3) *Why do you feel I should not be concerned about your having sat on a criminal case in the past?*

4) *This case is a civil case. What are the differences, as you understand them, between the following burdens of proof—preponderance of evidence and beyond a reasonable doubt?*

§ 16.9 'Natural' Power Brokers—Foreperson

Someone who has been the foreperson on a jury in the past will either feel he has an edge on being a juror, or other jurors will presume he does. It is important to ask what he thinks a foreperson's responsibilities ought to be and how that prior experience as foreperson may affect him in this proceeding. This will help reveal his interest in being the foreperson again. As mentioned earlier, jurors often take the path of least resistance and choose a foreperson based on their stereotypes of a leader or the fact she has taken a leadership role in the past. Someone who previously served as foreperson could easily be reappointed. You should therefore examine this person thoroughly as a potential power broker. The following questions will assist:

1) What do you think the role of a foreperson should be?

2) What did you like or not like about being a presiding juror in the past?

3) Would you like to be a foreperson in this case should you get on this jury, and why?

§ 16.10 'Natural' Power Brokers—Knows Courthouse Personnel

Explore whether any jurors know anyone who currently works or used to work in the courthouse. A juror may socialize with courthouse personnel and therefore know more about courthouse proceedings and personalities than the other jurors. The fact that this juror has an "in" at the courthouse will give her added power with the jury panel. She also could have lunch during trial with a staff person who may unintentionally divulge behind-the-scene information she should not know.

Most lawyers are good about asking whether or not jurors know anyone that works in the district attorney's office, any of the judges or any law enforcement officers. The support staff, however, is a critical area of inquiry that is often overlooked. For example, if a juror happens to know the judge's secretary or clerk and you are not getting along with the judge, that could have an adverse impact on your case. Conversely, if there is a juror who knows a clerk or a secretary and you happen to enjoy a good relationship with her co-workers, it could well benefit your case. By that we mean if a juror knows a secretary for another judge and learns that the secretary has a good relationship with you, the juror may well see you as a person who should be listened to.

We cannot stress enough how important it is to maintain good relationships with the court personnel as well as the court. Not only may you need their cooperation in a crunch, but many of the staff wield tremendous power in the courthouse and personally have lots of friends and acquaintances that serve on jury duty.

§ 16.11 'Natural' Power Brokers—Supervisor/Manager

People who are used to being managers on the job tend to want to be managers in other situations. In many instances they will find jury duty to be just another group of people to manage, and naturally become power brokers at trial. Ask supervisors how they view their job responsibilities and how they think that may influence them if they sit on a jury. Some managers perceive their job to be another way to help people be more organized and have a sense of job satisfaction. Other people see it as a way to get people to produce and to make money for the company or organization. The manager who says he supervises 25 hourly wage earners is a different kind of human being than the manager who says he makes people's jobs more fulfilling.

Depending on your case and client, look at how these people see the role of management. Should you be representing a corporate head whose employees are testifying that he was difficult to work for, you may want the juror who describes himself as a strict and hard-driving manager. He may perhaps relate to your client, all things being equal. On the other hand, should you be representing an employee whose manager testified against him, this kind of juror may not be a good choice. If it is a business case and one of the questions for the jury to decide is whether or not the business was properly run, compare the juror's management style with that of the corporation in question.

How people see their job will tell you a lot about how they will see their role as a juror. You will want to ask the following kinds of questions to get the manager's perspective:

1) *What are your main job responsibilities as a manager?*

2) *What do you like best and what do you like least about managing other people?*

3) *What parts of being a manager do you find to be the most fulfilling?*

4) *What parts of being a manager do you find to be the most frustrating?*

You might emphasize how important it is for supervisors to think about their employees' thoughts and feelings before interjecting their own. This is an especially vital point when you are leery about a potential power broker whom you want to encourage to consider other people's opinions if picked for the jury. Should you like the supervisor, reinforce his or her leadership experience as a candidate for foreperson.

The caveat is that some managers feel that when they are on jury duty it is their opportunity to sit back and let someone else run the show. It is important to find out whether or not this is a person who enjoys being manager in all situations or is only willing to take charge on the job. You may want to ask the following questions:

1) *Ms. Jones, I note that you are a manager at your place of business. Some people like to take charge in all situations. Others prefer to manage only at work. What is your preference?*

2) *I would presume, Ms. Jones, that because you are in a managerial position at work, it would be natural for you in other environments to do the same. What do you think?*

3) *Some people like being a leader and taking charge. Others feel it more as a burden and inconvenience. How do you see this, Ms. Smith?*

§ 16.12 'Natural' Power Brokers—Teacher/Guide

Some people, throughout their lives, aspire to be a guiding force for others. They like giving people direction and helping people see the way. In the courtroom, they will be notable as the people who tell other jurors how to proceed in a situation or during breaks, show people around or answer people's questions. If they direct people in a loving way, they could be a very powerful influence on the jury. If they appear to dictate how people should see things or do things, they could obviously be a negative influence.

A distinction must be drawn between a person who seeks to give guidance and a person who seeks to run the show. The following kind of questions may help ferret out the positive and negative guides:

1) *Some people feel that they are a guide in some situations. How do you see yourself in this regard?*

2) *In what kind of situations do you feel comfortable giving other people guidance?*

3) *How do you feel when you give someone guidance and he/she doesn't follow it?*

The person who has taught professionally naturally assumes the role of teacher. In many instances, he or she will also be a powerful juror. Look for the people who like to teach in a loving way as opposed to those who like to dictate. The following questions can help you ferret out the teachers:

1) *Have you ever taught a class in anything in your life? What was that class and what did you think about teaching?*

2) *What did you like most and least about teaching?*

3) *How do you feel when you are teaching something and you see that the class is understanding what you are saying? What is that like?*

4) Describe for me your favorite teacher. What was that person like? Do you identify or not identify with that person. Why?

Teachers can be a particular asset when they have experience in an area in which your experts will be testifying. They themselves could become "experts" on the jury because of their natural ability to teach others. They also could give the expert testimony more credibility by their identification with the experts as teachers.

Teachers, however, can also be extremely difficult jurors, depending on what type of person they are, what they teach, and their philosophy of life. A problem may also arise at the end of the school year when teachers have projects due and are preparing tests and grading papers. As with other professional people under pressure, determine whether or not you want this teacher on the jury or excused for hardship by the court. Should you want to keep the teacher, the following question will assist in clarifying if he or she will in fact be a good juror:

Ms. Smith, I understand that this is a tough time for you because it is the end of the school year. However, many of the other jurors also have problems regarding their job and I am sure that if called upon to serve on this jury, you can put that aside and do your duty. Tell me about your situation.

Once again, the object is to get opposing counsel to strike a juror you do not want or a juror you would like to keep who could be excused for hardship. This tack can also leave the impression that you like a juror that you do not like, in the hopes that opposing counsel will exercise the strike rather than having to waste one of your own.

§ 16.13 'Natural' Power Brokers—Politician

Politicians can be a problem whether they are elected officials or leaders of a civic club or religious organization, or people who just like to politic on a general basis. They can also be a very positive force on the jury if they understand your case issues and theory. The following questions can help you discover the people on the panel who know and love politics:

1) Who has ever run for office? Please tell me about that.

2) Who has a family member or friend who has ever run for office? Please tell me about that.

3) Who has ever worked in any kind of campaign?

4) Who has ever held any kind of office or headed any kind of club or religious organization? Please tell me about the club and your leadership position.

5) *Some people feel more comfortable in a leadership role than others. How about you?*

6) *Some people enjoy participating in intense discussions. Other people find that uncomfortable. How do you feel under those circumstances?*

§ 16.14 'Natural' Power Brokers—'Expert Witness' on the Jury

Should a prior job, family history or some other life experience cause a juror to have more information about the issues at trial than other jurors, you could have an "expert witness" on the jury. Jury duty is a microcosm of life. People who have experience in an area where others do not will naturally be looked to for guidance. You need to examine the people on your jury who could be the experts, given the facts and theory of your case, and whether or not they will be open-minded.

The following are examples of technical skills, direct knowledge and life experience that could give a juror "expert" status in different kinds of cases:

- Nursing or medical training in a case involving medical malpractice.
- Laboratory experience in cases involving medical malpractice.
- Having been a patient or having a relative in a hospital in a case involving medical malpractice.
- Engineering, metallurgy, chemistry or other relevant technical background in cases involving products liability.
- Family members in medicine in cases involving medical malpractice.
- Law enforcement background in a criminal case or a plaintiff's suit involving law enforcement officers.
- Mathematical or engineering training in cases where preponderance of the evidence or reasonable doubt is the standard of proof.
- Swimming, boating, fishing or other outdoor water sports in cases involving water incidents.
- Owners of stock or players of the stock market in cases involving securities issues.
- Frequent travelers in cases involving customs.
- Mothers, fathers and teachers in cases involving relationships between children and parents.

- Carpenters, laborers and union members in cases involving building construction.
- Homeowners and former homeowners in cases involving real estate.

Once you have determined that someone is a likely "expert," the following are sample questions to ask:

1) *Mr. Jones, I am concerned that because of your prior work experience in the field of medicine that you may have more influence than others in this case involving medical malpractice. What do you think about my concern?*

2) *How do you think your experience in the field of accounting may affect your judgment of this case which involves pension plans?*

3) *This case involves engineering issues. How do you think your engineering experience will affect you in this case?*

4) *My client's family experiences will have bearing on this case. You have been a mother for many years. How do you think that will affect how you see my client's family life?*

5) *You have worked with law enforcement, Ms. Jones. How do you think that will affect you in a case where law enforcement officers will be testifying?*

6) *There was a gun used in this case, Mr. Jones, and you said that at one time you ran a gun shop. How do you think that will affect you?*

The list can go on and on. The important thing is to examine each juror about possible expertise and then make a judgment as to how you think it will affect your case. Should you feel uncomfortable with anyone you think is an "expert" who will wield undue influence or somehow taint the evidence, try either to develop a challenge for cause or use a peremptory strike.

Also track down the jurors who sat on another jury and drew from life experiences in deliberating that case. Ask those jurors what experiences came into play in the prior jury service. Did, for example, their job, their family or a past experience figure into that case? You will want to know if they are inclined to use personal experience again to become an "expert witness." The following kinds of questions will assist:

1) *You say that you have been a juror on a case before and that your life experiences played a role. Please tell me about that.*

2) *This case involves medical matters. You are a nurse and you have prior jury experience. How do you think that will affect you in this case?*

§ 16.15 'Natural' Power Brokers—Mathematician, Engineer, Scientist

There is a theory that mathematicians, engineers and people in the sciences are generally not good jurors for plaintiffs or for defendants in criminal cases. You should avoid this knee-jerk thinking because many times they are the very best jurors. A case in point are the three engineers and one mathematician who led the way to a not guilty verdict in the 1976 trial of two American Indians charged with killing two FBI agents on the Pine Ridge Reservation in South Dakota. Many times people from a scientific or mathematical background are apt to evaluate more carefully the standard of proof in a case. They will consciously consider what reasonable doubt or preponderance of the evidence really means. As with all jurors, it is also important to find out how they feel about the case issues before you jump to any conclusion about them. The following questions will help you determine whether or not a juror in the sciences is going to be helpful:

1) *What does reasonable doubt mean to you?*

2) *Some people feel that "close enough" is an appropriate standard by which to judge things. For example, Mr. Smith, in your work if you are required to work out a problem and you can't get it exactly right, are you the kind of person who would be inclined to let it go and say, "Well, that's close enough." Or would you persist until you got the accurate answer. Please tell me what you think.*

3) *You realize, Ms. Smith, that in mathematics if something is one one-hundredths of a point different from something else, the answer is different. This is the same in a lawsuit. Someone has to tip the scales only by a preponderance of the evidence, as little as .001. What do you think about that?*

§ 16.16 'Natural' Power Brokers—Nurse

Nursing is a complicated profession that requires women and men in this line of work to play a number of roles simultaneously. They supervise patient care while taking orders from a doctor, and work as a team while being responsible for their own tasks. Most nurses have had not only medical training but some kind of training in social work and psychology. Therefore, they have more understanding than a lot of people about the inner workings of human nature, as well as their own judgments about appropriate and inappropriate behavior. You will want to know the effect of nurses' training, both in school and on the job, to determine if the juror can be open-minded in your case.

Emergency room nurses are exposed to a lot of violent crime. Should your case involve sexual molestation, rape, child abuse, a fight or fatality, they will undoubtedly have more information than other jurors and perhaps even know some of the experts and law enforcement officers. It is very important, if you are calling doctors or other medical-related experts with whom the nurse may have come into contact or know by reputation, to *voir dire* on the nurse's knowledge of the injuries in question, the weapons that may have been used and the experts and law enforcement officers who may testify.

§ 16.17 'Natural' Power Brokers—Insurance

Many people work in insurance companies as well as in related fields like law enforcement, real estate management, corporate business, or some other line of work that requires them either to have a lot of insurance or to deal with insurance companies. They are potential experts, not only about the insurance industry, but about the many areas covered by insurance. They could be a significant positive or negative influence in deliberating a range of cases, from auto accidents to medical malpractice, land claims to police brutality, to name a few.

Most Americans are ill-informed about insurance rates and blame the "insurance crisis" on plaintiff's lawyers. When representing the plaintiff, identify the jurors who have high insurance premiums, either personally or in business, and might attribute their high premiums to people like yourself who bring lawsuits. Out of self-interest, they may be reluctant to award your client damages to compensate for the full extent of the injury. Should you be in a state that allows you to *voir dire* on insurance, the following questions will assist:

1) *Have you or any family member ever worked for or in any way been affiliated with an insurance company?*

2) *Have you or any family member ever had an occupation that required you to deal with insurance companies? Please describe.*

3) *Who do you think is responsible for the fact that your insurance now costs more than it did a few years ago?*

4) *I have a concern that because my client is suing Ms. Jones and her insurance company in this case, some of you might feel that if you award the appropriate money, it will mean your premiums are going up. What do you think about my fear?*

Some pension funds and other investments are backed by insurance companies. Ascertain whether or not the jurors have any financial investment in an insurance company that could affect their attitude toward awarding damages. The following questions will assist:

1) *Have you invested in any funds that you believe to be backed by an insurance company? If so, please describe.*

2) *Some pension funds are backed by insurance companies. What about yours?*

3) Who feels, because of financial investments related to insurance companies, that they may be inclined not to award as high a verdict as they feel should be awarded for fear it could affect their investment? Please tell me about that.

(*See also* Section 12.12, *supra,* for additional ways to develop insurance as an issue in civil claims.)

§ 16.18 'Natural' Power Brokers—Claims Experience

Some people will say they have had no connection to insurance but they will say yes to having experience with claims. If you are operating in a state that does not allow questions pertaining to insurance, this is the best approach to getting insurance-related information without specifically asking for it. You should ask whether or not jurors or any family member or friends have ever worked in claims or had to deal with issues where people were making claims for money. Also be sure to ask whether or not they have ever been involved in making claims for property, working either as or with adjusters, appraisers, and other people who make their living in insurance-related fields.

If you are a plaintiff's lawyer trying a civil case, knowing each juror's insurance or claims-related experience is imperative because of the obvious tie with opposing counsel that could work against you. For a defense lawyer, this connection would, of course, be positive. If you are a criminal defense lawyer, you should be aware that people who are in the claims and insurance-related fields often deal with law enforcement. You will want to know what kind of contact they have ever had with law enforcement and how closely aligned they feel they are. The following questions will help ferret out claims-related people:

1) Have you ever worked in a company that made claims? If so, please describe.

2) Have you or any family member or friend ever worked in a claims-related field? Please describe.

3) Do you have any knowledge of claims? How did you get that knowledge?

4) How often have you or a family member or friend ever worked with law enforcement? In what regard was that work?

5) Some people feel that when they work in claims and insurance-related fields, they are in some way related to law enforcement. How about you?

§ 16.19 'Natural' Power Brokers—Broker

Being a broker can involve brokering mortgages, insurance, property, merchandise and serving as a go-between in any number of fields. When you have a case that involves brokering of any product, you should ask questions related to brokering in general, to ferret out who may have special knowledge. Brokers are accustomed to examining both sides of an issue, though most of them generally align with one side of the fence or the other. It is important to find out with whom they work the most and to whom, professionally, they feel their # 1 allegiance. The following questions will help:

1) *Have you, a family member or friend, ever worked as a broker? In what field?*
2) *What did you like most and least about that line of work?*
3) *What products did you broker most often?*
4) *Generally you are seen as being a go-between when you are a broker. How do you see that?*
5) *To whom were you ultimately responsible as a broker?*
6) *Who tended to give you the most business?*
7) *What did you feel were some of the difficult matters about being a broker?*

§ 16.20 'Natural' Power Brokers—Contract Experience

Someone who has been in a job that requires them to deal with contracts and resolutions will be a distinct voice in the deliberations of a case involving such matters. Real estate brokers, insurance agents, building contractors, and small business people are among the numerous professions that often have to deal with contracts. It is therefore important in a contract case to ferret out those who deal with contracts in their daily experience or have done so in the past. The following questions will assist:

1) *Have you or any member of your family ever had to deal with contracts in any part of your business? Please describe.*
2) *What experience have you ever had with contracts or resolutions?*
3) *Who do you think is responsible for making sure a contract is properly drawn up well before it is approved?*

§ 16.21 'Natural' Power Brokers—Patent/Copyright Information

People in journalism, electrical, mechanical or chemical engineering, the film, television or recording industry, and many other fields often deal with patents or copyrights. Also, any number of novelists, writers and inventors have sought copyrights and patents at some time in their career. Many times these people have not actually gone through the patent or copyright process but they have discussed or researched the issue. This indicates they may have a lot of information about the subject, certainly more than most jurors, or that they are lacking in information, but think they know more than they do.

Pay attention to those who claim knowledge in this field should your case involve a copyright or patent dispute. These questions will assist:

1) Have you or any member of your family ever attempted to get a patent or copyright? Please describe.

2) Have you ever wanted to get a patent or copyright but chose not to? Please describe.

3) Have you ever talked to a lawyer or anyone that knew something about patents or copyrights? Please describe.

4) Have you ever done any reading about patents, copyrights or trademarks?

pater

§ 16.22 'Natural' Power Brokers—Industrial Knowledge

People who work at plants, factories or have some other kind of industrial experience can be very influential in a case that involves machinery, chemicals or some factory-related mishap. Even if someone says he is a forklift operator and your case involves a chemical explosion, he may have at some point in time worked at a chemical plant and have knowledge about chemicals. Therefore, it is important that you know specifically what kind of plant someone has worked in and what that plant does.

Additionally, people who work in industrial situations may know a lot about government regulations and other matters that you may think are unrelated, but find to be important. For example, you may have a criminal case involving whether or not someone followed the guidelines and have an industrial worker on the panel who has to follow a lot of guidelines. Always look for the common ground and the differences between a juror's profession and the issues in your case. This becomes particularly important when you are dealing in areas where most jurors have little or no experience and by default may turn to the "expert."

§ 16.23 'Natural' Power Brokers—The Legal Connection

People who have been around the legal system as a client, party or family member of a party; people who have taken a law course; people who have worked in law offices; people who know lawyers or have family members who are lawyers are all people who tend to see themselves as being better acquainted with the jury system than others. In this category, as well, are those with past jury service as discussed previously. This connection is important because these people project themselves as being experts. Even if they do not, other jurors will see them as experts because the others have not had their experience.

Inquire about any experiences jurors have had with lawyers, courtrooms or the law. The following kind of questions will help you uncover the legal "experts":

1) *What experience have any of you ever had with the law?*
2) *Have you ever followed a case or ever been in a courtroom before? Tell me the situation.*
3) *Who knows lawyers either as friends, neighbors or relatives?*
4) *Some people like lawyers and others do not. How do you feel about lawyers?*
5) *What good or bad experiences have you ever had with lawyers? Please tell me about that.*
6) *Who has ever wanted to be a lawyer or work in the legal community? Why?*
7) *Who has ever been involved in law enforcement or some other related profession? Tell me about that.*
8) *Who has ever served on jury duty or had a friend or family member who did? Please tell me about that experience for you or them.*

Lawyers, too, can make the mistake of believing that jurors with a family member in the law know more about the law than they actually do. Not all families talk about work, or the juror may not have a good rapport with that relative. For example, should a juror have a brother who is a well-established lawyer in a field of law that would take the opposite side in your case, you might presume that the juror would talk to, or even take direction from, his or her brother. But what if the juror had a bad relationship with that brother and was diametrically opposed to anything he had to say? This juror could then be a positive force on the jury. The following questions zero in on the impact of having a family member in the legal profession:

1) *Do you have any relatives, either immediate family or cousins or in-laws, who are involved in the legal profession? What do they do? What is your relationship with them? How often do they talk about what they do? Please tell me about a case they worked on that you found interesting?*
2) *What do they say about what they do for a living?*
3) *What do you feel about what they do for a living?*
4) *As a result of having family members in the legal profession, what do you know about the law that you would not have known otherwise?*

Then there are those who dabble in the law vicariously. With the spate of television shows and bestsellers that portray the law as a glamorous profession, there are people who have developed a fascination with the law and tend to believe they know more than they actually do. Make sure that the juror questionnaire asks about all the popular television shows such as "People's Court," "L.A. Law" and "Matlock." If you do not have a questionnaire, you must request of the court the right to pursue that line of inquiry. The *voir dire* should include the following questions:

1) You seem to be interested in the law, Mr. Smith. Please tell me why.

2) You seem to know a lot about the law. How did you come to this knowledge?

3) Some people have always wanted to be in the legal profession. Others wouldn't be interested if the opportunity was handed to them. How do you feel about that?

4) Who reads books or watches TV shows or movies about lawyers?

5) What movie or book have you read about the law or a lawyer that stands out the most? What did you like or not like about how the law or the lawyer was presented?

§ 16.24 'Natural' Power Brokers—Used to Public Speaking

Jurors who are used to speaking in public through their work or hobbies will probably be more outspoken during deliberations. Because the number one fear in America is the fear of public speaking, these jurors will automatically have an impact on less vocal jurors. You will obviously want to note which jurors are comfortable speaking in the courtroom, but you should also explore which jurors are probably used to public speaking because of their job. The following questions will help you discover jurors who will not hesitate to let their views be known:

1) Mr. Jones, how often are you required to give speeches or to talk in public or in front of a group? How do you feel about doing this?

2) Some people like speaking in groups and others do not. How do you feel about it?

3) Some people are involved in managerial jobs where they are required to do a lot of public speaking. Others are not. How about you?

4) How often are you required to run meetings at your place of business? How do you feel in this role?

§ 16.25 'Natural' Power Brokers—The Perfectionist

Perfectionists often emerge as power brokers during trial. They are the ones who are precise in how they dress, how they talk and how they address issues. Their clothing may not be expensive, but everything is neatly pressed and carefully tucked in. They are very specific in how they talk, whether grammatically correct or less formal. They will also be very specific about what they say, and think through each word as they are speaking. Additionally, when they are asked how they deal with life, their answers will reflect very high standards.

A perfectionist on the jury would impose very specific terms on how things are dealt with in deliberations. Obviously, this can be positive if the juror understands your case issues and very damaging if the juror is against you. You must ask questions, as follows, to determine the effect of this perfectionist attitude:

1) *Ms. Smith, some people are very specific in their dealings in life and have been called perfectionists. How about you?*

2) *How does being a perfectionist affect how you judge situations?*

3) *You obviously have very high standards for dealing with things. How do you think that will affect you if you are a juror in this case?*

§ 16.26 'Natural' Power Brokers—The Social Leader

The social leader is someone who is easy to get along with and generally liked by others. Whether quiet or vocal, the social leader is often the power broker who wields more influence than anyone else on the jury. Many a social leader who did not have the education or other trappings of "leadership" have been handed the power because their personality was much more important than what they did for a living or where they went to school. When things got hot and heavy during deliberations, it was they who assumed the role of peacemaker and became a voice of reason among hostile reactions.

Court observers should look for people who seem to be listened to in the hallway and liked by other jurors. They will be the jurors who are quick to hand mints or gum to other people, have tissues ready, or are helpful in other ways to the rest of the jury panel. They will also be the ones the other jurors will pay attention to in deliberations because they like them and want their acceptance. It is important to abandon any stereotypes and evaluate the totality of who they are as human beings to decide whether or not you want their influence in your particular case.

§ 16.27 'Natural' Power Broker—The Power Lover

Some people have a desire to be powerful in all situations. They only feel good about themselves when they have power and others do not. You will find these people in "power jobs" like lawyering, consulting, banking, business management, jobs that basically require someone to tell others what to do. You can also see this desire for power in jurors who take control in the *voir dire* process or usher other jurors around at breaks or at lunch. This is the person who will only be comfortable as the foreperson or in an obvious leadership role during deliberations. Whether the display of power will come across abusively or kindly in the jury room will depend on the person. Should you like this juror, and after careful questioning feel he or she understands your case theory and is inclined to accept it, the result can be positive; if not, this can be a problem.

Open-ended *voir dire* is the key to these power-seeking jurors. If you talk to them in an honest, open manner and probe deeply enough, they will admit that at least one of the reasons they are in a "power job" or seek positions of power is because it gives them a sense of control. Giving them the opportunity to talk will make them feel acknowledged for their good thoughts and reasoned opinions, and allow you the opportunity to explore whether or not they should ultimately be selected for the jury.

§ 16.28 The Not-So-Likely Power Brokers—Generally

There are those people who want power, but in life do not take it or are not given the opportunity to take it. Lawyers have been known to overlook people in professions or walks of life who they believe do not wield power. In this category are housewives, laborers, mechanics, clerks and minority people, among others.

These people may have sought power unsuccessfully at various turns in their lives, but jury duty may be their first occasion to actually attain power. You will particularly want to ask these jurors how they think they would behave in a stressful situation like jury deliberations. You may phrase the questions as follows:

1) *Describe an instance in your life where you took charge and helped organize a situation.*
2) *How influential do you think you are in situations that require people making difficult decisions? Why?*
3) *Does your family say you are someone who sticks up for your own opinion or another's opinion when necessary? Or do they describe you as someone who tends to follow other people? Please tell me how you see yourself in this regard.*
4) *When called upon to do so, how do you deal with making sure that your thoughts and feelings are heard?*

§ 16.29 The Not-So-Likely Power Brokers—Minority Juror

Many lawyers have made the mistake of presuming that a minority person will not make a strong juror. This is another instance where it is very important to ask enough questions to determine whether or not someone is a power broker. Many minority people are used to being the underdog and, therefore, given the chance, assert even more power in the jury room to reverse this role. The following questions will assist in distinguishing the minority power brokers on the panel:

1) *Ms. Jones, how do you feel about asserting your position in a group?*

2) *Some people feel that their life experiences have made them more apt to speak up for what they feel in order to be heard. How do you think your life experiences have affected you in this way?*

Also, do not pass over minorities for older, educated white men or women in the questioning process. This can be a grave mistake because a very strong minority juror could hold opinions dangerous to your position. Additionally, you appear to be prejudiced when you do not question all the jurors. (*See* Sections 15.27 and 15.28, *supra,* for further discussion of how to evaluate minority jurors on the panel.)

§ 16.30 The Not-So-Likely Power Brokers—Homemaker

Housewives are accustomed to running a small business. Someone who takes the job of being a housewife seriously understands the basic tasks of an accountant, engineer, carpenter, legal assistant, social worker and numerous other professions. Dismissing housewives as not having job experience related to your case can therefore be a crucial mistake. The following questions will help you discover how this juror sees her job in the home and what experience she brings to the jury box:

1) *Ms. Smith, you tell me that you are a housewife. Please tell me what your main job responsibilities are?*

2) *This case involves carpentry. I am sure that as a homemaker you have had to deal with carpentry and maybe even do some carpentry yourself. Please tell me what you know about the subject matter.*

3) *What do you like best and least about your work in the home?*

Whether full-time or part-time, a housewife has many different roles that require her to be a leader. She can be your best leader or your most difficult one at trial. How she deals with decision making will be a key to her leadership on the jury. The following questions will assist:

1) *Ms. Jones, please tell me how being a homemaker has taught you to make decisions?*

2) *Ms. Brown, I note that you are a manager of a business as well as a homemaker. How would you say these roles affect your comfort in taking leadership?*

Be aware, when you ask jurors about leadership and decision making, that this gives them the go-ahead to be a leader if they are so inclined. Use these questions, in conjunction with case-specific questions, not only to uncover the power brokers, but to judge whether or not they are power brokers that will be open-minded to your case.

§ 16.31 The Not-So-Likely Power Brokers—Secretary/Note Taker

People who are in jobs that require them either to take shorthand or to write at a rapid pace are often strong leaders, especially in a case where the judge has allowed the jury to take notes. These people could end up having more power on the jury than you thought their profession would suggest. It is a well-known fact that other jurors tend to listen to the best note takers more often because they customarily refer to their notes, whether they are accurate or not. The jurors who have been more intent on listening, rather than taking notes, will many times be forced by other jurors to concede to the note takers because the American mind has been trained to believe that what is on paper is what is accurate. The following questions will help you learn more about the juror whose work requires note taking or who takes notes during the *voir dire:*

1) *How often are you required to take notes at work or in some other situation? How do you think that will affect you in this case where notes will be taken by the jury?*

2) *I noticed, Mr. Smith, that you were taking notes during jury selection. May I ask you which parts of the* voir dire *or which questions you were writing down, or were you writing about something else?*

3) *How accurate do you tend to believe your notes are at your place of business or in general?*

Additionally, secretaries, by definition, are used to making quick decisions for a variety of people in a variety of circumstances. Taking the lead is very common to them. They are accustomed to being the person who runs the office and directs the business matters of others. Do not, therefore, make the mistake of believing that because someone is a secretary or in some other clerical position, they are less likely to emerge as a power broker. Many secretaries have wound up as the foreperson and been the major decision maker on the jury. The following questions will help identify the secretaries who could influence your jury deliberations:

1) Ms. Jones, I note that you are a secretary. Please tell me what role decision-making plays in your everyday life?

2) What kind of decisions do you tend to make at your place of business?

3) How do you think making a number of decisions on a daily basis affects your comfort with being a leader?

Many times clerical people have experience in a range of businesses, schools and organizations, and know a lot about them. They are rarely credited with the knowledge they have accumulated. Someone who says she is a clerk-typist at a corporation should be asked what she has done in the past. You might find that she has been a clerk at a hospital and if you are in a medical malpractice case, this would be important to know.

Clerical people also tend to listen to what is going on and give out information to many people on the phone. Never underestimate a clerical person, or forget to ask the relevant follow-up questions. You could find yourself in a very difficult position with a juror having more power than you anticipated. Good follow-up questions are:

1) Ms. Smith, you say you are a clerk-typist. For whom do you work, what jobs have you held in the past and what have your main job responsibilities been?

2) I don't know your office, but my secretary runs my office. How about yours?

§ 16.32 Your Power Broker or Theirs?—Generally

Some jurors will be the power brokers for your opponent; others will be your power brokers. Question jurors carefully to determine how they fall on important case issues. Should you discover a power broker you feel will identify with your case theory, work at keeping that person on the jury. If, on the other hand, someone has opinions that concern you and has the mark of a power broker, try to get that person excused for cause or exercise a peremptory strike.

§ 16.33 Your Power Broker or Theirs?—If the Power Broker Is Yours

When you identify a power broker you believe will boost your case, try to reinforce that person's position on the jury. You can point out characteristics you see that could be helpful during deliberations and ask how the person thinks these characteristics may be of use. You can talk about persuasion and ask what that means and how the person thinks he or she would be able to persuade other jurors. The following questions will assist:

1) *Ms. Smith, you seem to be a kind, yet assertive person. How do you think these characteristics will assist you during deliberations?*

2) *Mr. Jones, you've had leadership experience on your job. How do you think that will affect you during jury deliberations?*

3) *You've worked in real estate and this case involves real estate. How do you think that will affect you during this case and how may it be useful to you?*

4) *Why do you think being persuasive and speaking your mind is important during jury deliberations?*

Many lawyers believe that if the *voir dire* uncovers a positive juror for their side of the case, they should automatically ignore that juror and go on to the next person. It can be dangerous to jump to a conclusion when, in fact, you may not have asked the questions necessary to determine the juror's true self. You should ask enough questions to get a sense of the whole person and to develop his or her expertise as a power broker to influence other potential power brokers. Take the opportunity to use this power broker to educate the rest of the panel, rather than move on to the next person.

Even if you are clear that someone is a good juror for your case, the other side has probably noticed as well. You might ask some questions about other issues that may make the person look not so good for you but good for the other side. This is the best way to hide a juror as opposed to going on to the next person and not fully developing the issue that you think makes the juror good for you. In asking additional questions, you might determine that your first impression was totally wrong, that this is a power broker for the other side, not for you.

§ 16.34 Your Power Broker or Theirs?—If the Power Broker Is Theirs

If you identify jurors as power brokers for the other side, you should still develop the issues that make them look good for the other side. In this way you may get them excused for cause and determine whether or not they are truly favorable to your opponent. Through careful questioning they could convert to your side. Ask how they think key matters will influence them. For example, should your opponent represent a corporation and there is a juror who was a corporate head, ask how that may influence her in this case. Be direct. Discuss your concerns that she may identify with your opponent. There could be something in the way she has dealt with her position that will make her look askance at how opposing counsel is presenting the case. Once again, do not jump to conclusions about jurors based on limited information.

§ 16.35 Getting Power Brokers to Work Together

One of the problems trial lawyers face is getting several strong leaders or power brokers on a particular case to pull together for their side as opposed to undermining one another during the deliberation process. *Voir dire* is fine territory to create a good working spirit among power brokers—you would like to see them help each other rather than fight each other. You must first point out common ground among the power brokers and explore how they think that may affect their ability to work together during the deliberations.

For example, if you have two jurors who are business executives, you may want to point out that both are executives accustomed to taking leadership, and ask how they think that will affect their ability to work together as a team. Should you have two teachers on a panel, ask them to talk about ways they are put in the position of deciding issues between people and getting other people to work as a group. Tell homemakers on the panel that you are aware that they have the most difficult job of all because they have to wear so many hats during the course of their day. Ask them how they think being a homemaker will affect them in deciding a number of different issues, since this is something that they have to do on a daily basis. Engineers should be examined about how they have to analyze situations and look for reasonable doubt or preponderance of evidence in making decisions on the job. Ask them how they think that will come into play in deliberations. Union members should be asked to talk about how they think being in a union and having to make decisions as a group will affect them in their role as a juror. These are but a few examples of assisting power brokers to view each other as advocates on the same team, rather than opponents of one another.

Once you have found common ground among power brokers, weave that experience into your opening statement, witness examination and closing argument. When at all possible during *voir dire,* note the common elements on a flip chart or blackboard to remind jurors how what they know about themselves and one another may have bearing on their views of the evidence.

§ 16.36 Choosing Power Brokers for a Hung Jury

Some lawyers are known to pick strong jurors who dislike each other and try to get them to "power broker" against one another during *voir dire.* This can be a major mistake. Choosing a strong person should not be an end in itself. The one thing power brokers may have in common is dislike for your client. You must be very careful in deciding whether or not you like the power brokers as individuals, and not just react to the feistiness in them that could lead to a mistrial.

A power broker who decides in the minority, however, can be very important in situations where the court is inclined to give an *Allen* charge. Under *Allen v. United States,*[1] a judge may encourage jurors to reach a unanimous verdict but cannot pressure them to abandon their individual views. The power broker can view the *Allen* charge as reinforcement for his or her position since it encourages jurors to re-examine their position, and if they come up with the same conclusion, to stick to that position. The power broker can also persuade other jurors to maintain their belief, even if it is a minority view.

The *Allen* charge has also come to be known as the "dynamite charge" because it forces jurors into a decision. As noted in *Jenkins v. United States,*[2] the *Allen* charge becomes coercive when a judge tells a jury that "you have got to reach a decision in this case." The appropriate constitutional inquiry is whether an *Allen* charge had an impermissible coercive effect "in its context and under all circumstances." The Eighth Circuit, when determining if there has been an impermissible coercive effect, has expanded the inquiry to: 1) the content of the instruction, 2) the length of the deliberation after the *Allen* charge, 3) the total length of deliberation, and 4) "any indicia in the record of coercion or pressure upon the jury." [3]

The use of the *Allen* charge has not been universally accepted. The Third Circuit rejected use of the *Allen* charge in *United States v. Fioravanti,*[4] which found that the *Allen* charge was an unwarranted judicial invasion of the province of the jury.[5] The Tenth Circuit uses a modified version of the *Allen* charge, known as the "Aldisert Charge," which calls upon every juror, not just the minority, to reflect upon the correctness of his or her preliminary appraisal of the evidence.[6] The D.C. Circuit also has a substitute, known as a *Thomas* instruction, taken from *United States v. Thomas.*[7] Adopting the ABA standard, the *Thomas* instruction strongly emphasizes that no juror should surrender honest convictions in lieu of other *Allen*-type charges.[8]

Most circuits have upheld the use of an *Allen* charge but review potentially coercive instructions on a case-by-case basis. Exemplary

§ 16.36

1. 164 U.S. 492, 17 S.Ct. 154, 41 L.Ed. 528 (1896).

2. 380 U.S. 445, 446, 85 S.Ct. 1059, 1060, 13 L.Ed.2d 957 (1965) (per curiam).

3. *United States v. Cortez,* 935 F.2d 135, 141–142 (8th Cir.1991), cert. denied ___ U.S. ___, 112 S.Ct. 945, 117 L.Ed.2d 114 (1992), quoting *United States v. Smith,* 635 F.2d 716, 721 (8th Cir.1980). *See also United States v. Foster,* 711 F.2d 871, 884–885 (9th Cir.1983), cert. denied 465 U.S. 1103, 104 S.Ct. 1602, 80 L.Ed.2d 132 (1984).

4. 412 F.2d 407, 417–420 (3d Cir.1969), cert. denied 396 U.S. 837, 90 S.Ct. 97, 24 L.Ed.2d 88 (1969).

5. *See also United States v. Graham,* 758 F.2d 879, 883 (3d Cir.1985), cert. denied 474 U.S. 901, 106 S.Ct. 226, 88 L.Ed.2d 226 (1985).

6. *United States v. Smith,* 857 F.2d 682, 684 (10th Cir.1988).

7. 449 F.2d 1177, 1184 n. 45, 1187 (D.C.Cir.1971) (en banc).

8. *See United States v. Dorsey,* 865 F.2d 1275, 1278 (D.C.Cir.1989), cert. denied 492 U.S. 924, 109 S.Ct. 3257, 106 L.Ed.2d 603 (1989).

cases are: *United States v. Jorge,*[9] where the court found no abuse of discretion when the judge gave a carefully tailored "modified *Allen* charge" after the jury communicated its inability to reach a verdict; *United States v. Levasseur,*[10] where the court found no coercion when deliberations lasted for three days after the judge gave a modified *Allen* charge before the jury returned a guilty verdict; *United States v. Sawyers,*[11] in which the court found no coercion in the use of the *Allen* charge, even though it was given after only slightly over three hours of jury deliberations; *United States v. Marchini,*[12] in which the court found no coercion when the trial judge commented on the expense of the trial and instructed the jury after four hours and forty minutes, to reconsider their positions and evidence with proper deference to the opinions of the majority, but not to surrender honest convictions simply because other jurors differed.

The *Allen* charge has been differently applied in state courts, as well as federal courts. For instance, in *State v. Howard,*[13] the *Allen* charge was found to be not a proper supplemental charge to be given to Ohio juries which become deadlocked on the question of conviction or acquittal; in *Veal v. Teleflex, Inc.,*[14] no coercion was found when jurors were merely encouraged to continue deliberating as long as there was a possibility that they could reach an agreement on the case; in *Stephens v. State,*[15] no coercion was found where, following the publication of the verdict, each juror was polled and each indicated that the verdict had been reached freely and voluntarily; in *Riddle v. State,*[16] no coercion was found where the jurors were told they would not be kept out all day, but were merely asked to make another effort to reach a verdict; and in *People v. O'Rama,*[17] the decision to withhold from defense counsel the contents of a substantive juror inquiry prior to giving the *Allen* charge was ruled reversible error.

In post-trial interviews, jurors routinely say that the *Allen* charge is misinterpreted to mean that they must make a decision. So that jurors do not believe there is something wrong with them for not being able to reach a verdict, attorneys should request five minutes of argument for both sides to clarify the true import of the *Allen* charge. Judges have granted the time, just because of the sheer novelty of the request and their desire to close the case.

9. 865 F.2d 6, 11 (1st Cir.1989), cert. denied 490 U.S. 1027, 109 S.Ct. 1762, 104 L.Ed.2d 198 (1989).

10. 816 F.2d 37, 45 (2d Cir.1987).

11. 902 F.2d 1217, 1220–1221 (6th Cir. 1990), cert. denied ___ U.S. ___, 111 S.Ct. 2895, 115 L.Ed.2d 1059 (1991).

12. 797 F.2d 759, 766–767 (9th Cir. 1986), cert. denied 479 U.S. 1085, 107 S.Ct. 1288, 94 L.Ed.2d 145 (1987).

13. 42 Ohio St.3d 18, 537 N.E.2d 188 (1989), rehearing denied 43 Ohio St.3d 703, 539 N.E.2d 166 (1989).

14. 586 So.2d 188, 192 (Ala.1991).

15. 261 Ga. 356, 405 S.E.2d 470, 471–472 (1991).

16. 580 So.2d 1195, 1202 (Miss.1991).

17. 78 N.Y.2d 270, 574 N.Y.S.2d 159, 161–162, 579 N.E.2d 189, 191–192 (1991).

When relying on power brokers to obtain a hung jury, make sure that the conflict is deep-rooted and irreparable, as opposed to some philosophical position that could be reversed for practical purposes.

§ 16.37 Don't Compete With Power Brokers

Another mistake that many lawyers make is trying to engage in a bullfight with a power broker. If the power broker is selected for the case because you run out of peremptory challenges, you are in a bind. Power brokers will then use their power to devastate you, simply because you embarrassed them in front of their peers. Always remember that they consider their peer group to be a lot more important than they consider you and your case.

True power brokers will hedge their position. If they have been on jury duty in the past, and see that you are trying to compete, they will be sophisticated enough to understand that they will probably be excused. In anticipation of this event, power brokers will often lobby during breaks and recesses to find other jurors who will agree with them and "get even with that lawyer" if they are not put on the jury. Unless your power broker is an absolute extremist, it rarely ever pays to get into a war of words. You and the client will invariably lose.

By the same token, this is not to say that you should not disagree with the juror. An appropriate way is to thank the juror for his or her honesty. Acknowledge that this is certainly one way of seeing the matter and that other jurors may view it differently. At that point, look for another juror who will disagree and let that juror engage in the battle with the power broker instead of you.

§ 16.38 Mock Trial Analysis—Generally

Mock trials can help you analyze what kind of jurors can be positive and negative for your case. The trial simulation can help you gain valuable information about how to present your case to different types of strong jurors. (*See also* Chapter 5 for an in-depth discussion of the use of mock trials.)

§ 16.39 Mock Trial Analysis—Filtering Power Broker Reactions

One of the real advantages of a mock trial is that it gives you insight into how different people in power positions will react to your case strategy. You may have determined in a civil case, for example, that corporate executives are more apt to respond well to your corporate client. In a mock trial, however, you may find that executives faced with similar decisions would be critical of how your client dealt with the situation. Mock trials have shown us that in many instances executives are judgmental of other people in power who do not dot their *i*'s and cross their *t*'s in a way that they would. On the other hand, outgoing and friendly people from the working force who have been loyal to their bosses have given a break or the benefit of the doubt to corporate clients—contrary to the lawyer's presumption that they would be judgmental and see this as an opportunity to get back at their bosses. The whole point is that once you identify the power brokers, you must analyze how they will react to your case.

As pointed out, by choice or by chance, conflicts can arise among power brokers. Should you have a case involving an engineering matter and it is in a community where you can expect to have engineers and executives on the jury panel, it would be important to determine whether or not the engineers would take a stronger stance than executives, vis-a-vis your client. Once again, a mock trial would be helpful to determine how different power brokers react to your case.

§ 16.40 Mock Trial Analysis—Clarifying Case-Specific Questions

A mock trial can also be very helpful in clarifying key *voir dire* questions. By conducting the appropriate *voir dire* at the beginning of the mock trial and then analyzing the responses of the mock jurors during deliberations, you will discover what additional questions should be asked to ferret out how power brokers react to the case strategy. For example, in the mock trial of a rape case, if a juror during *voir dire* admitted to being raped or knowing someone who was raped, you may be able to determine during the deliberations that there was something unique about this juror's reaction that could have been exposed during *voir dire* either to get her excused or to help her think more deeply about the differences between her situation and the situation involving your client and the alleged victim.

The mock trial may also suggest additional questions about views of work and decision making which could educate the panel about the case theory of supervisory responsibility. As an example, you may have an administrator on the panel who will soon be judging how someone did your corporate client's tax accounting. You may have assumed and tried to establish through *voir dire* that administrators would see it as an error that the company administrator did not know how the accounting was done. The mock trial may show, however, that the real issue is that the administrator did not carefully screen the person doing the company accounting. The mock trial may bring to light the perspective of a potential power broker that would otherwise have been miscalculated.

§ 16.41 Mock Trial Analysis—Weighing the Witnesses

It is important to give your power brokers as much ammunition as possible. The mock trial will provide insights into what other witnesses your case cries out for, which witnesses should not be presented and which should testify more fully. Many cases have been lost because power brokers wondered why a certain kind of witness was not called to give them information. They often conclude, erroneously, that such a witness was not called because one did not exist. Or they assume, also erroneously, that the lawyer for the case had interviewed such witnesses and none would agree with the theory of the case.

§ 16.42 Mock Trial Analysis—Perfecting Demonstrative Aids

It is a well-known fact that many people are visual learners and retain information when they are given something to look at that demonstrates the point that escaped them verbally. The mock trial will show you how the demonstrative aids are perceived by the power brokers and what other demonstrative aids are necessary. This becomes clear from points of confusion that remain, despite excellent opening and closing arguments and witness presentation during the mock trial. A simple chart will help clarify a matter in many instances; in other situations a video will do the trick; and sometimes you will need to resort to computer graphics. It is amazing how many lawyers are willing to spend thousands of dollars on expert witnesses and yet not give power brokers on the jury the necessary visual tools with which to understand their case theory.

In interview after interview post-trial, power brokers have commented that the most believable presentation was given by the side that used demonstrative aids. In criminal cases, this is often the prosecution. Jurors find the prosecution more believable because the charts and diagrams help them understand the prosecution theory of the case. Should the defense have incorporated demonstrative aids as skillfully, the accused would have gotten a fair trial. The same point has been made in interviews following civil cases.

The demonstrative aids, however, should not be too complex. They should convey the information at an eighth- or ninth-grade level. Demonstrative aids that are overdone or overly complicated only confuse the jury more. A mock trial can help assess whether or not your demonstrative aids are understandable, and correct the defects. It is obviously frustrating for lawyers who have spent a lot of money to redo a demonstrative aid that does not work, but rather than see it as money wasted, let it be a second chance to make your case.

§ 16.43 Mock Trial Analysis—Testing Jury Instructions

The phrasing and positioning of instructions can affect different power brokers in different ways. The mock trial will disclose how people from different walks of life respond to the way the instructions are organized and laid out. If you find, for example, that certain instructions confuse the issues for power brokers, these instructions should be redesigned, in discussion with the judge and opposing counsel, so that there are clear instructions the jury can follow. Once you review your mock trial deliberations, additional instructions may become evident for the power brokers to make sense of your case.

Lawyers have listened to instructions so often they sometimes become deaf to what people really hear as the instructions are being read. The mock trial opens their ears to the meaning and impact of the words. Of course, it is also important for all parties that the instructions go back to the jury room for consideration during the deliberations. In some jurisdictions this is allowed; in others, it is not.

§ 16.44 Aiming Portions of the Case at Power Brokers

The mock trial and *voir dire* should have singled out people who are going to wield power on the jury, one way or the other. Aim different parts of your case at these people. For example, during cases that involve tax issues, make eye contact with jurors who have had bookkeeping or accounting experience. Look at the strong social leaders when your client's relationships are discussed. Look at power brokers with family when mention is made of your client's family history and friends. Relate a part of the case to each of the power brokers and make eye contact with them.

This does not mean that you should avoid eye contact with other members of the jury. Many lawyers have made mistakes in identifying the power brokers and left someone out. During post-trial interviews, these jurors said they felt that the lawyer had paid no attention to them. You should make eye contact with all the jurors but aim specific portions of the case at specific people, based on what you learned about them during the juror investigation, *voir dire* and from the mock trial deliberations.

§ 16.45 Excusing the Power Broker for Cause

From the mock trial preview and the pre-trial juror investigation, you may isolate certain people who would be power brokers in your case. If, during *voir dire,* you discover a power broker who clearly is not in your camp, try to develop grounds for a challenge for cause. Because this person is in a position of power, not only with respect to other panel members, but potentially as a juror on your case, the challenge should be developed carefully so as not to offend the person. This can be done by raising what he or she has said about an issue and asking how that attitude may be manifested should the issue become a factor in your case. Explore how such an attitude has prompted his opposition or her strong feelings under certain circumstances. You should not begin by talking about strong feelings or opinions, however, until you have established that the juror indeed has those feelings or opinions. The following kinds of questions will set the stage for a challenge for cause:

1) Mr. Smith, you said that you feel an engineer has a responsibility to carefully oversee how his assistants are putting together a product. What would you think if an engineer did not oversee every part of a project?

2) What if you determined that on a regular basis the engineer hadn't overseen particular stages of a project?

3) What I hear you saying, Mr. Jones, is that you would feel that the person did not behave appropriately. Am I hearing you right? Tell me about that.

4) I have a concern because you have very definite feelings and high standards as to how people behave. Perhaps if someone behaved differently from what you feel would be appropriate, he might start out with a slight disadvantage in your mind. What do you think about that?

5) I'm afraid that you have an opinion that this is how someone should behave and you might be more fair to someone who had overseen a project more carefully. What do you think about my fears?

6) Don't you think that you might be more fair in a situation where these things were not at issue?

(*See also* Section 12.32, "Identifying Adversaries on the Jury," for further insight into the skill of developing cause challenges.)

§ 16.46 Ask Opposing Counsel for Help

You may have a power broker that you have determined is going to be a problem for you and your case and yet it is clear from what he has said, that he may be a problem for opposing counsel as well. You might ask opposing counsel to agree to excuse this person because it looks as if he will not be fair to either side. Your mutual agreement may make it easier to get the court to grant a challenge for cause and save you a peremptory challenge. The worst that can happen is that opposing counsel will say no; you then can pursue your questioning to affirm the negative aspects of this power broker, and hopefully push opposing counsel to exercise a strike. Opposing counsel may also loosen up and concede to joining in a challenge for cause. The point is to try every avenue to get someone excused for cause, before you use one of your peremptory challenges.

§ 16.47 Power Broker Sociogram

It is helpful when determining your jury strikes to draw a sociogram of which jurors will relate to each other. This can be done by arranging the jurors' names in a circle and drawing lines connecting who you believe will relate to whom. From the sociogram you can determine smaller groups which may form around different issues.

This is a key to the group process at work, which should always be taken into account.

Many times lawyers pick a jury thinking only of the individual jurors. Though this is the most important factor, you should also look at how the jurors function as a group. Try to design some kind of diagram or sociogram that identifies what jurors share in common. You should also look at how strong you think these ties may be, based on information gleaned from either a post-trial survey of a similar case or a mock trial.

§ 16.48 Ferreting Out the Foreperson

When you have a juror who you believe has the makings of a foreperson, draw out that person's leadership potential. Find out what he or she understands the responsibilities of a foreperson to be and what other qualities may come into play when dealing with such a heavy burden. You might ask how important the foreperson is in determining the outcome of a case and how comfortable the person would feel in this position.

You may want to follow this line of questioning with a couple of jurors who appear to be strong leaders and sow the seeds for the final decision in the jury room. They will be left with the feeling that they could fill the bill and, in most instances, will like you for having seen their leadership qualities.

§ 16.49 Just a Few People Run a Jury

In most instances, two or three power brokers are going to run most twelve-person juries. This is because both sides tend to strike many of the power brokers. Be clear, when you are carefully choosing the power brokers who will run your jury, that they are the ones with whom you feel comfortable. Do not make the mistake of striking all the powerful people. In most instances, it is generally not a good idea to have one or two people running a jury, which is what frequently happens. You are best having several leaders who are open-minded to your case strategy.

It is understandable to strike power brokers who are opposed to your case theory and very vocal in their opposition. Do not, however, begin randomly striking jurors just because they are intelligent, outspoken and head strong. If they tend to be somewhat open to your case theory, despite what their occupation or other demographics may suggest, they could turn out to be excellent jurors for you. Do not fall into the bad habit of striking people based only on demographics. Always listen to what they have to say with your eye toward having as many open-minded power brokers on a jury as possible.

§ 16.50 Who Will Follow?

To determine who will follow rather than lead, it is important to observe jurors both inside and outside the courtroom. Observers should note, when the jurors are talking out in the hallway, who tends to be quieter, more in a listening mode, and who tends to be more verbal, who is apt to give directions and who tends to follow those directions. This will help you gauge who is the leader and who is the follower. You can also identify followers in jurors who, during *voir dire,* respond to most questions with "I agree with the previous juror" or "I agree with what everybody else has said." If you find someone who tends to have no opinions of his own or to follow what other people have stated, that generally means he feels more comfortable with someone else making the decisions for him.

The danger, of course, is the follower who has had personal experiences that relate to your case and becomes outspoken in the more secluded setting of the deliberation room. Carefully probe, during *voir dire,* for personal experiences or opinions that may impinge on the follower's ability to hear your case fairly and provoke him to take a more active role on the jury.

§ 16.51 Self-Identified Follower

Just because people may identify with the word, *follower,* does not make them a follower. Perhaps they have a poor self-concept or have been told by others that they are more of a reticent, follower type. It could very well be that someone who is reserved and slow to speak up has come to see herself as a follower when in reality she is just slow to make up her mind. In most trials, this can be very helpful. Once again, it is important to ask enough questions to determine the true nature of the juror and what she thinks about the case issues. Otherwise, this so-called follower can abruptly surface as the leader of the group and exert an influence you may not have anticipated. Careful examination of the people who perceive themselves as followers or who recede into the group, is equally as important as talking to the very outspoken and verbal jurors.

§ 16.52 The Follower's Opportunity to Make a Statement

People who in their everyday life are not in a power position often seize the opportunity in jury duty to feel important. They can actively participate in the decision making and be recognized for their leadership. A 21-year-old baking assistant, who was normally quiet and felt he lacked self-confidence, was voted the foreperson of a jury in a recent civil trial. As a consequence, he became very verbal and outspoken and bragged to his friends and family about being the foreperson of a jury and making a very important decision. This was the first time in his life that he had ever had an opportunity to be a leader and he relished having the power. The defense lawyers had not properly explored his opinions or how he thought he would feel making decisions on a jury, and wrongfully jumped to the conclusion that he would not play a role in making the decision.

A courtroom is not everyday life. Although the way people behave in other situations is quite relevant, you need to determine whether or not jurors may use this new environment as a chance to step into a new role they can feel proud of. Always make sure that your questions focus on trial issues as opposed to how people generally see themselves.

§ 16.53 Personal Experience Can Make a Follower Into a Leader

Tapping into personal experience may transform a silent juror into someone who has a lot to say. In some instances this is a chance to express feelings, thoughts and impressions that have been festering, in an environment away from work or family where it is more comfortable to be outspoken. An analogy is the traveller who spends the train ride pouring out his heart to the stranger in the next seat.

You can bet, if someone has had a personal experience relevant to the issues in the case, though he may withhold his sentiments in the courtroom during *voir dire,* in the smaller, more intimate setting of deliberations he will be more forceful. He undoubtedly will have a positive or negative influence on the rest of the jury. Once again, this raises the importance of asking enough questions of each juror to expose people whom you normally would have dismissed as followers but, because of a particular experience, will drop their customary role and become verbal, opinionated jurors.

§ 16.54 Followers Can Be Social Leaders

One thing overlooked on occasion is that people who are followers by nature can become social leaders because they are good listeners and like to please other people. This is yet another reason to observe how the followers on the panel behave in the courtroom and in the hallway and whether or not they seem to be well liked by the other jurors. It is generally a good guess that if you and your staff like a follower, that person will also be liked by other members of the panel and could become more influential than what you first thought.

§ 16.55 Followers' Influence on Power Brokers

If there is a follower who knows something about issues in the case through work or other personal experience, he may gain the ear of the strong and vocal power brokers by dint of his expertise. His influence may be even greater if he and the power brokers have some knowledge of each other through work, their neighborhood or other community contact. Then, without being a vocal person on the jury, he can use his influence with the power brokers to lobby for his position. *Voir dire* should thoroughly address experience and expertise in key areas of the case that may give a follower status in the eyes of the power brokers on the jury.

§ 16.56 *Voir Dire* Questions for Followers—Generally

So that you do not form conclusions about someone you believe to be a quiet, shy follower, it is helpful to ask questions that reveal whether the person is quiet just in big groups, such as *voir dire,* or always holds his opinions to himself. It is critical to ask enough questions to ascertain if this is someone who first thinks through an issue or someone who tends not to speak at all. These questions will assist:

1) *Ms. Smith, please tell me how you express your opinions when you are in groups?*

2) *Some people do not see themselves speaking up in small groups and others feel more comfortable speaking in small groups. How about you?*

3) *Mr. Jones, you seem to be somewhat quiet. Some people would describe themselves as quiet and do not like to speak in groups. Others consider themselves quiet but feel that they should speak in groups. How about you?*

4) *Would you consider yourself to be a leader or a follower? Why?*

5) *In what kind of situations do you consider yourself to be a follower and in what situations do you consider yourself a leader?*

6) *Some people are considered quiet by their friends and family members, yet are known to stand up for their own opinions. Others feel they are seen as being quiet by their friends and family members and tend not to express themselves. How would you describe yourself and how would your friends and family members describe you?*

§ 16.57 *Voir Dire* Questions for Followers—Determining When a Follower Follows

It is important to determine in what situations a person is a follower because in other parts of his life he may be a leader. For example, someone may work in a high-powered corporation and out of intimidation or acquiescence, take more of a back-seat role. Once in a safer environment with fewer people, such as a jury, he or she may become a more vocal participant. To that end, it is important to ask the right questions to determine in what situations a person considers himself a follower. The following questions will assist:

1) *Please tell me in what situations do you consider yourself a follower and in what situations do you consider yourself a leader?*

2) *Some people feel the most comfortable in group situations letting other people be the supervisor or the leader. How about you?*

3) *Some people mistake quiet or shy people for followers. I believe this can be a misperception and is not the accurate way to observe people. What do you think?*

4) *In your mind, what does a quieter person contribute to a decision-making process?*

5) *When do you think it is important for someone, who generally is more comfortable allowing other people to lead, to emerge as a more vocal, outspoken person?*

§ 16.58 *Voir Dire* Questions for Followers—Reinforcing Followers to Stand up for Their Opinion

Should you have a follower who you feel will be a positive influence on the jury, it is important to bolster this person's feelings about being a juror. Make the person feel important and reinforce a sense of duty to stand up for his opinions, even if they differ from those of more vocal jurors. The person should first be questioned on the case issues to make sure he feels the way you thought he did. Once you have decided that he is a juror whose ideas could be favorable to your case theory, then you should begin encouraging him to express his thoughts and feelings. Many followers have never asserted themselves because they have never been encouraged to do so. Ask questions that will encourage them to talk about their desire to have their opinions heard and put into action. This is the trial lawyer's opportunity to exert a potentially positive force on the juror who would not feel his own strength without the lawyer's efforts to build his self-esteem. Most people want to be seen as a valuable member of society and view jury duty as a chance to do something for the community. Your goal should be to assist would-be followers to feel that they are serving their community by verbalizing their views and voting their conscience. This can be done by asking the following kinds of questions:

1) *Mr. Jones, some people realize, and I hope you are one of them, that it is important in serving the community to vote your conscience. What do you think about this?*

2) *It is important to realize that on a jury there are twelve individual verdicts, Ms. Smith. This means that each person should vote what she believes as opposed to what other people may want her to believe. What do you think about this?*

3) Why do you think there are twelve people on a jury as opposed to three or four?

4) Jury duty is a time to vote according to your true beliefs about an issue. This means that though there may be some members of the jury who are more outspoken than yourself, it is still important that you not allow them to convince you unless the evidence has done so. You should listen to what they say but should not allow any juror to push you into a position that goes against your belief system. What do you think about this?

§ 16.59 Don't Waste Strikes on Followers

Many a lawyer has been known to strike someone saying, "I don't want that person on my jury because he is too weak and will not have an influence on the jury." This is a valid perspective if you have enough strikes to eliminate all the followers as well as all the strong leaders who could adversely dominate the deliberations. This is rarely the case, however, and you waste a strike if you strike a follower just because you do not like his looks or vocation or simply the fact that he will not play a role in the jury room. Carefully examine whether or not this follower will have an impact on the case and if there is a good reason to exercise a strike. The guideline is generally to strike the strong, outspoken leaders or the followers who have had a deep personal experience related to the facts of the case—unless you have plenty of strikes and can strike anybody that you feel will not be favorable to your side. Again, this would be an extremely unusual situation in any trial.

§ 16.60 Strike Followers Who May Join Questionable Leaders

Should you have extra strikes after identifying the strongest people you feel must be excluded, your next target should be a follower who could join a questionable leader on the jury. The adage, "There is strength in numbers," is useful when you have a number of jurors who will follow a leader. This becomes a problem when you are ambivalent about a power broker with some good qualities who makes you want to take a risk. Obviously, there is no problem if you feel more comfortable with the leaders on the jury.

§ 16.61 Don't Have a Jury Full of Followers

There are generally a number of issues in any case where jurors must have the courage to vote their own conscience. This becomes a problem when you have a jury full of followers because they will generally follow the guidelines of the counsel they consider to be in a position of power, such as the prosecutor or the attorney representing the insurance company, or they will follow the lead of the court.

Moreover, when a jury is leaderless, it is easier for jurors to take the path of least resistance. This means they will do what they think is expected of them, as opposed to thinking through the issues in a comprehensive, searching way. To be sure, there are risks in seating a jury of power brokers, as mentioned earlier in this chapter, but there is a better chance with leaders than followers for a well-deliberated verdict.

Chapter 17
PEREMPTORY CHALLENGES

Table of Sections

---

§ 17.1 Overview

Prior to *voir dire,* it is important to determine how the court intends to handle challenges for cause and peremptory strikes. Lawyers often make the mistake of assuming that each judge in a jurisdiction uses the same process. In fact, there are many different methods, some with serious flaws. Always challenge the unfairness of any striking system in use that inhibits effective challenges. Suggest an alternative that maximizes your opportunity to strategize and select the best jurors possible.

§ 17.2 Striking Systems—Generally

There are numerous ways to handle peremptory challenges. Some judges use blind striking, which can lead to both sides challenging the same juror. Others recognize the benefits of the Arizona Struck System, which clears jurors for cause before peremptory challenges. There is also the procedure of seating one juror at a time and exercising peremptories as the jurors reach the jury box or striking after six or twelve jurors have been cleared for cause.

How, when and where to use your peremptory challenges requires thoughtful strategy and team planning. Consider also whether back striking will be allowed, how multi-party peremptories are to be handled and the number of additional strikes each party may request. Take nothing for granted in this final decision-making process.

§ 17.3 Striking Systems—Blind Strike

The most difficult way to exercise peremptory challenges is the blind strike. This is the system commonly used in Texas, a few other states and many federal jurisdictions. Under this process, each side is given a list of all jurors who have been passed for cause and goes into separate rooms to make their strikes. This is problematic because the same juror can be struck by both sides, wasting a strike that could have been used on another questionable juror. In a blind strike jurisdiction, you should file a motion requesting that the striking be done in a more efficient way.

§ 17.4 Striking Systems—Arizona Struck System

The Arizona Struck System is the ideal way to strike jurors. With this process, the number of jurors and alternates to be seated, plus the number of peremptories available to each side, are cleared for cause. A list is put together and passed back and forth between the two sides. Each side makes one strike or several strikes at a time until all peremptories have been exhausted. The first twelve jurors not struck become the jury and the next jurors in order become the alternates. The logical strategy in the Arizona struck system is to organize your peremptories so the last people you strike are those you reasonably believe the other side will strike before you. Request that strikes be made one at a time rather than several at a time, to assure the best consideration of your options. (*See also* Section 7.9, *supra*, for discussion of the Arizona Struck System and Appendix 7D for a sample motion requesting its use in jury selection.)

§ 17.5 Striking Systems—Back Striking

Some courts allow back striking and others do not. Always clarify with the court beforehand that if you do not strike a particular juror in the box and pass, then opposing counsel makes his strikes and does not strike that juror, you can go back and strike that juror on a subsequent round. You do not want a juror to be accepted when your understanding was that after strikes were made and the box was filled with new jurors, you could go back and strike jurors who were in the box before new seats were filled.

§ 17.6 Striking Systems—Multi-Party Litigation

Multi-party trials involving numerous counsel attempting to select the same jury can become a circus if not properly coordinated. It is essential that there be a key person, preferably a jury and trial consultant, to organize a discussion of the striking process to propose to the judge, and one lawyer, in consultation with the consultant, to take the lead on how to exercise the strikes. As in other cases, the Arizona Struck System is most effective.

Counsel should request additional strikes because of the multiple parties involved, and particularly if there are divergent case theories among the parties. Make a point of telling the court that conflicting case strategies exist and different members of the team will want to strike different jurors as a result.

Once the number of strikes has been determined, organize your strikes to maximize the possibility of the most favorable jury, and hopefully cause the other side to strike some of the jurors that you want struck. Inevitably, in multi-party litigation, conflicts will arise on the team as to which jurors to strike. It is very important to discuss these conflicts thoroughly and reach a consensus. If necessary, request a lengthy break or overnight recess to talk through the team's thoughts about the pros and cons of each juror. In the rare instance where there is adamant disagreement over the strikes, it should be brought to the court's attention, put on the record and additional strikes should be requested.

Jury and trial consultants can play a big role in assisting counsel in multi-party litigation. They may be hired by one, several or all parties on a side. With their experience, they can help hammer out the decisions, keep tempers at bay, and maintain an organized and focused jury selection. They are especially helpful when there are a number of attorneys and clients present, which can complicate the process.

Should the lawyers in a multi-party case not have hired a jury and trial consultant, one of the team must be appointed to take the lead on jury selection—in the same way that they would allocate cross-examination of different witnesses and experts or other parts of a case. It is the authors' contention that jury selection is critical to the case and should be given equal, if not more, attention than other parts of the case.

§ 17.7 Number of Strikes

Always clarify with the court the number of strikes each side is allowed. Request additional strikes on any grounds that you can justify: in multi-defendant cases with conflicting defenses; if your case has received any publicity; or if a challenge for cause was denied and you have been forced to strike an objectionable juror. Remember to request additional strikes when you see the need, particularly when a large number of jurors are objectionable or the composition of the panel is not a cross-section of the community. For instance, you may have a minority client and a mostly white panel, and feel that in order to reach some of the minority jurors on the panel, you will have to strike additional whites.

Have the law at hand to justify the additional peremptories and make your record before you actually begin your strikes. Requests for additional peremptories should be made before jury selection begins and again, on other similar grounds, before the striking process begins. Once the strikes have been made and before the jurors are identified and sworn, renew your desire for one or more additional peremptories, putting your reasons on the record along with the appropriate law. (*See* Appendix 7F for a sample motion, with authorities, for additional peremptory challenges.)

§ 17.8 Keeping Strikes Straight

Having a visual means of determining strikes will expedite the process. It is recommended that you have a flip chart, an easel and several colored magic markers for the out-of-court decisions regarding the striking process. Plaintiff's counsel, for instance, should devise a chart comprising several columns, including from left to right: Plaintiff Keep; Grey Area; Plaintiff Strike; Defense Keep; and Defense Strike. As each juror is discussed, jurors that everyone on your side agrees should be kept should be put in your Keep column. Those on whom you disagree should be put in the Grey column for later discussion. Those whom everybody agrees are definite strikes for your side should be put in your Strike column. Those that you believe the other side will definitely strike should be put in their Strike column and those whom you think the other side will definitely keep should be put in the their Keep column.

This gives you some basis for analysis. You can look at those you are definitely going to keep and those you assume they will definitely keep, and end up with an educated guess as to who the jurors will be. The object is to look at who you believe the other side will strike and rank them low on your strike list, while causing the other side to strike as many jurors that you want struck as possible. The Grey area will take a while to narrow down as you move people out of the Grey into either the Keep or Strike columns.

Once you have determined all the people you want to strike, you then need to order your strikes, with the top of the list being those that you definitely know the other side will not strike, and gradually working down to the questionable ones who they may or may not strike, then to the ones you are fairly certain they will strike.

Before making the final decision, carefully go through the jury chart and your notes on each juror. You can keep up with your impression of jurors with a number-coding system, one being least desirable and ten most desirable. Also, as you complete each juror interview, put down your possible keep, your definite strike, their possible strike and their definite strike, to correlate with the jury chart. If you are under time pressure, this is the easiest way to pull out what you have learned about the jurors and rank them. Remember, you have carefully *voir dired* or had the court carefully *voir dire* the panel. If the court conducted the *voir dire* poorly, you still need to avoid striking along standard stereotypical lines. Carefully analyze what you have learned about each juror other than race, occupation and age, and get the impressions of each person on the trial team as to each juror. Look for indications of who the jurors are, as opposed to only their demographic group.

In military court, the *voir dire* process is exacerbated by the fact that each side is given only one peremptory strike, and challenges for cause must be meticulously developed to achieve the fairest cross-section from the constellation of military jurors. Make sure that the person you strike is the one who truly has values that conflict to the greatest degree with the way you will be presenting your case.

§ 17.9 Striking Strategy—Generally

Once you have developed your jury chart and carefully thought through your striking strategy, beginning at the top of your list with those that you know that the other side will definitely not strike and moving down to those they possibly could strike and those you believe they will strike, you might consider challenging a juror for cause that you would like to keep but whom your opposing counsel would like to strike. Make sure when you challenge this juror that you are willing to lose the juror should the court grant the challenge. This requires that you understand how lenient or how strict the court is on challenges for cause. Sometimes these challenges for cause will leave the other side believing that you do not like the juror and this juror will make it onto the jury.

§ 17.10 Striking Strategy—Forcing the Opponent's Strikes

Putting the jurors you believe your opponent will strike at the bottom of your list is a way of forcing the opponent's strikes. Hopefully you have fully developed things your opponent would not like about a juror, through open-ended questions during *voir dire*, to hammer down their need to strike this person. Meanwhile, you and your trial team should send the signal that you like this juror, to reinforce the impression that your opponent should exercise a peremptory.

§ 17.11 Striking Strategy—The Importance of Alternates

Some lawyers forget the importance of the alternates in the striking process. Carefully *voir dire* the jurors who will likely become alternates so that they are never unimportant. Some lawyers rush *voir dire* of the alternates and pay them little attention, only to have a juror get sick and one of the alternates begin serving on the jury. Since alternates have the potential of playing a major role, especially in a long trial, carefully examine them as you would any other juror.

To determine who the alternates will be as much in advance as possible, ask the court whether or not the jurors are seated in the order in which they will move into the box. This should be discussed before you make your peremptory strikes so that you can decide whether or not to strike less objectionable jurors in order to reach a juror who you would prefer in alternate seat one or two. Fight against jurors being seated in random order because of the problem of having to consider the whole group, as opposed to the first few jurors, in your striking strategy. If you know the seating order, you can use more strikes on the first jurors to insure the alternates of your choice as first and second replacement jurors.

If there is a reason that you can justify to the court, request additional peremptories to strike the alternates. In multi-party litigation or a highly publicized case, you can reasonably expect the court to give you an additional strike for the alternates if you have put forth the proper record. There may be other reasons in your particular case that would persuade the court that additional strikes for alternates are appropriate.

§ 17.12 Striking Strategy—Jury Game

You may also want to play the jury game. Put each juror's name on a 3 × 5 card and then go through a mock striking process several times to see who may be the real jury. It is helpful to role play the strategy to prepare for what could actually happen in the striking process.

§ 17.13 Challenging Improper Use of Strikes—Generally

The peremptory challenge as defined in Black's Law Dictionary 1136 (6th ed. 1990) is "[t]he right to challenge a juror without assigning a reason for the challenge." For most of America's legal history, use of the peremptory challenge has been unreviewable. The United States Supreme Court stated this long-held view less than thirty years ago in

Swain v. Alabama,[1] overruled, in part, by *Batson v. Kentucky,*[2] The Swain Court reasoned:

> *[W]e cannot hold that the Constitution requires an examination of the prosecutor's reasons for the exercise of his challenges in any given case. The presumption in any particular case must be that the prosecutor is using the State's challenges to obtain a fair and impartial jury to try the case before the court ... Any other result, we think, would establish a rule wholly at odds with the peremptory system as we know it.*[3]

This view, however, has crumbled over five years. Now criminal defendants, as a result of *Batson,* civil litigants, as a result of *Edmonson v. Leesville Concrete Co.,*[4] and prosecutors, as a result of *Georgia v. McCollum,*[5] may attack their opponent's invidious use of peremptory challenges. These attacks may challenge, under an equal protection analysis, the improper exclusion of prospective jurors based on race or ethnic heritage, regardless of the race or ethnicity of the complaining party.[6] In addition a party may, in certain situations, be able to contest the improper use of peremptory challenges under a fair cross-section analysis. Cases of note are: *People v. Wheeler,*[7] which found the California constitutional guarantee to a jury drawn from a representative cross-section violated by invidious use of peremptory challenges; *Booker v. Jabe,*[8] which held that *Batson* could not be applied retroactively; and, conversely, *Holland v. Illinois,*[9] which rejects the argument that the fair cross-section requirement of the Sixth Amendment of the United States Constitution applies to use of peremptory challenges. Trial attorneys must understand the different theoretical foundations for the proper and improper use of peremptory challenges so that they are able to apply this reasoning as either a shield or a sword.

§ 17.14 Challenging Improper Use of Strikes—Equal Protection Analysis

Any equal protection analysis of the use of peremptory challenges must necessarily start with the landmark decision, *Batson v. Ken-*

§ 17.13

1. 380 U.S. 202, 85 S.Ct. 824, 13 L.Ed.2d 759, (1965).

2. 476 U.S. 79, 106 S.Ct. 1712, 90 L.Ed.2d 69 (1986).

3. 380 U.S. at 222, 85 S.Ct. at 837.

4. ___ U.S. ___, 111 S.Ct. 2077, 114 L.Ed.2d 660 (1991), on remand 943 F.2d 551 (5th Cir.1991).

5. ___ U.S. ___, 112 S.Ct. 2348, 120 L.Ed.2d 33 (1992).

6. Powers v. Ohio, ___ U.S. ___, 111 S.Ct. 1364, 113 L.Ed.2d 411 (1991).

7. 22 Cal.3d 258, 148 Cal.Rptr. 890, 583 P.2d 748 (1978).

8. 775 F.2d 762 (6th Cir.1985), vacated and remanded sub nom. *Michigan v. Booker,* 478 U.S. 1001, 106 S.Ct. 3289, 92 L.Ed.2d 705 (1986), remanded in light of *Allen v. Hardy,* 478 U.S. 255, 106 S.Ct. 2878, 92 L.Ed.2d 199 (1986).

9. 493 U.S. 474, 110 S.Ct. 803, 107 L.Ed.2d 905 (1990), rehearing denied 494 U.S. 1050, 110 S.Ct. 1514, 108 L.Ed.2d 650 (1990).

tucky.[1] In *Batson,* an African American defendant challenged the prosecutor's exercise of the state's peremptory challenges which excluded all four African American jurors from the venire in his trial for second-degree burglary and receipt of stolen goods. The defendant argued that the state's improper use of its peremptory challenges violated his right, under the Fourteenth Amendment, to equal protection of the laws, and his right, under the Sixth and Fourteenth Amendments, to a jury drawn from a cross-section of the community. Batson acknowledged that under the current standard, as stated in *Swain v. Alabama,* he had not met his burden of demonstrating the state's systematic exclusion of a cognizable racial group over a lengthy period of time necessary to substantiate his equal protection claim. He argued, however, that he should be permitted to put forth an equal protection claim based solely on the prosecutor's invidious use of peremptory challenges *in his own case.* The Supreme Court accepted the equal protection argument and reversed his conviction.

The Court found that *Swain* had imposed a "crippling" burden of proof on defendants challenging a state's purposeful discrimination during jury selection.[2] To remedy this, the Court held that if a defendant could establish a prima facie case of discriminatory use of peremptory challenges in his own case, then the burden shifts to the state to provide a nondiscriminatory reason for excluding particular jurors. To establish a prima facie case, a defendant must demonstrate that:

> *(1) he is a member of a cognizable racial group;*
>
> *(2) the state is using peremptory challenges to exclude members of this racial group; and*
>
> *(3) these facts and other relevant circumstances raise an inference that the prosecutor used peremptory challenges to exclude the veniremen from the jury on account of their race.*[3]

Although the Court did not provide much guidance as to exactly what is a constitutionally acceptable, racially-neutral reason for excluding jurors sufficient to rebut the prima facie case, it did "emphasize that the prosecutor's explanation need not rise to the level justifying exercise of a challenge for cause."[4] Thus, a criminal defendant of a cognizable racial group could now attack a state's purposeful discrimi-

§ 17.14

1. 476 U.S. 79, 106 S.Ct. 1712, 90 L.Ed.2d 69 (1986).

2. *Batson v. Kentucky,* 476 U.S. 79, 92, 106 S.Ct. 1712, 1720, 90 L.Ed.2d 69 (1986). *See also* Note, "The Use of Peremptory Challenges to Exclude Blacks from Petit Juries in Civil Actions: The Case for Striking Peremptory Strikes," 4 Rev. of Litigation 175, 182–84 (1984), which lists cases where defendants were unable to meet the *Swain* burden.

3. *Id.* at 96, 106 S.Ct. at 1723.

4. *Id.* at 97, 106 S.Ct. at 1723.

nation in using peremptory challenges to exclude jurors of the defendant's race at his own trial.

The Supreme Court has expanded *Batson's* equal protection application in recent years. In *Powers v. Ohio,*[5] the Court addressed the issue of whether a white criminal defendant could challenge a state's discriminatory use of peremptory challenges against prospective Afro–American jurors. In deciding for the defendant, the Court reasoned that wrongly excluded jurors would be unable to adequately protect their own equal protection rights and, therefore, the defendant was in the best position to raise the claim. The Court also narrowed the three-prong test enunciated in *Batson* for establishing a prima facie case by eliminating the first prong, that the defendant is a member of a cognizable racial group. Now any criminal defendant can object to the invidious use of peremptory challenges to exclude a racial group. Later in the same term, in *Hernandez v. New York,*[6] the Supreme Court added that a prosecutor's discriminatory use of peremptory challenges to exclude Latinos from a jury, due to their ethnicity, would violate *Batson.*

In *Edmonson v. Leesville Concrete Co.,*[7] the Supreme Court again expanded *Batson* by extending its protection to civil litigants. The *Edmonson* Court found that a civil litigant's use of the state trial system, combined with state-provided peremptory challenges and trial judges, formed the necessary "state action" to invoke the equal protection rights of the Fourteenth Amendment. The Court then applied *Batson,* as modified by *Powers* (and presumedly *Hernandez*), to the invidious use of peremptory challenges in a civil trial setting. However, *Edmonson* left one last litigant unable to put forward an equal protection claim in jury selection: the state in criminal prosecutions. This issue was addressed in *Georgia v. McCollum,*[8] in which the Court determined that a state may challenge a defendant's use of peremptory challenges. *McCollum* also called into question the continuing viability of peremptory strikes.[9]

Having established who may bring the equal protection claim, the next issue is for whom may the claim be made. In other words, what is a cognizable group protected under an equal protection analysis?

Under *Batson,* and its progeny, a complaining party must first show that the excluded juror is a member of a cognizable "racial" group. This is more easily said than done. Although it is clear that a

5. ___ U.S. ___, 111 S.Ct. 1364, 113 L.Ed.2d 411 (1991).

6. ___ U.S. ___, ___, 111 S.Ct. 1859, 1864, 114 L.Ed.2d 395 (1991).

7. ___ U.S. ___, 111 S.Ct. 2077, 114 L.Ed.2d 660 (1991), on remand 943 F.2d 551 (5th Cir.1991).

8. ___ U.S. ___, 112 S.Ct. 2348, 120 L.Ed.2d 33 (1992).

9. *See* S. Puiszis, "*Edmonson v. Leesville Concrete Co.:* Will the Peremptory Challenge Survive its Battle with the Equal Protection Clause?" 25 J. Marshall L.Rev. 37, 42 n. 27 (1991).

cognizable racial group is narrower for equal protection analysis than for a fair cross-section analysis, the Supreme Court has analyzed this question inconsistently.

In 1987, the Supreme Court twice analogized "race" with "identifiable classes of persons" intentionally subjected to intentional discrimination due to their ethnicity or ancestry for the purpose of civil rights analysis. In *St. Francis College v. Al–Khazraji,* [10] the issue was discrimination against Arab–Americans; in *Shaare Tefila Congregation v. Cobb,* [11] the issue was discrimination against Jews. The Court held that although Arab–Americans and Jews may now be considered members of the Caucasian race, at the time of the passage of the civil rights laws (1866), the term *race* included various ethnic groups.[12] Since the Fourteenth Amendment was passed at roughly the same time, the test would seem to be whether the proffered group was considered a race in the mid-nineteenth century.

In *Hernandez v. New York,* [13] however, where the prosecutor excluded jurors who were Hispanic, the Court seems to have applied a different standard. Noting that the parties used the terms *Hispanic* and *Latino* interchangeably in the lower courts, the Court accepted the characterization that the excluded jurors were Latino and found *Batson* protection. This analysis cites "ethnicity" as the controlling factor.[14] Later, in *Edmonson v. Leesville Concrete Co., Inc.*[15] the Court seems to have broadened the test to also include "ancestry."

Lower courts have found *Batson* protection for various groups, including: Italian–Americans, [16] American Indians, [17] Hispanics, [18] Navajo, [19] Mexican–Americans, [20] French–Canadians [21]. At least one case,

10. 481 U.S. 604, 107 S.Ct. 2022, 95 L.Ed.2d 582 (1987), rehearing denied 483 U.S. 1011, 107 S.Ct. 3244, 97 L.Ed.2d 749 (1987).

11. 481 U.S. 615, 107 S.Ct. 2019, 95 L.Ed.2d 594 (1987).

12. *St. Francis College,* 481 U.S. at 611–612, 107 S.Ct. at 2027 (including Arabs, Jews, Swedes, Norwegians, Germans, Greeks, Finns, Irish, Italians, Spanish, Mongolians, Hungarians and Russians).

13. ___ U.S. ___, ___, 111 S.Ct. 1859, 1864, 114 L.Ed.2d 395 (1991).

14. *Id.;* accord *United States v. Duran De Amesquita,* 582 F.Supp. 1326, 1328 (S.D.Fla.1984) (questioning whether Spanish-speaking persons constitutes a common cultural background).

15. ___ U.S. ___, ___, 111 S.Ct. 2077, 2088, 114 L.Ed.2d 660 (1991), on remand 943 F.2d 551 (5th Cir.1991).

16. *United States v. Sgro,* 816 F.2d 30, 33 (1st Cir.1987), cert. denied 484 U.S. 1063, 108 S.Ct. 1021, 98 L.Ed.2d 986 (1988).

17. *United States v. Chalan,* 812 F.2d 1302, 1313–1314 (10th Cir.1987).

18. *United States v. Alcantar,* 832 F.2d 1175, 1179–1180 (9th Cir.1987), appeal after remand 897 F.2d 436 (9th Cir.1990).

19. *United States v. Bedonie,* 913 F.2d 782, 795 (10th Cir.1990), cert. denied ___ U.S. ___, 111 S.Ct. 2895, 115 L.Ed.2d 1059 (1991).

20. *Bueno–Hernandez v. State,* 724 P.2d 1132, 1133–1135 (Wyo.1986), cert. denied 480 U.S. 907, 107 S.Ct. 1353, 94 L.Ed.2d 523 (1987).

21. *Commonwealth v. Gagnon,* 16 Mass. App.Ct. 110, 118–119, 449 N.E.2d 686, 691–692 (1983), affirmed on other grounds sub nom. *Commonwealth v. Bourgeois,* 391 Mass. 869, 465 N.E.2d 1180 (1984).

United States v. Biaggi, [22] analogized the equal protection analysis with the fair cross-section analysis. In *Biaggi* the Court found that a cognizable group under *Batson* "(1) [is] definable and limited by some clearly identifiable factor; (2) share a common set of ideas, attitudes or experiences; and (3) share a community of interests, such that the groups interests cannot be adequately represented if the group is excluded from the jury selection process." [23]

Courts are generally unwilling to extend this analysis to gender-based challenges, as evidenced in *Brown v. North Carolina,* [24] *United States v. Hamilton,* [25] (excluding three Afro-American women because the fact they were women does not violate *Batson*); *State v. Culver,* [26] (refusing to extend *Batson* to sex discrimination); *Stariks v. State,* [27] (refusing to extend *Batson* to gender). There are exceptions, however: *United States v. De Gross,* [28] *Di Donato v. Santini,* [29] *People v. Irizarry,* [30] and *State v. Gonzales,* [31] which was decided on the basis of the New Mexico Constitution rather than the federal Constitution.

In any event, an attorney must be ready to use any or all of the following tests to demonstrate to the court that the race, ethnicity or ancestry of the excluded juror is a cognizable group and thus protected, for equal protection analysis, under state or federal law. If the trial court determines that the proffered group is not a constitutionally protected one, counsel must be certain to preserve the record for appeal. Counsel must object in a specific and timely fashion, that is, before the jury is sworn, [32] and must make certain there is sufficient evidence in the record, through preserved testimony or written materials like juror questionnaire cards, that a reviewing court can identify the excluded juror's race, ethnicity or ancestry.[33]

22. 673 F.Supp. 96 (E.D.N.Y.1987), affirmed 853 F.2d 89 (2d Cir.1988), cert. denied 489 U.S. 1052, 109 S.Ct. 1312, 103 L.Ed.2d 581 (1989).

23. 673 F.Supp. at 100.

24. 479 U.S. 940, 941–942, 107 S.Ct. 423, 423–424, 93 L.Ed.2d 373 (1986) (O'Connor, J., concurring in denial of certiorari).

25. 850 F.2d 1038, 1040 (4th Cir.1988), cert. dismissed 489 U.S. 1094, 109 S.Ct. 1564, 103 L.Ed.2d 931 (1989).

26. 233 Neb. 228, 444 N.W.2d 662, 666 (1989).

27. 572 So.2d 1301, 1302–1303 (Ala. Crim.App.1990).

28. 913 F.2d 1417, 1426 (9th Cir.1990), rehearing granted 930 F.2d 695 (9th Cir. 1991).

29. 232 Cal.App.3d 721, 283 Cal.Rptr. 751, 761–762 (1991).

30. 165 A.D.2d 715, 560 N.Y.S.2d 279, 280 (1990).

31. 111 N.M. 590, 808 P.2d 40 (App. 1991), cert. denied 111 N.M. 416, 806 P.2d 65 (1991).

32. *See, e.g., Weekly v. State,* 496 N.E.2d 29, 31 (Ind.1986) (specific objection necessary to preserve issue for appeal); *People v. Evans,* 125 Ill.2d 50, 125 Ill.Dec. 790, 794, 530 N.E.2d 1360, 1364 (1988), cert. denied 490 U.S. 1113, 109 S.Ct. 3175, 104 L.Ed.2d 1036 (1989) (objection must be made before jury empaneled); *Clark v. State,* 562 So.2d 620, 624 (Ala.Crim.App.1989).

33. *People v. Evans,* 125 Ill.2d 50, 125 Ill.Dec. 790, 530 N.E.2d 1360 (1988), cert. denied 490 U.S. 1113, 109 S.Ct. 3175, 104 L.Ed.2d 1036 (1989) and *People v. Wheeler,* 22 Cal.3d 258, 148 Cal.Rptr. 890, 906, 583 P.2d 748, 764 (1978) (listing methods to establish race and preserve record).

Once a party claims that his opponent has used peremptory challenges in a discriminatory fashion, the court must hold an evidentiary hearing, known as a *Batson* hearing, to determine whether the claimant can establish a prima facie case of discrimination based on race, ethnicity or ancestry. The party must first demonstrate that the excluded juror is a member of a cognizable *Batson* group, then must show that the "facts and other relevant circumstances" raise an inference of purposeful discrimination.[34]

The Court in *Batson* gave some guidance as to which "facts and other relevant circumstances" to look for in determining whether a prima facie case has been made: (1) a pattern of strikes against a specific race or ethnic group of jurors; (2) the attorney's questions and statements made during *voir dire;* and (3) the level of representation of the venire of a specific ethnic group compared to the representation of that group in the jury.[35] Lower courts have cited other factors, including whether a disproportionate number of peremptory challenges were used to exclude jurors of a specific ethnic or racial group,[36] and whether excluded jurors were a heterogenous group sharing race as their only common characteristic.[37]

The claimant's burden to produce evidence to substantiate a prima facie case, as in other areas of law, is not great, since the exclusion of just one juror on the basis of race, ethnicity or ancestry mandates reversal of a conviction.[38] As articulated in *Tompkins v. State,* [39] the standard is "the minimum quantum of evidence necessary to support a rational inference that the allegation of fact is true." However, since the determination of the trial court as to whether the party has sustained its burden of establishing a prima facie case is, by and large, a finding of fact, a reviewing court will give great deference to the trial court and will overturn this finding only if it is "against the manifest weight of the evidence," [40] or "clearly erroneous." [41] Accordingly, trial attorneys must present to the trial court sufficient evidence to meet the

34. *Batson v. Kentucky,* 476 U.S. 79 at 96, 106 S.Ct. 1712 at 1723.

35. 476 U.S. at 93, 97, 106 S.Ct. at 1721, 1723.

36. *State v. Gilmore,* 103 N.J. 508, 511 A.2d 1150, 1164 (1986).

37. *People v. McDonald,* 125 Ill.2d 182, 125 Ill.Dec. 781, 787, 530 N.E.2d 1351, 1357 (1988).

38. *See,* for example, *People v. McDonald,* 125 Ill.2d 182, 125 Ill.Dec. 781, 789, 530 N.E.2d 1351, 1359 (1988); *United States v. David,* 803 F.2d 1567, 1570–71 (11th Cir.1986), on remand 662 F.Supp. 244 (N.D.Ga.1987), judgment affirmed 844 F.2d 767 (11th Cir.1988).

39. 774 S.W.2d 195, 201 (Tex.Crim.App. 1987), affirmed 490 U.S. 754, 109 S.Ct. 2180, 104 L.Ed.2d 834 (1989), rehearing denied 492 U.S. 933, 110 S.Ct. 16, 106 L.Ed.2d 630 (1989).

40. *See,* for example, *People v. Hooper,* 133 Ill.2d 469, 142 Ill.Dec. 93, 107, 552 N.E.2d 684, 698 (1989), cert. denied ___ U.S. ___, 111 S.Ct. 284, 112 L.Ed.2d 239 (1990); *People v. McDonald,* 125 Ill.2d 182, 125 Ill.Dec. 781, 788, 530 N.E.2d 1351, 1358 (1988).

41. *See,* for example, *United States v. Alston,* 895 F.2d 1362, 1366 (11th Cir.1990).

prima facie standard, thereby shifting the burden of proof to opposing counsel.

Once a complaining party has met his burden of establishing a prima facie case of discriminatory exclusion of jurors, the burden then shifts to the opposing party to give racially "neutral" reasons for exclusion.[42] A racially neutral reason, as defined in *Hernandez v. New York,* [43] is one "based on something other than the race of the juror," and should be accepted by the court unless it finds discriminatory intent. In determining whether the reason for exclusion is acceptable, the trial court should analyze: (1) the specificity of the explanation; (2) whether the reason is rationally related to the juror's qualifications or bias; and (3) whether the explanation is given in good faith. The trial court is the fact-finder and must evaluate not only the proffered explanations for exclusion, but also the credibility of witnesses, that is, the challenged attorney.[44] Counsel should always request that the notes opposing counsel took regarding jurors should be copied, examined and made part of the record. Counsel should also examine the opposing lawyer regarding the reasons for striking some jurors even though there were other jurors who gave similar answers but were not struck. The notes of opposing counsel could corroborate your argument.

Courts have found numerous "race neutral" reasons for juror exclusion. Although the reason need not rise to the level of a challenge for cause, the closer the proffered explanation comes to a challenge for cause, the more likely a court will accept the explanation as racially neutral.[45] Courts have found constitutionally acceptable reasons where: 1) the proposed juror knows one of the parties, attorneys or witnesses; [46] 2) the juror doubts his ability to sit in judgment or to be impartial; [47] or 3) the juror is hesitant or unwilling to follow the court's instructions.[48] In addition, courts have consistently found race-neutral

42. *Batson v. Kentucky,* 476 U.S. 79 at 97–98, 106 S.Ct. 1712 at 1723–1724.

43. ___ U.S. ___, ___, 111 S.Ct. 1859, 1866, 114 L.Ed.2d 395 (1991).

44. *People v. Hall,* 35 Cal.3d 161, 197 Cal.Rptr. 71, 75, 672 P.2d 854, 858 (1983); *Slappy v. State,* 503 So.2d 350, 356 (Fla. App.1987), decision approved 522 So.2d 18 (Fla.1988), cert. denied 487 U.S. 1219, 108 S.Ct. 2873, 101 L.Ed.2d 909 (1988).

45. *Hernandez v. New York,* ___ U.S. at ___, 111 S.Ct. at 1868.

46. *People v. Brown,* 152 Ill.App.3d 996, 106 Ill.Dec. 91, 95, 505 N.E.2d 397, 401 (1987), appeal denied 125 Ill.2d 568, 130 Ill.Dec. 483, 537 N.E.2d 812 (1989) (party); *United States v. Cartlidge,* 808 F.2d 1064, 1070 (5th Cir.1987) (attorney); *Williams v. State,* 507 N.E.2d 997, 998–999 (Ind.App. 1987) (attorney); *United States v. Love,* 815 F.2d 53, 54 (8th Cir.1987), cert. denied 484 U.S. 861, 108 S.Ct. 177, 98 L.Ed.2d 130 (1987) (witness).

47. *Thorne v. State,* 509 N.E.2d 877, 881 (Ind.App.1987), judgment affirmed 519 N.E.2d 566 (Ind.1988); *People v. Ortega,* 156 Cal.App.3d 63, 202 Cal.Rptr. 657, 662 (1984); *Wilder v. State,* 498 N.E.2d 1295, 1297 (Ind.App.1986).

48. *People v. Davis,* 189 Cal.App.3d 1177, 234 Cal.Rptr. 859, 870 (1987); *Rijo v. State,* 721 S.W.2d 562, 564–565 (Tex.App.—Amarillo 1986).

reasons where 1) the proposed juror has a criminal conviction;[49] 2) where the juror's relative had been a criminal defendant;[50] or where the juror had been arrested by the same police department.[51] Courts have also accepted as race neutral: 1) the age of the juror;[52] 2) a juror who is unreceptive to a party's theory of the case;[53] 3) the sex of the juror;[54] 4) the juror's religious beliefs;[55] or 5) the occupation of the juror.[56]

Even the non-verbal communication and body language of the prospective juror have been deemed by some courts to be race neutral. Reasons proffered by prosecutors have included lack of eye contact, lack of rapport and appeared to fall asleep,[57] poor attention, recollection and attitude.[58] A juror who looked gentle was deemed a racially neutral explanation[59] for exclusion as was a juror who slouched during the entire *voir dire.*[60]

Courts have found acceptable challenges based on a valid jury selection strategy;[61] however, the strategy must have a logical connec-

49. *Thorne v. State,* 509 N.E.2d 877, 881 (Ind.App.1987), judgment affirmed 519 N.E.2d 566 (Ind.1988); *People v. Jones,* 201 Ill.App.3d 440, 147 Ill.Dec. 112, 115, 559 N.E.2d 112, 115 (1990), appeal denied 133 Ill.2d 565, 149 Ill.Dec. 330, 561 N.E.2d 700 (1990); *Ward v. State,* 539 So.2d 407, 408 (Ala.Crim.App.1988); *but see Maloney v. Washington,* 690 F.Supp. 687, 691 (N.D.Ill. 1988) (exclusion of juror convicted of disorderly conduct found to be pretext for discrimination), mandamus granted on other grounds, sub nom., *Maloney v. Plunkett,* 854 F.2d 152 (7th Cir.1988).

50. *People v. Harris,* 129 Ill.2d 123, 135 Ill.Dec. 861, 884, 544 N.E.2d 357, 380 (1989), cert. denied 494 U.S. 1018, 110 S.Ct. 1323, 108 L.Ed.2d 498 (1990); *United States v. Vaccaro,* 816 F.2d 443, 457 (9th Cir. 1987), cert. denied 484 U.S. 914, 108 S.Ct. 262, 98 L.Ed.2d 220 (1987).

51. *People v. Woods,* 184 Ill.App.3d 688, 133 Ill.Dec. 154, 157, 540 N.E.2d 1020, 1023 (1989).

52. *People v. Kindelan,* 213 Ill.App.3d 548, 157 Ill.Dec. 674, 678–679, 572 N.E.2d 1138, 1142–1143 (1991), appeal denied 141 Ill.2d 552, 162 Ill.Dec. 500, 580 N.E.2d 126 (1991); *Harrell v. State,* 555 So.2d 263, 268 n. 1 (Ala.1989), appeal after remand 571 So.2d 1269 (Ala.Crim.App.1990), writ quashed 571 So.2d 1270 (Ala.1990).

53. *People v. Chambie,* 189 Cal.App.3d 149, 234 Cal.Rptr. 308, 311–312 (1987).

54. *People v. Hooper,* 133 Ill.2d 469, 142 Ill.Dec. 93, 110–111, 552 N.E.2d 684, 701–02 (1989), cert. denied ___ U.S. ___, 111 S.Ct. 284, 112 L.Ed.2d 239 (1990).

55. *United States v. Clemmons,* 892 F.2d 1153, 1157 (3d Cir.1989), cert. denied 496 U.S. 927, 110 S.Ct. 2623, 110 L.Ed.2d 644 (1990); *People v. Malone,* 211 Ill. App.3d 628, 156 Ill.Dec. 108, 113, 570 N.E.2d 584, 589 (1991), appeal denied 142 Ill.2d 660, 164 Ill.Dec. 923, 584 N.E.2d 135 (1991).

56. *People v. Harris,* 129 Ill.2d 123, 135 Ill.Dec. 861, 885, 544 N.E.2d 357, 381 (1989), cert. denied 494 U.S. 1018, 110 S.Ct. 1323, 108 L.Ed.2d 498 (1990); *People v. Ortega,* 156 Cal.App.3d 63, 202 Cal.Rptr. 657, 662–663 (1984).

57. *Holman v. State,* 772 S.W.2d 530 (Tex.App.—Beaumont 1989).

58. *Dennis v. State,* 772 S.W.2d 525 (Tex.App.—Beaumont 1989).

59. *Barnett v. State,* 771 S.W.2d 654 (Tex.App.—Corpus Christi 1989).

60. *Smith v. State,* 734 S.W.2d 694 (Tex. App.—Houston 1987).

61. *See,* for example, *Haynes v. State,* 103 Nev. 309, 739 P.2d 497, 502 (1987); *People v. Mack,* 128 Ill.2d 231, 131 Ill.Dec. 551, 557, 538 N.E.2d 1107, 1113 (1989), cert. denied 493 U.S. 1093, 110 S.Ct. 1170, 107 L.Ed.2d 1072 (1990), rehearing denied

tion to the theory of the case and the juror exclusions must be executed consistently.[62] A party justifying its juror exclusions based on a jury selection strategy should be prepared to explain such a plan to the court.[63] Where disclosure of a jury selection strategy would reveal confidential trial strategy, the challenged counsel should request an *ex parte, in camera* hearing,[64] since the court may order the attorney's *voir dire* notes to be produced.[65]

Although a nondiscriminatory reason for exclusion, given in good faith, should be accepted by a trial court, certain explanations have been consistently held unacceptable. For example, *United States v. Brown* [66] held that presuming African American counsel would have an unfair advantage with an African American juror is not race-neutral; *People v. Pagel* [67] found excluding African American jurors because opposing counsel struck white jurors unacceptable; *Clark v. City of Bridgeport* [68] held that assuming bias and prejudice of an excluded African American juror is unacceptable. However, as established in *People v. Harris,* [69] good faith alone will not rebut a prima facie case.

Once a party has rebutted the prima facie case, the burden then shifts back to the challenging party.[70] For the challenger to prevail he must show that the explanations for juror exclusion were a pretext for discrimination.[71] This can be accomplished by demonstrating that the excluded jurors had only race in common, as in *People v. Moss,* [72] or by comparing the characteristics of selected and rejected jurors, as in

494 U.S. 1092, 110 S.Ct. 1841, 108 L.Ed.2d 969 (1990).

62. *See,* for example, *Townsend v. State,* 730 S.W.2d 24, 26 (Tex.App.—Texarkana 1987).

63. *See,* for example, *People v. Mack,* 128 Ill.2d 231, 131 Ill.Dec. 551, 557, 538 N.E.2d 1107, 1113 (1989), cert. denied 493 U.S. 1093, 110 S.Ct. 1170, 107 L.Ed.2d 1072 (1990), rehearing denied 494 U.S. 1092, 110 S.Ct. 1841, 108 L.Ed.2d 969 (1990); *People v. Gregory ZZ,* 134 A.D.2d 814, 521 N.Y.S.2d 873, 874–875 (1987), appeal denied 71 N.Y.2d 905, 527 N.Y.S.2d 1014, 523 N.E.2d 321 (1988).

64. *United States v. Tucker,* 836 F.2d 334, 338–340 (7th Cir.1988), cert. denied 488 U.S. 855, 109 S.Ct. 143, 102 L.Ed.2d 115 (1988); *United States v. Thompson,* 827 F.2d 1254, 1259 (9th Cir.1987).

65. *Salazar v. State,* 795 S.W.2d 187, 193 (Tex.Crim.App.1990), appeal after remand 818 S.W.2d 405 (Tex.Crim.App.1991); *but see People v. Mack,* 128 Ill.2d 231, 131 Ill.Dec. 551, 559–560, 538 N.E.2d 1107, 1115–1116 (1989), cert. denied 493 U.S. 1093, 110 S.Ct. 1170, 107 L.Ed.2d 1072 (1990), rehearing denied 494 U.S. 1092, 110 S.Ct. 1841, 108 L.Ed.2d 969 (1990) (attorney's notes protected from disclosure).

66. 817 F.2d 674, 675–676 (10th Cir. 1987).

67. 186 Cal.App.3d Supp. 1, 232 Cal. Rptr. 104, 108 (1986), cert. denied 481 U.S. 1028, 107 S.Ct. 1953, 95 L.Ed.2d 525 (1987).

68. 645 F.Supp. 890, 893–894 (D.Conn. 1986).

69. 129 Ill.2d 123, 135 Ill.Dec. 861, 863, 544 N.E.2d 357, 379 (1989), cert. denied 494 U.S. 1018, 110 S.Ct. 1323, 108 L.Ed.2d 498 (1990).

70. *Batson,* 476 U.S. at 97, 106 S.Ct. at ——.

71. *Id.* at 98.

72. 188 Cal.App.3d 268, 233 Cal.Rptr. 153, 157 (1986).

Gamble v. State, [73] and *Ex parte Branch* [74]. Since there are often many variables to consider in determining whether to accept or reject a particular juror, the challenging party has a formidable task to overcome the presumption that the opposing counsel properly exercised such challenges.[75]

§ 17.15 Challenging Improper Use of Strikes—Fair Cross-section Analysis

In addition to a party's right, under the equal protection clause of the Fourteenth Amendment, to protect against the discriminatory use of peremptory challenges, a criminal defendant has certain similar rights under the Sixth Amendment's right to a fair and impartial jury. The Sixth Amendment of the Constitution provides, in pertinent part, that, "[i]n all criminal prosecutions, the accused shall enjoy the right to a ... public trial, by an impartial jury...." U.S. Const. amend. VI. The Supreme Court, in *Taylor v. Louisiana,* [1] has interpreted this to mean that a criminal defendant has a right to a jury chosen from a representative cross-section of the community. This guarantee is likewise imposed on the states through the Fourteenth Amendment.[2] The right is generally thought to apply equally to civil litigants.[3]

State and federal courts have interpreted this right to apply to the invidious use of peremptory challenges.[4] However, the Supreme Court's recent decision in *Holland v. Illinois,* [5] has narrowed the application of this right. In *Holland,* the Supreme Court held that a defendant's right to a jury composed of a fair cross-section of the community applied only to the venire, the panel from which the jury is ultimately chosen, and not to the jury itself. Accordingly, the Sixth Amendment right, under the federal Constitution, to a representative cross-section of the community does not apply to the use of peremptory challenges.

73. 257 Ga. 325, 357 S.E.2d 792, 795 (1987).

74. 526 So.2d 609, 621–625 (Ala.1987), on remand 526 So.2d 634 (Ala.Crim.App. 1988).

75. *See People v. Young,* 128 Ill.2d 1, 131 Ill.Dec. 78, 80, 538 N.E.2d 453, 455 (1989), cert. denied ___ U.S. ___, 110 S.Ct. 3290, 111 L.Ed.2d 798 (1990), rehearing denied ___ U.S. ___, 111 S.Ct. 16, 111 L.Ed.2d 830 (1990).

§ 17.15

1. 419 U.S. 522, 525–526, 95 S.Ct. 692, 695, 42 L.Ed.2d 690 (1975).

2. *Duncan v. Louisiana,* 391 U.S. 145, 147–150, 88 S.Ct. 1444, 1446–1448, 20 L.Ed.2d 491 (1968), rehearing denied 392 U.S. 947, 88 S.Ct. 2270, 20 L.Ed.2d 1412 (1968).

3. *See Thiel v. Southern Pacific Co.,* 328 U.S. 217, 66 S.Ct. 984, 90 L.Ed. 1181 (1946).

4. *People v. Wheeler,* 22 Cal.3d 258, 140 Cal.Rptr. 890, 904, 583 P.2d 748, 762 (1978); *McCray v. Abrams,* 750 F.2d 1113, 1128–1130 (2d Cir.1984), reconsideration denied 756 F.2d 277 (2d Cir.1985).

5. 493 U.S. 474, 110 S.Ct. 803, 107 L.Ed.2d 905 (1990), rehearing denied 494 U.S. 1050, 110 S.Ct. 1514, 108 L.Ed.2d 650 (1990).

This does not, however, end the inquiry. Several states have found that their state constitutions prohibit the discriminatory use of peremptory challenges which infringe on a party's fair cross-section rights.[6] Thus, an attorney must be ready to argue state-guaranteed rights when contesting the discriminatory use of peremptory challenges under this analysis.

The fair cross-section analysis is quite similar to an equal protection one.[7] The claimant must show a prima facie case of discriminatory use of peremptory challenges based on a cognizable group, as provided in *Biaggi* and *Wheeler*. Then the opposing party must rebut the prima facie case and, if this is done, the claimant must then show that the opponent's reasons are pretextual under *Wheeler*.

There is, however, one important difference in the fair cross-section analysis. A party's equal protection right against the invidious use of peremptory challenges is limited to race, ethnicity and ancestry. But a party's right to a jury chosen from a fair cross-section of the community includes various cognizable groups, including women,[8] wage earners[9], Native Americans,[10] age.[11] Accordingly, where state constitutional guarantees include the right to attack an opponent's discriminatory use of peremptory challenges under a fair cross-section analysis, counsel should be prepared to define a cognizable group and apply the reasoning of *Batson* and its progeny.

One way to avoid, or at least attempt to avoid, a skewed panel is to file a motion for a special venire that represents a cross-section of the community. (*See* Appendix 17A for a sample motion filed in a Georgia death penalty case.) You may also want to protest the procedures used to summon and excuse prospective jurors if you find they do not comply with statutory requirements designed to provide a jury pool selected from a fair cross-section of the population of the area served by the court. (*See* Appendix 17B for a sample declaration of counsel in

6. *See,* for example, *People v. Wheeler,* 22 Cal.3d 258, 148 Cal.Rptr. 890, 896, 583 P.2d 748, 754 (1978); *State v. Gilmore,* 103 N.J. 508, 511 A.2d 1150, 1158–1159 (1986); *Fields v. People,* 732 P.2d 1145, 1151–1155 (Colo.1987) (listing jurisdictions applying Sixth Amendment analysis); *Ex parte Jackson,* 516 So.2d 768, 770–773 (Ala.1986), on remand 516 So.2d 774 (Ala.Crim.App. 1987), appeal after remand 553 So.2d 647 (Ala.Crim.App.1989); *People v. Thompson,* 79 A.D.2d 87, 435 N.Y.S.2d 739, 746–752 (1981).

7. *See United States v. Biaggi,* 673 F.Supp. 96, 100 (E.D.N.Y.1987), affirmed 853 F.2d 89 (2d Cir.1988), cert. denied 489 U.S. 1052, 109 S.Ct. 1312, 103 L.Ed.2d 581 (1989).

8. *See,* for example, *Taylor v. Louisiana,* 419 U.S. 522, 531–533, 95 S.Ct. 692, 697–699, 42 L.Ed.2d 690 (1975); *Duren v. Missouri,* 439 U.S. 357, 99 S.Ct. 664, 58 L.Ed.2d 579 (1979).

9. *See,* for example, *U.S. ex rel. Barksdale v. Blackburn,* 610 F.2d 253, 272 (5th Cir.1980), cert. denied 454 U.S. 1056, 102 S.Ct. 603, 70 L.Ed.2d 593 (1981).

10. *See,* for example, *United States v. Brady,* 579 F.2d 1121, 1131 (9th Cir.1978), cert. denied 439 U.S. 1074, 99 S.Ct. 849, 59 L.Ed.2d 41 (1979).

11. *See,* for example, *Julian v. State,* 134 Ga.App. 592, 215 S.E.2d 496, 499–450 (1975).

support of a motion to dismiss the jury panel for lack of representativeness.)

Once into jury selection, however, any *Batson* challenge should be made before the striking process begins. It is preferable to invoke *Batson* early in the *voir dire* to discourage opposing counsel from excluding minority jurors who would be potentially good jurors for your side of the case.

(*See also* § 15.62, *supra,* for further discussion of the *Batson* case and its use in obtaining additional peremptory challenges or reversal of the verdict.)

§ 17.16 Challenging Improper Use of Strikes—Need to *Voir Dire* in Federal Cases

In light of the *McCollum* decision, an argument should be made by civil and criminal litigants in federal court that counsel cannot intelligently exercise peremptory strikes nor can racially neutral explanations for such strikes be provided to the Court unless counsel is allowed an adequate opportunity to *voir dire* the jurors. *Batson* and its prodigy specifically look at the words used by the juror, the interaction between the lawyer and the juror and the lawyer's sense and feelings about the juror. It is impossible to gain a meaningful impression of a potential juror unless counsel is given the chance to interact with the juror. If peremptory strikes are going to be attacked, the Court must give the litigants a reasonable opportunity to form impressions and draw out information. This can only be accomplished if counsel is allowed to participate in the *voir dire* process.

§ 17.17 Including the Client in the Striking Process

Always include your client in the striking process so the jurors see that you value your client's input. Not only does this help humanize your client, but it can be instructive as well. Clients naturally observe which jurors look at them with interest, disdain, anger, kindness, or understanding and sense feelings that may affect jurors' perceptions of the case. Many times clients come up with an idea about a juror that you had not thought about. Specifically ask your client how jurors appear to be looking at him and why he feels good or bad about each juror. In the process, you will do wonders for your client-attorney relationship that will last throughout the trial.

§ 17.18 Where to Strike—Generally

There are various options not only about *how* to exercise strikes but *where.*

§ 17.19 Where to Strike—In Court

It can be difficult deciding your strikes in front of the panel, especially if more people than just you and your client are involved in the striking process. It can resemble a madhouse if all of you are scurrying around the table discussing each juror, and there is the potential for jurors to feel singled out when you look at them in order to remember who they are. For purposes of identification, however, it is advantageous to have all the jurors in the courtroom when the striking occurs. Just remember to leave the courtroom to discuss the jurors after a final look, to put names and faces together.

§ 17.20 Where to Strike—Out of Court

The problem with striking jurors outside their presence is that you often cannot remember as much about them as you could if you had a face to put with your notes. Again, discuss the jurors outside the courtroom and then come in for a final observation before making your strikes. To assist with putting names and faces together, you may want to consider having someone do a rough profile sketch of each juror.

§ 17.21 Where to Strike—In the Presence of the Jury

Request that the court allow you to make your strikes at the bench after you have discussed the jurors out of court and have observed them in court. If you are required to stand up and state the strikes in front of the panel, you should always thank and excuse each juror as you strike them.

§ 17.22 Where to Strike—Overnight

The best of all worlds is to have the panel in the courtroom at the end of the day so you can review the jurors, then have overnight to discuss the panel with the rest of the team and come up with a list of strikes. When you return the next day, you can quickly make the strikes. Your argument to the court should emphasize that rather than going in and out of the courtroom after each strike to discuss the next strike, it will save time if you are allowed overnight to discuss the strikes, especially in a multi-party case. If the court forces you to proceed, nonetheless, request that you have the opportunity to go out of the courtroom after each striking round, rather than rush a decision about a strike.

§ 17.23 Where to Strike—Over Lunch

Some judges will not allow you to have overnight but will give you a break or the lunch recess. This is the second best option for the legal team to have a chance to discuss the appropriate strikes. The important thing is not to allow the court to speed up your striking time to the point where you are not putting thought or energy into the appropriate strikes.

§ 17.24 If the Judge Imposes a Time Limit

Should the court limit the amount of time to discuss the strikes, make a record. The record should state that you have been hampered in jury selection because there was not adequate time to discuss each juror and intelligently exercise your peremptory challenges. Have other members of the team file affidavits stating how rushed you were. In a multi-party case, the affidavits must emphasize the lack of opportunity for all counsel to discuss among themselves the strikes that you felt should have been made. There have been situations where some lawyers were in one corner of the room discussing the strikes and others were in another and the strikes were never tabulated in an organized fashion. This should all be put in affidavit form and filed promptly.

§ 17.25 If a Juror Is Erroneously Struck

If you accidentally strike a juror whom you did not intend to strike, immediately draw it to the court's attention and ask that you be allowed to strike the appropriate juror. Generally this happens when you have a name confused with a face or when the jury panel is not in the courtroom and someone on your trial team brings the mistake to your attention. Most courts will allow you to change the strike within a reasonable period of time after you made the erroneous strike or if the jury has not yet been sworn. If more than a few minutes have passed, however, most courts will not allow you to change the strike. It never hurts to ask, so ask if you feel you have made a mistake.

§ 17.26 When to Swear in Jurors

After all motions (including *Batson*) have been made, all requests for additional strikes voiced, and the panel dismissed or mistrial requested, the jurors should be sworn in. However, should you feel that something occurred during jury selection that would warrant a mistrial, a hearing should be requested and held prior to swearing in the jurors and excusing the panel. This will adequately protect the record and keep the issue from being waived. The swearing-in should take place immediately after the peremptory strikes and the jurors should be cautioned by the court not to talk to anyone about the case, including family members, court staff or other jurors. If you have not made all of your motions and fully developed the record, request that the jurors not be sworn in until your record is complete.

Chapter 18

DEATH PENALTY *VOIR DIRE*

Table of Cases

---

§ 18.1 Overview

In a death penalty case the entire courtroom is more emotionally charged than in any other kind of case. The jurors are more nervous, the judge is on guard, the defense team is fearful of the potential consequences should the jury return a death verdict, and the prosecutor feels especially driven because of community sentiment and the vengeful feelings of the victim's family. Of course, the client is terrified about what faces him.

The defense must be aware of this heightened emotional state and bring it out in the open in the course of *voir dire*. You should first express your feelings about the magnitude of representing someone facing a life or death sentence so the jurors understand how seriously you take your job. Should there be obvious conflicts or anger between the defense and the prosecutor, talk to the jury about how the emotions between the attorneys may be high because of your concerns about the case. Should there be problems communicating with the court, you may need to explain that you and the judge may not always be in agreement on some matters. To defuse any negative reactions toward you or your client, as a result, you might ask how they feel about that disagreement. Also ask jurors how they would feel if they were on trial for their lives. Talk to the jurors about these feelings to prepare them for their reactions to the case and at the same time help them understand where your feelings lie.

The more you disclose your feelings about situations that arise during a death penalty *voir dire*, the more the jurors will feel free to do the same. Feelings belong in all cases, especially death penalty cases. If you feel scared or nervous, tell the jury about that. If you feel embarrassed, say so. If you become concerned that you may have offended a juror, tell the juror, "I feel you are a little bit angry with me. Let's talk about it." Initially, when you discuss your feelings, the court may be upset and the jurors may feel that feelings should not be talked about. You will find, however, that the longer the *voir dire* goes on, the more comfortable everyone will feel communicating this way and the closer you will be to getting jurors to say what they honestly think and feel. This, of course, will make challenges for cause easier to develop.

After months of pre-trial preparation, you will wind up functioning at an emotional level that is impossible to sustain alone. You must anticipate the exhaustion that is inevitable with a lengthy *voir dire*, compounded by pressure from the judge to rush the process and challenges by opposing counsel to in-depth questions. To take on a death penalty *voir dire* without the assistance of competent co-counsel to share the burden can be disastrous. *Voir dire* has become noticeably shorter and less probing, and gross errors have been omitted from the record when counsel has chosen to play Lone Ranger at trial. Co-counsel can help to take the heat off and can assure that the *voir dire* is not diluted over time and that a full record is made to preserve every possible appeal. Each attorney who, during the course of the trial, will examine witnesses, make arguments or be in any other way involved in presenting the case, should participate in jury selection. Remember, *voir dire* is your opportunity to establish a rapport with the jury panel so that they feel comfortable with you and know that you are sincere in your mission to save your client. (*See* Sections 12.17 through 12.26 for the various ways to share *voir dire* with co-counsel.)

A clear head is essential for what the authors would argue is the most important part of a death penalty case—the jury selection. Take several days off beforehand to relax and become centered. Once jury selection has begun, do not dismiss the value of exercising, being with those who love and support you, "escaping" to your hobbies periodically and taking at least a day off every week or two to unwind in order to avoid exhaustion. Almost all lawyers who try death penalty cases on a regular basis will tell you that the exhaustion factor is one that you must work to avoid, or else you risk missing things and becoming overly saturated with the case. Do whatever is necessary to take care of yourself during the preparation and trial of a death penalty case, so that you always think with a clear head.

Given the present status of our higher courts, winning at the trial level has become even more important in a death penalty case. Remember a life verdict is usually a win in a capital case. Take care of yourself, so you can breathe life into the courtroom.

§ 18.2 Building Rapport

You must build as much rapport with the jurors as you possibly can during *voir dire* because it is easier for them to give a defendant the death penalty if they feel no connection with the attorney. At the same time you are building a bridge to your client. You must help the jurors feel a human response to your client as opposed to only seeing a brutal murderer who must be punished. Unless the jury perceives the client as a human being, they are not apt to give life. Look at your client and occasionally touch him, and always refer to him by first name. Standing behind him as you broach questions about his background, or placing your hands on his shoulders, can evoke the jurors' empathy while personalizing your own relationship. If it is appropriate, you may also want to have your client appointed co-counsel so that he can ask one or two questions during *voir dire* and develop a one-on-one relationship with members of the jury panel.

Questions about your client's background and appearance will either enlarge the jurors' one-dimensional view or point out their prejudices. Talk to the jurors about how your client looks, to expose those jurors who feel that some people look like killers because of the color of their eyes, their bad complexion, race, or size. You might ask the jurors, while putting a hand on your client's shoulder, "[Client's name] has a scar across his forehead and some people believe that someone with a big scar is more apt to be a dangerous person than someone without. What do you think about that?" If your client has tattoos on his hands or face, ask the jury panel what impression they leave.

Diffuse the negative parts of your client and play up the good. Should your client have been a good father or cared about even one person in his life, explore in depth what gives life meaning. Strongly emphasize that if someone has been good even in a small part of his life, there is reason to weigh the value of that life and not assume that the person is useless to society.

In order to avoid arguments with your client, or risk him being surprised or feeling betrayed because of the personal nature of your questions, always discuss with him what you are going to ask beforehand. Some questions that have caused dissension, because the client was not told they would be raised, pertained to the client's background, relationships, alcohol or drug abuse, and how the client looked—evidence that the lawyer was trying to defuse. Clients have been known to become visibly angry, look shocked at the question or in some way exhibit what could be misinterpreted as an aggressive stance. You do not want to make your client angry with you and leave the impression with the jury that here is a person who can be violent even with his ally in the courtroom—you, the lawyer.

You will definitely want to consult your client during *voir dire* so that the jury sees that you value his input. That also shows you are working with your client and leaves the lasting impression that your client is cooperative and not necessarily dangerous. Your client, meanwhile, will feel that he has an active part in the decision-making process and may contribute some important insights into the jury selection.

The only caveat, as mentioned earlier, is that you should not allow the client to look at the juror questionnaires, if granted. Jurors have expressed discomfort with the client having access to this confidential information. Keep the questionnaires in a box next to counsel table where only you can look at them in front of the jury. Should the court allow the client access, it is still best that the client refrain from looking at the questionnaires in the presence of the jury panel.

Death penalty work is very serious business. The trial team should express an interest in the client and concern for his or her feelings and not act out at counsel table by shuffling papers noisily, making a lot of fuss pouring water or otherwise distracting counsel during *voir dire.* It is also quite important that your demeanor inside the courtroom be the same outside the courtroom. If the jury sees you laughing in the hallway after an intense session in court, they may think you are merely playing a role. Team demeanor should be consistent so that the jurors see you as people who are very serious about the business at hand. This does not mean you should go around with glum faces everywhere you go; you should most certainly be cordial and warm. Socializing or laughing out in the hallway with the prosecutor, however, is taboo. It leaves the damaging impression with jurors that this is all a game.

§ 18.3 A Consultant's Role—Generally

A jury and trial consultant can be quite helpful in any case, but especially in a death penalty case. The following sections identify just a few of the situations where a consultant's expertise can make a significant difference:

§ 18.4 A Consultant's Role—Identify Case Themes

Some consultants have participated in more death penalty cases than any ten lawyers would ever imagine doing during their career. This means that they have had the advantage of learning from the best, and learning from a variety of cases. They can be helpful in isolating the themes of your case and how those themes can be discussed during *voir dire.* A good consultant will always advise you to engage in discussion with the jurors, as opposed to lecture.

§ 18.5 A Consultant's Role—Frame *Voir Dire* Questions

The effective consultant will work with you on how to ask open-ended questions and how to do appropriate follow-up that will get the jurors to say honestly what they think and feel and give examples that explain their feelings.

§ 18.6 A Consultant's Role—Propose Follow-up Questions

In court the consultant will be seated next to you and can pass you appropriate follow-up questions, which are paramount in a death penalty *voir dire.* You are so busy listening to the jurors, dealing with objections and having discussions with the judge about the kind of questions that should be allowed that many times follow-up questions can be missed. The consultant can help you keep up with what could be vital follow-up. Regard the consultant as a trained set of eyes and ears who can see and hear things differently because she is not on the firing line like you and can therefore focus on good questions.

§ 18.7 A Consultant's Role—Review Questionnaires

The consultant can review the questionnaire of a juror being questioned to suggest appropriate follow-up questions which the questionnaire indicates are necessary. Should there be a difference between the juror's answer in court and on the questionnaire, the consultant's job would be to point out the discrepancy and pass you follow-up questions to elicit the juror's true thoughts and feelings. (*See* Sections 8.19 through 8.23 for further discussion on follow-up questions from questionnaires.)

§ 18.8 A Consultant's Role—Encourage the Lawyer to Build the Record

A trained consultant will have seen the record made in other cases and be able to suggest points for you to make as the *voir dire* proceeds. She will advise you on how to make the record and the tone in which to make the record. (*See* Section 11.20 for ideas on how to build a record in non-capital cases.)

§ 18.9 A Consultant's Role—Assist in Developing Challenges for Cause

Once again, because they are the listener and not the questioner, consultants can apply their accumulated knowledge of a juror to develop ways to challenge the juror for cause. With some jurors you need to be tough and somewhat leading; with others you need to be open-ended and bring out a variety of feelings and thoughts. Each juror is different as to the correct stance to take when developing a challenge for cause. The consultant can help you in deciding the tone to use and the kinds of questions to ask. (*See* Section 12.34, *supra,* for further discussion on challenges for cause.)

§ 18.10 A Consultant's Role—Assist in Exercising Strikes

The more input you have to assist in exercising your strikes, the better job you will do. The intelligent use of peremptory challenges requires a thorough airing of the trial team's impressions of each juror. The consultant's role would be to lead everyone who has been involved in the jury selection in an open-ended discussion about the pros and cons of all the jurors. (*See also* Chapter 17, *supra,* for an in-depth discussion of the use of peremptory challenges and how to develop a striking strategy.)

§ 18.11 A Consultant's Role—Testify About *Voir Dire* Conditions

You may need your consultant to take the witness stand before you begin jury selection to educate the court on such matters as juror questionnaires, open-ended questions, lawyer-conducted, individual sequestered *voir dire* or death qualification. During jury selection you may want to call the consultant to testify about problems that may have arisen in court, such as: the judge leaving the impression that trial counsel is doing something incorrect and the spillover this could have on the jury panel members; why the group *voir dire* is not reaching the bias and prejudice of this particular panel; why certain questions need to be asked in order for counsel to get a clear understanding of a juror's thoughts and feelings relevant to the case. Use your imagination as to the different ways the consultant could assist in making the record.

§ 18.12 A Consultant's Role—Eliminate Stereotypes

The consultant should assist in defusing stereotypes so that you *voir dire* every juror thoroughly. This would include any stereotype you may have about jurors based on age, race, occupation, and initial answers to death qualification. The consultant's job is to encourage you to continue asking questions to develop as complete a picture as possible of each juror.

§ 18.13 A Consultant's Role—Provide Emotional Support

Consultants play a very active role as a support system for both you and your client. They should perceive their job as listening to you about your frustrations regarding the process and assisting the client in remaining calm at counsel table and understanding what is happening. The consultant wears many hats, one of which is being a good listener for lawyer and client.

§ 18.14 A Consultant's Role—Write Affidavits

Consultants can write affidavits, prior to, during and post-jury selection, to supplement the record. The affidavits can pertain to questionnaires, attorney-conducted individual sequestered *voir dire,* the judge's or prosecutor's demeanor, or the elimination of scrupled jurors and retention of automatic death penalty jurors. (*See* Section 7.27 for further discussion of the scope of expert affidavits from jury and trial consultants.)

§ 18.15 A Consultant's Role—Introduction of Consultants

It is always important to introduce a jury and trial consultant in a way that will not intimidate the jurors. This is easiest done by talking to the jurors about how lawyers do not learn in law school how to interview effectively and that, as they well know, many lawyers do not listen well. Tell the jurors that they are the most important people in the courtroom, and because it is hard to ask questions, listen well and take notes simultaneously, you have asked someone to assist you during jury selection to make sure you ask all the necessary questions so that no stone is left unturned. This person will be a second pair of ears and the person who takes your notes so you can listen at the highest level possible.

§ 18.16 The Pros and Cons of a Bifurcated Trial

There has been much written about the wisdom of having two juries in a death penalty case, one to decide guilt/innocence and upon conviction, another to decide life/death. It is documented that when the jury that decides guilt/innocence also decides punishment, the jurors are predisposed toward conviction because the process of talking about punishment suggests from the beginning that the defendant is guilty and the guilt/innocence phase becomes perfunctory. On the other hand, if a separate jury decides life/death, they have not had the long involvement with you and your client and may be less hesitant to give the death penalty. There is something in the theory that people warm up to counsel during a lengthy death penalty trial, which can affect their inclination to give the death penalty.

Courts rarely grant requests for separate juries for the guilt/innocence and penalty phases of a trial. If your request is granted, there is one definite caution. A judge may order that the penalty phase jury be present to hear testimony regarding the nature and circumstances of the crimes and the special aggravating and mitigating circumstances. Counsel should aggressively oppose this simultaneous presentation of evidence. Experience has shown that simultaneous presentation invariably operates to the detriment of the defendant, predisposing the guilt/innocence phase jurors to receive and interpret evidence in a way favorable to the prosecution. Seeing the penalty phase jurors sitting "like vultures on a fence," the guilt/innocence phase jurors feel absolved of the responsibility of making an independent judgment. Appendix 18A contains a sample motion opposing simultaneous presentation, with points and authorities.

Some consultants and lawyers believe that though you may want to make the record in favor of two juries, in reality you should keep the same jury to maximize the opportunity to develop a relationship with the jurors. There may be one or two jurors who feel that there is a doubt about guilt/innocence and use that later as leverage to bargain with the other jurors for a life verdict. At the guilt/innocence stage, you should stress the point that the jury could find your client not guilty or could convict on a lesser charge. There is no assumption that the client will be convicted of anything. Appendix 18B contains suggested remarks to jurors to preserve the presumption of innocence, as provided in *Hovey v. Superior Court,* 28 Cal.3d 1, 168 Cal.Rptr. 128, 616 P.2d 1301 (1980). In addition, you may want to file a motion requesting the court to conduct *voir dire* of the guilt/innocence phase jury prior to *voir dire* of the penalty phase. (*See* Appendices 18C and 18D for sample motions with points and authorities in support.)

If your case is truly a reasonable doubt case or one where you can argue reasonable doubt without appearing to speak out of both sides of your mouth, then address the issue of reasonable doubt during *voir dire*. Be particularly cautious during the penalty phase, however, because you do not want the jurors to feel that you are criticizing their guilty verdict; you are merely asking them to think about any lingering doubts they may still have. Talk about the enormous burden of deciding whether or not someone lives or dies and how any lingering doubt should point toward a life sentence because they would not want to make a mistake.

§ 18.17 Penalty Phase Only

When you are trying a case that involves only the penalty phase and this is the second trial after a reversal on a penalty phase, carefully analyze how to conduct your *voir dire*. Add questions such as,

> *There's no doubt that my client killed this person with premeditation and malice aforethought. Another jury has already decided her guilt. The only thing that we will be discussing in this case is whether or not she should get life or death. What do you think about that?*

In the rare circumstance where there is some potential for reasonable doubt about whether the defendant should have been convicted of first degree murder, you can say,

> *My client has been convicted of killing a man. As the penalty phase unfolds and you begin to understand something about what occurred in this case, if you feel some doubt as to whether or not* [client's name] *should have been convicted, that would be appropriate grounds to consider as mitigation.*

This statement should obviously be made only in a case that has some reasonable doubt.

Do as thorough a *voir dire* in penalty phase cases as you would in a bifurcated case. Explain all the mitigating and aggravating circumstances and ask how they would figure into the equation, given the law of the jurisdiction. Do the jurors see the evidence pointing toward life or death? The standard in each state is different, so carefully examine your state's laws concerning aggravation and mitigation and conduct *voir dire* accordingly. The war on crime has also spurred the call for ongoing changes in the federal law, of which you should keep apprised.

Good sources of information on the status of death penalty law and tools for conducting a capital case are the state and federal public defender departments in your jurisdiction. The National Association of Criminal Defense Lawyers also has a death penalty task force which can be contacted through the chairpersons of the task force or the national NACDL headquarters at 1110 Vermont Avenue NW, Suite

1150, Washington, D.C. 20005, (202) 872–8688. In addition, there are twelve capital case resource centers throughout the country, including the states of Tennessee, Georgia and New York.[1]

§ 18.18 Guilt/Innocence Jury Versus Life/Death Jury

A jury that may acquit your client is not necessarily a jury that would give life should they convict. Carefully consider, with your client, whether or not you truly have facts to argue reasonable doubt and give you a shot at a not-guilty verdict. If the evidence does not support your claim of innocence, the jury can feel deceived and, though originally open to a defense such as self-defense, for instance, will be quick to vote for death.

It is also possible to get a false impression about how a juror feels about the death penalty or life imprisonment. Always clarify your impression by asking the jurors to tell you all the things that they feel about the death penalty and all the things that they feel about life imprisonment. You should ask them specifically what they like and dislike about each punishment to be sure you do not misjudge a juror.

Just because a juror claims to be in favor of the death penalty during *voir dire* does not mean the juror will automatically vote for death in the jury room. Many times jurors who say that they are in favor of the death penalty turn out to be the best jurors for the defense, if you explore this issue in depth. Ask jurors what would make them hesitate to vote for the death penalty, what kind of things they would consider, and why they would consider them. The following questions will assist:

1) *You say that you are in favor of the death penalty. Please tell me why.*
2) *What are the things about the death penalty that you agree with and when would you disagree with imposing the death penalty? Please describe.*
3) *What do you feel are the advantages of life imprisonment versus the death penalty? Please tell me about that.*

§ 18.19 Avoiding Stereotypes

Never resort to stereotypes when picking a death penalty jury, though, admittedly, stereotypes do exist. A well-known stereotype is that minorities are more apt to give life than death. Accepting this thesis and not adequately exploring a juror's feelings along racial lines

§ 18.17

1. Capital Case Resource Center of Tennessee (CCRC), 1225 17th Avenue, S. Nashville, TN 37212, (615) 327–8791; Southern Center for Human Rights (SCHR), 83 Poplar Street, NW, Atlanta, GA 30303–2122, (404) 688–1202; and NAACP Legal Defense and Education Fund, Inc. (LDF), Suite 1600, 99 Hudson Street, New York, NY 10013, (212) 219–1900.

can get you into a lot of trouble. If you remember that African Americans are the object of more violence than whites, you will recognize the fallacy in believing that just because someone is a minority, he or she will be less apt to feel that the death penalty is the appropriate sentence in a murder case. Also, there can be as many differences within races or ethnic groups as there are between them. (*See* Chapter 15, "Basic Biases: Gender, Race, Religion, Age, Socio–Economic Status.")

The stereotype that social scientists and artists are more liberal and therefore inclined to vote for a life sentence is also misguiding. The majority of our society is in favor of the death penalty and that means that even people in the more "liberal" professions harbor these feelings. Talk to the jurors about books that say people in the arts and social sciences tend to favor a life sentence, and ask what they think about that description of their profession and whether or not they fit that description. Likewise, you should not assume that military people, engineers, scientists and farmers are more inclined toward the death penalty. Many of the best jurors for the defense have come from these professions.

Another stereotype is that motherly, older women are much more apt to be pro-life. This same person, however, could identify with the mother of the victim or could have had a family member or friend killed over whom she still grieves. Always ask enough questions to determine whether or not a juror or any family member or friend has been the object of violence or relates to a family member who has lost a loved one through violence.

It is also important in a death penalty case to ask jurors whether or not they or any members of their family know someone who has suffered the recent death of a loved one. This person may still have some lingering feelings about that death and might relate to the alleged victim's family. Ask in a sensitive manner how that person died. Should that person have been murdered or died an unexpected death, you need to probe how the juror felt about losing that person suddenly and what effect the juror's personal loss would have in a case where the defendant is accused of murder. He or she will no doubt empathize with the tragic loss of someone unexpectedly and may not be able to give a murder defense a fair hearing.

If the juror feels that this recent death would influence how he or she views the case facts, find out specifically what role it may play. The following questions will help:

1) *I'm concerned that the recent death of your loved one may affect you in this case. What do you think about my fear?*

2) *The mother of the person who died in this case will be testifying. How might you relate to her?*

3) *If you had not recently suffered the death of a loved one, would you feel differently about serving on this case? How do you think your loss will affect you?*

The key is not to jump to conclusions about someone based on their profession, age, sex, race, religion or any other demographic or personal experience. You should ask each juror all questions in an open, non-judgmental way, listen carefully to the answers and weigh those answers with everything else you have learned about the juror.

§ 18.20 Non-verbal Responses

It is also critical in a death penalty case to "listen" carefully to what the jurors are saying with their bodies, tone of voice and choice of words. They may say, for instance, that they are opposed to the death penalty but there is a hesitancy in their voice. Follow up the discrepancy by asking such questions as:

1) *Ms. Smith, you say you are against the death penalty; however, I hear some hesitancy in your voice. Please tell me about that.*

2) *I detect, Mr. Jones, that there may be some situations where you feel the death penalty is appropriate. Please tell me about that.*

Jurors who are predisposed toward the death penalty may say that they can consider life, but you notice that they are staring hard at your client, their voice is strained, their body is tightly closed and turned away from you, or in some other non-verbal way they are indicating to you that there may be more to their answer. You may want to ask the following questions:

1) *Mr. Jones, you say that you are able to consider a life sentence, however, you seem unhappy or uncomfortable about something. Please tell me about that.*

2) *It seems to me, Ms. Smith, from what you have said that though you say that you think you can consider life imprisonment, you would be much more inclined to favor the death penalty. Please talk to me about this.*

(*See* Chapter 14, "Voice Inflection, Body Language, Non–verbal Communication" for an in-depth discussion of how to read non-verbal responses in *voir dire.*)

§ 18.21 Questions to Ask and How to Ask Them—Generally

Ask as many open-ended questions as possible, questions that begin, "what do you feel," "what are your thoughts," "what are your perceptions," "why do you feel that way," "please describe that," "please tell me about that," "give me an example." The more open-ended questions you ask, the more apt you are to get to the bottom of a juror's feelings. It is always the question that you do not ask that gets you into trouble.

Closed-ended questions are necessary when you need to develop a challenge for cause. You should take this tack only after you have asked enough open-ended questions to find out what the juror feels and believes. Then use leading questions in a sensitive tone of voice to encourage the juror to admit what he or she thinks and feels about issues at hand. In addition to probing the impact of prejudicial publicity, you should ask about religious and racial biases, prior experiences and personal knowledge. The death sentence was set aside in several cases where the court failed to allow adequate inquiry into pervasive pre-trial publicity: *Irvin v. Dowd,*[1] where the death penalty was set aside due to pre-trial publicity regarding the defendant's confession, other criminal activity, his offer to plead guilty to avoid the death sentence, and the promise of a sheriff to secure the death sentence in another state if he was not sentenced to death in this case; *Rideau v. Louisiana,*[2] where the trial was considered a "hollow formality" after a twenty-minute interview in which the defendant confessed to the crime was broadcast three times; *Coleman v. Kemp,*[3] and *Isaacs v. Kemp,*[4] where death sentences were set aside due to the trial court's failure to grant a change of venue based on pre-trial publicity in a rural Georgia county; and *Jones v. State,*[5] where a conviction and death sentence were reversed because of denial of a change of venue, when a change of venue is to be granted if the defense makes a substantial showing of the likelihood of prejudice by reason of excessive pre-trial publicity.

§ 18.22 Questions to Ask and How to Ask Them—Exploring Religious Influences

Many people consider their religious and moral upbringing when deliberating the death penalty. Some adhere to the biblical concept "an eye for an eye," that someone who killed someone else should also be killed. You may want to ask jurors what they think about the concept of "an eye for an eye" and what that means to them. They may not have thought through its full implications. Does that mean that everyone who commits a murder should be killed by the state? If they say no, this is a good opening to talk about mercy, and suggest life in prison as an alternative punishment. You might want to bring up the New Testament, and Jesus' advice to "turn the other cheek." "An

§ 18.21

1. 366 U.S. 717, 722, 81 S.Ct. 1639, 1642, 6 L.Ed.2d 751 (1961).

2. 373 U.S. 723, 83 S.Ct. 1417, 10 L.Ed.2d 663 (1963), on remand 246 La. 451, 165 So.2d 282 (1964).

3. 778 F.2d 1487 (11th Cir.1985), cert. denied 476 U.S. 1164, 106 S.Ct. 2289, 90 L.Ed.2d 730 (1986).

4. 778 F.2d 1482, 1484 (11th Cir.1985), cert. denied 476 U.S. 1164, 106 S.Ct. 2289, 90 L.Ed.2d 730 (1986).

5. 261 Ga. 665, 409 S.E.2d 642 (1991).

eye for an eye" has been interpreted the same as "you reap what you sow" but that does not have to mean that the accused should be put to death if the victim died.

Another factor to explore is the position a juror's church has taken on the death penalty. Some jurors will follow their church unwaveringly. Others believe that no matter what their church thinks they have their own personal feelings about the death penalty and what is correct. Of course, the local church may adopt a different stance than the denomination nationally.

The following questions will help you sort out these issues. You should be sure to broach this subject sensitively and tell the jurors that you are not trying to invade their privacy, but because religion often plays a big role in how people make final decisions, like giving someone the death penalty, it is important that these issues be discussed.

1) *What do you feel about the saying "an eye for an eye"? What do you think that means?*

2) *Some people feel that the saying "an eye for an eye" means that if a person kills someone else, his life should also be taken. Other people feel that it means that if a person kills someone, he also should be punished but not necessarily by death. What do you think? Give me examples of the kinds of crime you believe warrant life in prison and those you believe warrant the death penalty.*

3) *Ms. Smith, you have told us that you are a Baptist, which means that you believe in the New Testament. Jesus said, "I have come to free you from the law," which means that he would have been opposed to the "eye for an eye, tooth for a tooth" concept. What do you think about that?*

4) *You say that you are a Roman Catholic. What is your understanding as to how the Catholic Church feels about the death penalty? How does that fit with your views?*

5) *Are you aware that the Catholic Church has said that it is opposed to the death penalty? How does that affect your feelings about the death penalty?*

6) *Every major religion in the United States has come out against the death penalty. What are your thoughts about that? Why do you think that all religions oppose the death penalty?*

§ 18.22A Questions to Ask and How to Ask Them—Developing Impressions of Potential Witnesses

Voir dire the jurors on all of your key witnesses, including your client's parents, fact witnesses and character witnesses. Ask about negative or positive reactions to opposing counsel's witnesses. Anything about how a witness may be perceived by the jury is important. For example, if the client's parents are going to testify, and the mother is a nurse and the father is a truck driver, ask the jurors what they know about truck driving, or if they or any family members have ever been in nursing. Should opposing counsel be putting on an eyewitness who works as a bartender, ask jurors what they think about the business of bartending and whether or not they, any family member or friend have ever worked as a bartender. These are obviously just a few examples, but you should explore everything you know about the witnesses on both sides of the case to see if the jurors have some connection with, or opposition, to any witness.

If you intend to call experts at trial, ask the jurors what knowledge they have of the subject matter and how they feel about experts in that field. It could turn out that you are using a psychologist, and a juror may have had a bad experience with a psychologist, and therefore would not trust the psychologist's testimony. Or a juror could have some medical training and should you be calling a pathologist, may listen more intently because of that training. The key is to *voir dire* on all consultants and experts to find out what knowledge, experiences or thoughts the jurors have about people in that profession and any kind of specialized training they personally may have had in that profession.

§ 18.23 Questions to Ask and How to Ask Them—Diffusing Heinous Events

It is well known that the more jurors hear about the ugly facts of a case during *voir dire,* the less impression those facts will make when raised in the course of the trial. *Voir dire* on gory pictures and, if possible, show them to the jurors to gauge their reactions. Talk about disturbing facts such as stabbings, rape, beatings or any other events that could inflame the minds of the jurors. Ask, for instance, how they would react to the fact that the victim was brutally beaten and if that fact would make them feel more inclined toward the death penalty. Describe the facts in detail—talk about stab wounds, the kind of knife that was used, how many other instruments were used against the victim. Be as specific as you possibly can so the jurors will have heard all of the negative information before the prosecution gets a chance to stand up and give their opening statement. This disturbing evidence should be sensitively explored with jurors by saying that you wish they did not have to be exposed to it but you must know how it might affect them.

§ 18.24 Questions to Ask and How to Ask Them—Underscoring the Systematic Bias Against Minorities

America has a long history of racial discrimination in the infliction of the death penalty.[1] "Legal lynchings" through perfunctory capital trials replaced the mob lynching of the post-Civil War Years.[2] The criminal justice system seems to be the institution in many states least affected by the civil rights movement of the Sixties and Seventies. Minorities continue to be excluded from full participation as judges, prosecutors, jurors and defense attorneys. No wonder that race, like poverty, continues to play a critical role in determining who is sentenced to death. In 1990 the U.S. General Accounting Office published the findings from 28 studies establishing a pattern of racial disparities in the charging, sentencing and imposition of the death penalty in the statutes adopted after *Furman.*[3] The case law is equally as glaring. In *Amadeo v. Zant,* [4] a death sentence was set aside after it was discovered that the prosecutor conspired with jury commissioners to under-represent women and African American people in the jury venires. In *Horton v. Zant,*[5] the Court found that the prosecutor had used his peremptory jury strikes against African Americans 96% of the time in capital cases involving an African American defendant and a white victim. This history, along with other discriminatory actions by the prosecutor, satisfied the burden under *Swain v. Alabama*[6] of showing systematic practice of intentional racial discrimination in jury selection. Relief is not always granted, however. In *Dobbs v. Zant,*[7] relief was denied even though Dobbs was called "colored" and "a colored boy" by the judge at his trial, the prosecutor called him by his first name, his court-appointed defense lawyer stated that he believed that blacks are good primarily as basketball players, have inferior morals and are less intelligent than whites, and jurors expressed distrust and fear of black people. Likewise, in *Edwards v. Scroggy,*[8] the death sentence was upheld and carried out, although the prosecutor in Jackson, Mississippi admitted that it was his "policy" to "get rid of as many" African–Americans as possible in jury selection.

§ 18.24

1. *See,* for example, *Furman v. Georgia,* 408 U.S. 238, 249–252, 92 S.Ct. 2726, 2732–2733, 33 L.Ed.2d 346 (1972), rehearing denied 409 U.S. 902, 93 S.Ct. 89, 34 L.Ed.2d 163 (1972) (Douglas, J. concurring), *Id.,* at 309–310, 92 S.Ct. at 2762–2763 (Stewart, J. concurring), *Id.,* at 364–366, 92 S.Ct. at 2790–2791 (Marshall, J. concurring) (1972).

2. *See* D. Carter, *Scottsboro: A Tragedy of the American South* (LSU Press Rev. ed. 1979) and G. Wright, *Racial Violence in Kentucky, 1865–1940: Lynchings, Mob Rule and "Legal Lynchings,"* (LSU Press 1990).

3. *See* U.S. General Accounting Office, *Death Penalty Sentencing: Research Indicates Pattern of Racial Disparities* (1990).

4. 486 U.S. 214, 108 S.Ct. 1771, 100 L.Ed.2d 249 (1988), on remand 259 Ga. 469, 384 S.E.2d 181 (1989).

5. 941 F.2d 1449 (11th Cir.1991), rehearing denied 948 F.2d 729 (11th Cir. 1991).

6. 380 U.S. 202, 85 S.Ct. 824, 13 L.Ed.2d 759 (1965).

7. 720 F.Supp. 1566 (N.D.Ga.1989), affirmed 946 F.2d 1519 (11th Cir.1991).

8. 849 F.2d 204, 207 (5th Cir.1988), cert. denied 489 U.S. 1059, 109 S.Ct. 1328, 103 L.Ed.2d 597 (1989), rehearing denied 490 U.S. 1032, 109 S.Ct. 1772, 104 L.Ed.2d 207 (1989).

Since everyone knows that a disproportionate number of minorities are charged with the death penalty, it is the challenge of defense counsel to prevent racial bias from entering into the prosecutor's decision to seek death and the ultimate determination of whether death is imposed. If you have an African American, Hispanic, Asian or Native American client facing the death penalty, you should particularly raise this aspect of racism in our society. The following kinds of questions should be added to your general *voir dire* on racial attitudes:

1) *It is clear that if you are African American in this country you are more apt to be charged with the death penalty than if you are white. What do you think about this?*

2) *Why do you think this occurs?*

3) *What I am saying is that in a situation with the same set of facts, a white person is less apt to be charged with the death penalty than an African American person. What do you think about this discrepancy? Who do you think is responsible for this occurring?*

4) *What do you think should be done?*

§ 18.25 Questions to Ask and How to Ask Them—Encouraging Jurors to Vote Their Own Conscience

It is important to encourage jurors to vote with the courage of their conviction, especially when the decision is life or death. You should ask what it means to them when they are told, "vote your own conscience." Explain to them how important it is to deliberate with other jurors and listen to others' thoughts and feelings, but when everything is said and done, the responsibility of each juror is to vote what he or she believes is appropriate. At the guilt/innocence phase and again, if necessary, at the sentencing phase, each juror is ultimately on his or her own. You will especially want to reinforce the prolifers on the panel to be their own person. The following questions will assist:

1) *I am sure, Ms. Jones, that you are a person who has the courage to say what you feel. Is this true? Tell me why.*

2) *Why is it important in a case involving whether someone lives or dies that you as a juror carefully weigh all of the evidence and then vote according to what you believe is correct? Why do you think that is important?*

3) *There may be a lot of disagreement in the deliberation room. Sometimes tempers flare. How are you going to react if you are one of the only people who believe that a particular sentence is appropriate? Will you continue to hold to your opinion after you have listened to everybody else's?*

4) Do you agree or disagree that it is important that intelligent, fair-minded people differ on important decisions? How will you react to the differences of opinion? Will you be able to form your own opinion and stick to that opinion? What would make you sway from your opinion?

5) Why do you think there are twelve people on the jury as opposed to four or five?

6) Why do you think the law says that in order for there to be a unanimous verdict, there must be twelve individual verdicts that are the same, meaning twelve jurors who all agree? This means that you may or may not agree. How would you feel if you were the only person who was not in agreement with the other folks?

7) Give me an example in your life where you were the only person who felt one way and everybody else felt another. How did you feel about holding to your own opinion? Looking back on it later, are you still happy that you chose to stand up for what you believe in?

8) Why is it important in life to stand up for what we believe after we've listened to other people's thoughts and opinions?

§ 18.26 Aggravating and Mitigating Circumstances—Generally

When you mention mitigation in *voir dire,* some jurors tend to think you are saying that the accused is not responsible for his or her actions because of childhood neglect, alcohol or drugs, or some painful experience. You will often hear jurors say, "That is no excuse for killing someone."

Think through the mitigating factors you will argue even before you begin trial. If you are admitting the murder but begging for your client's life, introduce your *voir dire* on mitigation by saying that you are not implying that these mitigating factors are an excuse, or that they make your client any less responsible for his or her actions. On the other hand, if you are not admitting the alleged murder and still have to *voir dire* on mitigation and aggravation, ask the jurors what effect certain factors would have on their choosing life versus death, should they find the defendant guilty. You should be absolutely clear that you are not suggesting that they *should* find your client guilty. This is an important fact to emphasize: You are not admitting your client's guilt, but by law you must ask how the jurors feel about the mitigating factors in order to determine who may be open to life as an appropriate verdict in this case. Either way you need to tell the jurors that these are not factors to make them feel sorry for the client; rather they are factors that by law the jurors can weigh to determine whether life or death is the correct sentence. You also need to explain that only one mitigating factor is required to reduce the death sentence to a sentence of life without the possibility of parole or life imprisonment.

Be equally thorough in exploring the aggravating circumstances. Find out whether or not jurors automatically feel that because your client has a prior criminal record or has abused people in the past, he should get the death penalty. Your goal is to diffuse the aggravation, or in the alternative, to clarify that the aggravation would make the juror feel that the appropriate punishment is death and develop a challenge for cause.

Under the pressure of *voir dire,* lawyers have been known to cut corners by neglecting to ask what jurors think of different mitigating or aggravating circumstances and how they would figure in either mitigating or aggravating the alleged crime. Some lawyers, for example, will ask a juror what they think about the death penalty and if the juror expresses hesitance, will move on to the next topic or the next juror without developing out how the juror would relate to the specific aggravating or mitigating circumstances of the case. This can be quite dangerous because some jurors might say that they have some hesitation about the death penalty but when they hear the aggravating circumstances, may determine that this is the case where they will feel comfortable giving the death penalty. On the other hand, this same juror may feel that a bad childhood, the defendant's age or some other mitigating factor will play no role in how they would see the alleged crime. Cutting corners, therefore, is never advisable in a death penalty case.

§ 18.27 Aggravating and Mitigating Circumstances—Transforming Aggravation Into Mitigation

Creativity is the keystone of all cases, but especially of death penalty cases. Use your imagination freely to turn the prosecution arguments to your advantage. The prosecution, for example, may imply that because your client was voluntarily under the influence of drugs or alcohol, this becomes an aggravating circumstance. Should you, in turn, present testimony that your client had an addiction to drugs or alcohol, that could be argued as mitigation. Or the prosecution may try to bring in your client's prior criminal record as aggravation. You should develop your client's negative experiences in prison that you believe affected his ability to become a healthy member of society. The testimony of inmates, other ex-convicts, prison guards, family members and/or experts can reinforce the view of incarceration as a mitigating factor if you develop your client's prior brush with the law as one more experience in his life that made him feel useless and unworthy and turned his pain into anger. This transformation can be made in *voir dire* by asking such questions as:

1) *My client has a criminal record and has served time in the state penitentiary. How do you think serving time in a penitentiary would affect someone's feelings about herself?*
2) *If a person was beaten or raped while in prison, how do you think that would affect his feelings about himself?*
3) *Some people feel that when someone is the victim of violence in prison, he will first feel horrible about himself, then turn angry. What do you think about that?*
4) *Have you ever heard of the saying, "Anger is nothing more than pain which is unresolved." What do you think about that statement?*

These are just a few ways to turn aggravation into mitigation, and humanize the pathological picture the prosecution would sooner paint of your client.

§ 18.28 Individual, Sequestered and Attorney-Conducted *Voir Dire*

It is imperative in a death penalty case to seek individual, attorney-conducted *voir dire* in a sequestered setting, particularly on the death penalty, publicity, racism and other highly charged issues in the case. (*See* Appendix 18E for a sample motion with authorities.) To make it easier for the court logistically, you may want to request that the *voir dire* be conducted in the jury room so that there is a place to put the panel in the interim. The jury room also allows everyone to sit at the same level and tends to create a more relaxed atmosphere. It may also be a refuge from the electronic media in this day and age of cameras in the courtroom. Given the potential intimidation factor, for jurors and witnesses alike, we would suggest that it is not in your client's interest to have electronic coverage of any part of the trial proceedings, but particularly of the *voir dire*. There is case law to back up this contention: In *Mississippi Publishers Corp. v. Coleman,*[1] the Mississippi Supreme Court upheld the closure of the pre-trial proceedings to avoid more prejudicial publicity prior to retrial of a capital case; and in *Georgia Television Co. v. State,*[2] a trial court's refusal to permit electronic and photographic coverage of pre-trial proceedings in a highly publicized case was upheld. Appendix 18F contains a sample motion to prohibit electronic coverage in a death penalty case, with points and authorities in support. Appendix 18G specifically addresses exclusion of the press from sequestered *voir dire*, suggesting, in the alternative, press access to daily transcripts.

You will find that individual sequestered *voir dire* is the best forum for getting jurors to be the most honest. They are more relaxed and

§ 18.28

1. 515 So.2d 1163 (Miss.1987).

2. 257 Ga. 764, 363 S.E.2d 528 (1988).

less apt to take cues from their peer group as to what are the right or wrong answers. It is also time for you to develop a rapport with each juror. Be gentle and open in your questioning and sensitive to what each juror thinks and feels about the issues. This is your chance to be seen as a strong force in the courtroom because most likely you will be the person who asks the most questions.

Once a juror has been passed for cause during the sequestered part of the jury selection, it is important to allow the juror to leave so there is no opportunity for other members of the panel to discover what questions are being asked and formulate their answers. Should the court refuse to dismiss the jurors who have been questioned individually, request that they be escorted to a separate area. Even if the court insists that the jurors return to the panel, it is *still* to your client's advantage to have individual sequestered *voir dire.* The court should be reminded to instruct the jurors not to discuss the questions and answers with anyone in the panel or outside the panel.

A two-part *voir dire* is helpful and expedient, where you initially conduct individual sequestered *voir dire* on the death penalty, publicity, racism and other sensitive issues and then bring back the jurors in a group for the open-ended educational questions relevant to the case. After a lengthy *voir dire* it is often difficult to remember all the jurors. This process gives you a first impression of the jurors one-on-one and then a second view in the panel, to observe their group dynamics. Also, you may be able to ask questions of the group that the court felt were inappropriate to ask of individuals.

If you are in a state that does not automatically allow individual sequestered *voir dire* in death penalty cases, you need to make a strong argument to the court. Instructive cases are: *Jordan v. Lippman,*[3] which found that *voir dire* must be adequate to "unearth such potential prejudice in the jury pool"; and *Coleman v. Kemp,*[4] which found group *voir dire* inadequate where there was a need to question about pre-trial publicity. More recently, however, in *Mu'Min v. Virginia,*[5] the Supreme Court found that *voir dire* procedures were not constitutionally inadequate where jurors were asked whether they had been exposed to media coverage, and whether they could put what they had seen aside, but they were not asked what they had seen. To reinforce the need for individual sequestered *voir dire,* you should request a hearing and introduce affidavits of experts discussing the difference between how people behave in a sequestered environment as opposed to a group. Present testimony from jury consultants, attorneys and anybody else

3. 763 F.2d 1265, 1273 (11th Cir.1985).

4. 778 F.2d 1487, 1541–1542 (11th Cir. 1985), on remand 257 Ga. 126, 355 S.E.2d 644 (1987).

5. ___ U.S. ___, 111 S.Ct. 1899, 114 L.Ed.2d 493 (1991), rehearing denied ___ U.S. ___, 112 S.Ct. 13, 115 L.Ed.2d 1097 (1991).

you feel could educate the court on the relevance and importance of this form of *voir dire* in this kind of case.

Should the court deny your motion for individual sequestered *voir dire,* renew your motion before and after each juror, emphasizing that the panel *voir dire* is not reaching the bias and prejudice and true feelings of this juror. Be specific as to what you feel you did not get as a result of the panel *voir dire.* Put on the record the juror's non-verbal language that indicated he was holding back or not being totally candid, as well as indicators that the juror was less than comfortable being *voir dired* in the big group. Remind the court that the number one fear in America is the fear of public speaking and that when jurors are interviewed in a big group about sensitive matters, their fear of embarrassment becomes, in many instances, more compelling than their desire to express what they truly think and feel. (*See* Sections 7.2 and 7.3 for further discussion of individual sequestered and attorney conducted *voir dire.* *See also* Sections 12.14 and 15.17, *supra,* regarding the use of individual sequestered *voir dire* for sensitive issues.)

§ 18.29 Death Qualification—Generally

To sit on a death penalty case, a juror must be able to consider both life and death as a punishment for the crime on trial. Death qualification is the process that discloses if jurors *can* consider both punishments. The task at hand for defense counsel is to artfully save pro-lifers and successfully challenge for cause those who would automatically impose death.

Most lawyers know how to save, or "rehabilitate," jurors who would be challenged for cause because of their belief in life in prison. Follow-up questions can confirm their belief in a cross-section of the community sitting in all cases, reinforce their ability to consider all opinions on all issues in life, and underscore their willingness to accept that we never know absolutely what we will do in the future.

There are many jurors, however, who feel if someone did something this terrible, the only appropriate sentence is the death penalty. Getting those jurors excused for cause who would automatically vote for the death penalty requires establishing their immovable position in *voir dire.* You may need to develop the heinous nature of the crime or adopt a softer touch, to show that no matter what the district attorney, the judge or the law says about considering life and death, they cannot overcome their resolve that the death penalty is right in this kind of case. (*See* Section 18.36, "Challenging Automatic Death Penalty Jurors for Cause," *infra,* for specific questions that may assist in hammering down a juror's thoughts and feelings.)

In the old days, judges paved the jury box for these death-prone jurors by routinely granting the prosecution's challenge for cause with respect to prospective jurors who had reservations about the death penalty. This practice was disapproved in *Witherspoon v. Illinois*,[1] in which the Court held that such jurors could be excluded for cause only if they made it "unmistakably clear (1) that they would *automatically* vote against the imposition of capital punishment without regard to any evidence that might be developed at the trial of the case before them, or (2) that their attitude toward the death penalty would prevent them from making an impartial decision as to the defendant's guilt."[2] Violation of the requirements of *Witherspoon* was per se reversible error.

While *Witherspoon*, on its face, dealt only with exclusion of jurors who opposed the death penalty, its rationale came to be applied to defense cause challenges to prospective jurors who strongly favored the death penalty. Just as the prosecution could not get rid of prospective jurors absent an unmistakably clear showing of absolute opposition, so too, the defense could not get rid of those favoring the death penalty absent an unmistakably clear showing of their commitment to the death penalty for murders.

Seventeen years later, in 1985, the Supreme Court took another look at *Witherspoon* and relaxed its exacting standard. In *Wainwright v. Witt*,[3] the Court established that a prospective juror could be excused for cause if his views on capital punishment "would prevent or substantially impair the performance of his duties as a juror in accordance with his instructions and his oath." *Witt* reaffirmed *Adams v. Texas*,[4] which lowered the standard of certainty, and altered the traditional *Witherspoon* test by dispensing with the reference to "automatic" decision making and the requirement that a juror's bias be proved with "unmistakable clarity." A trial judge can now excuse a juror based on a definite impression that the juror would be unable to faithfully and impartially apply the law, specifically with reference to the imposition of the sentence of death. Ironically, *Witt* increases *both* the number of people who can be excluded for cause because of their *opposition* to the death penalty and the number of people who can be excluded for their *support* for the death penalty. It is a sword available to the defense and prosecution alike. For defense counsel, it means not only identifying and challenging those who would "automatically" impose the death penalty but those whose support for the death penalty would prevent them from following the law on sentencing—those who would be unwilling to consider evidence presented in mitigation.

The judge can be helpful in setting the stage for open and honest responses during the death qualification process. Appendix 18H con-

§ 18.29

1. 391 U.S. 510, 88 S.Ct. 1770, 20 L.Ed.2d 776 (1968).

2. *Id.* at 523 n. 21, 88 S.Ct. at 1777 n. 21.

3. 469 U.S. 412, 424, 105 S.Ct. 844, 852, 83 L.Ed.2d 841 (1985).

4. 448 U.S. 38, 100 S.Ct. 2521, 65 L.Ed.2d 581 (1980), on remand 624 S.W.2d 568 (Tex.Crim.App.1981).

tains remarks from the bench to prospective jurors prior to a death qualification *voir dire* in the Superior Court of California. The process itself can mean the difference between a life or death verdict for your client. Defense counsel should assure that the death qualification is done consistent with the law. Appendix 18I contains a succinct sample trial brief on the standards to be applied in death-qualifying jurors in California that can be adapted to other states. If the proper standards are not followed, the death qualification process becomes additional grounds for appeal by building a record of the jurors inappropriately excused and those the court has erroneously allowed to remain. In *Gray v. Mississippi,*[5] for instance, the Supreme Court found that the erroneous exclusion of a juror because of attitudes regarding the death penalty is not subject to harmless error analysis even when the prosecutor has an unexercised peremptory challenge at the end of jury selection, nor can improper exclusion serve as a remedy for the erroneous denial of the prosecution's challenge of another juror. *Alderman v. Austin*[6] found that a juror who could not sign the verdict form was improperly excluded under *Witherspoon.* The death sentence was set aside in *Pope v. State,*[7] in which a juror indicated on *voir dire* that he would vote for the death penalty if the defendant was convicted.

§ 18.30 Death Qualification—Judge-Conducted Versus Attorney-Conducted *Voir Dire*

Whenever possible, you should avoid having the court death-qualify the panel. The problem with judge-conducted death qualification is that the court may ask three or four standard questions and tie the juror down before you have had a chance to rehabilitate him or her. The lawyer will be able to get a more complete picture of what the jurors think about the death penalty.

In a jurisdiction where the court generally does the death qualification, file a motion that you be allowed to do the death qualification and request a hearing. At that time, present your jury consultant, out-of-state affidavits of lawyers and judges who believe in attorney-conducted death qualification and any studies or other expert testimony that will make a case in point for the court. Should the court deny the motion and insist on doing the death qualification, you will want to respond sensitively to those who have said they are either opposed to the death penalty or have not owned up to the fact that they would automatically give the death penalty. Make sure that you have the opportunity to go back and pose some open-ended questions about the jurors' ability to

5. 481 U.S. 648, 107 S.Ct. 2045, 95 L.Ed.2d 622 (1987).

6. 663 F.2d 558 (5th Cir.1981), adhered to en banc 695 F.2d 124 (5th Cir.1983) (en banc).

7. 256 Ga. 195, 345 S.E.2d 831 (1986), appeal after remand 257 Ga. 32, 354 S.E.2d 429 (1987), cert. denied 484 U.S. 873, 108 S.Ct. 207, 98 L.Ed.2d 159 (1987).

consider the death penalty or conversely, their ability to consider life in prison, should the defendant be found guilty of murder.

§ 18.31 Death Qualification—Saving Scrupled Jurors

One of the most difficult tasks that any death penalty lawyer has is saving scrupled jurors during the *voir dire* process. Often scrupled jurors want to confess that they cannot be fair because they do not want to judge another human being or could never give someone a death sentence. They feel they are helping if they admit the fact that they could not vote for the death penalty or else equivocate on the issue. It is the lawyer's task to try to save these jurors and force the prosecution to use a strike. To gracefully allow these people to remove themselves is verging on ineffective assistance of counsel in a death penalty case. There are several approaches to keep a scrupled juror on the panel. (*See* Sections 18.32 through 18.35 for a representative sample.)

§ 18.32 Death Qualification—Saving Scrupled Jurors—Community Standard

Explain that a defendant is entitled to a jury chosen from a fair cross-section of the community, including people who represent the whole range of attitudes toward the death penalty. The following questions will assist:

1) *I am sure you would agree that it would be fair that a cross-section of this community serves on any case, including a death penalty case. This means that both people who believe and do not believe in the death penalty should sit on the jury because that would be fair in determining whether or not the defendant lives or dies. Do you agree with this or not? Why?*

2) *How would you feel if someone who was faced with the death penalty was tried only by people who strongly believe in the death penalty?*

3) *Given how you feel about the fairness of being tried by a cross-section of the community, would you put aside your opposition to the death penalty? Could you be fair in a death penalty case and decide whether someone should receive capital punishment or life without the possibility of parole?*

§ 18.33 Death Qualification—Saving Scrupled Jurors—Fair Person

Many scrupled jurors consider themselves to be fair in all circumstances. You should play up their sense of fairness and ask the following questions:

1) Would it be correct to say that you consider yourself to be a fair person, Ms. Smith?

2) Given this fair perception of yourself, you would be fair no matter what you were deciding, isn't that correct?

3) As a fair person, can you be fair enough to consider all the evidence as to whether or not someone was guilty of a crime and then decide and vote your conscience in a case involving the death penalty?

§ 18.34 Death Qualification—Saving Scrupled Jurors—Ability to Judge

Many religious jurors and fair-minded people feel it is unfair for them to judge whether or not someone lives or dies. You must help them realize that their ability to judge does not mean their ability to consider evidence. The following questions will assist:

1) Ms. Jones, you have told us that you feel it is unfair for someone to judge another human being. However, wouldn't you think it would be unfair for someone to be judged by twelve people who are all very judgmental?

2) If a loved one of yours was on trial for his life, wouldn't you think it would be fair to have someone on that panel who considers herself unfit to judge? Given this, do you think you could put aside your fear of judging and say that you could listen to evidence, deliberate and talk with other people about your feelings and then vote your conscience not affected by what other people think is right or wrong?

§ 18.35 Death Qualification—Saving Scrupled Jurors—Obey the Law

Many scrupled jurors, though morally opposed to the death penalty, will feel bound to follow the law, as instructed by the judge. It is your job to make the distinction clear with such questions as:

Under law, your conscientious or religious feelings about the death penalty are not, in and of themselves, cause for removing you from this jury unless you state unequivocally that under no circumstances will you follow the instructions of the court and fairly consider the imposition of death as a punishment in this case. Do you feel that you would not be able to follow this court's instructions and fairly consider the death penalty?

There are any number of ways to deal with scrupled jurors. You can remind them of their civic duty to do jury service, or on a more personal level, explore whether or not they can separate their emotions from their ability to listen and consider the evidence. The touchstone is that you be creative, look at the person, hear what they are saying about their feelings in opposition to the death penalty, and on the basis of their feelings, build a substructure which will allow them to deliberate and vote their own conscience. Most scrupled jurors just want to be fair and do not want to hurt anyone. Your job is to create an opening where they can consider the death penalty and yet not feel as if they are being overly punitive.

§ 18.36 Challenging Automatic Death Penalty Jurors for Cause—Generally

A death penalty *voir dire* is all about getting automatic death penalty jurors excused because, in most or at least many instances, scrupled jurors excuse themselves or the trial judge is, unfortunately, more comfortable excusing them than excusing those who are inclined toward the death penalty. You will obviously use your peremptory challenges to excuse the jurors who are strongly pro-death. Through your cause challenges, which you should develop creatively for the appellate record, point out the court's tendency not to excuse those who are inclined toward the death penalty while arbitrarily excusing those who are opposed.

In most jurisdictions, the preponderance of jurors are inclined toward the death penalty and a small group are opposed. Therefore, death penalty jury selection requires that you artfully develop cause challenges to diminish the number of death penalty-prone and broaden the base of those who fall in between the pro-death penalty and scrupled jurors. The closer this comes into equilibrium, the closer your client comes to a life verdict.

The art of getting automatic death penalty jurors excused demands great patience and skill. You cannot accuse a juror of wanting to kill someone and expect her to say, "You're right. May I be excused?" You will have to develop the fact that if she should feel the evidence supports a first-degree conviction, she would believe the appropriate sentence is death. Of course, in exploring the issue, avoid the word *death* and instead use the socially acceptable term *capital punishment.* The more people feel they are in line with public sentiment and are not being perceived as dispassionate human beings, the more apt they are to agree with your characterization of their position and feed into your challenge for cause.

Once the prosecution and the judge realize that you are developing a number of cause challenges of automatic death penalty jurors, they will up the ante and try to circumvent you. The following questions will help solidify the automatic death penalty jurors in order to preserve the record and nail down jurors' feelings and thoughts before the judge and the prosecution does.

1) *Ms. Smith, what I hear you saying is that should the evidence show that the defendant with premeditation and*

malice aforethought murdered this person, you would feel the appropriate verdict to be capital punishment. Am I correct? Please tell me what you feel.

2) *Mr. Jones, I hear you saying that if you found my client guilty beyond a reasonable doubt, you would feel that the appropriate sentence would be capital punishment. Is that correct?*

3) *The fact that my client had a bad childhood, was young and was under the influence of drugs would play no part in what you would feel would be the appropriate sentence. Have I been hearing you correctly?*

4) *This tells me that if the district attorney asked whether or not you could consider this evidence, though you may think about this evidence, you would still feel that the appropriate sentence would be capital punishment, notwithstanding the age of my client, what drugs he was taking or any other mitigating circumstance. Have I heard you correctly?*

5) *This also means that no matter what the judge may say to you, you would still feel that considering all the evidence, the appropriate sentence would be capital punishment. Is that correct?*

It is quite important when you are questioning the automatic death penalty jurors that you defuse the mitigating circumstances. Mitigation is obviously the easiest route of rehabilitation for the prosecution. Before you begin a closed-ended cause challenge, however, you must first establish how people feel about the mitigation evidence. Many lawyers have thought a juror was automatically pro-death penalty, only to find, upon asking about mitigation, that the juror began to back down from his or her position. You should therefore hold off on developing a cause challenge until you have explored how the juror feels about the death penalty, the mitigating circumstances and the appropriate sentence.

§ 18.37 Challenging Automatic Death Penalty Jurors for Cause—Developing Cause Challenges Without Alienating the Panel

Should you be in a jurisdiction that requires you to conduct the death qualification in front of the panel, you must develop your challenges for cause so as not to alienate the other jurors. This does not mean, however, that you should hesitate to remove the people that deserve to be removed for cause. In the long run the jurors who get on the jury will see themselves as the chosen ones and will not hold it against you that you had to get other people excused.

There are ways to aggressively develop cause challenges without making an out-and-out attack. You can sensitively point out the jurors' feelings and why you think this is not the appropriate case for them. Assure them that they could be a great juror in every other trial in the courthouse. Tell them that there is nothing wrong with feeling that they would automatically impose the death penalty should they find guilt, that a lot of people feel that way, so that they know they are part of a group and not an odd ball out. The more you develop a friendly discussion with jurors so everybody feels free to say what they think and feel, the more apt you are to develop challenges for cause. The strategy is to make getting excused a badge of courage as opposed to a rejection notice.

Should you be discussing a sensitive area where you think a juror may be embarrassed, you should always say to that juror, "Would you feel more comfortable discussing this up at the judge's bench or back at the judge's chambers?" If the juror says yes, then politely ask the court if this can be discussed in a more personal setting. Almost all judges will allow a juror to approach the bench or go into chambers rather than risk the juror being embarrassed.

If, after every effort, the court denies your challenge for cause, you have the option of filing a motion to reconsider, with the transcript of that portion of the *voir dire* that establishes the basis for your challenge and the legal authority in support. (*See* Appendix 18J for a sample motion to reconsider filed in the Superior Court of California.) Obviously, in this instance, particularly, and throughout a lengthy death penalty case, a daily transcript is invaluable. If the expense is not an issue, or an issue that can be overcome, you should request a daily transcript of the trial proceedings. Your motion is more likely to be granted in capital cases. (*See* Appendix 18K for a sample motion with points and authorities.)

§ 18.38 Establishing Error

One of the saddest things in death penalty cases is when a transcript is reviewed and it is discovered that the lawyer was initially developing error in a way that the appellate court suggested was necessary and at the very end dropped the ball or did not go far enough. Make sure that you or co-counsel are aware of the cases relevant to death penalty *voir dire* so that, if necessary, they can be cited fully at trial. (As a guide, *see* Appendix 18L for a sample memorandum of law regarding the proper scope of *voir dire* in capital cases, that if limited may constitute judicial error.) Each time a juror is removed for being pro-life or kept after claiming to be pro-death, or you are not allowed a particular question, you will want to be able to instantly refer to the appropriate case law to establish the judge's error for the appellate record. (*See also* Section 18.29, *supra,* for cases and pleadings pertaining directly to death qualification.)

This is one of the real arts in a death penalty case, and knowing that you are entering a death penalty case with a fully developed record from jury selection can relieve some of the pressure. Also, when error has been appropriately developed during *voir dire,* prosecutors sometimes realize the wisdom of pleading the case for a life sentence, or even a lesser-included offense such as second-degree murder or manslaughter. Do your homework and have co-counsel prepared to pass follow-up questions that will give you and your client a safety net. Always keep in mind, a capital case *voir dire* is your most powerful tool at trial and for appellate purposes.

§ 18.39 Affidavits of Excused Jurors

When the court has conducted the death qualification or when the court has not allowed you to do an adequate rehabilitation of a juror, you may want to have an investigator, jury consultant or someone from your staff interview the excused jurors, if possible, before they leave the courthouse and after they are excused from jury duty. Ask them some of the more open-ended questions you were not allowed to pursue and find out from the jurors what they might have said, had they been allowed to answer those questions. For example, ask pro-life jurors whether or not they see themselves as fair and whether or not they would have considered other people's opinions during the deliberation process. Ask whether or not they could have put aside their feelings regarding the death penalty and deliberated with the other jurors and then voted their conscience. You might also want to ask whether or not in the right case they could consider the death penalty, though they may not vote for it. When you uncover information that would suggest a juror should not have been excused, you or your jury consultant should then write a short affidavit in the courthouse and ask the juror to sign it. If the juror refuses to sign the affidavit, then have the person who interviewed the juror do an affidavit and file it immediately with the court. At that point you have the grounds to ask for another hearing on the issue and should continue building your record as to why you should be allowed attorney-conducted death qualification. This was a successful method of expanding the death qualification in the 1980 New Mexico prison riot cases defended by Mike Stout, Mark Donatelli, Richard Winterbottom and other members of the National Association of Criminal Defense Lawyers.

§ 18.40 *Batson* Challenges

It is imperative in a death penalty case that *Batson* challenges be made whenever you find a cognizable group that the prosecutor is excluding from the panel. For example, if the prosecutor seems to be using strikes more on African Americans or Hispanics, make a *Batson* challenge to prevent this group from being eliminated from the panel. You may also want to point out to the jurors during *voir dire* that the prosecutor is excluding African Americans or Hispanics more than he is any other group, and ask what they think about that. This is important because it not only puts the prosecution and judge on notice, but could forestall the prosecutor from systematically excluding those people so as not to be obvious about striking along racial lines in front of the jury. In many instances the African American and Hispanic jurors will also make more of an effort to stay on the panel in order not to lose their representation.

Be creative about your use of *Batson*. For example, if your client is a Vietnam veteran and the prosecutor is systematically excluding people who either served in the war or have family members who did, bring a *Batson* challenge. Should you have the rare instance where your client is upper middle class or upper class and the prosecutor is systematically excluding people from this class, *voir dire* the jury on what they think about the prosecutor excluding all people in a similar economic bracket as your client, and of course, bring a challenge to try to prevent this from happening. Whether it works tactically or not at the time, it is still a viable strategy for reversal. (*See also* Sections 17.13 through 17.15, *supra*, for a legal analysis of *Batson v. Kentucky* and its application in non-death penalty trials.)

§ 18.41 Clarification of Instructions

Jurors tend not to understand instructions in any kind of case, and especially in a death penalty case. In post-trial interviews it is often noted, for instance, that the jurors did not know what *mitigating* or *aggravating* meant. *Voir dire* to carefully develop the meaning of *mitigation* and *aggravation*, as well as other confusing parts of the law that will have bearing on the jury's verdict.

§ 18.42 Verdict Forms

Examine the verdict form to make sure that there is nothing in the wording or layout to suggest a particular verdict. Objectively look to see if there is some way that the jurors might feel more comfortable checking guilty or checking the death penalty, and explore different formats that would avoid encouraging any verdict.

§ 18.43 Polling Jurors With the Verdict Form

Should the jury return a guilty verdict, poll the jurors to see whether or not that was truly their verdict. Note which jurors seem to express some hesitancy by their tone of voice or non-verbal language. During the penalty phase of the case direct some of your strongest arguments to these jurors.

Should the jury return a death verdict, again, poll the jurors, using the verdict form and each of their names. This will help determine which jurors you will want to interview post-trial in jurisdictions that allow post-trial interviews.

Be sensitive, not angry, when polling the jurors post-verdict. As in jury selection, the jurors feel your emotions. Sadness and disappointment are feelings jurors can accept from you. They will be more inclined to grant you an interview if they feel accepted by you, not rejected. You can disagree with their verdict and still remain a sensitive person.

CONCLUSION

Openness, flexibility and courage on the part of attorneys are what make communication during *voir dire* and trial accomplish your aims. The art of human relationships is a very demanding one. It is filled with flaws and mistakes because understanding someone and how he or she feels is one of the most difficult and unpredictable tasks in the world, yet fulfilling when valued. Most people never really know even the people with whom they are closest, such as their spouse, their family and their friends. During the client interview, *voir dire* and other aspects of trial practice, the complications of human interactions become compounded and require highly developed skills in the art of listening, perceiving and intuiting. Time, effort and practice must go into using these skills. A sense of balance emerges after many clumsy moments. The ultimate lesson is to evaluate your ability to relate to others, discover strengths and weaknesses in yourself, and encourage feedback from anyone who is willing to help. Developing skills of relating, educating and persuading in *voir dire* and elsewhere is the touchstone of strong advocacy. This book has sought to convey that people educate one another and lawyers are best served listening.

This guide is by no means exhaustive. Time and space allowing, other areas would have been broached or amplified. Forthcoming supplements will cover other important areas that were not included in this body of ideas. Supplements will reflect the evolutionary nature of jury consultation as we see change in the courts, the law and the jury pools. As the field grows and experience broadens, so will the topics for discussion. As we said in the beginning, the courtroom is our laboratory, and each trial experience refines our thinking.

This guide is just that—a guide. We seek to be your companions in the courageous pursuit of protecting all of our rights. We value the honor of serving the legal profession and encouraging you in the face of negative public sentiment towards the legal profession. The fact you have read this book says you are special in your field because you focus on the people involved in your work. Our warmest respect for you has motivated our writing of this book.

We want to express the joy we had in putting this book together for you. It has been a moving experience to recall courtroom and out-of-courtroom moments that have been the thread of this work. As colleagues of yours, we have the deepest hope that in some small way we have made your difficult job a little easier, more complete, more successful and full of life. Let us know if we can ever help.

Cat and Robert

TABLE OF CASES

*

TABLE OF STATUTES

UNITED STATES

UNITED STATES CONSTITUTION

Amend.	This Work Sec.	Note
5	9.38	
6	17.15	
14	9.38	
	17.15	

UNITED STATES CODE ANNOTATED

26 U.S.C.A.—Internal Revenue Code

Sec.	This Work Sec.	Note
6103(h)(5)	9.39	
6103(h)(9)	9.39	

28 U.S.C.A.—Judiciary and Judicial Procedure

Sec.	This Work Sec.	Note
636(b)(3)	11.3	2

STATUTES AT LARGE

Year	This Work Sec.	Note
1968, Oct. 17, P.L. 90–578, 80 Stat. 1108	11.3	2

*

TABLE OF COURT RULES

FEDERAL RULES OF CIVIL PROCEDURE

Rule	This Work Sec.	Note
16(b)(2)	5.65	5
19	5.65	
26	5.65	
26(b)	5.65	
26(b)(3)	5.65	
	5.65	4
	5.65	10
	5.65	36
26(b)(4)(A)	5.65	15
	5.65	17
26(b)(4)(B)	5.65	23
27—36	5.65	
29(b)(4)	5.65	
30	5.65	1
33	5.65	
	5.65	1
34	5.65	1
35	5.65	1
36	5.65	
37	5.65	
48	12.13	
48A	12.9	

FEDERAL RULES OF CRIMINAL PROCEDURE

Rule	This Work Sec.	Note
24A	12.9	
43(a)	7.32	

FEDERAL RULES OF APPELLATE PROCEDURE

Rule	This Work Sec.	Note
10(b)	7.32	
11(a)	7.32	

*

INDEX TO TEXT & APPENDICES VOLUMES

References are to Sections in Main Text (e.g. "§ 1.1") or to Appendix number (e.g. "1A") in Appendices Volume

INDEX

INDEX

INDEX

INDEX

INDEX

†